ONSCREEN / OFFSCREEN

Based on over a decade of ethnographic fieldwork in the South Indian state of Tamil Nadu, *Onscreen/Offscreen* is an exploration of the politics and being of filmic images. The book examines contestations inside and outside the Tamil film industry over the question "what is an image?" Answers to this question may be found in the ontological politics that take place on film sets, in theatre halls, and in the social fabric of everyday life in South India, from populist electoral politics and the gendering of social space to caste uplift and domination.

Bridging and synthesizing linguistic anthropology, film studies, visual studies, and media anthropology, *Onscreen/Offscreen* rethinks key issues across a number of fields concerned with the semiotic constitution of social life, from the performativity and ontology of images to questions of spectatorship, realism, and presence. In doing so, it offers both a challenge to any approach that would separate image from social context and a new vision for linguistic anthropology beyond the question of "language."

(Studies in the Anthropology of Language, Sign, and Social Life)

CONSTANTINE V. NAKASSIS is an associate professor of anthropology and of social sciences in the College, resource faculty in Cinema and Media Studies, faculty associate in Comparative Human Development, and core faculty on the Committee on International Relations at the University of Chicago.

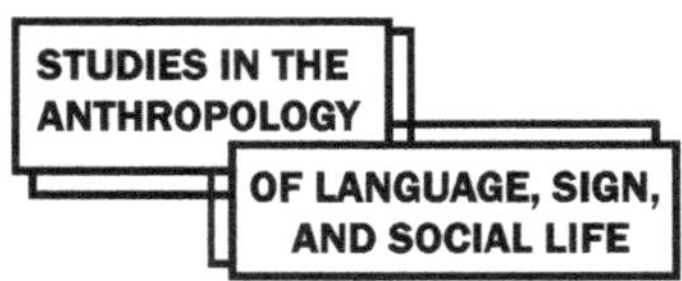

Studies in the Anthropology of Language, Sign, and Social Life focuses on cutting-edge developments in the analysis of linguistic and semiotic processes within a comparative, ethnographic, and socio-historical context. The series provides a home for innovative, boundary-pushing scholarship in linguistic anthropology, as well as work in sociolinguistics, the sociology of interaction, and semiotics. Including both ethnographic monographs and theoretical explorations, books in this series present new ways of understanding the centrality of language and other sign systems to social and cultural life.

Editor: Jack Sidnell, University of Toronto

ONSCREEN/OFFSCREEN

CONSTANTINE V. NAKASSIS

UNIVERSITY OF TORONTO PRESS
Toronto Buffalo London

Toronto Buffalo London
utorontopress.com

ISBN 978-1-4875-4177-4 (paper)
ISBN 978-1-4875-4180-4 (EPUB)
ISBN 978-1-4875-4179-8 (PDF)

Studies in the Anthropology of Language, Sign, and Social Life

---

Library and Archives Canada Cataloguing in Publication

Title: Onscreen/offscreen / Constantine V. Nakassis.
Names: Nakassis, Constantine V., 1979–, author.
Description: Series statement: Studies in the anthropology of language, sign, and social life | Includes bibliographical references and index.
Identifiers: Canadiana (print) 20220396523 | Canadiana (ebook) 2022039654X | ISBN 9781487541774 (softcover) | ISBN 9781487541804 (EPUB) | ISBN 9781487541798 (PDF)
Subjects: LCSH: Motion pictures and language – India – Tamil Nadu. | LCSH: Motion pictures – Semiotics – India – Tamil Nadu. | LCSH: Motion pictures – Political aspects – India – Tamil Nadu. | LCSH: Motion pictures – Social aspects – India – Tamil Nadu. | LCSH: Motion picture industry – India – Tamil Nadu.
Classification: LCC PN1995.4 .N35 2023 | DDC 791.4364 – dc23

We wish to acknowledge the land on which the University of Toronto Press operates. This land is the traditional territory of the Wendat, the Anishnaabeg, the Haudenosaunee, the Métis, and the Mississaugas of the Credit First Nation.

University of Toronto Press acknowledges the financial support of the Government of Canada, the Canada Council for the Arts, and the Ontario Arts Council, an agency of the Government of Ontario, for its publishing activities.

Canada Council for the Arts
Conseil des Arts du Canada

Funded by the Government of Canada
Financé par le gouvernement du Canada

For my infinite girl, Anastasia Eléa Danielle Nakassis, a fan of "Baashaa" like her older sister and father.

And for the late Michael Silverstein, in whose guiding path and in whose thought this book dwells and follows in pale echo.

For K. Senthil Saravana Kumar, இப்புத்தகத்துக்கான ஆராய்ச்சியின் ஆரம்பத்திலிருந்து என்கூட பயணம் செய்தவர், என் அன்பு தோழர் மற்றும் அண்ணன்.

And for E. Annamalai, that most generous scholar who has shared so much with so many of us for the pure love of knowledge, teaching, and all things Tamil.

Contents

Illustrations

Figures

Tables

Acknowledgments

This book is based on research dating back to my very first fieldwork as a green graduate student interested in, but rather ignorant of, Tamil cinema. Along the way, now over fifteen years later, I have accumulated many intellectual debts and made and strengthened many relationships, collegial, friendly, and familial, all of which have made possible and shaped this book. Considerably grayer, I happily remain green (though not as vividly as before, I hope; colourlessly perhaps), honoured by all those thanked below who have helped me along the way by showing me, and encouraging me to push beyond, the limits of my knowledge and understanding.

Primary among those are mentors, colleagues, and students who read, listened to, and commented on parts of the manuscript at various stages: Asif Agha, E. Annamalai, Indira Arumugam, Richard Bauman, Christopher Ball, the late Bernard Bate, Susan Blum, Quentin Boitel, Charles Briggs, Claudia Brittenham, Brigitta Busch, Cécile Canut, Jim Chandler, the late Venkatesh Chakravarthy, Lily Chumley, Francis Cody, Li Cornfeld, James Costa, Whitney Cox, Colleen Kim Daniher, Sonia Das, Melanie Dean, Sara Dickey, Sascha Ebeling, Swarnavel Eswaran, Allyson Field, Daniel Fisher, Luke Fleming, Mi-Cha Flubacher, Anton Ford, Susan Gal, Tejaswini Ganti, Suzanne Gruca, Joseph Hankins, William Hanks, Kathryn Hardy, Nicholas Harkness, Jonas Hassemer, John Haviland, Manon Him-Aquilli, Erika Hoffmann-Dilloway, Stephen Hughes, Judith Irvine, Kajri Jain, Damodaran Karthikeyan, Gwendolyn Kirk, Rajan Krishnan, Amrutha Kunapulli, Michael Kunichika, Emily Kuret, Gabrielle Lear, Martin Lefebvre, Isabelle Leglise, Sabine Lehner, Alaina Lemon, Michael Lempert, Michael Lucey, Rochona Majumdar, Kaley Mason, Bertrand Masquelier, William Mazzarella, Tom McEnany, Anand Pandian, Jennifer Pranolo, V. Rajesh, Karthick Ram Manoharan, Vasu Renganathan, Justin Richland, Ricardo Rivera, Kamala Russell,

Llerena Searle, Susan Seizer, Susan Philips, Shubham Shivang, David Shulman, Maria Sidorkina, the late Michael Silverstein, Salomé Aguilera Skvirsky, Jürgen Spitzmüller, Ravi Sriramachandran, S.V. Srinivas, Perundevi Srinivasan, Marth Umphrey, Anubhav Vasudevan, Anna Weichselbraun, Christopher Wild, Kristina Wirtz, Perry Wong, Kathryn Woolard, and Alice Yao. Discussion with the Michicagoan Faculty Seminar in May 2019 helped me articulate certain of the stakes and commitments of the project. N. Govindarajan provided some last-minute translation advice. Priya Nelson lent generous support during the initial stages of the project. Jack Sidnell offered an enthusiastically engaged scholarly push and boost of confidence that helped move the project forward at a critical juncture; and Jodi Lewchuk helped guide it from there. Meghanne Barker, Daniel Morgan, the late Nancy Munn, Jack Sidnell, and Amanda Weidman generously read drafts of the whole manuscript at various points. Each offered numerous helpful, challenging, and detailed comments that have left deep impressions on my thinking and in this text. All the chapters were graciously read, many times over and at various stages over the course of the writing process, and once as a whole draft, by my fellow writing-group members, E. Summerson Carr, Julie Chu, and Jennifer Cole. Their comments thoroughly improved the book at every level, from writing style to analysis to theoretical formulation. Several anonymous reviewers at various stages greatly helped to improve the book. Many, many thanks to all.

Friends in India and the United States helped the project along in various ways. K. Senthil Saravana Kumar was instrumental in supporting me as a research assistant, a conversational partner about all things Tamil, and as a friend and brother. Dr. Bharathy, Dr. Jayanthi Kannan, Anusha Hariharan, Aravind Kumar, Kedharnath Sairam, Shaktisree Gopalan, Santhosh, Tony James, and the many college students and friends in Madurai and Chennai who spent time watching and talking about Tamil films with me made this project pleasurable to carry out. Venkat Prabhu and his directorial team at the time (Sripathi Rangasamy, Pa. Ranjith, Suresh Mari, A.N. Pitchumani, Senthil Velayudham, Venkateshan R., Basha, Shanoob Karuvath) were incredibly welcoming, opening up their office, sets, and homes to me. Many thanks to Kalyan Kumar, Sakti Saravanan, "Stunt" Silva, Vaibhav Reddy, Shakti Rajan; A.M. Ratnam, Selvaraghavan; Simran Bagga; John Vijay, Madhavi Elango, Vadivukkarasi, Ashok Balakrishnan; C.S. Amudhan, S. Sashikanth, "*Akila Ulaga* Superstar" Shiva, Manobala, Rambala, Suriya Narayanan, Sudhish Kamath; Balaji Sakthivel, Sasikumar; the late K. Balachander, the late Balu Mahendra, the late C.V.

Rajendran, Chitralaya Gopu, Gangai Amaran, K.S. Ravikumar, Mysskin, P.C. Sriram, Pushkar and Gayathri, Rajiv Menon, Sasi; the late "Film News" Anandan, B. Lenin, G. Dhananjayan, Kalyana Devan, K. Hariharan, Uma Vangal, and many, many others, who were incredibly generous with their time, speaking with me about their work and experiences in and of Tamil cinema.

Emily Kuret did a masterful job annotating and designing key transcripts and figures in the book and, more generally, prompted me to think more creatively about design. Ruhi Sah, Sean Maher, and Jackson Cyril, at various points in this project, provided invaluable research assistance. All four helped me see new things about the materials in this books that have illuminated my analyses. Janice Evans and Carolyn Zapf managed the production and copy-editing of the manuscript at its end stage beautifully. Chris Fitzwater perfectly pictured the book in its cover, transposing the painterly aesthetics of Tamil cinema into a painting that brilliantly captures the film image's simultaneous flatness and depth; I am honoured that he did so.

Thanks to my family for their unwavering support and generous advice – Anastasios and Carmen Valenzuela Nakassis, Dimitri Nakassis and Sarah James, Magda Nakassis (who aided in editing the manuscript and helped me clarify my writing and thinking throughout) and Damon Jackman, and especially to my daughters – Carmen Cassandre and Anastasia Eléa, who eagerly watched (and demanded that we watch) many, many Rajinikanth and Vijay films with me in the United States, in India, and on the plane in between – and my dear wife, Julie Cousin, who listened to me prattle on endlessly about everything in the manuscript and nevertheless always had something helpful and insightful to say that improved my thinking. She supports me in innumerable and not-often-enough acknowledged ways, ways I myself often fail to understand and sufficiently appreciate. I am ever grateful. Thank you.

The research and writing of this book were supported by funding from the American Institute of Indian Studies, the Marion R. and Adolph J. Lichtstern Fund for Anthropological Research at the University of Chicago, the Franke Institute of the Humanities at the University of Chicago, and the Committee on Southern Asian Studies (COSAS) at the University of Chicago. COSAS generously made the open-access publication of this book possible. The Lichtstern Fund generously supported manuscript preparation costs.

Chapter 1 expands the article "The Hero's Mass and the Ontological Politics of the Image," published in the *Journal of Cinema and Media Studies* 60, no. 1 (2020):70–91. Versions of this chapter were presented at the workshop "Ideologies of Communication: Practices, Scales, and Modes," held at the University of Vienna (3 July 2019); Amherst College, Center for Humanistic Inquiry (27 March 2019); the University of California – Berkeley Sawyer Seminar on Linguistic Anthropology and Literary and Cultural Studies (14 November 2018); Unité Mixte de Recherche du CNRS, de l'INALCO et de l'IRD (8 June 2018); the Chicago Tamil Forum, the University of Chicago (26 May 2018); Conference of the Society for Linguistic Anthropology (10 March 2018); Indiana University – Bloomington's Dhar India Studies Program (9 March 2017); New York University's Media, Culture, and Communication Department (8 December 2016); the University of Chicago's Mass Culture Workshop (2 December 2016) and Linguistic Anthropology Lab (27 May 2016); and the University of California – Berkeley's Linguistic Anthropology Working Group (4 December 2015).

Parts of Chapter 2 were published as "A Tamil-speaking Heroine" in *Bio-Scope* 6, no. 2 (2015):165–86, published by SAGE, and, with Amanda Weidman, as "Vision, Voice, and Cinematic Presence" in *differences: A Journal of Feminist Cultural Studies* 29, no. 3 (2018):107–36, republished by permission of the publisher, Duke University Press. Versions of, or materials from, this chapter were presented at the Conference of the Society for Linguistic Anthropology (8 April 2022); the IV Annual International Conference of Caesurae Collective Society (27 March 2021); the Department of Anthropology and the South Asia Studies Program Colloquium, the University of California – San Diego (13 April 2015); the Franke Institute of the Humanities, the University of Chicago (6 April 2015); the Chicago Tamil Forum, the University of Chicago (31 May 2014); the Department of Anthropology and Liu Institute for Asia and Asian Studies, University of Notre Dame (20 March 2014); Berkeley Tamil Studies Conference, the University of California – Berkeley (21 April 2012); Tamil Studies Working Group, the University of Chicago (2 March 2012); and "Audible Intimacies: A Symposium on Song in South Indian Cinema," the University of Chicago (16 February 2012).

Chapter 3 expands the article "The Ontological Politics of the Spoof Image in Tamil Cinema," published in *New Review of Film and Television Studies* 17, no. 4 (2019):423–55, available online at https://doi.org/10.1080/17400309.2019.1667056. Versions of this chapter were presented at the Chicago Tamil Forum, the University of Chicago (21 May 2016); and at the 2015 Annual Conference on South Asia (Madison, WI) for the panel "Tamilness in Cinema: Deconstruction, Interrogation, and Entrenchment of Stereotypes" (25 October 2015).

A section of Chapter 4 was published as "Realism, On and Off the Screen" in Anand Pandian, ed., *Subramaniyapuram: The Tamil Film in*

English Translation (Chennai: Blaft Publications, 2014), pp. 217–23, used with permission. Materials from and drafts of this chapter were presented at the panel "Images of Otherness, Othering Images" at the annual American Anthropological Association meeting (22 November 2019); "Sense and Semiosis: Creating Conversations across Linguistic and Visual Anthropology," the University of Chicago (27 September 2019); the workshop "Ideologies of Communication: Practices, Scales, and Modes," University of Vienna (2 July 2019); Atelier de Recherche en Anthropologie du Langage, the University of Paris Descartes, Centre de Recherche sur les Liens Sociaux (26 June 2019); and Amherst College, Center for Humanistic Inquiry (27 March 2019).

Note on Transliteration, Quotation, Names, and Transcripts

I indicate Tamil language material with *italics*, with words of English origin retaining their canonical English spellings and all others transliterated following a modified Madras Lexicon system (as per Nakassis 2016a:xiii–xv). When used within otherwise Tamil speech, linguistic forms of English origin that are not normalized as Tamil are left unitalicized. For the transliteration of Tamil proper names (of people, places, texts, films), I follow general usage in unitalicized font (for example, Madurai instead of *Maturai*), unless they are titles of films, in which case I italicize them (for example, *Mankatha* instead of Mankatha or *Maṅkāttā*). For direct quotations in the original language, I use double quotation marks. For English translations of quoted Tamil discourse, I use single quotation marks. Except for place names, film titles, character names, and publicly known figures, all names in this book are pseudonyms. In some transcripts, I use the following symbols:

(#)	# second pause
(.)	short pause (fewer than 0.2 seconds)
//…//	overlapping speech
=	no pause between turns of talk
-	interruption, break in speech
a::	elongated vowel or sonorant
↓	falling intonation
SMALL CAPS	louder volume
( )	implied, elided, or contracted linguistic material
[ ]	referent of anaphor or other term
< >	description of nonlinguistic action
{ }	description of audience behaviour
(( ))	speech that is unclear or uncertain in a recording
(h)	aspirated burst of laughter within an utterance

...	elided speech
* *	non-diegetic sound (*bleep*)
[EXCL.]	exclusive 'we' (speaker plus non-addressee[s])
[INCL.]	inclusive 'we' (speaker plus addressee[s])
[+HON.]	honorific linguistic form ("polite" pronouns, verb endings, address terms)
[-HON.]	non-honorific linguistic form ("impolite"/familiar pronouns, verb endings, address terms)

ONSCREEN/OFFSCREEN

Introduction: Ontological Politics of the Image

If the term "ontology" is combined with that of "politics" then this suggests that the conditions of possibility are not given. That reality does not precede the mundane practices in which we interact with it, but is rather shaped within these practices. So the term *politics* works to underline this active mode, this process of shaping, and the fact that its character is both open and contested.

– Annemarie Mol, "Ontological Politics: A Word and Some Questions," 1999

All these examples of (magical) realism in which image and contact interpenetrate must have the effect of making us reconsider our very notion of what it is to be an image of some thing, most especially if we wish not only to express but to manipulate reality by means of its image.

– Michael Taussig, *Mimesis and Alterity*, 1993

Introduction

I first began coming to South India in 2003, pursuing an academic interest in the close connection between formal electoral politics, ethno-linguistic identity, and cinema in the state of Tamil Nadu. In particular, and like many, I was intrigued with the way in which a number of popular South Indian film stars – such as the "*Puraṭci Talaivar*" (Revolutionary Leader) M.G. Ramachandran, or MGR for short, in Tamil Nadu – succeeded in segueing from the silver screen to the state Secretariat (Hardgrave 1973, 1993[1975]; Sivathamby 1981; Pandian 1992; Dickey 1993a, 1993b). While such imbrications of cinema and electoral politics were, and are, still present in Tamil Nadu, just as striking when I began doing fieldwork were the hopeful, if also perhaps anxious and frustrated, declarations by the press, by upcoming directors, and by many, typically middle-class, young viewers that a new kind of Tamil cinema had arrived or, at least, was just on the horizon. Critics and viewers alike pointed out how small-budget films like *Sethu* (1999, dir. Bala), *7/G Rainbow Colony* (2004, dir. Selvaraghavan), or *Kaadhal* (2004, dir. Balaji Sakthivel) were outperforming blockbuster films by the current generation of so-called mass heroes – such as the "Superstar" Rajinikanth or his heirs apparent, "*Iḷaiya Taḷapati*" (Young General) Vijay and the "Ultimate Star" *Thala* (Chief) Ajith Kumar – many of whose films were flopping at the box office. Such "new" films, critics announced with an air of relief, were driven by the "story" rather than "hero worship" of the star. Their aesthetic style was realist and their characters authentic to everyday life, viewers insisted, rather than fantastical and unbelievable. They also took up social issues – such as caste violence and women's sexuality – in frank, unapologetic ways, affirmed their directors, rather than glossing over them or neatly resolving them into the infallibility of the hero and his heterosexist narrative. Was the cine-political hero dead (Kurai 2012; Prasad 2014, 2020)? Had I come too late?

The same death knell was sounded when I conducted my dissertation fieldwork in the late 2000s. And it sounded yet again after the fieldwork for this book finished in the mid-2010s, when another new generation of directors, technicians, and actors began making (again) women-centred films, self-reflexive parodies, hero-less films, and films articulating Dalit rights and historical subjectivity, all featuring a panoply of new tropes and narrative genres that were loosening the hold and altering the star image of the ever-disappearing, ever-present mass hero.

Real changes had occurred, of course. These included the rise of the satellite television and the internet, the displacement of the single-screen theatre by the multiplex (and then by over-the-top digital streaming), new film genres and styles, as well as the waning centrality of cinema celebrities in major political parties. Yet what threads these two decades (and the decades before and the decades to come) and their real and imagined newnesses is something more constant, indeed, constitutive: *an ontological politics of the image* – those claims and counterclaims on and for and by the moving film image, contestations about what an image *is* or *is not*, should or should not *be*.

In the Tamil case, as elsewhere, such contestations turn on the question of whether the image is a representational sign or performative act, realist shadow or real presence, just as they turn on the spectator for whom an image is one or the other – a liberal, modern subject who sees the shadows on the cave for what they are or the illiberal idolater in the present-past who clutches at their chains and confuses sign for referent (Mitchell 1986). Consider some examples from the Tamil case:

- The mass hero appears onscreen. He's greeted by the audience with whistles and screams. Fans touch his image, call to it. And he, the actor, responds. Through a close-up of his face and eyes looking at the camera, he stares back at us, speaking to us, pointing at us. Not simply playing a character, this hero-star looms present in the theatre. Outside, large posters of him, appearing as a king and intimating at fans' political aspirations for him, drip with milk and other expensive liquids echoing Hindu rituals of consecration. Media commentators marvel and scoff at the fan excess, even as they too wonder about the hero-star's political plans.

- A character actor is cursed when appearing onscreen in the theatre and later on the street by upset fans of the film's hero-star for hitting and insulting him in the course of the fictional film, an act for which he apologizes in public. A middle-class friend, also a fan of the hero, dismisses such fan responses as the "stupid" thinking of irrational, implicitly low-class fans who, unlike him, can't tell that it's "just a movie" and instead see it *as* its referent.
- Public outcries of obscenity follow the release of a publicity poster for a new film that features its hero (who is also its director) and heroine with lips locked, as well as other images with the hero-director's head lying on the heroine's breast. The heroine, in response, insists that she never "actually" kissed the hero-director, that the image was created using a computer. For his part, the hero-director justifies any so-called obscene images by insisting that the "storyline" demanded them.
- A director of "serious," "class" film laments the frustrating difficulty of making movies in the Tamil industry without compromising with producers to include vulgar, sexist "commercial" elements or with heroes to cater to their demands to add lines or particular shots to "build up" their star images. In the next breath, he says that he wants to do something truthful, that he wants to do something real with his films, not just make "cinema." His producers laugh at him, tell him not to talk mad, tell him to earn money.

In all such cases, at stake are the heterogeneous possibilities of the image, a struggle about what an image is, how it is to be crafted and taken up, and who is responsible for it: the presencing of a star or the representation of a character, fantastical propaganda or truthful text, the act of the actor or the expression of a director, "just a movie" or the prolegomenon to a political career or a spoiled identity, and so on. *Onscreen/Offscreen* is a study of these multiple claims on and for the film image. By bringing together ethnographic fieldwork on the Tamil cinema with the analytic approach of linguistic anthropology,

I explore how such claims manifest as images, as a tension immanent to images between their representationality and performativity, two Janus faces, in dialogue and contestation, split and stitched with a vertical, coronal cut down the flaky tissue of the screen. Such ambivalent images, as we will see, are complexly textured phenomena, both precipitate and process unfolding in multiple modalities – aurally, visually, tactilely – in and across time and space, contested and contesting. What are the politics by which images like these come into being, in which they participate, and which they enact? And what are the semiotic processes and social relations that constitute them? Indeed, what *is* a film image such that it could mediate such effects, processes, and social relations? Such that it could be, at one and the same time, or at one time or another, a realist fictive representation and/or a real performative act? As evidenced above, these are acute, pressing concerns that pervade the Tamil industry, worried about by Tamil directors, actors, producers, technicians, critics, and viewers, and the images that they make, watch, comment upon, and come to bear (or not bear) responsibility for.

From Ontologies to Ontological Politics

The question of what an image is, of course, is not peculiar to debates within the Tamil film industry of South India.[1] It is the foundational question of Western film theory itself, most closely associated with the writings of the French film critic and theorist André Bazin and his commentators and critics. Is the filmic image an emanation of its object, made from the camera's inscription of the profilmic reality that stands before it? Or is it a spectral illusion that affords a mere "impression" of reality in its positioning of its spectator? Does such an image open up a liberal, and liberatory, politics of ethical humanism, where viewers can experience the contingency and ambiguity of the world anew in its re-presencing, where they can make meaning for themselves from its screened shards? Or does it promote a fascist politics of authoritarianism or a patriarchal heterosexism, where meaning is overdetermined and ideology is naturalized through the apparatus's alibi of the real? And thus, should film abide by a realist aesthetic style or attempt to break the smooth surface of the text through modernist refusals of it?[2]

Such theoretical debates in film studies and related fields offer many insights into what an image is and can do. I draw upon them heavily in the chapters that follow. But we should also see these debates for what they are beyond what they denote: namely, situated claims and counterclaims on and for the image, not different in kind from those that haunt and mediate the Tamil cinema (or, for that matter, Hollywood, Nollywood, Bollywood, or any number of other industries; Hansen 1991; Larkin 2008; Ganti 2012). What if, then, we take up this question – what is a film image? – as an empirical object in its own right, examining how it is articulated by various stakeholders (for example, directors, actors, producers, viewers, state organizations, but also film theorists) and with what effect?[3] In this, I follow W.J.T. Mitchell (1986) by asking *when*, *for whom*, and *relative to what ideologies* does this question have political stakes and pragmatic entailments (Branigan 2006:67–8; Alloa 2011; Moxey 2011; Gal and Irvine 2019).

Shifting from the ontological question to the empirical, pragmatist question reveals that the image is not a coherent, pregiven object of analysis. As art historians and visual studies scholars have suggested, we find instead a myriad of theories (*-logia*) of images and their being (*ōn-*, *ont-*), which is to say, claims on and ideologies about what images are (Mitchell 1986:9, 1994; Manghani et al. 2006:3; Elkins and Naef 2011).[4] One is, perhaps, in a position not dissimilar to that faced by the great Genevan linguist Ferdinand de Saussure (1986[1916]:8–11; compare Metz 1974[1971]:9) in confronting what might serve as the object of study for a science of language. And like Saussure, one is led to conclude that to determine an object of analysis like *image* (or *language*) is to take a particular theoretical point of view on it (Goodman 1976; Agha 2007b), that is, to approach it with a particular purpose and methodology in mind. Of course, we need not agree with Saussure's choice of *langue*, the language "system," as the methodological and theoretical basis for a science of language or semiology, or look for any such structuralist equivalent for a science of images. Indeed, quite the opposite, as I argue in what follows.

But, as noted above, it is not only analysts who must, implicitly or explicitly, take a particular theoretical position among others in order to open up a horizon for their inquiry. Anyone who experiences and engages an image must as well. The ontological question of what an image is – and, most importantly, the diverse, shifting, and contentious ways it is put into play – is an immanent feature of all encounters with images, be it by film critics in Paris or Chennai, anthropologists in Chicago or filmgoers in Madurai, or even by non-human semiotic agents in the so-called cloud. And this feature makes the question of the being of images not just an empirical issue but a *political* fact. Contestations about what an image *is*, is the very nature of images. This means that attending to empirical questions about the politics of images is a preliminary to, and not a substitute for, the ontological question about the being of images. It is a way – and to my mind, the most productive way – of asking that question.[5]

Modes of being of film images, and their ontologies, in short, are the outcomes of *ontological politics* (Mol 1999; Chumley 2017) as they come to be institutionalized in and across the textual surfaces of film images, in industrial modes of production and cultures of spectatorship, and in the technological apparatuses of the cinema.[6] From this point of view, neither the mode of being of an image nor its ontologies are sited *in* or *of* the image, its spectators, or its apparatus. Rather, we must approach them as the distributed effects and achievements of the work of variously situated social projects, projects that make the being of images "a terrain of political struggles" (Strassler 2020:12), dialogic becoming, and even stabilization. Such projects constitute, though do not overdetermine, the being of images.

Such ontological politics of the image manifest in multiple, interrelating ways. In South India, the question of what an image is or could or should be has everything to do with elections, populist mobilization, and state power (as discussed in more detail later); with the political economy of the industry (the politics of distribution, production, financing, censorship, taxation, industry unions, and so on); with the politics of what can be filmed and put onscreen; with the politics of gender, caste, kinship, and age and status that regiment how images are made, who or what is held responsible for them, who may engage them and how; and, above all, with the processes through which the sensibility and the meaningfulness of film images are imagined, interpreted, circulated, contested, and transformed. The phrase *ontological politics* captures each of these entangled dimensions (electoral, economic, industrial, sociological, inter/textual, interpretive) as they come to construe and produce – or "perform," as Annemarie Mol (1999) puts it – the reality of images, images as they come into existence and in their capacity to semiotically represent/presence the real.

At the same time, each of these dimensions and the semiotic processes that constitute them reach far beyond cinematic images into wider sociocultural and political worlds, worlds that must be taken into account to understand the nature(s) of images. Contestations in South India over caste domination or equality, the (im)propriety of Tamil femininity, the fates of regional political parties or ethnolinguistic identity, among other issues, each play out in a wide variety of media. Yet all serve as a critical backdrop in this study for the question of what a film image is or could be, and vice versa. As we see across the various chapters of the book, film images are a central node for how these social fields are manifested, represented and enacted, reproduced and transformed. To ask after the politics of caste (Chapter 4), gender and sexuality (Chapters 1, 2, 4), kinship (Chapters 2, 3), electoral representation (Chapters 1, 3), ethnolinguistic identity (Chapter 2), and so on is to ask after the politics of what a film image is and can do, just as to ask what an image is or should be requires appeal to those wider worlds in which "the screen is nothing but one object among many" (Casetti 1998[1986]:129). While an ontological politics, thus, might appear as one *kind* of politics of the image among others, it is also – whether implicitly presupposed or explicitly foregrounded – *the* political ground for whatever other ends or means images participate in mediating, encompassing every other kind of image politics as a dimension of it.

Towards a Linguistic Anthropology of Cinema

To theorize the political and semiotic work of the ontological politics of the image requires, as I suggested above, not simply a different theoretical conceptualization of our object of study but also – or what amounts to the same thing – a different methodology and analytic strategy. In this book, I provide this by drawing on the ethnographic methods, analytic tools, and semiotic theory of linguistic anthropology.[7] Below, I describe in general terms what such an approach – what I call *a linguistic anthropology of cinema* – entails and how it illuminates the study of film and cinema.

A central commitment of linguistic anthropological analysis is the close attention it pays to the semiotic dimensions of social life in and as anchored to the contexts of their happening (that is, to their *pragmatics* or *indexical* grounding). Linguistic anthropological analysis unpacks the processes by which sign activity unfolds in and across events and, further, the ways those pragmatic processes are mediated by reflexive semiotic activity (which is thereby *metapragmatic* in scope, often ideologically so). There is a genuine, if non-resolving dialectical relationship between these dimensions, between semiotic processes in and across events, their form and their pragmatics, and between such processes and the metapragmatics that mediate them and arise from them. A linguistic anthropology of cinema is the study of these dialectical relations, on and off the screen, as they give rise to images and the social worlds and ontologies they mediate and are mediated by.[8] It is, to adapt a phrase variously used by Émile Durkheim, Marcel Mauss, and Michael Silverstein, the study of the *total semiotic fact of cinema* (Nakassis 2016b).

A linguistic anthropology of cinema, thus, focuses on cinema and film not as made up of symbolic "codes" – as did an older generation of structuralist film semiology (Metz 1974[1971], 1991[1971], 2016[1986]; Lotman 1976; Bellour 2000[1979]; compare Worth and Adair 1972:133; see note 7 in this chapter) – but as contingent and emergent events of by-degrees institutionalized iconic indexical practice as they traverse the screen. (*Entextualization* and *interdiscursivity* are the technical terms used by linguistic anthropologists to capture the emergent coherence of and connections made between events of semiosis.[9]) Of interest to such an approach, thus, are not simply the moving images on the screen (as autonomous text, sui generis code, and so on) but the real-time, performatively efficacious and socially meaningful practices (and social relations, participation frameworks [Goffman 1979], and the like) they occasion and that occasion them – that they *are* – wherever and whenever they take place.

Studying such events, practices, and relations – and how they shape and are shaped by images, by images-as-events – requires ethnographic fieldwork. It requires being party to and involved in such events, practices, relations, and images so as to understand them in their contingent particularity and social and cultural significance. The analyses and theoretical arguments in the various chapters of this book, for instance, emerge out of and are informed by thirty-six months of ethnographic research over eight research trips in Tamil Nadu, India, from 2004 to 2018. This research involved fieldwork – on film sets, in production offices and post-production suites, at industry events (audio launches, parties, award ceremonies), in television studios, film theatres, college dormitories, and people's homes. It involved recorded interviews (totalling 125), and countless more informal conversations, with directors, producers, actors, technicians (cinematographers, editors, fight choreographers, dance choreographers, stylists, dialogue writers), publicists, film critics, fan-club members, and everyday viewers, as well as close analyses of select films and press and industry metadiscourses about them (press releases, film reviews, trade reportage, gossip publications). Guiding this research was the analytic question of how the practices of these dispersed yet entangled social projects (of filmmakers, producers, actors, fans, politicians, film critics, journalists, and film theorists, among others) relate to each other in and through images, how they mediate and are mediated by the filmic images that they mutually orient to, engage, and ontically manifest; and, further, how we can detect these relations in and beyond the image, just as we can trace such images in and beyond these relations (Nakassis 2016a:227–37).

This way of conceptualizing and studying images as the medium and outcome of the dialectics of indexical practice has a number of wider implications. The first is that filmic text and cinematic context are mutually constitutive *precipitates* of semiotic activity. They are not pregiven. They are dynamically emergent. This implication undermines any notion of an absolute "inside" of the image or text that could be read or analysed – for example, for its spectator positions, style, performative force, representational content, being – independent of its constitutive "outsides," independent of those empirical moments and sites in which it takes (its) place. Such an approach, thus, presents more than familiar critiques of text-internalist approaches to film, avowals of empirical studies of cinematic "reception" or "production," or even a plea for their additive combination (Kuhn 1984; Casetti 1998[1986]:13; Gledhill 1999[1988]; Metz 2016[1986]:§83; Gunning 1991:10–13; see Nakassis 2016a:184–7, 231–7). Neither text nor context alone, our object of analysis is the porous, dialectical "interface" (Casetti 1998[1986]:129) between the two; indeed, our object is the very process by which they come to be. In this book, this plays out through a necessary tacking back and forth between close analysis of select films (indeed, particular scenes and image-acts) and a selective interrogation of their making, circulation, and uptake so as to theorize this relation of onscreen/offscreen.[10]

Second, approaching images as relational processes that transpire in and across events, on and off and across the screen, requires that we actively resist delimiting medium specificities (or the singular media they presuppose) as the basis or boundary of our analyses or their empirical foci, including, and especially, in our interrogation of the being of the image. Without denying such specificities, a linguistic anthropology of cinema is concerned with semiotic processes and relations that give rise to and breech them at one and the same time. Such processes are not peculiar to any one medium. (Nor are they peculiar to any particular modality. As should be evident from this discussion, images are not only visual but occur in many, perhaps all, modalities; see Nakassis 2019 for discussion.) There is no route to medium specificity or the delimitation of a medium – epistemologically and, I would add, ontically – that is not already mediated by attention to the empirical pragmatics/politics of image-events/acts. Such events and acts are multimodal and transmedial. And it is they that demand our study.

The third implication, which follows from the other two, is that a concern with the (meta)pragmatics of film and cinema requires that our analytic encounters with film and cinema always be framed through attention to empirical situations that implicate us as analysts but outstrip our own subjectivities. We cannot assume to know what a film image is as such, or for anyone in particular, independent of analysis of the wider sociocultural worlds within which images circulate, especially given the historical, cultural, and situational variability and diversity of cinematic worlds. For an approach such as that described here, methodological individualism will not suffice.

As the chapters that follow demonstrate, a linguistic anthropology of cinema can help reframe a number of issues that span film studies, visual studies, and visual and media anthropology, offering up fresh answers and avenues of exploration to enduring questions and debates, from the ontology of the image to questions of realism, spectatorship, style, and performativity, among others. In addition, a turn to the cinema offers up a provocation for rethinking the field of linguistic anthropology itself. In the Conclusions of the book, I argue that *Onscreen/Offscreen* is not simply a work that draws *on* linguistic anthropology but is a work *of* linguistic anthropology, despite (and in a way, *because of*) not focusing on "language." In so arguing, I draw out how this claim on the book implies the necessarily open boundaries and multiple, interlocked centres of linguistic anthropology in relation to the wider intellectual worlds in which it traffics.

/ / /

In the rest of this Introduction, I turn to the history of cinema in South India, mapping the terrain of the ontological politics that concern the remainder of the book. In outlining this history, I give special attention to those tensions on and off screen that the chapters that follow interrogate: between story and hero, character and actor, director/studio and star, and, above all, the tensions and confluence between presence and representation, performativity and narrative.[11] I focus, in particular, on the post-Independence emergence of the "mass hero" – a type of populist, and thus often caste-unmarked, hero-star endemic to South India, whose auratic presence enables forms of charismatic power in electoral politics – and his filmic discontents: in particular, advocates for filmic realism and alternate ontologies and politics of the image. I conclude the Introduction with an outline of the chapters.

A Brief History of Tamil Cinema

Cinema arrived in Bombay months after, and in the Madras Presidency a year after, the first commercial screening in Paris in 1895 (Baskaran 1996; Hughes 1996:27). As Stephen Hughes (1996) has shown, cinema took root in South India as a form of European variety entertainment – what Tom Gunning (1986, 1991) and André Gaudreault (2009[1999]) have called the "cinema of attractions" – that was only available to elite European and Indian audiences in Madras City (now, Chennai). Yet with the growth of touring cinemas and permanent cinema houses in the first two decades of the twentieth century, the audience for film spread – beyond European elites to the Indian working classes and beyond Madras City to provincial towns – just as more and more Indian-produced films – mainly based on Hindu religious mythology (Baskaran 1996) – began to be made for Indian audiences.[12]

By the 1920s, cinema had come to be perceived as a decidedly "mass" medium: low-class, vulgar, stigmatized/ing (Ganti 2012). Yet it was not until the 1930s, with the advent of "talkies," that Indian films began to dominate local exhibition and displace American and European imported films (though neither ever disappeared from Indian theatres). With sound came a number of transformations in the Indian industry. The most important of these for my discussion are the movement of theatre artists and stories into the cinema and the eventual regionalization of India's film industries in the 1930s; the articulation of the "Tamil" film industry to an ethnolinguistic identity politics in the 1940s and 1950s; and the emergence of a class-linked discourse of realism and a South Indian star system in the 1930s and its transformation by regional identity politics in the 1950s and 1960s. This history evinces a particular ontological politics that serves as the backdrop to my fieldwork in the twenty-first century, the central thread of which is the tension between the presence and representationality of the image.

For a "Tamil" Cinema

From the mid-nineteenth century up until the 1930s, the primary mass entertainment medium in South India was dramatic musical theatre. With the advent of sound in film and the possibility of addressing mass audiences, Indian film producers in the 1930s increasingly turned to staged musical drama for content and personnel, bringing South Indian drama troupes to Bombay, Pune, and Calcutta to perform their plays for the camera. While the development of an infrastructure of silent cinema exhibition and local cultures of filmgoing in the 1920s was critical to this remediation (Hughes 1996), equally important was the parallel emergence of a gramophone record industry based on recording the singing stars of the theatre.[13] The emergence of so-called talkie films capitalized on such theatre and recording stars, with up to 80 per cent of three-to-four-hour feature films filled with song (approximately fifty to sixty songs per film; Dungan and Smik 2001:56).

By the mid-1930s, a number of sound studios emerged in Madras, resulting in an increased number of films more specifically targeting South Indian audiences (Sivathamby 1981:23) and the eventual emergence of a "Tamil" film industry. Yet the creation of such an industry was not a simple, automatic result of the introduction of sound. While sound made it possible for India's film industries and language communities to be aligned in new, regionally defined ways, the ideological and institutional emergence of a "Tamil" film industry (and in constitutive contrast to a Telugu industry, a Hindi industry, and so on; compare Hardy 2014) was an outcome of the interests and practices of a number of industry stakeholders, as well as part of the ongoing formation of a Tamil language community out of what had been (and continues to be) a deeply multilingual speech community (Annamalai 2011; Shulman 2016).[14] Into the 1930s, what it meant to address or produce a film for a specifically South Indian, or even a Telugu or Tamil, audience was less than clear (as reflected in the multilingual films produced during that era).[15] It was, however, increasingly becoming an object of contention for critics, audiences, and filmmakers. By the second half of the 1930s, a clear sense of a differentiated "Tamil" film type and "Tamil" film industry took hold (Hughes 2011).[16]

A critical condition of possibility for this ideological suturing of film industry to language community was the very concept of a monoglot *Tamil* language community composed of persons who could be addressed by films *as* Tamils, which is to say, as subjects whose identity was linguistically defined. This concept was itself a historical novelty.

The nineteenth and twentieth century witnessed a major transformation in ethnolinguistic imagination in the Madras Presidency. Colonial philological research into the relatedness of what became known as the Dravidian language family (Trautmann 2006; Mitchell 2009) proved that the South Indian languages came from a different genetic stock than the North Indian languages (as members of the equally novel Indo-Aryan/European language family), which, in turn, grounded the claim that its speakers, as later scholars and political actors argued, were of a different ethno-racial and cultural-historical population. Alongside a literary renaissance and re-"discovery" of ancient Tamil texts came a religious resurgence of South Indian Saivism (Ramaswamy 1997), as well as, at the beginning of the twentieth century, the emergence of the non-Brahmin movement, a consortium of elite, upper-caste non-Brahmin South Indians – initially organized as the South Indian Liberal Federation and, later, the Justice Party – that protested Brahmin monopoly on colonial positions of power (Pandian 2007). The outcome of this movement was a new hegemonic form of identity: a Dravidian – and more specifically,

Tamil – identity that was explicitly and primarily based in language, region, and ethnicity. While this identity, of course, had a caste and religious component – as non-Brahmin, Saivite or atheist – it was ideologically predicated on subsuming and transforming older forms of identity based on caste, kin group, local polity, religious community, or literary community of practice into an ethnolinguistic dispensation.

In the first half of the twentieth century, these distinct but entangled threads – the so-called Dravidian movement – came to be channelled through the rationalist, reformist efforts of "Periyar" (The Great One) E.V. Ramasamy (1879–1973). Periyar, along with his lieutenants, "*Ariñar Aṇṇā*" (Learnèd, Older Brother) C.N. Annadurai (1909–69) and "*Kalaiñar*" (The Artist) Mu. Karunanidhi (1924–2018), agitated against social injustice and promoted a Dravidianist political consciousness. They did this work initially through the Self-Respect Movement (which merged with the Justice Party in 1939) and the Dravidar Kazhagam (Dravidian Federation, or DK for short, formed in 1944), and later through the Dravida Munnetra Kazhagam (Dravida Progress Federation, or DMK for short), an explicitly electoral political party formed in 1949 when Annadurai and Karunanidhi split from Periyar and the DK.

The narrative that underwrote the Dravidian movement described an autochthonous, egalitarian and secular, ethnolinguistically pure Dravidian/Tamil community (which the DK, and later the DMK, defended and represented), which was and continued to be, they inveighed, unjustly dominated by an Aryan, Sanskritic, and casteist Brahminical culture and political party – the Indian National Congress – from the north. What was necessary, they argued, was to uplift the poor and low-caste, abolish religious (that is, Brahminical) superstition, purify the Tamil language (from Sanskrit) and restore it to the greatness of antiquity, and keep Hindi out of the state (for example, in education, bureaucracy, public signage, and so on).

In the 1930s and into the 1940s, the Dravidian movement made extensive use of the popular media of stage oratory (Bate 2009) and theatre, holding large public meetings and staging socially reformist plays that didactically propagated the DK's rationalist and at times iconoclastic ideology in efforts to politicize their audiences.[17] After the Second World War and the concomitant downturn in the film industry,[18] this message moved to the cinema, as cautious film producers turned to the popular plays of the time for source material (as they had with mythologicals with the advent of sound in earlier decades). Such producers increasingly began to make films penned by Dravidian ideologues such as Annadurai and Karunanidhi, whose plays had flourished during wartime.[19] But it was not just writers – in the 1940s and 1950s the

Tamil film industry teemed with Dravidianist lyricists, directors, and actors who brought their politics (and politicized language style) to their films.[20]

By mid-century, Tamil cinema had wed mass politics to mass entertainment and the fate of ethnolinguistic identity to the fate of the screen.

Realism and the Mass Hero

In transforming the cinema's cultural value from an elite form of (anglicized) entertainment to a form of (Indian) mass entertainment, the shift to sound cinema in the 1930s also set a challenge to South Indian elites. Such elites, as M.S.S. Pandian (1996) argued, found it increasingly necessary to engage with, and participate in, what they had otherwise ignored as an uncouth medium marked by its popularity among (excessively) enthusiastic low-class audiences (Baskaran 1996:1–11; compare Gaudreault 2009[1999]:131),[21] its (vulgar) performance by artists from stigmatized, lower-caste theatrical backgrounds, and its remediation of (fantastical) folk tales and religious mythological topics from popular theatre.[22]

In this context, filmic realism emerged as a strategy of class and caste distinction among urban elites, both as an aesthetic style produced within the industry and as an ideological valuation of films. Such elites advocated in and out of the industry for forms of Western-style filmic realism – plausible narratives, contemporary themes, authentic depictions of everyday people, understated acting, absence of songs – against what they saw as the patently unrealistic theatrical aesthetics and associated modes of excited and participatory reception favoured by subaltern audiences. Such advocacy was akin to the "gentrification" (but with less success perhaps) that Miriam Hansen (1991:64) and others have discussed in the context of the emergence of "classical" Hollywood cinema (Dyer 1998[1979]:22; Gunning 1991; Casetti 2009: 59; compare Ganti 2012 on the gentrification of Hindi cinema in the 1990s).[23] In the 1930s and 1940s, realism took the form of what was called the "social" – a film genre whose everyday characters facing contemporary issues in secular, modern timespaces (Vasudevan 1995) contrasted it to the so-called mythological.

While I discuss this enregisterment of realism in more detail in Chapter 4, critical here are two things. First, the Tamil cinema as an ethnolinguistically specified mass medium emerged alongside an ontological politics of realism. The two are co-constitutive. This politics of realism has enjoyed a longevity from the 1930s to the present across rather drastic stylistic, generic, and technological transformations, characterized by its insistent opposition between fantastical "mass" cinema for subaltern crowds and "serious" realist "class" cinema for liberal, middle-class subjects. Second, this politics of realism quickly became articulated, in complex and at times contradictory ways, to the Dravidian identity politics – and later electoral politics – that arose alongside and through the co-emergence of Tamil cinema and its ontological politics.

In the 1940s and 1950s, the Dravidianist use of cinema produced what became known as the "DMK film," after the eponymous political party whose ideology such films espoused. Such films voiced the DMK's rationalist political ideology through the "social's" form of social realism (the influential screenwriter and politician C.N. Annadurai, for example, was deeply influenced by Italian neorealism and classic Hollywood realism).[24] The canonical DMK film, *Parashakti* (1952, dir. Krishnan–Panju), provides a striking example of the ontological politics at stake in this moment (Pandian 1991). The film, penned by Mu. Karunanidhi, famously articulates Periyar's idol-smashing iconoclasm in a now-legendary scene of the protagonist, Gunasekaran (played by the then-debutant Sivaji Ganesan), denouncing the immoral hypocrisy of a Brahmin priest who tried to rape his sister in the sanctum sanctorum of the temple. Castigating the priest, who has mistakenly taken Gunasekaran's voice as that of the deity herself, Gunasekaran responds to the priest's invocation of the eponymous Goddess by saying, in contempt: 'It [the idol] won't speak, it's a stone' (*Atu pēsātu. Kal*). At precisely this moment of unveiling the real presence of the idol as mere inanimate representation, however, the soundtrack where Gunasekaran/Sivaji enunciates "*kal*" (stone) was silenced by the state's censor board. Gunasekaran/Sivaji's lips, however, are visible and hyperarticulated (Venkatachalapathy 2018:31–2), a proleptic (visual) response perhaps to an act of (aural) censorship (by the then–Congress-controlled government) that construed this cinematic act of representation – itself a critique of performatively presentist idolatry – as a performative act of sacrilegious propaganda.

The social realism of the DMK film was also inflected by the DMK's aims to mobilize the masses under the sign of Tamil identity and its purist language politics. Critically important to this project was the way in which the "social" genre favoured speech over song as the narrative engine and mode of attraction (Krishnan 2009:158–9; Eswaran Pillai 2015). This predilection shifted the narrative economy of Tamil film by focalizing the speaking hero as the centre of the narrative diegesis in contrast to, as had been the case in the 1940s, a more diffuse, disjointed narrative carried by the songs of male and, especially, female singing stars (Weidman 2015, 2021).[25] The DMK hero, however, didn't simply speak; he efflorescently delivered mellifluous, pro-DMK monologues (Pandian 1991). And he did so in the signature style of Dravidian political oratory, *sentamiḻ*, that register of "refined" and "beautiful," "pure" and antiquated Tamil, which, through the efforts of the Dravidian movement, came to indexically invoke a Tamil antiquity imagined to predate contact with Brahminical Hinduism and Sanskrit, a time of Tamil kings ruling a Tamil land (Bate 2009). When this hero spoke, he spoke within a Dravidian world, in and as a Tamil, and – as we'll see – *for* the Tamil people and on behalf of their (putative) party, the DMK.

In short, the DMK film grafted an elite, aesthetic register of realism onto its populist ethnolinguistic identity politics (Gal 2018); and in so doing, afforded new forms of spectatorial identification (with the figure of the hero) and thus star value (for the male actor and his political party; Prasad 2014). This grafting came to radically alter the politics and the mode of being of the filmic image.[26]

The rise of the DMK film brought about a new crop of politically affiliated hero-actors – most important of them being M.G. Ramachandran (1917–87) and Sivaji Ganesan (1928–2001) – who replaced an earlier generation of politically non-affiliated singing stars (for example, M.K.T. Bhagavathar and P.U. Chinnappa).[27] Such new stars rode but also carried forth the popularity of the Dravidian movement (Hardgrave 1973, 1993[1975]), enunciating its ideologies onscreen but also participating in party activities offscreen. Stars like Sivaji Ganesan and MGR were regular attractions at public party meetings and served in party posts. MGR, for example, was a DMK party member from 1953, a DMK member of the Madras Presidency Legislative Council from 1962 to 1967, a DMK member of the Tamil Nadu Legislative Assembly from 1967 to 1971 (when the DMK swept the National Congress Party out of the state), and DMK party secretary from 1969 to 1972.[28] He acted all the while.

Yet if MGR's films initially promoted DMK party ideology, as K. Sivathamby (1981) and M.S.S. Pandian (1992) have noted, the narratives of his swashbuckling folkloric but also socially realist films in the 1950s and 1960s increasingly held out a space especially for *him* as *the* hero who would bring social justice to the Tamil masses, rather than being simply the mouthpiece for the party and its dialogue writers. Instead of (relatively) realist social critique voiced by the hero-character (which implied the DMK as its offscreen solution), in MGR's films such critique increasingly found its resolution fantastically personalized in his infallible star image. This transformation of the DMK film into the

MGR film ironically reversed the iconoclastic social realism of the former into a semiotics of star adulation that entangled character and actor, onscreen and offscreen, cinema and politics in new and complex ways (Dickey 1993b).

Political leaders within the DMK – such as Sampath and Neduchezhiyan, and eventually Karunanidhi himself – early on realized the implications of this ontic transformation. While they benefited from the propaganda function and star value of hero-stars like MGR, they came to see such film stardom as a political threat (Sivathamby 1981:40; Pandian 1992:122–3). When the DMK party leader and chief minister of the time, C.N. Annadurai, died in 1969, tensions between his successor Mu. Karunanidhi and the wildly popular MGR led to the latter leaving the DMK in 1972 to form his own party, the Annadurai DMK (later AIADMK). Before and after MGR's split, DMK leaders attacked the image that they had a hand in giving rise to, both by launching Karunanidhi's eldest son as a film rival to MGR (a miserable failure; Venkatachalapathy 2018:38) and by attempting to "break this overlap between the cinematic and the real" (Pandian 1992:120), insistently arguing to the general public that image and referent, character and actor, were not one and the same (for example, through booklets with titles such as *Cinema Soru Poduma* [Is Cinema Enough to Feed Us?]).[29] Neither tactic worked. MGR was voted into power in 1977 until his death in 1987, after which his onscreen and offscreen consort, the heroine J. Jayalalitha, after an internal power structure with MGR's wife, took over the AIADMK (see the book's Conclusions).

M. Madhava Prasad (2014) has termed this close relationship between cinematic representation and populist electoral representation *cine-politics*. As he argues, cine-politics in South India emerged out of a particular historical conjuncture, wherein ethnolinguistic regional aspirations for recognition and sovereignty (for example, Periyar's call for a separate Dravida Nadu) were threatened by their subordination to the postcolonial Indian nation-state and thereby consigned to a precarious state of potential "political inexistence."[30] While one site where this was worked out was the demand for linguistic and regional autonomy, as expressed by successful agitations against Hindi (for example, in the 1930s and 1960s) and for linguistically defined states (in the 1950s), another was the figure of the mass hero himself.[31] Thwarted aspirations for regional sovereignty lived on by being displaced into the imaginary diegetic worlds of the cinema, in films wherein the hero-star was narratively emplotted and extra-narratively taken up as a representative of – indeed, the leader (*talaivar*) of – the masses, the Tamil people[32] (hence, in general, the importance of such hero-stars' caste unmarkedness, which allowed them to represent the caste-heterogeneous "masses" via their putatively shared ethnolinguistic belonging). According to this argument, the election of the MGR as chief minister of the state was the actualization of a shadow sovereignty and structure of political relationality that already existed on the screen as a virtual political community demanded by his fan-spectators (Krishnan 2009; Srinivas 2009).[33] The possibility of this cine-politics was itself, this being the critical point, a particular ontological politics of the image, enabled by a particular kind of performatively present filmic image that not only represented on the screen but also acted and transacted beyond and across it.

It is relative to this cine-political and ontological dispensation that the subsequent history of Tamil cinema from the 1970s to the present has unfolded. As we see across the book's chapters, it is around the populist, charismatic figure of the mass hero (and his fan) that other image types, political projects, and subjectivities have orbited, constituting the field of Tamil cinema as an oscillatory tension between presentist performativity and realist representationality, between desires for and anxieties about cine-populism and the fate of postcolonial liberal democracy.[34] As Sivaji and MGR's dominance began to wane in the 1970s – with Sivaji's box office steadily reducing and MGR's retirement from cinema in 1978 (Sundar Kaali 2000; Eswaran Pillai 2012; Chakravarthy 2018:270) – a new kind of auteur-director emerged in the late 1970s that operated outside of the star system and studios that supported it.[35] Such directors, as I discuss in more detail in Chapter 4, produced a new kind of cinema: realist, hero-less, and deeply cynical of the promises of Nehruvian nationalism and regional Dravidianist social revolution.

Out of this brief, transformational moment (itself an echo of the ontological politics of a generation past) came the next crop of stars – "Superstar" Rajinikanth and "*Ulaga Nayagan*" (World Hero) Kamal Haasan pre-eminent among them – who through popularity garnered from such realist films reasserted dominance over the commercial film industry in the 1980s and into the 1990s.[36] By the end of the millennium, expectation had reached a fever pitch that Rajinikanth – MGR's cinematic heir – would enter electoral politics (Nakassis 2017, 2019). He did not, and the new millennium began with another set of crises and transformations surrounding the political and economic viability of the existing hero-stars, as well as the rise of a new generation of actors, directors, and technicians. In this historical moment, long-standing debates about the status of the Tamil film image – what it is and could be – and the possibilities of a new, realist cinema were reinvigorated (again) with new force. It was at this moment that I began my first research into

Tamil cinema and where *Onscreen/Offscreen* picks up, interrogating the ontological politics of the image in the first two decades of the twenty-first century.[37]

Overview of the Chapters

Onscreen/Offscreen is organized into two parts – Part I: Presence/Representation and Part II: Representation/Presence, each of which comprises two chapters – followed by the book's Conclusions.

Chapter 1, "The Hero's Mass," focuses on the performative presence of the mass-hero figure and his populist political potency as it intersects with competing ontological claims on the image as realist representation. The chapter works through a close analysis of a particular sequence in the 2011 film *Mankatha* (dir. Venkat Prabhu) and its uptake, alongside interviews with its director, cinematographer, fight choreographer, actor, and fans of its hero, Ajith Kumar. In this scene, a character (played by Vaibhav Reddy) slaps the film's hero (played by the popular hero-star Ajith Kumar). Shot in a realist style that amplifies the profilmic actuality of the slaps, this sequence angered Ajith's devoted fan following, who threatened Vaibhav, the actor, with violence offscreen. The chapter unpacks this fan anger and the semiotic ideologies that subtend it, revealing how questions of gender, age, and status, as well as aesthetic style and narrative framing, participate in the profaning potential of diegetic acts of violence towards the sacred hero-star. Further showing the ways that the film and its makers dialogically anticipated this uptake by fans, Chapter 1 illuminates the constitutive tension that weaves the sequence's textual surface between the hero's massive presence and the realism of the director's narrative text. This tension, I argue, encapsulates the politics and political economy of the wider Tamil cinema and, indeed, film images in general. Engaging with André Bazin on questions of the film image's presence and being, the chapter concludes that images harbour ontological multiplicities that problematize any attempt to theorize THE being of the image as anything other than a tenuous, ideological, and institutional achievement.

Chapter 2, "The Heroine's Stigma," focuses on the semiotics and politics of vision as they envelop and emanate from images of film heroines and so-called item dancers (film artists who perform in racy, one-off song-and-dance sequences). Focusing on one song sequence in the 2004 film *7/G Rainbow Colony* (dir. Selvaraghavan), and drawing on ethnographic research and interviews with film viewers and the film's director and dance choreographer, as well as interviews with actresses in the industry, this chapter explores the stigmatized performativity of women's acts of appearing onscreen and how filmic textuality and narrative form variously exploit or bracket such performative presence. Extending Chapter 1, here we see how the image's actness (its capacity to performatively act) and narrativity (its capacity to narratively represent) efface and absent as much as they presence. Engaging classic work in feminist film studies on spectacle, narrative, and structures of looking, I show how a particular mode and chronotope of vision – conditioned not by the filmic apparatus per se but by more general ideologies of publicness, kinship, and femininity – tangles onscreen and offscreen, presence and absence. This chronotope and mode of vision conditions the sociology of actresses (who, since economic liberalization in the 1990s, have increasingly tended to be non-Tamil and unmarried) and the division of cinematic labour in the industry (between non–Tamil-speaking screen actresses who appear but are unheard and Tamil-speaking voice actresses – or "dubbing artists," as they are known in the industry – who are heard but not seen). This ethnolinguistic/gendered distribution, I argue, plays into a masculinist culturalist politics of Tamil identity within and outside of the film industry, namely, the widely circulating discourse that "our" girls are too modest to act onscreen. The chapter's epilogue concludes with reflection on the emergence in the late 2010s of women-centred films that attempt to displace the performative economy of stigma, which places actresses and the heroine/item at the margins of the text, industry, and society.

If Part I of *Onscreen/Offscreen* focuses on the performativity of the film image and the particular modes of being, vision, and textual strategies that subtend and contest it, Part II takes up concerted attempts within the commercial Tamil film industry to instate alternate modes of being, production formats, and modes of spectatorship, namely, realist, narrative-driven, and director-authored texts. Chapter 3, "The Politics of Parody," focuses on the industry's first full-on spoof film, *Thamizh Padam* (Tamil Film; 2010, dir. C.S. Amudhan). Through close analysis of the film and interviews with its producer, director, screenwriter, and actors, I detail the ontological politics of the spoof image: its liberal yearning for a more "serious," more realistic, story- and director-driven cinema. Here, parody attempts to instate a representationalist "regime of imageness" (Rancière 2007, 2009) in lieu of the performative presence of the populist mass hero that it lampoons, producing the real through its (inter)textual excess. And yet, as I show, the onscreen politics of *Thamizh Padam* was only possible, and took the textual form it did, because of the offscreen, illiberal political connections of its producer. Every ontological politics, the chapter argues, turns on the dialectical relation between the politics *of* an image and the politics *for* that image; in other words, between those politics borne by images and those that give rise to them, enable them to circulate, and condition their uptake. One medium and result of this dialectical relation, I suggest, is the image itself, ambivalent and fraught in its internal textuality and perlocutionary force, resulting in images that ask us to construe them in their representationality only to reinscribe the performativity they otherwise disavow.

Chapter 4, "The Politics of the Real," is based on the analysis of a number of low-budget, non–hero-centred realist films that emerged in the 2000s, in particular the 2004 film *Kaadhal* (Love; dir. Balaji Sakthivel). Drawing on interviews with directors, producers, and viewers of such films, as well as on ethnographic accounts of filmgoing, this chapter looks at how films like *Kaadhal* bear an ambivalent politics that is, at one and the same time, an ontological politics of the image and a class and caste politics of spectatorship. In particular, its attempts to critically depict caste patriarchy risked eliciting negative, even violent, reactions from casteist viewers who would construe the image *not* as realist representation but as a performative image-act issued by the director. By attempting to foreclose such an entextualization of the image – which would effectively undermine the film's critique of caste – *Kaadhal* avoided the taboo performativity of what it censored from its textuality (namely, depicting the sexuality of the dominant-caste heroine). As such, the performativity of the image, and the illiberal uptake it anticipated, organized the text in its absence and thereby participated in the ongoing conventionalization – or, more technically, *enregisterment* (Agha 2007a) – of realism and caste. Here, again, we see how the performative potentiality of the image erupts out of it, even when (and especially when perhaps) it is attempted to be bracketed by a purely representationalist framing. The chapter ends with a reconsideration of Bazin's account of realism as an ethical stance towards the being of the image. I affirm Bazin's account while arguing that *what* such a being entails has to be thought differently from Bazin's formulation, indeed, has to be thought as an ontological politics of realism.

The book's Conclusions begins by reflecting on the tension and complicity of narrative and performativity, presence and representation that are at issue throughout the book, here posed in the context of the seeming breakdown and revival of cine-politics in the late 2010s with the death of J. Jayalalitha and Mu. Karunanidhi, the shambles of the Dravidian political parties, and the descent of a number of star actors – in particular, Rajinikanth and Kamal Haasan – into the political arena. I briefly focus on two commercial films made by activist Dalit filmmaker Pa. Ranjith with Rajinikanth, *Kabali* (2016) and *Kaala* (2018).

Such films, I show, metonymize and exemplify the complex ontological politics at issue in Parts I and II of the book: questions of the "production format" (Goffman 1974, 1979) of the image (who authorizes it, who is responsible for it?) and the multiple potentials that it may manifest (as realist representation, as performative act). At the same time, such films attempt to bring about the "death of the hero" (Kurai 2012) in the narrative pulverization of his body in films that were, for all that, still star vehicles in the wake of which came a new wave of cine-politics. In the second half of the Conclusions, I reflect on the problematic of the film text, not as theoretical object but as methodological entry into analysis. Here, I reiterate my call for an empirical approach that would deconstruct the text as a boundary object with an inside and an outside, and instead treat the text as the precipitate of event-based, perspectival processes that both fold the text's (putative) exteriors *into* it while projecting what is "inside" of it beyond itself. This approach provides the basis for my explication of what the phrase *a linguistic anthropology of cinema* might mean as a (re)conceptualization of the field of linguistic anthropology itself.

The cases discussed in these chapters collectively reveal the tenuousness of the film image, the performative and representational capacity of images (and all signs, more generally) to be and become, and thus to mediate and act as, the fulcrum of the real and the political and social worlds through which images circulate and of which they are constitutive elements. To theorize the image (and semiosis more generally) in this way is to be open to those capacities in their own openness, to follow them as they unfold out of images(/signs) and are folded up into them, institutionalized and deconstructed, assembled and dispersed, transformed and conjured, as they make claims and have claims made on them, in their name and in the names of others.

PART ONE

Presence/Representation

Chapter One

The Hero's Mass

A shot of this kind by virtue of its dynamism belongs with the movement of a hand drawing a sketch ... In such a case the camera movement is important. The camera must be equally as ready to move as to remain still ... The Italian camera retains something of the human quality of the Bell and Howell newsreel camera, a projection of hand and eye, almost a living part of the operator, instantly in tune with his awareness.

– André Bazin, "An Aesthetic of Reality," 2005[1948]

The notions of the importance of the close-up, and of the role being less important than the performer in the cinema, can be related to the aesthetic of realism with which the cinema has predominantly been burdened, the belief that film, like photography, "captures" or "reflects" reality. That is, despite their extravagances and extraordinariness, the stars are an aspect of realism because what is foregrounded is their person as much as the characters they play.

– Richard Dyer, *Stars*, 1998[1979]

In politics as in films, the star arrives only because the fan-spectator was whistling interminably.

– S.V. Srinivas, *Megastar*, 2009

Introduction

In early September 2011, I went to a bar in southwest Chennai to meet up with Suresh, a middle-class friend in his early twenties. After a few rounds, we ended up back at his one-room apartment. We ate and watched a talk show special on the Tamil television station Sun TV (*Mankatha Sirappuk Kaṇṇōṭṭam* [*Mankatha*, A Unique Perspective], 11 September 2011), dedicated to the recent release of *Mankatha* (2011, dir. Venkat Prabhu), the fiftieth film of Ajith Kumar (b. 1971), Suresh's favourite actor and one of the pre-eminent hero-stars of the Tamil film industry. The show featured discussions with *Mankatha*'s director and writer Venkat Prabhu (b. 1975) and its main actors, though not Ajith, who is known to avoid media appearances. Each of the guests was introduced by the host, comedian-actor Shiva (b. 1982), and invited to the sound stage.

When Shiva came to one of the film's actors, Vaibhav Reddy (b. 1980), however, he introduced him cryptically as the other guests smiled and laughed. With a smirk, Shiva said in Tamil:

> *Aṭuttatāka inta paṭam* release *ākuṟa varaikkum cinna vayasuleruntu ellā kaṭaikkum pōyiṭṭu tēvaiyāna* items *nallā vāṅki sāppiṭṭuṭṭu irunta Vaibhav, inta paṭattukku appuṟamā orē oru* scene-*kku appuṟam kaṭaikki pōṟatukku kūṭa appaṭiyē kai kāl ellām utaṟutu avarukku. Ēnnā inta paṭattule paṇṇina oru* scene *appaṭi.*

> Up until the release of this film, from a young age Vaibhav would go to whatever stores he wanted to buy things and eat them. But after this film, and after one scene in particular, even when going to the store, his [+HON.] hands and legs shake with fear. Because in this film (he) did a scene like that.

There's a "justification" for why/how he did it, Shiva continues in Tamil, 'but before that, let's welcome Vaibhav!' Vaibhav doesn't materialize, however, and Shiva and Venkat Prabhu have to playfully coax him into coming out from backstage: 'Come on [-HON.] dear, be brave and come out, there's no problem at all, come!' (*Vā mā, tairiyamā vā, oṇṇum piraccanai illai, vā!*). With seeming trepidation, Vaibhav appears with a shy smile on his face. Later in the show, Shiva makes good on his promise and turns to the scene that supposedly gave, and continued to give, Vaibhav fits of fear.

The scene that required "justification" occurs nearly two hours into the film. It involves the protagonist Ajith Kumar (as Vinayak), Vaibhav Reddy (as Sumanth), and one other character actor, Ashwin Kakumanu (as Ganesh).[1] Vinayak, Sumanth, and Ganesh are part of a gang of five men that has just robbed Arumuga Chettiar, a local gangster who runs a gambling ring. Discovering the theft, Chettiar kidnaps Sumanth's wife, threatening to kill her unless Sumanth gets his money back to him. Fearing for his wife's life, Sumanth reveals where the gang hid the money. Before Chettiar or Vinayak can get to the cash though, the other two gang members steal it and go on the run. When Vinayak, Sumanth, and Ganesh arrive to retrieve the money, they discover it's gone. Following a violent run-in with Chettiar's men, who have also come for the money, the three escape to the dusty train yard where the scene in question takes place.

Overhearing Sumanth on the phone with Chettiar, Vinayak discovers Sumanth's betrayal and confronts him (0:00–0:13 in Figure 1.1).[2] Unhinged by the loss of the money, Vinayak tries to get Sumanth to help retrieve it, first by angrily screaming at him (0:14–0:19), then by gently placating and pleading with him (0:21–0:26), and finally by vulgarly suggesting that if they had the money, Sumanth could have not just one but a thousand wives like his own (0:26–0:33). At this grave insult, Sumanth grabs and shoves Vinayak, cursing him (0:31–0:34 in Figures 1.1 and 1.2). A scuffle ensues wherein Sumanth slaps a passive Vinayak twice (0:34–0:35; 0:39–0:40 in Figure 1.2). Vinayak finally strikes back, savagely knocking Sumanth to the ground with a single blow (0:43–0:44). Vinayak then draws a gun and shoots at Sumanth. Ganesh tries to stop Vinayak, and in the confusion Sumanth escapes.

What about this scene had Vaibhav seemingly so scared, weeks after the film was released, months after the scene was filmed? He was, after all, simply acting out a scene, playing a character in a fiction. Vaibhav explained in the Sun TV special that Suresh and I watched what the television audience already knew but wanted to hear about all the same: that he was terrified of Ajith's legions of fervent fans who were furious with him, a relatively junior actor – just a *cinna paiyan* (little boy), as another Ajith fan in his mid-twenties, Anbu, put it to me – for having dared to slap the face of their *Thala* (Chief; literally, the head), their *talaivar* (leader; literally, headman).[3] In contrast to a cooler, liberal sensibility that could laugh about it, if always a bit nervously, in this small-screen narration and others like it Vaibhav humorously invoked the stock figure of the credulous, illiberal fan-spectator (Hansen 1991; Gerritsen 2012:46–50; Mazzarella 2013; Nakassis 2016a:274n21), unable to distinguish reel from real and out to give him a beating in retribution.[4]

And while such humorously framed narratives got laughs, it was no joke (see Pandian 1992:121). When Suresh, Anbu, and others I knew saw the film on its opening day, audiences immediately responded to the slaps, booing and screaming obscenities in an overwhelming roar: 'Hey! How the hell can you [-HON.; Vaibhav] hit our [EXCL.] *Thala*?!' (*Ēy! Ep[paṭi]-ṟṟā eṅka Thalaye nī aṭippe*!), as Anbu reported, (politely) voicing fans' reactions.[5] Ultimately, however, Vaibhav never received any physical retribution for his slaps, though he was and occasionally continued to be, he told me in 2016, verbally harassed by Ajith fans in public.[6]

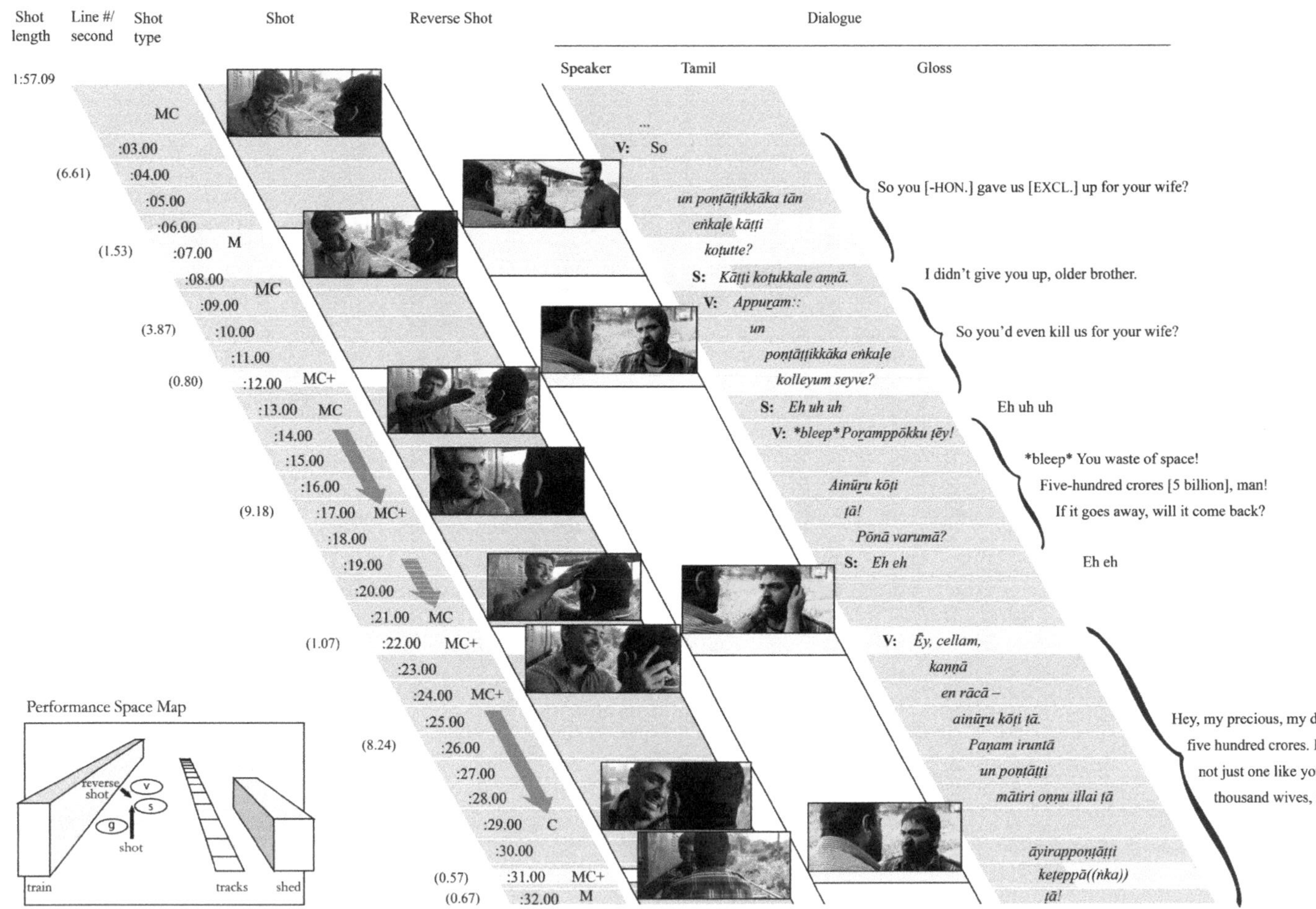

Shot length
Line #/ second
Shot type
Shot
Reverse Shot
Dialogue
Speaker
Tamil
Gloss
1:57.09
MC
:03.00
(6.61)
:04.00
:05.00
:06.00
(1.53)
:07.00
M
:08.00
MC
:09.00
(3.87)
:10.00
:11.00
(0.80)
:12.00
MC+
:13.00
MC
:14.00
:15.00
:16.00
(9.18)
:17.00
MC+
:18.00
:19.00
:20.00
:21.00
MC
(1.07)
:22.00
MC+
:23.00
:24.00
MC+
:25.00
(8.24)
:26.00
:27.00
:28.00
:29.00
C
:30.00
(0.57)
:31.00
MC+
(0.67)
:32.00
M
...
V: So
un poṇṭāṭṭikkāka tān
eṅkaḷe kāṭṭi
koṭutte?
So you [-HON.] gave us [EXCL.] up for your wife?
S: Kāṭṭi koṭukkale aṇṇā.
I didn't give you up, older brother.
V: Appuṟam::
un
poṇṭāṭṭikkāka eṅkaḷe
kolleyum seyve?
So you'd even kill us for your wife?
S: Eh uh uh
Eh uh uh
V: *bleep* Poṟamppōkku ṭēy!
Ainūṟu kōṭi
ṭā!
Pōnā varumā?
bleep You waste of space!
Five-hundred crores [5 billion], man!
If it goes away, will it come back?
S: Eh eh
Eh eh
V: Ēy, cellam,
kaṇṇā
en rācā –
ainūṟu kōṭi ṭā.
Paṇam iruntā
un poṇṭāṭṭi
mātiri oṇṇu illai ṭā
āyirapponṭāṭṭi
keṭeppā((ṅka))
ṭā!
Hey, my precious, my dear, my king – it's five hundred crores. If we had the money, not just one like your wife, you'd have a thousand wives, man!
Performance Space Map
reverse shot
v
s
g
shot
train
tracks
shed

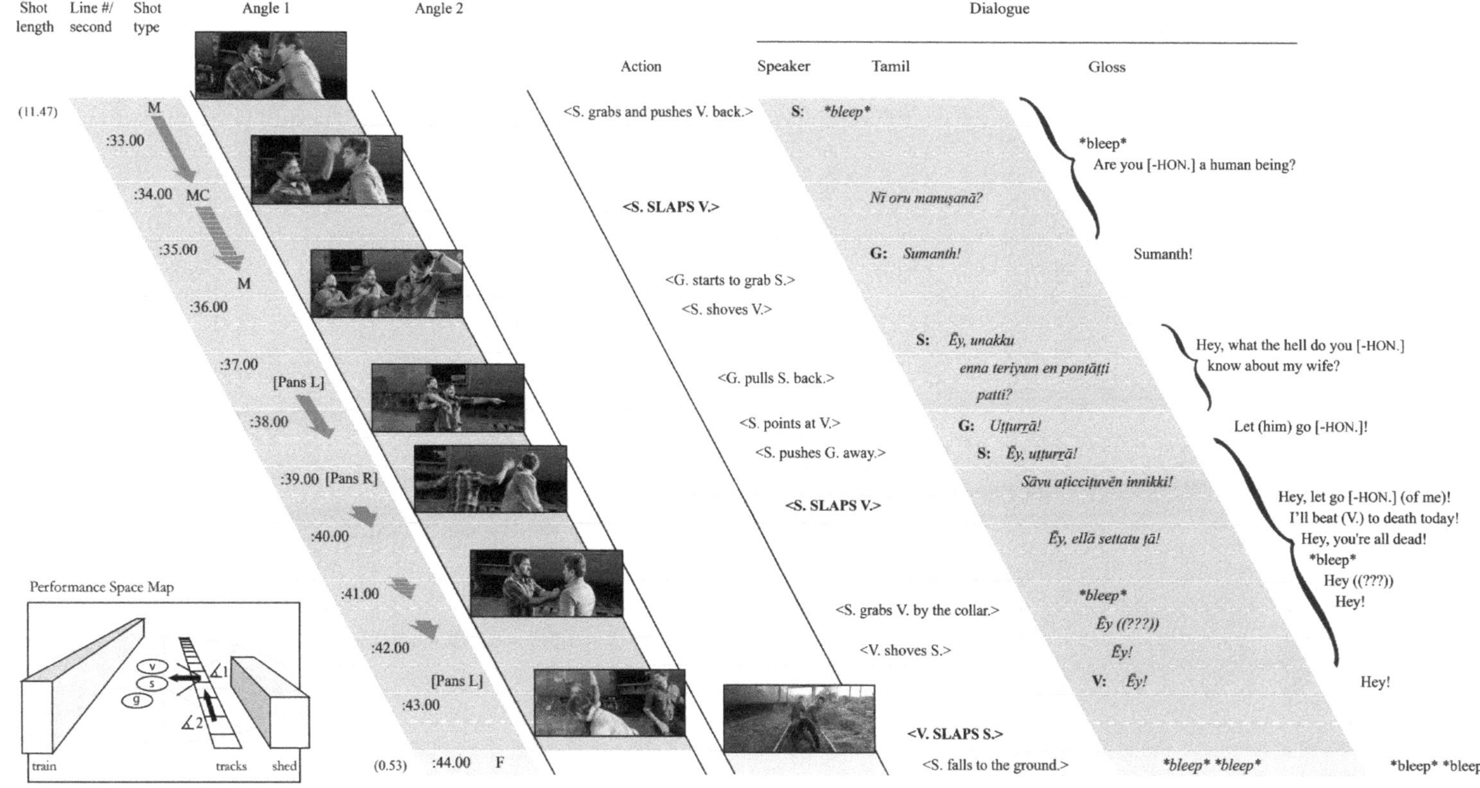

Figures 1.1 and 1.2. Top (p. 30) – *Mankatha's slap* sequence (2011, dir. Venkat Prabhu), Transcript 1 (shot/reverse shot); bottom (p. 31) – *Mankatha's* slap sequence, Transcript 2 (Sumanth's/Vaibhav's slaps)

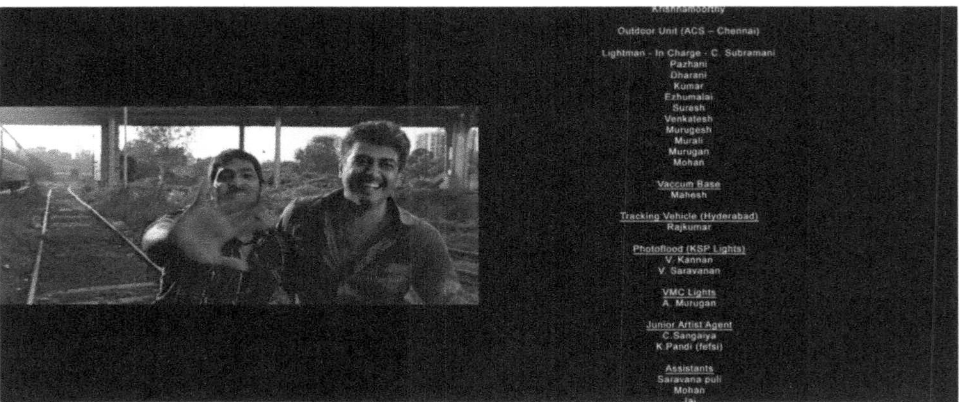

Figure 1.3. *Mankatha*'s end credits: Vaibhav anxiously apologizing to the audience: 'I didn't (really) hit him! I didn't (really) hit him!'

Mankatha already anticipated and inscribed into its textual form the performativity and affective charge of Vaibhav's slaps as potential and blockage, as something that it both embraced and resisted. In the end credits of the film, we see on-set documentary materials, mainly bloopers. About three-quarters in, we see what putatively followed the take of the slaps that made it onto the screen. Following a seamless cut from the rushes of the scene, Vaibhav and Ajith's bodies slip out of their aggressive encounter in the diegetic world to face the camera. Vaibhav clings to a grinning Ajith. With a pleading smile and whimpering voice, Vaibhav says to the camera/audience: 'I didn't (really) hit him! I didn't (really) hit him!' (*Nān aṭikkale! Nān aṭikkale*!), while waving his palm back and forth in negation (Figure 1.3). They filmed this out-take, Vaibhav told me, just to be on the "safer side."[7]

In this blooper, Vaibhav disavows (and thus acknowledges) the reality of his act. Breaking away from the narrative frame, this apologetic image attempts to bracket the slaps' performativity and reframe them as a mere representation, a fictional image.[8] On the Sun TV special that Suresh and I watched that night in September, Shiva concludes the segment by asking Vaibhav for an "official announcement." Turning to look at the camera, Vaibhav points with his index finger through the screen and says to the televisual audience: 'Everyone please stay until the end of the film to see the bloopers. You'll see there that I said I didn't hit him. And *Thala* was smiling, so I didn't hit him' (*Kaṭaisi-le ellārum anta* bloopers-*e pāttuṭṭu pōṅka. Atule vantuṭṭu nān sollirukkēn, nān aṭikkale nnuṭṭu. Appuṟam Thala siriccukiṭṭiruntāru*, so *aṭikkale*). Ultimately, as the out-take and small-screen expiation suggested (and yet controverted at one and the same time), it was Ajith and his smile who determined the reality of the profilmic and fictitiousness of the filmic.

/ / /

What kinds of filmic images are these that slide between the diegetic world of the fiction, where one character slaps another, and the profilmic moment of its recording, where one actor slaps another? What is this image that is not only of a past act of slapping recorded by a camera but also an act of offence unto itself in the moment of its exhibition and apperception, an act whose animator bears the responsibility (or *principalship*, as Erving Goffman [1979] would have put it) for what is shown, for what subtends the representation: the act of acting itself? And who is the anchoring figure of these image-acts, *Thala* Ajith, whose auratic, affecting presence (Armstrong 1971, 1981; Power 2006) and forceful masculinity breaks through the bracketing citational marks of the narrative, the character, and the cinematic apparatus such that to touch his character is to touch *him*, not simply once in front of the camera but with every subsequent exhibition of the image onscreen?[9] Such that what is depicted is enacted and comes to be?

In addressing these questions, this chapter broaches two problematics, the image's *being* and the image's *doing*, its ontology and its performativity.

To the first, my departure point and main interlocutor is André Bazin (2005[1945]) and his seminal discussion of "the ontology of the photographic image." While Bazin was a figure to be repudiated in much 1970s and 1980s American and European film theory as variously either a naïve realist, an idealist, or an empiricist (Morgan 2006, 2013), recent decades have seen something of a Bazin revival and a return to engaged discussions of the ontology of the filmic image. This return is the result of a number of factors: the waning of post-structuralist film theory, the emergence of film history as central to film theory, as well as, perhaps most importantly, film studies' self-critical interrogation of its object of study in the face of the digital (Morgan 2006; Gunning 2008; Hassan 2017).[10] My interest in Bazin, however, is slightly different than the motivations behind this return. For me, thinking with Bazin and his commentators is productive in three ways. First, Bazin's account of the ontology of the photographic image in cinema uncannily resonates with, and yet radically differs from, the aesthetics and cultural phenomenology of the Tamil film image that concern this book. As such, Bazin's ontology helpfully illuminates what is empirically in need of explanation in the cases I explore. Second, Bazin and the discussion around his work exemplifies a number of symptomatic investments and tensions in film studies regarding mediation and immediation, representation and realism, and the liberal or illiberal potentials of the filmic image. These tensions exemplify the political field of being at issue, both for film studies and for the stakeholders in the image that I discuss in these chapters. As such, third, Bazin's ontology stands as a productive example of the ontological politics that concern this book (a politics not wholly unrelated to the ontological politics of the Tamil cinema) and thus helps clarify the in-principle entanglement of the political in the ontological and the theoretical.

The second problematic this chapter broaches – which stands in a dialectical relationship to the first – is that of the performativity of images, their actness. Here, I speak to concerns among critical theorists, art historians, and visual and media anthropologists about how images do not simply represent but enact; the ways in which images of various kinds, in various contexts, may "want" or "demand" something from us, as W.J.T. Mitchell (2004) and Karen Strassler (2020) have put it, and thus have their own agency and efficacy (Armstrong 1971; Freedberg 1989; Gell 1998; Pinney 2004; MacDougall 2006; Jain 2007; Mazzarella 2013; Bredekamp 2018[2010]).[11] Such concerns echo classic work in the philosophy of language (Austin 1962) and its reanalysis in linguistic anthropology (Silverstein 1979, 1993, 2004; Lee 1997; Agha 2007a; Stasch 2011; Nakassis 2013a; Fleming and Lempert 2014) concerned with the semiotics of performative speech and ritual. Thinking these literatures together, as I do in this chapter and the next, affords us a productive way to theorize what images are and can be, and how they come to bear the dynamic, multiple potentialities and capacities we observe them to have as we find them. Doing so, I argue, allows us to rethink questions of what an image *is* such that it can *act*.

Articulating these problematics of being and doing, ontology and performativity in the context of the cinematic image is the question of *presence*.

The Presence of the Film Image

In Bazin's (2005[1945]) classic essay, the "ontology of the photographic (film) image" turns on two aspects of cinema: on the one hand, a particular desire and existential condition on the part of the spectatorial subject; on the other hand, the technical apparatus of the cinema and the way in which it inscribes and gives over its images to that subject. As Bazin argues, the plastic arts have long attempted to grapple with and preserve duration, driven by a desire to arrest time (and death) that has taken the form of mummies, death masks, relics, religious icons, portraiture, and into the nineteenth and twentieth century, photography and film. Critical for Bazin is how, in each of these cases, something evenemential of the past is carried forth in the image-artifact, an indexical connection that, he argues, speaks to our desire for the presencing of the past.[12] Film, on this account, appears as a fuller, indeed, as the telic realization of this desire, precisely because of the way in which it constructs its image through pieces of concrete reality in their durative flux (see also Mitry 1997[1963]:15, 17).[13]

In doing so, Bazin suggests, film less represents than re-presences its object to the subject. The "automatic fixing" (Bazin 2005[1945]:12–13, 19) of light onto the "tin foil" (2005[1951]b:97) of the camera allows for, Bazin argues, a (relatively) autonomous inscription of the material surface of the natural world with which the camera was in an existential relation of co-presence (see also Cavell 1979; Barthes 1981:115). Like a decal or a death mask, the film image maintains a real (indexical) connection with that which it also thereby (iconically) depicts.[14] On this view, the film image is a kind of transduction (Silverstein 2003b), a "transference of reality from the thing to its reproduction" (Bazin 2005[1945]:14), which confers to the film image a kind of ontological *identity* with its object (Morgan 2006). Not just a *re*-presencing, then, the film image put us in the continuing presence of what it "embalms," that is, with itself, or at least with a part or past phase of itself that has been suspended in time and made continuously available to those who apprehend it (Schoonover 2012:32–41, 58–67). Bazin (2005[1945]:14) writes: "The photographic image is the object itself, the object freed from the temporal contingencies that govern it ... [I]t shares, by virtue of its becoming, the being of the model of which it is the reproduction; it *is* the model."[15]

This capacity of film images to put us in the presence of their objects – which is to say, to cater to our desire for such presence – has an ethical and political implication for Bazin, for it allows the image to reveal something of the world to us in its contingent and ambiguous, yet integral reality. Deeply influenced by Bergson, Sartre, Merleau-Ponty, and Mounier's personalism (Staiger 1984; Hassan 2017), Bazin suggests that this ambiguity – which film's apparatus, by its machinic, indexical automaticity and its historically emergent techniques and stylistics, can re-produce and foreground – can put us into a particular relationship to the world, allowing for an attunement to – precisely by staging for us an encounter with – its alterity and open-ended possibility. It allows for a form of freedom for the subject to make meaning out of the underdetermination of cinematic experience (Bazin 2005[1948], 2005[1955], 2005[1958]), creating a space to see the world afresh in its "virginal purity" and without that "spiritual dust and grime" and "piled-up preconceptions" of everyday experience (Bazin 2005[1945]:15; see also Kracauer 1960). Bazin's view here is that film allows subject and object to encounter each other in a non-dominating, liberating, transcending way.

Or, at least, the right kind of film can. Bazin calls such films *realist*; his examples famously include Italian neorealism (Bazin 2005[1948], 2005[1951]a, 2005[1955]), Orson Welles's and Jean Renoir's films (Bazin 2005[1958]), and even Charlie Chaplin's comedic sequences (Bazin 2005[1951]b).[16] Such films respect the being of the image (as Bazin defines it): the presence of the image and its ability to put the spectator into the particular relationality to experience, meaning, and the world that Bazin valued. This is in contrast to films that are not aesthetically realist enough, such as German expressionism (Bazin 2005[1958]), or that foreclose openness to the contingency of the world (and the meanings makeable in it), as in Soviet montage films. In this latter category, Bazin also included films that are presentist and realist in the wrong way, as in pornography and filmed executions (Bazin 2005[1957]; see Williams 1989:184–228; Schoonover 2012:13, 62), and authoritarian, propaganda films (Bazin 1985[1950]; see Hassan 2017). Rather than respect the ontic possibilities of the cinema, such films leverage realism for presumably obscene ends and in so doing alienate us from the profilmic rather than implicating us in it (as in pornography and "snuff films"); or alternatively, naturalize a singular vision of history, disallowing any critical space to engage with either image or reality (as with, for example, the filmic figure of Stalin). As is apparent in such contrasts, realism for Bazin is less an aesthetic style than a normative, liberal, and anti-authoritarian stance actualized in (a particular style of) images – one that Bazin ambivalently vested in the capacity of the image to presence its object for the spectator-subject (see also Chapter 4).

Bazin's writings about the presence of the image uncannily characterize what is at stake in *Mankatha*'s slap sequence and its performativity. Indeed, it is precisely the insistent *presence* of the film image and its referent that is at issue in Vaibhav's slaps of Ajith, the way in which the filmic image exceeds its representational and narrative status and thereby disrupts ideological assumptions about, and commitments to, the idea of film as merely a shadow, distant from and undemanding of us. And entangled with the question of presence in this scene, as with

Bazin, are a set of aesthetic norms and their political implications. Yet, as I show in this chapter, this presence is not and perhaps is never singular or pregiven, nor does it simply follow from the mechanical processes of the filmic apparatus or the metapsychology of "the" spectator. Neither is the presence of the image necessarily realist or liberal in its politics. Instead of a determinate being, we find an uneasy tension and contention in the image unfolding dialectically across the screen. Here, we see how presence (or better, presencing) is a complex and tenuous achievement, one shot through by a panoply of ontic tendencies and potentials, and distinct positionalities and perspectives. In *Mankatha*'s image-act of the slaps, we find a heterogeneous and ambivalent set of presencings in dialogic tension, some of which resonate with Bazin's own political and aesthetic sensibilities (namely, realism, liberal humanism) and others that stand in startling indifference, even opposition, to them. Such distinct presencings enact distinct politics for and of the image that intersect in the image, standing in opposition and amplifying each other at one and the same time. This case reveals the image to be a contact zone, a site of struggle between different claims on the being of images, illuminating the multiplicity of ways that reality, aesthetics, and politics – that is, different modes of being – can be conjoined in one and the same image.

In short, thinking with Bazin – and centring the question of the being of the image in its relation to the ontological politics of presence and the image's performativity/representation – helps us consider the semiotic work and political effects that *Mankatha*'s slap sequence accomplishes. But if being follows ontological politics and not only the other way around, as I argue in this chapter, then a thinking together of Bazin and the mass hero requires a reconsideration of the being of the image and how we might study it. In effect, it requires us to decentre and provincialize[17] Bazin's account of "THE" ontology of the filmic image so as to open up the complex empirical ways in which images come to be and act.[18] Here, I echo Brian Larkin's (2008:80) attempts to intervene into "debates about the origins of cinema" and the social and historical basis of its ontology by looking at "sites outside of the West [in his case, Nigeria] … (so as) to rethink some classical ideas about the nature of cinema." Discussions of the ontology of the film image, as I hope the reader will see, can benefit from a study of the Tamil (and Nigerian and …) cinema, not as a peculiarity or particularity that can be set aside in its curiosity but in how it illuminates – indeed, demands a rethinking of – general questions at the core of the study of cinema (and mediation more broadly).

To begin addressing these issues, in what follows I interrogate *why* the image-act of Vaibhav's slaps was so potent, feared by its animator, and repudiated and cursed by its fan viewers. I begin with the masculine figure of the "mass hero" *Thala* Ajith Kumar, that auratic, affecting presence that serves as a kind of cinematic black hole whose clawing gravity threatens to transform all representational images of him into performative acts involving him. Drawing on fan discourse, I show how this presencing is linked to a *sociological realism*, the way in which the social reality and history of the actor is transferred to his screen image (Dyer 1998[1979]:16; Aumont et al. 1992[1983]:108; Metz 2016[1991]:69). I then turn to the aesthetic and narrative features of *Mankatha*'s slap sequence. Drawing on interviews with *Mankatha*'s director and cinematographer, I look at how the sequence's aesthetic style entextualizes a liberal, representationalist politics of the image that runs counter to but also curiously intensifies both the mass hero's presence and the fan fury in seeing that presence profaned. The intercalation of these different aesthetics and claims on the image reveals a complex ontological politics rippling across and beyond the surface of the text.

The Gravity of the Hero's Mass

Within India and beyond (see, for example, Romig 2015), the Tamil film industry is infamous for its so-called mass heroes, bombastic and fantastically hyper-masculine celebrities, larger than life and larger than the screen. In their film worlds, mass heroes are all powerful – able to dispatch dozens of bad guys with a single blow, stare down a bullet, and fly through the air. They are not superheroes, however, since that implies some supernatural capacity within a world of everyday physics. Rather, the very warp of the worlds the mass hero inhabits are bent around him: to his will, his status, his power, his personage, his *mass*. Moreover, this world is not simply some fiction projected on the screen, standing apart from us in space or time. His world encompasses the space and time of its exhibition (Nakassis 2017). Projected *out* of the screen, the mass hero is always potentially present to us, standing above and in front of the narrative and the film text. He is both onscreen and offscreen, hero and star at once. This projection contrasts, as the discussion below elaborates, with character actors, who are typically englobed within each film's narrative world, shielded by the characters they animate, the stories they act out, and the directors who author them.[19]

A mass hero has gravity. He has "*weight*," a near synonym of the similarly English-borrowed "*mass*," both terms denoting in Tamil the influence and importance of a powerful, dominating person. As such, he is also a hero *to* "the masses." Heroes like Ajith Kumar are not simply auratic, presenced bodies to be seen and desired in images. They are also political bodies on whom demands for representation may be made, a point forcefully made by M.S.S. Pandian (1992), M. Madhava Prasad (2014), S.V. Srinivas (2009), and others (Dickey 1993a; Chakravarthy 2002; Pongiyannan 2015; Rajanayagam 2015). The "mass" of the hero, then, is not simply a property of him; it is a socially constituted relation with his fan publics, one that makes him responsible, and vulnerable, to them by representing them politically.

As noted in the book's Introduction, electoral politics in Tamil Nadu is often a direct extension of cinema, where popular actors are expected to become, and often do become, political leaders. The mass hero onscreen, thus, is always a sovereign in potentia offscreen, his mass anticipating some future political horizon beyond the screen. Mass-hero films cultivate this *cine-politics* (Prasad 2014), addressing audiences not simply as fans but as *followers* of their *talaivar* (leader), the hero-star.[20] It is precisely this populist cine-politics – and the figure of the illiberal, cinema-affected fan in particular – that activates in postcolonial South India a liberal anxiety about democracy (and its limits), one implicitly evidenced in the knowing, anxious laughs in the television recountings of the slap sequence discussed above and, as I suggest below, in *Mankatha*'s textual form itself.

Indeed, *Mankatha* was not a typical mass-hero star vehicle (though it was a star vehicle all the same). Nor did it conform to Ajith's mass-hero image at the time. Ajith Kumar's film career began in the 1990s and followed a pattern typical of other mass heroes (see Nakassis 2016a:196–203). He began by acting in narrative-driven, relatively realist (so-called class) films as a romantic male lead. After a series of successful hits (for example, *Kadhal Kottai* [1996, dir. Agathiyan], *Ullaasam* [1997, dir. J.D. & Jerry]), by the end of the decade Ajith had garnered critical praise as a gifted actor and developed a large and dedicated fan-club base. His 1999 blockbuster *Amarkalam* (dir. Saran) introduced him as the "Ultimate Star," a citational reference to the "Superstar" Rajinikanth, the pre-eminent mass hero of Tamil cinema since the 1990s (Nakassis 2017, 2019). This interdiscursive gesture made claim to a level of stardom that Ajith capitalized on in the 2000s, releasing increasingly commercially oriented action films like *Dheena* (2001, dir. A.R. Murugadoss), a film that earned him his second sobriquet, *Thala* (Head, Chief) – the nickname of his character in the film (Dheena). During this period, Ajith's films promoted his "mass," shifting him from a character actor to a hero-star, whose films "build up" and adulate his star image.

While Ajith's early films invited realistic identification with his characters, his later films offered the fan-spectator what M. Madhava Prasad

(1998:76) calls symbolic identification, a relation founded not on representational similarity (he is like me) but on hierarchical difference.[21] At this stage of stardom, films that do not conform to the mass-hero formula – such as Ajith's 2007 *Kireedam* (dir. A.L. Vijay), a relatively realist film in which the hero fails to achieve his goals – risk being met coolly, even outright rejected, by fans and often fail at the box office. (For both reasons, after its initial release, *Kireedam* was recut so the hero triumphs [*IndiaGlitz* 2007; compare Srinivas 2009:38–9].) This situation is what M.S.S. Pandian (1992) has called the mass hero's "image trap," a phrase that points not simply to a set of textual strictures on the hero-star (for example, those that bar certain realist modes of representation) but also to the star's responsibility to fan expectations (for example, that his infallible image not be tarnished on and off the screen).[22]

In this context, Ajith's choice of Venkat Prabhu as director of his landmark fiftieth film was highly significant. At the time, Venkat Prabhu was a director known for making non–hero-centred films with a dash of Hollywood-esque realism and hero-parodying comedy (see Chapter 3). For many, then, *Mankatha* was an example of Ajith's ongoing struggle to break out of his image trap (compare Dyer 1998[1979]:100; Srinivas 2009:65–6). Indeed, just the year before, Ajith publicly announced that he would no longer use his epithet "Ultimate Star" in title credit sequences.[23] And months before *Mankatha*'s release, on his birthday (a major day for fan activity), he disbanded his large network of fan clubs.[24] As one director observed to me, all this was Ajith trying to say to his fans and the wider public: "I'm not planning on entering politics; I am just an actor."

In a state where actors continually intimate on and off the screen their imminent entry into electoral politics (and where they often subsequently do enter politics), such image work is not inconsequential, which makes *Mankatha*, and its slap sequence in particular, a rich site to explore the ontological politics of the image. To unpack this politics, I begin with the potent presence of the mass hero's image for his viewing publics and its textual and sociological underpinnings. It is such presence, as we will see, that is at issue in the competing claims on the image in *Mankatha*.

Presencing Mass in Mankatha

Consider a particular ethnographic scene of presencing (or rather, a montage of such scenes culled from fan videos posted on YouTube, supplemented by my own experiences of similar scenes from my research on Tamil cinema) – *Mankatha*'s first day, first show.[25]

It's just after dawn, 13 August 2011. The theatre premises are packed with young male bodies, some frenetically celebrating the film's release by dancing, yelling, whistling, or setting off firecrackers, others grinningly looking on, participating vicariously while waiting for the theatre to open. The space is saturated, dense with bodies, sounds, and visual displays appropriate to and entailing the "bigness," the *mass* of the hero-star (compare Mines 2005:157, 162–4; Bate 2009:78–83). Huge billboards of him loom outside, sponsored by fan clubs and garlanded by them with flowers and perhaps still moist from milk, beer, or maybe even soda having been poured over them in citations of Hindu rituals of idol purification (Pandian 2005; L. Srinivas 2016:199; Nakassis 2017:218–19). As the doors open, bodies flood inside. The crowd is antsy in anticipation and breaks into whistles when the government's censor board certificate appears onscreen, an image of a document that announces the projector is on and the hero-star is, as it were, in the building. Producers' banners come and go. *Mankatha* begins.

Most mass-hero films, including Ajith's, begin with a title credit sequence: the hero-star's name and epithet flashed onscreen so as to herald his arrival and lay claim to what follows – the film proper – as in his names (Nakassis 2017). In a telling deviation from this norm, *Mankatha* begins with something else: a cloudless sky and the phrase "A Venkat Prabhu Game" (Figure 1.4), a reference to the betting card game, mankatha, at the centre of the film's heist plot.[26]

Having announced the director's claim on what follows, the camera pans down to reveal an arid, desert landscape where a henchman of the don Arumuga Chettiar, Faizal (played by Aravind Akash), is tied up on his knees (Figure 1.5). With this image, audience members whistle and scream, calling out Ajith's name, anticipating and demanding his arrival (Srinivas 2009:37–8, 127). Some stand right in front of the screen, able to touch its projected images.

The narrative progresses, and the crowd simmers down slightly (though does not remain silent, some contingent of the crowd continuing to whistle and yell). Our ears strain to hear that Faizal is about to be executed by local thugs hired by crooked cops. Forty seconds into the scene, a gun is raised and pointed at Faizal, the trigger cocked. We then hear the loud revving of an engine as the film again cuts to the cloudless, blue sky. Out of the left edge of the frame, a jeep flies across the screen in slow motion (Figure 1.6). The film's theme music kicks in. *Thala* has finally arrived! The theatre erupts. Full-throated screams and ear-piercing whistles rip through the room as young men jump up and down, shirts and towels twirled over their heads, confetti thrown in the air.

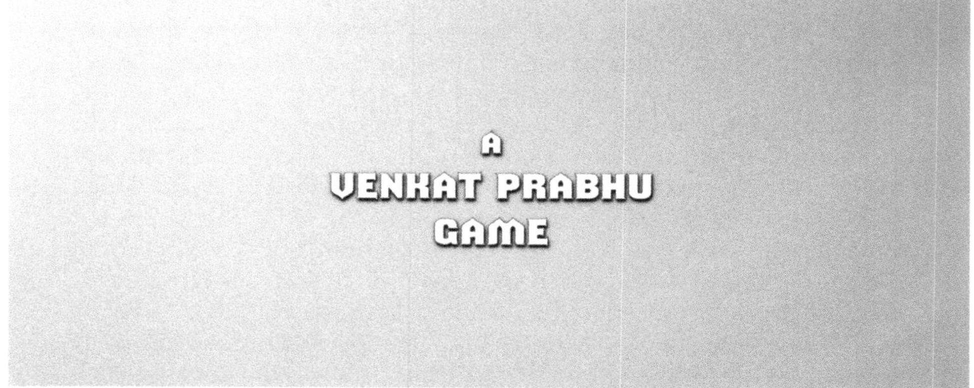

Figure 1.4. Opening frame of *Mankatha*: "A Venkat Prabhu Game"

Figure 1.5. The opening of *Mankatha*'s diegesis: The introduction of Faizal (played by Aravind Akash)

Yet even though Ajith's presence is palpable in the timespaces of the diegetic scene and theatre, the camera defers showing him. In the sequence that follows, the camera lingers on the flying car in slow motion, interspersed with shots of the awestruck faces of the police, hired thugs, and Faizal (Figure 1.7).

Only after sufficiently deferring our desire to *see* Ajith does the screen reveal his body, but not yet his face, as he emerges from the jeep in a low-angle, medium-long shot, the image even going dark for a split second as if we are blinking in disbelief that he is finally here (Figure 1.8). What's finally unveiled is the hero in his full plenitude: his rugged face in a tight, frontal, slow-motion close-up (Figure 1.9 – top). Following this image, we see his body shot from various angles and then multiplied onscreen in a visual metaphor of his mass (Figure 1.9 – bottom).

Figure 1.6. Ajith's entry in *Mankatha*; note the scalar aesthetics that are enacted upon the character/actor Faizal/Aravind Akash (top right, bottom left) upon Ajith's entry into the narrative/theatre (compare Figure 1.5)

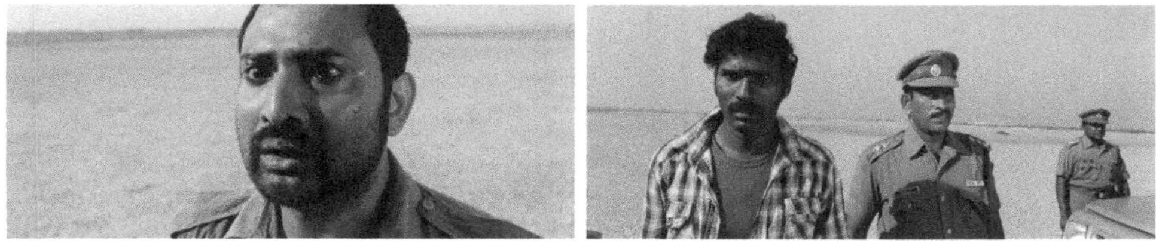

Figure 1.7. Shocked and awed character-spectators, prefiguring our own wonder at seeing the arrival of the hero-star, *Thala* Ajith Kumar

Figure 1.8. Deferring our vision, kindling our desire; note the flickering of the image, which pales (left), goes to black, then returns to colour (right) as a trope of the blinking awe of the camera/spectator

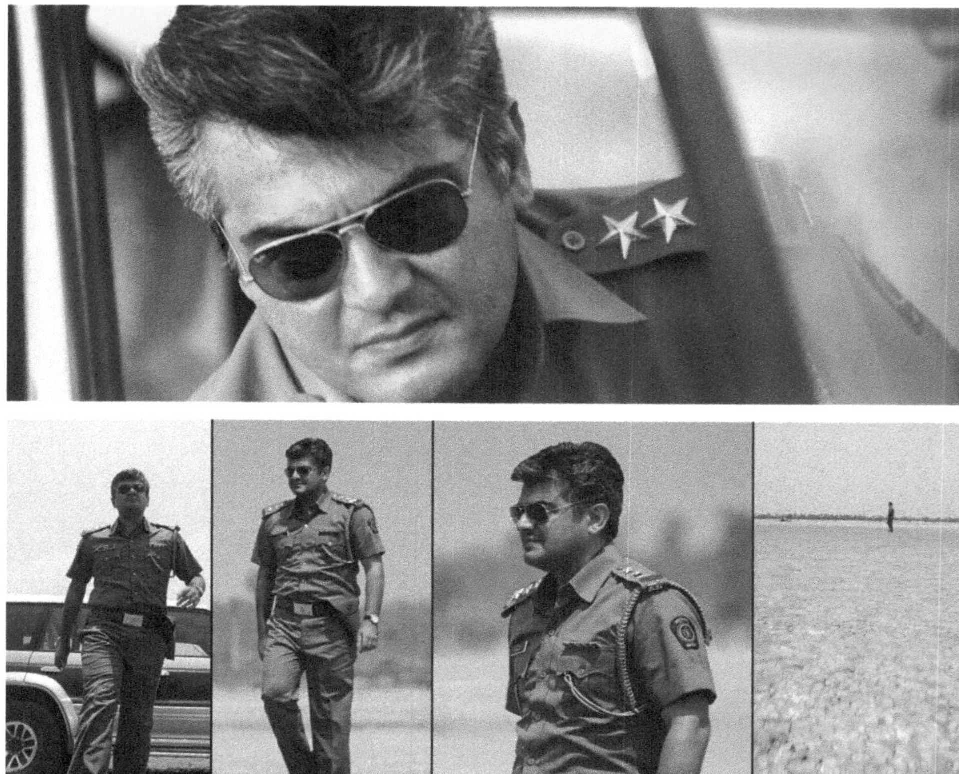

Figure 1.9. Top – Ajith's revelation, his face and eyes in close-up; bottom – Ajith in quadruplicate in one frame onscreen

Ajith's first appearance is not just a sight to behold. It is, in a sense, *him* – the hero-star, *Thala* Ajith Kumar – before us, letting us see him and take him in. As we've seen, this presence offers an occasion for interaction with the screen: whistles, yelling, touching, and addressing the hero-star. And to these adulating responses, this image responds in turn (Nakassis 2017; compare Dagrada 2014:34–9; Metz 2016[1991]). The arrival of the mass hero almost always takes the form of an aesthetics of frontality that accedes to the fan-spectator's desire to see and be seen by him.[27] This is an image that doesn't simply represent. It *acts*. It directly addresses its viewer. And through it, the mass hero looks and points at the viewer and, in many such films, speaks to him. (In

Figure 1.10. The beginning of Ajith's title sequence in *Mankatha*: his transtextual persona, *Thala*, as the cumulation of his "film history"

theatres on first-day shows, it is almost always a *him*, insofar as fan clubs and the carnivalesque timespace of the first-day show are almost exclusively male.) Here, the screen does not offer us a substitute, surrogate world apart from our own, a world emanating from some past moment, as Bazin (2005[1951]b:108–9) or Cavell (1979:23–5) suggest. Rather, it is our world, simultaneous and contiguous with us. This is the mass hero's *presence*.[28]

What follows this revelation is a fight sequence that demonstrates Ajith/Vinayak's physical dominance. He thrashes the police and hired thugs in a precisely choreographed spectacle of slow-motion shots, punches thrown and bodies flung, alternating with rapid action sequences quickly spliced together. Glossy and effect-laden, brightly lit and in shallow focus, these images culminate at the end of the fight with a return to Ajith's face in a close-up shot that poetically recalls his first appearance (as shown in Figure 1.9 – top). Ajith then turns around to face away from us, and the screen cuts to a grid of images as the film's theme music comes in (Figure 1.10 – left).

Each box of the grid offers a film clip from one of Ajith's previous forty-nine films. The shot pulls back to reveal the grid as one side of a cube, one among many flying towards Ajith (Figure 1.10 – right). As the boxes near the back of Ajith's head, he turns back around and the cubes congeal together *as* his face, encircled by a gold band (Figure 1.11 – left). The filmic image is replaced with, or rather it (self-)absorbs, this multitudinous collage of his previous films (compare Srinivas 2009:95–6, 234). *Thala* Ajith here is presented as the cumulative "build-up" and interdiscursive telos of his film history, every single image sequence of his oeuvre but a molecular instance of his self-same, transfilmic being. The image then flips around, revealing its Janus face to be a gold gambling chip (Figure 1.11 – right). Emblazoned on the chip is "Thala 50," that is, *Thala*'s fiftieth film.

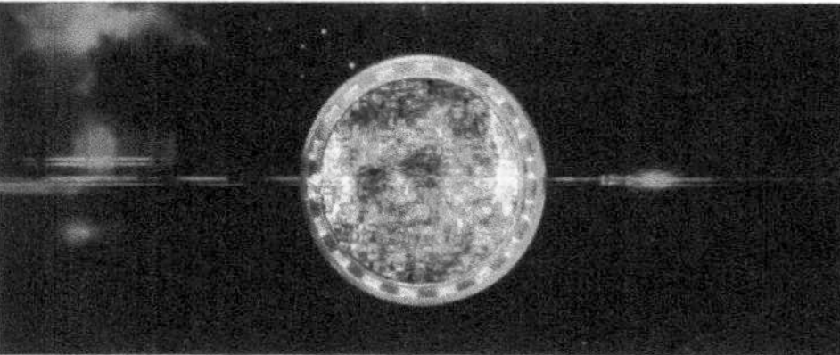

Figure 1.11. The end of Ajith's title sequence in *Mankatha*: Ajith's face (left) and name (right) as currency and value; note the absence of Ajith's other sobriquet, "Ultimate Star," which had heralded his arrival in his films from 1999 to 2010

This deferred title sequence announces what we already knew all along. This is not just "A Venkat Prabhu Game." It is Ajith's film. (As Vinayak/Ajith maniacally screams later in the film: "This is *my* fucking game!"[29]) *Thala* presenced, the film's name appears onscreen. The opening credits roll, and the story resumes.

/ / /

Here, note two key points. First, this film is a spectacle, a spectacle of *him*. The opening scene turns on the hero-star's "entry," not simply his specular revelation on the screen but his spectacular perforation of the theatre's fourth wall. Furthermore, this revelation/perforation emerges out of a narrative setup (saving Faizal as a way into his gang) that cannot contain it. The extreme close-ups of Ajith's face set in bright lighting, the slow-motion shots and computer-graphic effects spliced with frenetic jump-cuts, the gratuitous shots of his *stylish* gait and awesome strength – this tropology serves not the story per se but to presence *Thala* himself. This rupture, like the title sequence that follows it, serves to envelop and subsume the narrative text and diegetic world (and ultimately the audience and its world) to the hero-star's massive image. It is also, thus, a spectacle of masculinity. Presented in his "to-be-looked-at-ness" through a series of looks – from other characters, from the camera itself, but also from the hero-star who looks back *at* us and solicits our gaze in ways not formally dissimilar (if with key differences, of course), as we see in the next chapter, from those Laura Mulvey (2009[1975]) and others have identified for the patriarchal image of women in classical Hollywood film (Willemen 1994; Williams 1989) – this image serves to build the hero up as the object of the spectator's attention, amazement, and erotic adulation/identification (Neale 2000[1983]). This world is the mass hero's world and his alone. In his objectivity, he is its subject, and when it ceases to be exclusively his, when he has to face up to the resistance of a reality that is not his own (for example, in the figure of the villain, the act of a slap, or the realist emplotment of the narrative), such breaches must be resolved, either onscreen (for example, by narratively punishing the transgressors [compare Mulvey 2009[1975]:22] or by ensuring the hero's triumph) or offscreen, as by angry viewers exacting retribution on particular individuals (such as Vaibhav) or by rejecting the film itself (as with Ajith's *Kireedam*).[30]

Second, not all actors can anchor such worlds. While the character actor Aravind Akash *acts* as Faizal in the diegesis, it is Ajith Kumar qua *Thala* who *is* onscreen in the theatre. While the screen veils Aravind Akash with his character, with images of Ajith we see *through* the screen and character to what undergirds it: on the one hand, to the actor's personage as *Thala* and, on the other hand, *as Thala*, to all of Ajith's previous films. Ajith's title credit in *Mankatha* is an explicit figuration of this compulsive and avowedly formulaic intertextuality, a visual trope that underscores that every character played by the actor Ajith Kumar *is Thala*, that transtextual being who sutures together through the rigid designators of his identity (his names, his face, among other film fractions that he travels through) a film oeuvre to a biographical person (Ajith Kumar, distinct from but blurred into his star personage *Thala*), and vice versa.[31]

Every such avatar adds to the hero-star's mass, growing with every film into a roaring chorus. It is this chorus that is met with the deafening cries of his fan audiences when *Thala* is presenced in the theatre (as with Ajith's title sequence in *Mankatha*). Caught in this feedback loop, this "image trap" (that which traps images and spectators; Gell 1998), every instance of the mass hero *is* him in his transcendent, nomic totality, not as a shadow representation of an absent self but as a semiotic agent in action, reflexively calibrated to the moment of his theatrical appearance.[32] He is a celestial body holding all others in his wake (fans, filmmakers, other actors, other characters, and so on); they orbit him in an iterated, circular trajectory, their motion bent to his, their fates determined by his. This is the hero's *mass*.

The Image-Act of the Slaps, Again and Again and …

We can now begin to understand why the character Sumanth slapping the character Vinayak constitutes a problematically performative image-act of the actor Vaibhav slapping the actor Ajith. Events entextualized within the ambit of the mass hero always potentially count as more than representations, for Ajith is (reflexively) present in his image. Here, the representational bracketing of the image – the ideological notion that a film is just a shadow representation, a mere fiction – is denatured and superseded by a different ideology of the image, by an insistent presencing *in* the present of its imaging. It is this substantial presence – the fact that the slaps hit not just Vinayak's but Ajith's cheek, and not just in some (reportive) profilmic past in front of the camera but also in every moment of its exhibition – that enables this cinematic representation to be an act unto itself, an image-act that affronts the body and (nomic) personage of *Thala* Ajith himself.

But the intensity and performative effect of Vaibhav's slaps are not simply a function of Ajith's status as a mass hero. They are also linked to a sociological, industry-internal relation between Ajith and Vaibhav as "senior" and "junior" male artists, respectively, as well as to the aesthetic form and narrative framing of the scene itself. I explore each in turn.

Vaibhav's Audacity and the Sociological Realism of the Image-Act

At issue in Vaibhav's slaps are two kinds of indexicality and two kinds of realism: one that reportively articulates a profilmic timespace to an image (to slap Vinayak onscreen is to have slapped Ajith in front of the camera) and another that reflexively articulates the former relation to the timespace of the image's exhibition (to have slapped Ajith/Vinayak on film is to slap Ajith in the theatre). The former presupposes the kind of causal, physical, indexical relations and logics that have long concerned film theorists of realism like Bazin and Mitry (the photographic image as "trace" of some past event; film as composed of representations that reproduce their object qua slices of "concrete reality").[33] Here, images emanate from the physical reality of the profilmic. The latter, by contrast, is underwritten by the offscreen sociological status of the celebrity hero-star as an image-immanent being. Here, images emanate from the (metafilmic) reality of the actor's status.[34] I call this the *sociological realism* of the image-act (see Dyer's epigraph at the beginning of this chapter).[35]

Recall one of the main reasons that Suresh and Anbu gave for why fans were so upset by Vaibhav's slaps: Vaibhav was just a 'little boy.' When I asked Suresh why Vaibhav was so afraid to act in this scene, why Vaibhav had to apologize, and why he, Suresh, got upset when he saw the scene, Suresh said it was because Vaibhav is just a "junior artist" in comparison to Ajith, who is a "senior artist."[36] Part of the anger, then, is Vaibhav's audacity: Who is *he* to dare hit our *Thala*? What are his qualifications? What gives him the right to do so?[37] Here, we can see how the mass hero's intertextuality, his "film history" as it is called in the Tamil industry, has its corollary in a spectatorial logic that evaluates the presence of the film image against the offscreen industry status of those who animate it: Who is this actor to appear on and in front of the screen? Is he a 'little boy' or a 'big man' (*periya āḷ*), a "new face" or an established star with many hit films to his name (see Nakassis 2016a:196–202)? Vaibhav himself explained fans' anger in this way, saying to me:

> It's like, uh, "*Iva(n) yār-ṟā, ivan Thala mēle kai vaikkiṟān?!*," *anta mātiri.*
> [Who the hell is he (-HON.) raising a hand to *Thala*?!, like that.]
> That was the thing … I was just only three movies old.

Here, Vaibhav voices, in an English-framed Tamil reported-speech construction, fans' response to his slaps. He then explains it, codeswitching back to English, with a trope of age: "I was just only three movies old." An impetuous cinematic toddler, Vaibhav scales his lower status to Ajith – nine years his chronological elder, forty-seven films his cinematic elder – as a developmental progression of maturation.[38] Just as children shouldn't raise their hands and voices to their elders, so too junior (character) actors shouldn't raise a hand or voice to senior artists/mass heroes.

This fan voice, however, was not just an externalized body animated by Vaibhav, kept within distancing quotation marks. It was also *his* own interior voice. Earlier in our conversation, Vaibhav said:

Ajith periya star, first of all. So:::	First of all, Ajith is a big star. So:::
atukku first when Prabhu was, you know, reading the scene, uhm::	when (Venkat) Prabhu first was, you know, reading the scene (to me), uhm::
"*Atu- Itulerentu inta mātiri Ajith varuvāru. Vanta uṭanē Vaibhav* character *vantu Ajith* slap *paṇṇaṇum* because he's talking bad about his wife. So, you have to slap,"	"It- From this Ajith will come this way. Immediately after coming, the Vaibhav character has to slap Ajith, because he's talking bad about his wife. So, you have to slap,"
appaṭi nnu sonnāru.	he said like that.
Sonnatukku appuṟam I thought, ((???))	After he said that, I thought, ((???))
"See, he is a big star, you know, and I'm just coming up. So, *nallā irukkātu paṇṇā*,"	"See, he's a big star, you know, and I'm just coming up. So if I slap him, it won't be nice,"
appaṭi nnu solli sonnēn.	like that I said (to Venkat Prabhu).

By 'it won't be nice,' Vaibhav indicated that it was unseemly to hit someone whom he respected and looked up to, because as he then explained, *he himself* was an Ajith fan. The issue, then, wasn't simply about fan retribution. When I prompted Vaibhav by saying, in Tamil: 'So, if it wasn't for the fans, you wouldn't have a problem hitting Ajith?' he laughed and said: "*Appaṭi ille, ānā* [It's not like that, but] but uh *iruntālum* [even so] he's a very big star, no? I mean <mouth click> I've been watching his films since childhood," again underlining how hierarchies of age, generation, and status underwrite the image, both in its becoming (production) and its perpetual affective charge (reception). Vaibhav continued:

> Obviously, obviously (I'm a fan). ((Because)) if suddenly if someone calls me and says, you know, (for) example, "Rajini sir [an even bigger, more senior mass hero than Ajith] next *paṭattule vantu* [in his next film] you have to push him or you have to, you know, hit him and all" *sonnavuṭanē* [immediately after they say that] obviously we'll feel "No, no, no, *māttaṇum*" [No, no, no, (the scene's) got to be changed].

It's got to be changed because fans don't hit their idols, and little boys don't step to big men, at least, not without receiving their comeuppance.

A comparison here with *Mankatha*'s climactic fight sequence is instructive. In this spectacular sequence, Vinayak comes head to head with the police officer who has been gunning for him, Pritviraj, played by the "Action King" Arjun Sarja (b. 1962), a senior artist and former hero in his own right. In this scene, Arjun and Ajith exchange blows in a dazzling set of highly stylized, choreographed sequences. But everyone with whom I spoke (from the film's stunt choreographer "Stunt" Silva to fans like Anbu) emphasized that no one would get mad at Arjun, even if they don't like seeing Ajith hit by him. There are a number of reasons for this response – including aesthetic and narratological ones, to which I turn below – but a central one is that Arjun, while not of equal standing with Ajith, is of the "same category and level," as Anbu put it. He too is a hero-star and heavyweight in the industry. By contrast, Vaibhav, Anbu went on to say, 'doesn't have as much worth' compared to Arjun, who has "a lot of experience." Naren, a close friend in his late thirties, similarly explained in 2016: Arjun is a 'big actor,' whereas Vaibhav is just an 'ordinary guy' who would have only acted [-HON.] in a few films (*Vaibhav sātāraṇamāna āḷ tān, oru paṭam, renṭu paṭam tān naṭicciruppān*). Voicing the fan, Naren said: 'Being new, who the hell are you [-HON.] to threaten my leader?!' (*Putusā vantu ennaṭā en talaivan miraṭṭuṟe*?!).

Aesthetic Realism and the Event of the Slaps

In comparison with its introductory sequence and climactic fight sequence, most of *Mankatha* has a gritty, naturalistic feel. Sitting down to watch the slap sequence with Sakti Saravanan (2016), the film's cinematographer, in his home, I spoke with him about the look of the sequence and how he achieved it. Filmed in a naturally dusty location, Sakti emphasized the "rawness" of the sequence and the film in general: 'There's nothing refined in the film … There is a real chaos to everything' (*Romba* fine-*ā vantu etuvumē irukkātu intappaṭattule … Ellāmē vantu romba oru* chaos *irukkum, oru* rawness *irukkum*). "We wanted to record that chaos," he emphasized, making sure that the camera work was "dynamic" to reflect the unstable, changing nature of Vinayak, who first appears in the film as something of a good guy but is revealed in the slap sequence to be a 'really bad guy.' This sequence lays bare Vinayak's true colours: consumed with greed, he is willing to do and say anything for money.[39]

When I asked Sakti what they did to achieve this rawness and chaos, he invoked a naturalist ideology of the image, saying, matter of factly: 'Nothing at all' (*etuvumē paṇṇale*). No camera tricks, no special effects, no editing effects. They never curated the image (but see note 39 in this chapter), leaving it intentionally without any "balance" in its composition (*Inta paṭam* total-*ā* shoot *paṇṟappavē* balanced-*ā vantu eṅkēyumē irukkātu*). They didn't use any "fine lighting," opting for natural lighting ('whatever was available') in outdoor locations (rather than sets). In addition, in the slap sequence and the larger scene of which it was a part, Sakti used a lightweight, handheld camera (Arriflex 235) with a short zoom that easily allowed him to move with the camera, both physically and with the lens. Equipped with a wide-angle lens rather than a long lens (long lenses allowing the object of focus to be foregrounded and appear larger relative to other objects in the frame), this camera setup allowed Sakti to cover as much of the performance space as possible while maximizing the camera's proximity to the action. Additionally, this setup optically flattened Ajith's image (and thereby elevated Vaibhav; compare Figure 1.6), putting Vinayak *into* the scene rather than projecting Ajith out of it.

Echoing Bazin's writings on cinema's capacity to maintain the phenomenological reality and spatiotemporal coherence of the profilmic event (for example, through long shot-length, deep focus, transparent editing, natural locations, and the like), these intentional production choices (certainly not 'nothing at all') aimed to capture the *event* of slapping in its entirety, spatially and temporally. As *Mankatha*'s director, Venkat Prabhu (2016), explained to me, it was important to use a wide shot with long shot-duration – in particular, when showing the slaps themselves (see Figures 1.1 and 1.2) – so that the viewer can 'see everything,' so that the "full action" of the conflict between the characters was highlighted as a single continuous event (compare Branigan 2006:9).[40]

For Sakti Saravanan, however, recording this event in its performed reality was not just about being there as a detached observer to "document" the performance (as he also framed it in our discussion). It also involved being part of it, being *in it* – which is why, Sakti indicated, he used a single handheld camera with long-duration shots (rather than multiple cameras and quickly edited shots, as in the spectacular fight scenes such as the climactic fight with Arjun).[41] As Sakti explained, if you use more than one camera, "you're not free." You're located, fixed in time and space, unreactive. When you use a handheld camera, you can move, react. With a handheld camera, Sakti(/the camera/the spectator) could enter deeper into the scene, allowing for a dynamic transaction with the event.

This approach was particularly important since, in order to guarantee the "natural output" of the performance (Sakti Saravanan 2016), the filmmakers intentionally did not choreograph the altercation in the slap sequence or use set positions (as is typical in fight scenes, including those in *Mankatha*).[42] As Sakti said, he had no real idea what the actors were going to do. It was, as he put it, "extempore": 'Whatever occurred to me at that time, that's what I shot. I didn't plan (my movements) at all.'[43] He continued: 'I was reacting to the dialogue, to the "mood."' Echoing the improvisational and open-ended approach to creativity documented in Anand Pandian's (2011, 2015) ethnography of Tamil filmmakers, not simply recording what was in front of it, on this view the camera transduces the profilmic performance in/as the image's own dynamic form/framing, interacting with the actors' performance and thus becoming part of the performance itself (see Bazin's epigraph above; MacDougall 2006:26–7). Critical here is Sakti Saravanan's use of short zooms, pans, and subtle physical movements. Such participatory, interactive movements have a dance-like feel,[44] iconically echoing the facial expressions, volume, timbre, and dialogue of the characters (see 0:13–0:22 of Figure 1.1 in particular), creating a poetic resonance across modalities of expression that show us both the (objective) action and its (subjective) affective charge at once.[45] Each camera movement – each shake, zoom, dip – Sakti claimed, had his "touch," capturing his own reactions to Ajith and Vaibhav's acting, to the drama, emotion, and contingency of the event.

While for Bazin, the importance of realism was how it enabled the subject's freedom to make meaning out of the open-ended contingency of the profilmic world, for Venkat Prabhu and Sakti Saravanan, more important was how a vérité style shaped and amplified the narrative flow and dramatic pathos of the scene, in particular (and in a Metzian vein), as they impacted the viewer's voyeuristic involvement. As Venkat Prabhu noted, the narrative development – in particular, Vinayak's vulgar insult of Vaibhav's wife (truly shocking for a mass hero to say, Venkat Prabhu emphasized) – prompts the anxious question for the viewer: "What is he [ambiguously, Vaibhav, Sumanth] going to do?" It is this drama that necessitates, Venkat Prabhu averred, a realist style that allows the viewer to get *inside* the spatiotemporal envelope of the diegetic event. 'It should make him feel like he's standing there with them, watching them,' Venkat Prabhu said (*Aṅkē iruntē pākkuṟa mātiri irukkaṇum. Oruttan ninnu ippaṭi pāttuṭṭu irukkān appaṭiṅkuṟa mātiri oru* feel *taraṇum*). 'Without you knowing it at all,' he continued, 'you've been brought inside of the scene, which builds up its tension' (*Uṅkaḷukkē teriyāme uḷḷē vantu uṅkaḷukku vantu oru cinna* tension *oṇṇu* build up *ākum*; compare Aumont et al. 1992[1983]:123; MacDougall 2006:251).

The desire for an emotionally intense "natural output" also explains why Vaibhav slaps Ajith rather than punches him. As Vaibhav Reddy (2016) noted, "punch will be like a fight, action thing. Slapping is different. It's personal. Slapping is different, you know. When something happens between two friends it's- Punching is different, it'll be a fight. Slapping is a bit, it will hurt you (emotionally), you know? … Yeah, emotionally, they'll say, you know, *Areñceṭṭān maccān enne*! [Bro, he slapped me!]."[46] By contrast, as Venkat Prabhu (2016) and "Stunt" Silva (2016), the film's stunt choreographer, both noted to me, a punch is something that happens in "cinema," that is, it is choreographed, unspontaneous.[47] A punch in this affectively charged scene between former male friends would make the scene become unrealistic and fake (*poyyā iruntirukkum*), as Venkat Prabhu put it.

Equally critical for these filmmakers was that the voyeuristic presence and affect this representationally realist aesthetic enables is independent of Ajith's star image and, moreover, in distinction to his auratic presence. Not simply realist in the sense that it respects the spatial and temporal coherence of the profilmic event, or that it voyeuristically sutures the spectator into the narrative scene, this scene is realist for these filmmakers because of its *intertextual opposition* to the spectacular aesthetics of the typical mass-hero film (see Chapter 4), an aesthetics that *Mankatha* itself selectively deployed (for example, in the introductory scene, the fight scene with Arjun; see Table 1.1). The whole idea, Sakti

Table 1.1. Formal contrasts between *Mankatha* and Ajith's "typical" mass films

	Mankatha / *Mankatha*'s slap sequence	Typical mass-hero film / *Mankatha*'s introductory scene, climactic fight
Camera	Handheld (single)	Steady (multiple)
Lens/Zoom	Wide/Short	Long/Long
Depth of field	Deep, flat	Shallow
Composition	Unbalanced, jittery	Balanced, "smooth"
Découpage & mise en scène, Performance	Unplanned, "extempore"	Planned, choreographed
Editing	Long single shots	Rapid multiple shots
Lighting	Natural, "rawness"	Artificial, "fine"
Colouring of image	Dark, greenish	Bright, colourful
Post-production	No special effects	Special effects

Note: These distinctions are fractally reinscribed within *Mankatha* between the slap sequence and other key scenes (for example, the introductory scene, climactic fight scene with Arjun).

Saravanan and Venkat Prabhu repeatedly insisted, was that this scene (and *Mankatha* overall) should *not* be like Ajith's other mass films.

Like Bazin's own liberal humanism and the realism he saw (potentially) expressing it, here the filmmakers' ideologies of realism stand in tension with, and even oppose, the aesthetics of the mass hero's spectacle and its implied authoritarian, populist politics. Yet while Bazin's realism turned on recognizing and cultivating a presence that exceeds representation, in *Mankatha* it is precisely the performative presence of the mass hero that the filmmakers attempt to dampen with the sequence's representationalist realism, that is, by entextualizing, through their "touch," an affectively intense and immersive voyeuristic fiction.

The ambivalence of this image – which must put into play what it attempts to forestall: Ajith's presence – reflects precisely the ambivalence of presence itself (and thus Bazin's ontology), a fact not lost on Bazin, who warned of the political risks of the presentist, realist filmic image of an authoritarian figure like Stalin, whom Bazin likened, with irony, to the cinema "star" (Bazin 1985[1950]:32; Hassan 2017; a concern Walter Benjamin [1968(1935)] was also alive to). Just as Bazin articulates his realism, and the ontology it presupposes and the politics it entails, through a differentiation from other types of images (for example, certain kinds of propaganda films, pornography, German expressionism) and other politics (for example, fascism), here too we find multiple realisms, aesthetics, and politics – indeed, multiple ontologies of the image – in contestation. Such heterogeneity is not only distributed across images, however. It is inscribed *within* them.

The image of Vaibhav's slaps is one such ambivalent, polyphonic image. Note how the representational realism of the slap sequence, precisely by bracketing Ajith's presence, simultaneously forces the viewer beyond the representational enclosure of the image to the star actor's auratic body. This, in turn, amplifies Vaibhav's slaps of Ajith as a profilmic event, entextualizing them as (image-)acts that really took place. Not just defeasing Ajith's presence, then, here the representationalist realism and photographic indexicality of the scene also entails it (compare Pinney 2004:66; Lefebvre 2021:18), activating the sociological realism of Ajith's (star) image by transgressing it. In an era of digital images, where the spectacle of the mass hero's presence is ever more exaggerated through various non-realist film techniques (including the painterly aesthetics of CGI graphics; compare Pinney 1997:138–9), the slap sequence's realist aesthetic treatment (and, we might add, the way in which it entextualized the image not as Ajith's but as the "touch" of its filmmakers) was itself a stinging offence.[48] As I discuss below, the narrative realism of the sequence itself, like its aesthetic realist style, was entextualized by some viewers as an image-act.

Ambivalent Realisms

Like the film's (selectively) realist style, the narrative of *Mankatha* also entailed and voided the slaps' performativity at once, offering up different, competing positions to engage the image. As Venkat Prabhu (2016) noted, during the filmmaking process it was an open question whether audiences would accept *Mankatha* with all its deviations from the mass-hero formula. It was a gamble, he said. Particularly risky was the way the narrative positioned Ajith, the spectatorial site for fan attention and affective investment, as anything but a typical hero. Not only did he appear his age in this film, with his natural, salt-and-pepper hair (atypical for heroes of his stature and age, who while well into middle-age when they reach their critical mass almost always act as youth), he also eschewed his signature handsome, stylish appearance by wearing the same dark-coloured, sweat-stained, torn shirt for nearly all of the film's second half (also atypical).[49] But most of all, he played a completely unredeemable character. Would anyone accept Ajith cursing, vulgarly insulting innocent women, unabashedly greedy and violently ruthless, scheming and deceitful? (Even one of Venkat Prabhu's assistant directors vigorously protested this depiction, pleading with the director on the shooting spot to change Ajith's dialogue in the slap sequence.)

The slap sequence most acutely staged this reversal, functioning as the plot's "turning point," as Venkat Prabhu (2016) put it to me, where not only has the hero turned out to be the villain but where we are also asked to emotionally sympathize with a lesser actor/character and ratify his righteous anger *against* the hero-star.[50] Venkat Prabhu justified this structure of identification, and the need for Sumanth/Vaibhav to slap Vinayak/Ajith, by appealing to the logic of the story and its characters:

Ānā itu avan aṭiccatukku oru niyāyam paṭuttaṇum, le? Avan summā aṭikkale, le? Anta niyāyam vantu correct-*āna niyāyam appaṭiṉṟatanāle perisā Vaibhav-kku* effect *ākale.*	But it [the story] should justify his [-HON., Sumanth] hitting (Vinayak), right? He didn't hit (him) for no reason, right? Because that justness is correct, the effect [that is, fan's anger] on Vaibhav wasn't as much (as it would have been).

Like the vérité shooting style and its optical flattening of Ajith's image, here the narrative demotes the hero-star to a character; or at least, by putting the moral right on the side of Sumanth, it fails to conserve and build up the hero-star's mass, instead giving some of it over to Vaibhav.[51] Indeed, as Venkat Prabhu noted, it "was a scene for Vaibhav," to showcase his emoting and foreground his character.[52] This diegetic moral economy conspires against the fan's anger by suggesting that, if anyone, it is Vinayak/Ajith with whom we should be angry. To Venkat Prabhu's mind, this narrative logic – and the realist identification with Sumanth it invited – (should have) worked against the fans' anger at Vaibhav. But curiously, in doing so, it also amplified it.

Consider Anbu's narration of fans' anger. Like many, perhaps most, film-star fans in Tamil Nadu, Anbu was ambivalent about his fandom (see Dickey 1993a, 1993b, 2001; Gerritsen 2019, 2021). Coming from an upwardly mobile, lower-middle-class background, educated in a prestigious Chennai college, and with some experience as an assistant film director, Anbu voiced a familiar elitist discourse differentiating those who can see that it's "just acting" and those who take the image too seriously.[53] When I prompted him by saying that Vaibhav/Sumanth slaps Ajith/Vinayak for a good reason (namely, Vinayak's vulgar insult of

Sumanth's wife), Anbu responded by derisively voicing the stereotypical fan's response: 'Beyond the reason [that is, ignoring the motivating reason provided by the narrative], they'll sort of think a little stupidly, like, How could you [-HON., Vaibhav] hit (Ajith)? There may be a thousand good reasons. Ajith said [+HON.] it, so what?' (Beyond the reason *vantu, Nī vantu eppaṭi aṭikkalām? Āyiram [kāraṇaṅkaḷ] irukkaṭṭum, Ajith tān sonnāru appaṭi nnu koñca muṭṭāḷtanamā yōsikkiṟāṅka*). On this thinking (as given voice by Anbu), narrative logic and fictional framing are rejected as irrelevant concerns; indeed, they are themselves entextualized as *acts* that threaten the hero's personage.

Yet even if this fan response turns on rejecting the film's narrative justifications, the slaps' sting – and the intensity of fans' repudiation – worked itself through this very narrative logic. Anbu continued by noting that if minor characters hit Ajith (for example, in fight sequences), no one would care too much because, as he noted, they're "just passing" through the story. But with Vaibhav's character, he continued, 'he's in half of the film. He's a character that travels throughout the film with Ajith ... so the impact is more (intense).' Not just a dampening of fan affect, the intimacy of Sumanth and Vinayak – and the importance given to Sumanth, and thus Vaibhav, by the narrative – makes Vaibhav's slaps of Ajith an unforgivable betrayal. Reanimating the fan voice that Anbu animated above, there may have been a thousand narrative reasons for Sumanth to hit Vinayak, but how could *Vaibhav* hit *Ajith*?

Authorizing the Slaps, or the Principal of Animation

As we've seen, commercial Tamil film, not unlike other film industries, presents its viewers with a set of overlapping tensions – between "class" and "mass" films (Srinivas 2009; Ganti 2012:282, 295–301), story and star, character and actor, presence and representation – whose intersections are, on the one hand, the film image and, on the other hand, the performative effect/affect anticipated and engendered by that image (Dyer 1998[1979]; King 1985). These tensions also suffuse the profilmic event. How, in fact, does such an image come into being in the force field of the mass hero? If realist images and mass-hero images articulate different politics, what politics are necessary for such an image to be conceived, performed, recorded, and exhibited? How could Vaibhav have done it?

Consider the televised 2012 birthday special for Ajith (Aj) on Vijay TV (*Happy Birthday Ajith*, 1 May 2012), wherein Vaibhav (V) narrated the filming of the slaps in *Mankatha*:

Morning *vantu* Venkat Prabhu [VP] *avaru vantuṭṭu* shooting spot-*ukku pōnavuṭanē appō nān appaṭiyē vantēn.*

(V:) *"Eh, enna sār nīṅka enna eṭukkiṟīṅka?" appaṭi nnuṭṭu.*

Prabhu vantu sonnāru:

(VP:) *"Inta mātiri vantuṭṭu nī Ajith sār-e vantu aṟaiyaṇum" appaṭi nnuṭṭu.*

(V:) *"Sār, enna viḷaiyāṭuṟīṅkaḷā? Atellām muṭiyātu sār ennāle" appaṭi nnu.*

Appaṭi pinnāṭi ninnu kēṭṭiṭṭu irukkāru <imitates Ajith with his hand over his chin stroking it>. *Nāṅka pākkale. Appaṭiyē ((ninnu))* <imitates reading the script>,

(Aj:) *"Enna pēsuṟīṅka reṇṭu pērum?" appaṭi nnu.*

(VP:) *"Ille-(a)ṇṇa(n) inta mātiri* scene-*u vantu"-*

<Sits up a little bit and speaks louder, inhabiting Ajith:>

(Aj:) *"Inta* scene *vantu nān paṭiccuṭṭēn. Inta* scene-*le oru* dialogue *kūṭa* miss *āyiccunālum Prabhu nān summā irukkamāṭṭēn" nnuṭṭu.*

(VP:) *"Illa-(a)ṇṇa(n) nān appaṭiyē eṭutturēn. Enakku oṇṇum* problem *illa.* But *ivan tān vantu uṅkaḷai aṭikkamāṭṭēn appaṭi nnu solli solṟān."*

(Aj:) *"Nān ivvaḷō nāḷ* sweet-*ā tān iruntu pātte. Nī ippa māṭṭum naṭikkale nnu vaccukkō inta kaile* <looks down at hand, raised up to strike> *aṭippēn pāru atē kiḻe* train-*le iṭiccu((kkuvēn)) pāru" appaṭi nnuṭṭāru.*

In the morning, I came to the shooting spot immediately after (the director) Venkat Prabhu [VP] came. I asked him:

(V:) "What are you [+HON.] going to shoot today, sir?"

Prabhu then said,

(VP:) "I'm gonna do this scene, where you're [-HON.] gonna have to slap Ajith sir."

I said,

(V:) "Sir, are you playing around? I can't do all that, sir!"

He [+HON., Ajith] is standing behind us <imitates Ajith with his hand over his chin stroking it>. And we didn't see him. Standing like that <imitates reading the script>,

(Aj:) "Hey, what are you two talking about?," he said.

(VP:) "No older brother, a scene like this-"

<Sits up a little bit and speaks louder, inhabiting Ajith:>

(Aj:) "I've read this scene. If there's even one dialogue missing from it Prabhu, I'm not going to let it slide."

(VP:) "No older brother, I'll shoot it like that. I don't have a problem. But he [-HON., Vaibhav] is saying that he won't hit you [+HON.]."

(Aj:) <to V.> "I've been sweet for all these days. But if you [-HON.] don't act now (as it's written), with this hand <looks down at hand, raised up to strike> I'm going to beat you and smash you against the train," he said [+HON.].

{audience laughs} (V:) <soft voice:> *"Sari okay."*	{audience laughs} (V:) <soft voice:> "Alright, okay."
First time *vantu* light-*ā* <gestures a pat on the cheek> *appaṭiṇṇēn.*	The first time (I hit him) lightly <gestures a pat on the cheek> like that.
(Aj:) *"Nān enna sonnēn unakku?" appaṭi nnu.*	(Aj:) "What did I tell you [-HON.]?"
(V:) *"Aṭikka sonnīṅka-(a)ṇṇā."*	(V:) "You [+HON.] said to hit (you), older brother."
(Aj:) *"Ippa inta* take *maṭṭum* okay *akale nnu veccukkō appuṟam semma aṭippēn Vaibhav. Oḻuṅkā naṭi!" ṇṇāru.*	(Aj:) "If this take isn't okayed, I'm going to beat the hell out of you, Vaibhav. Act [-HON.] properly!," he said [+HON.].
Aṭicca muṭiñcavuṭānē,	Right after hitting (him):
(Aj:) "Very good *ṭā. Itān.* This is what I expected" *appaṭi eṇṇāru.*	(Aj:) "Very good, man. That's it. This is what I expected," like that he said [+HON.].

While, ultimately, Vaibhav agreed to do the scene, as he told it to me (Vaibhav Reddy 2016), he struggled to bring himself to slap Ajith, to see Ajith *as* Vinayak. It took Vaibhav, as Venkat Prabhu (2016) recalled, eight to ten takes for Vaibhav to sufficiently slap Ajith, with Ajith continuing to complain that he wasn't getting "the real feel of the slap," that Vaibhav was "just acting," "just only touching me."[54]

Consider Ajith's ambivalent position here: on the one hand, he enjoys ultimate authority and authorship over but not principalship (that is, responsibility) for the filmic image.[55] This authority is not only with respect to the actor Vaibhav (the animator of the slap), who will only act if physically intimidated to do so by Ajith. It is also with respect to the director (the slap's putative author), who felt he needed to ask Ajith's permission to even include such a scene, as Venkat Prabhu reported in the Sun TV special.[56] On the other hand, what Ajith insists on is for Vaibhav to not consider the act that subtends the act of acting – namely, slapping him – and instead focus on the craft of "acting properly," in other words, that Vaibhav do his job as an actor: to animate a character in the script, the script the way the *director* wrote it. But therein lies a further irony, for as Venkat Prabhu told me in 2016, he hadn't originally written the scene this way, nor was Ajith's character as villainous. He had originally toned it down. "You tend to mellow it down a bit (with big stars)," he said, "because you don't want the fans to go mad." But Ajith wanted more. He wanted more slaps.[57] And he wanted a more negative character. As Venkat Prabhu told me in 2010,

Ajith wanted to do something like Heath Ledger in *The Dark Knight* (2008, dir. Christopher Nolan), a telling comparison since it was suggested by some English-language media that Ledger's role as the Joker was a tragic coup of so-called method acting,[58] of the actor *becoming* his character (beyond the frame of the film) rather than simply "playing" it (versus every character being swept up as another avatar of the mass hero; King 1985:47).

Ultimately, in the orbit of the mass hero, to act as a character *requires* an order of authority beyond the script and the story, beyond the director's authorship. It requires, quite literally, an order given by the mass hero himself.[59] While Ajith demands that Vaibhav show fidelity to the story/script's representational economy and *not* to the economy of his mass, such a demand is waged, and must be waged, from within that very star economy. This authority hovers before and after the image; it envelops that image, even in moments when the hero's mass is leveraged to open up space for a type of image that does not (or is not supposed to) orbit around the mass hero, that attempts to discard his graven image and its compelling power.

Of course, as Vaibhav's insistent refusals, fans' recalcitrant anger, and the filmmakers' own hesitations indicate, Ajith's auratic star image is not so easily displaced by either the representational quotation marks of the director's narrative or Ajith's permission for such a bracketing to hold. The mass hero does not have the authority to authorize the ontic transformation of his image, the power to effectuate his own (or others') escape velocity from the gravity of his mass, on the set or in the theatre. As Vaibhav told me, in the slap sequence he could never fully bring himself to act as his character, just as some viewers could not bring themselves to forgive his transgressions or accept the narrative's justifications for them.[60]

/ / /

Let me conclude this section with two points. First, as we've seen, a fundamental ambivalence suffuses this image-act of the slaps (Mitchell 2004:19–20). This image harbours a confluence of disjointed forces (aesthetic, sociological, narratological) that variously play into and against each other, a series of ideological claims and counterclaims played out in the image about what that image is/should be. This ambivalence inheres in the multiply tiered textuality of the scene itself, in how the slaps are shot in a realistic style that reflexively invokes, and exploits, that which it implicitly contests: Ajith's star image and its presentist aesthetics. But this ambivalence also emanates from and travels beyond the screen, from and beyond the profilmic moment. It appears in the anxiousness in Vaibhav's voice in the end credits; in the fact that the director had to ask the hero's permission to direct the scene as he wrote it (or didn't write it); and in Ajith's violent insistence on set that he and Vaibhav act just as characters in a story rather than in the thrall of his star image. It appears in the way that Vaibhav is called on to repeatedly and publicly narrate his fear and reluctance to even consider such a scene. And finally, we hear it in the anxious, mediatized (middle-class) laughs that surround these public, televised narratives, in the fascination of television hosts and audiences (and anthropologists) who want to hear about credulous, fanatical fans who *really* got upset, who *really* wanted to beat Vaibhav, inscribing their own distinction as sensible, liberal viewers who only see the film image as a representation and nothing more.

Second, these ambivalent forces and counterforces problematize the question of responsibility and authorship of the image, the question of what "footings," to use Goffman's (1979) term, are distributed vis-à-vis some image. Complexifying and deconstructing the notions of speaker and hearer, Erving Goffman used the phrases *production format* and *participation framework* to denote the heterogeneous and multiple kinds of stances, or "footings" (we might even say, subjectivities), that participants may inhabit vis-à-vis some stretch of semiosis – in the case of production format, as *author* (the person who composes/originates the stretch in question), *animator* (the person who enacts or carries it out), or *principal* (the person responsible for it and whose position is staked by it), and so on (Goffman 1974, 1979).[61] As we've seen in this chapter, such fractions are not simply analytic descriptors of objective social or interactional facts but objects of ideological contention and negotiation that are perspectival in nature. Indeed, part of what is being struggled over in the making and uptake of the slap sequence is precisely *who* and *what* authorizes the image. Who is its master, in control of its becoming and its effects? And who is responsible for its perlocutionary effects? The director? The script? The story/diegetic world? "Reality"? The hero-star? The audience?[62] While ultimately it is in the name of the director-script-story-character that the mass hero authorizes the image, the question of responsibility, as we have seen, remains an essentially open and contested one, for what is at stake for Vaibhav Reddy (but not Venkat Prabhu or Ajith Kumar) is that for some section of the audience, no amount of hedging and disavowal – be it the narrative's interpellation of us as sympathetic viewers to Sumanth's rage; the film's end credit out-takes where Ajith and Vaibhav disavow the illocutionary actuality of the slap; or even the hero-star's and the director's exhortation that Vaibhav *must* do it – can fully suspend the performativity of *Vaibhav*'s slaps. Vaibhav is never a mere animator, but always also the one responsible for, the Goffmanian principal of, the image-act of the figure (Sumanth) he animates.

In this configuration is a particular conception of agency and image, one that a final interrogation of the fans' anger at Vaibhav elucidates. When I asked Anbu and Naren why fans don't get mad at directors, who write and direct the scripts that have character actors like Vaibhav hit mass heroes like Ajith, they both voiced the same logic. Anbu said: 'Vaibhav is to blame (and not the director) ...Where did your [-HON., Vaibhav] sense go? <mouth click> Where did your intelligence go? If he [-HON., Venkat Prabhu] says (to hit Ajith) will you hit (him)? It'll go like that' (*Vaibhav tān tappu ... Unakku eṅkē pōccu butti?* <mouth click> *Unakku eṅkē pōccu aṟivu? Avan sonnā aṭippeyā?" appaṭi pōkum*). Naren (N) put it to me (CN) this way (in his case, discussing his favourite hero in his youth, Rajinikanth):

N: *"Talaivane pōy etukku ṭā nī tiṭṭina aṭicca?!" nnu solliṭṭu.*	N: "Why the hell did you [-HON.] scold and hit (our) leader, man?!" I'd say like that.
CN: *Sari, avaru "Nān naṭikar tānē. Katai appaṭi tān irukku" appaṭi nnu solliruntā?*	CN: Okay, but what if he said "I'm just an actor. The story is written like that"?
N: *"Inimē appaṭi naṭikkātē. Sonnāl kūṭa nī naṭikkātē ... Naṭikkamāṭṭēn nnu sollu ṭā! Atukkāka en talaivanai tiṭṭuṟuviyā?! ... Tiṭṭuṟa mātiri* scene *iruntā anta paṭattule nī naṭikkamāṭṭēn nnu solliru* (director-*kku*)."	N: (I'd say) "Hereafter don't act [-HON.] (in scenes like that). Even if they tell you to, don't act (in them) ... Say that you won't act, man! You hit my leader just because someone told you to?! ... If there is a scene where you have to scold him and all, tell (the director) that you won't act in that film."

Here, whatever else may have been impinging upon the becoming of the image, this fan reaction presupposes and imagines the agentive *choice* of the actor-as-animator to (not) refuse, to (not) appear, and to (not) act (a spectatorial logic that we will see again in later chapters). So ideologically construed, this choice serves as a moral evaluation of responsibility *for* the image, saddling the most visible and most immediate cause with the image's ultimate effects.

Conclusion

In Vaibhav's slaps, and in *Mankatha* as a whole, we see an ontological politics working itself across the image's textual surface, its various paratextual commentaries, and its extratextual peregrinations. This ontological politics manifests in each of these sites as a tension between a liberal yearning for a representationalist, realist image and the gravitational pull of the auratic presence of the hero's mass, whose image is always liable in this context to bleed into populist electoral politics. These competing images forestall and enable each other, simultaneously stoking their iconophilia and iconoclasm (Mitchell 1986:157–8; Keane 2009). As such, these cinematic images are potent sites of ambivalence and anxiety, distinction and desire, which play out not just in/through these polyphonic film images but in the subjects implicated therein, including and especially the fraught star image of ~~Ultimate Star~~ *Thala* Ajith.

This is a political terrain – aesthetic and electoral, liberal and populist, representationalist and performative, onscreen and offscreen – waged in images. This politics itself forms, as we noted, the political economy and genre organization of the Tamil film industry more generally, whose productions are roughly split between politically potent, big-budget "mass" films and realistic, representationalist, small-budget "class" films, the latter of which take inspiration from, among other things, a global film culture shaped by Bazin's own legacy of film criticism and theory (Andrew 2011; Majumdar 2016, 2021). *Mankatha* internalizes this tension in/as its textual form, as perhaps do all Tamil films to varying degrees, the poetics of their filmic images evincing a struggle for the dominance of (even "dominant" of; Jakobson 1987[1935]), and balance between, different modes of being.

But if so, to theorize this politics is not to pluralize ontology and being (Mol 1999; Chumley 2017), as if the issue were simply to move from ontology to ontologies, being to modes of being, parcelling out being and difference to kinds of images (performative versus representational), films or genres (mass versus class), filmic cultures (Tamil versus Euro-American), or epochs ("primitive" versus "classical"), each with their "own" ontology or mode of being. Rather, this analysis pushes us to approach images as always bearing multiple ontic potentials and impulses.[63] We have to see how this ontological politics inheres in even a single film, even a single image-act, even a single motion of a hand slapping a cheek onscreen. Here, the image – and its ontologies – opens up as a multiplicity of heterogeneous impulses and tendencies, a multiplicity of capacities and "voices" (to extend Bakhtin's [1981] and

Vološinov's 1986[1929] trope) that abut and interact with each other.[64] Such variegated impulses and tendencies, capacities and voices are within and yet also elsewhere than images, immanent to a field that includes but exceeds the images that constitute it.

This multiplicity does not imply that images do not have modes of being to be enquired after. Rather, it implies that any inquiry into the nature of images has to contend with the fact that their being is constitutively mediated – in its multiplicity – by various, contentious ontological claims, be they by fans, filmmakers, or film critics and theorists, as they come to inhere in but also beyond the image. Ontologies are political facts – is there nothing more political than a claim about being, about what is or is not? And images are a critical medium of such claims. I take this point to be one of Bazin's most profound insights. But rather than normatively adjudicate such claims in the name of being (on moral, aesthetic, or philosophical grounds), another avenue, I have argued, is the empirical study of the processual pragmatics of such ontological politics and their entailments, that is, the study of how social actors (like Bazin, Anbu, Venkat Prabhu, and film texts themselves) engage with images and the effects generated therein (see Odin 2018:104).[65] From this point of view, Bazin's ontology is not simply an uncanny account of the Tamil image, its presence and its realism, but also an empirical datum, a situated ontological politics criterial to the ongoing unfolding of the (still-contested) being of at least some filmic images, one that has had and continues to have its own consequences on and off the screen (see Andrew 2011).[66] Any mode of being of an image is caught in this reflexive loop, as the medium, object, and outcome of particular claims on/accounts of the being of images.

This point bears on the question of the image's performativity as well. For while it has been rightly suggested that images should not be thought of as inert objects, simply reflecting, simply depicting, or simply denoting that which they are not, and instead must be treated as affective acts with animated agencies of their own, this performativity too is a complex semiotic achievement and not a pregiven fact. Further, this potency is not a property of the image as such – at least, not the image as we typically construe it, as a decontextualizable, localizable chunk of (audio-)visually mediated signs – but is interdiscursively distributed across images, actors, and audiences (among other stakeholders still: for example, producers, financiers, state bureaucrats, film critics, theorists) as they orient to and intersect in any particular image or series of images.

In even a single image, we find a play and tension of multiple indexicalities – physically inscriptional and citationally characterological – and multiple realities, rather than a single, ambiguous reality. If the "realism of the cinema" is inherent to it, as Bazin suggested, it is perhaps only because there may be more than one way for something to be and become real. Cinema in these cases *is* indeed "based on the inalienable realism of that which is shown" (Bazin 2005[1951]b:108) – for example, slapping the hero – but not simply because of film's sui generis facticity or ontological identity with its referent-object (as relayed by the physical indexicality of the apparatus across time and space) but because of a heterogeneous set of social and (inter)textual indexicalities embedded within a complex of onscreen/offscreen linkages and industry-internal social hierarchies, what Linda Williams (1989:45) has called the "social apparatus" of performativity. And as we've seen, the image's ability to *be* and *act* in the world follows from its ontological and political multiplicity, and the ideological tensions therein, its existence and its charge galvanized from those antinomies that weave its textual surface and their offscreen emanations.

All this shows how an image, and an ontology of the image, is always radically decentred from itself, only locatable as a fetish metonym of a larger network of social relations and practices of which it is an entextualized and interdiscursive part and effect, exploded as the dynamic, shifting intersection point of ongoing and conflictual practices that are elsewhere and elsewhen but are commonly oriented willy-nilly *in* and *as* particular images (Nakassis 2019). Any such mode of being, thus, is a dynamic, shifting relation between different practices and projects as it manifests in/as images. Such practices and projects are political. They are an ontological politics.

As this implies, rather than a settled, or even in-principle settleable, question (be it by the analyst or anyone else), the being of the image and the image's performativity are open questions that are up for grabs. If and when some such impulses become regimented and institutionalized, thickened and separated out as seemingly stable, selfsame, and singular modes of being – so as to be neatly formulated in theoretical discourse; experienced as the self-evident nature of images; or inscribed in and presupposed by technological apparatuses, political economies, or cultural norms – it is the historical achievement of situated and interest-inflected political processes that are ongoing and tenuous and in dialogic relation with those other urges, movements, and countermovements that images bear in their contested being. Not a provincial example, the Tamil hero's mass shows all this in its exemplary generality.

Chapter Two

The Heroine's Stigma

The presence of woman is an indispensable element of spectacle in normal narrative film, yet her visual presence tends to work against the development of a storyline, to freeze the flow of action in moments of erotic contemplation. This alien presence then has to be integrated into cohesion with the narrative.

– Laura Mulvey, "Visual Pleasure and Narrative Cinema," 2009[1975]

Whenever the movie screen holds a particularly effective image of terror, little boys and grown men make it a point of honor to look, while little girls and grown women cover their eyes or hide behind the shoulders of their dates ... Another excellent reason for the refusal to look is the fact that women are given so little to identify with on the screen ... she exists only to be looked at.

– Linda Williams, "When the Woman Looks," 1984

I can recall asking my parents, at the age of four or five, whether the people in movies were really kissing. The question involved a moral dilemma, and it revealed a paradox: in fact, actors both do and pretend, sometimes at one and the same moment – hence the potentially scandalous nature of their work. In certain contexts, their actions can become *too* real, breaking the hold of illusion.

– James Narenmore, *Acting in the Cinema*, 1988

The film may be a fiction but the bodies are not.

– David MacDougall, *The Corporeal Image*, 2006

Introduction

Being onscreen is being seen. On a hot April afternoon in 2009, the film crew with whom I was working on the Tamil film *Goa* (2010, dir. Venkat

Prabhu) was milling about, waiting for the frenzy that would descend as soon as we started the next shot. We were shooting a sequence for the first third of the film in a village in Theni, an agricultural district to the west of Madurai. The assistant directors were looking for a couple of extras for the shot. The scene needed village women, so they asked the woman whose house we were using for one of the indoor locations if she would like to be in the scene (a non-speaking, background role, as I recall). In her early thirties, married, and with two small children, her face betrayed interest, though she was reticent and equivocated. Her husband, who came a couple of minutes later, spoke in her stead: No, she wouldn't be participating. The assistant directors, seeming to understand immediately, dropped the issue, wandering off to find someone else. I persisted, though, and asked him: why not let her? He responded, tersely, by motioning to the dubious morality of acting and the cinema. Thinking he was talking about stereotypes of sexual misconduct on sets, I countered: but you'll be here the whole time. You would know that she hadn't done anything wrong. He responded, as if to indicate that I misunderstood him: it wasn't proper because she would be *seen* onscreen, in a theatre, by an open-ended but not quite anonymous set of viewers. That was enough to trigger local gossip that would impugn not just her, but his honour as well. This assumption that to be onscreen is to be seen, however, was conditioned by who she was offscreen. It mattered that she was a middle-class woman, still of reproductive age. As he mentioned before we parted ways, men, babies, and old women can appear in films, and no one will talk badly about them.

Being seen seeing a filmic image. During my dissertation fieldwork I would screen, and then hold discussions about, Tamil films for those college youth with whom I was conducting research. In early February 2008, I screened a film called *7/G Rainbow Colony* (2004, dir. Selvaraghavan) at a Madurai women's college. It was a popular youth film, already several years old, which many of the young women had seen before. Watching the film in a screening room in one of the college's academic centres, the film viewing was going smoothly until the critical juncture of the narrative. The heroine, her marriage to another man looming in the near future, takes her lover, the protagonist, to a lodge in a mountain resort town. There she explicitly explains her love for him, and more importantly, her desire to have sex with him. For the first time while watching the film, an absolute quiet descended. The laughs and side conversations that had peppered the viewing up until then went completely silent, a shift in spectatorship indicating a seriousness and engaged attention accorded to a scene of consequence. As the dialogues transitioned into an erotic song-and-dance sequence representing the sex act, an exodus began. About half of the crowd rushed out of the room, standing outside of the door waiting for the song to finish, at which point they came back in. The remaining women reoriented their gaze away from the screen. They turned to their college papers in their laps or to each other. (By contrast, when I screened the film in the all-male Madurai college hostel in which I lived, my hostel mates turned the volume on the television all the way up, the song-and-dance affording a ludic and raucous fraternity of heterosexual, homophilic desire.) As became clear to me from speaking with some male and female friends about the incident later, it wasn't necessarily the sexualized images per se that the young women couldn't bear – it was me, an older, unrelated, and unmarried man watching those images with them in a semi-public space amid a crowd of their peers. (On a later screening with a different group, I made sure to leave the room before the scene, which kept attendance much higher.) To see such filmic images entailed being seen seeing them; it meant bringing the corporeal imagery onscreen too close to our bodies on *this* side of the screen. In co-presence with each other, caught in the screen's and each other's sight lines, our mutual orientation to the sex act and erotic display onscreen became uncomfortable, implicating us in the represented acts, not just as voyeurs but also perhaps as displaced proxy participants.

/ / /

In both these vignettes, the filmic image, anticipated and actual, erupts from the screen, its presencing radiating in two directions: towards the profilmic (to the body and self of the actress) and towards the moment of its exhibition (to the bodies and selves of her viewers). In both cases, this eruption is met by an absenting and a blockage – prevented from being seen by the camera, preventing one's own eyes from seeing. In both cases, at issue is a politics of vision and its relationship to (im)proper femininity.

In this chapter, I look at how this politics of vision enables the performativity of images of women and the ways in which the sociological organization and cultural phenomenology of this performativity leaves its traces on and off the screen. I begin by focusing on what are called in South Asian film industries "item numbers" or "item songs" – sexually charged, stand-alone song-and-dance sequences like the one intercalated into *7/G Rainbow Colony* – and other erotic filmic imagery – such as kissing and romantic scenes – that exploit and also disavow the performative potentials of the screen. In the second part of the chapter, I turn to how such potentials play out offscreen, shaping the sociological backgrounds and statuses of the actresses who appear in such images.

As in Chapter 1, I am especially concerned to show how narrative form and performative force interact in film and the cinema, as well as the ways in which responsibility for the onscreen image is thereby variously distributed offscreen.[1] What I develop in this chapter in particular, however, is an analysis of how the performativity of presence and the representationality of narrative work alongside and through processes of absenting and occlusion. In the chapter's conclusion, I take up Teresa de Lauretis's (1984) argument that the effacing of historical women in cinema is the precondition and effect of the presence and representationality of images of woman, and of cinematic images more generally. Absenting, like presencing, however, I argue, is never singular, as a phenomenon or in its effects; in the Tamil cases I discuss, absenting ambivalently functions as both heterosexist inscription of and protective response to the presence of the image.

One such absence in my analysis, I should note, is that of the female spectator and her desires; indeed, my focus in this chapter is largely on heterosexual, masculinized spectatorship, though questions of female (heteroerotic and homoerotic) desire and spectatorship are certainly at play in the images discussed in this and the previous chapter (most obviously in the way that mass heroes are objects of desire for many female spectators – most famously in the case of MGR, perhaps [Pandian 1992:81–3; Dickey 1993a:169; Rajanayagam 2015:33ff.] – to say nothing of male spectators). Part of this absence is due to issues of ethnographic access, given my own status at the time as a young, but older unmarried man, as evinced in the second vignette; but it is also because, as also indicated by that same vignette, modes of heterosexual, masculinized spectatorship form the dominant, normative frame of public vision and visibility in Tamil cinema, an institution and set of social spaces that in the time of my fieldwork had become increasingly oriented to young male audiences and their desires, a fact that structures the dialectics of representation and performativity that this chapter focuses on and, as I indicate below, the fissures in this frame's otherwise hegemonic status.

The Item's Interruption

Talk about commercial Tamil cinema has long focused on "glamorous" song-and-dance sequences – earlier, "cabaret" songs and during my fieldwork, so-called item numbers – as a disturbingly powerful and vulgar part of Tamil film. More generally, female dance in film has historically been seen by conservative viewers as morally problematic. Yet it was not always so. As Amanda Weidman (2016, 2021:27–30) has shown, in the early era of sound cinema being strictly a ("classical") dancer *or* singer onscreen was preferable to inhabiting "character roles." The latter was associated with lower- and mixed-caste, hereditary *devadāsī* performers, so-called dancing girls, who sang *and* danced onscreen. From the mid-nineteenth and into the twentieth century, reformist movements succeeded in legally rebranding *devadāsī* courtesan traditions as prostitution, thereby pushing such women to the margins of society, including into work in popular theatre and later, with the advent of sound cinema, into film (Weidman 2003; Ramamurthy 2006:215; Soneji 2012, 2021).[2] In such a context, narrative emplotment bore stigma to the actress while classicized dance (which is to say, dance that disavowed its *devadāsī* roots; Krishnan 2019; Iyer 2020:78), especially when it had nothing to do with the plot, was relatively respectable ("relatively," since cinema as a whole was by then marked by disrepute and stigma for all involved; see Introduction).

With the rise of nationalist themes and Dravidian identity politics in post-Independence Tamil cinema and, relatedly, with the centralization of the Tamil industry around its male heroes (rather than male and female singing stars), this regime of value reversed. Women's stand-alone dancing – in particular, sexualized modern or folk song-and-dance – became a primary site of cinema's impropriety and stigma. In this dispensation, the respectability of the heroine-star turned on her general avoidance of "glamorous" dance. In her stead, the figure of the vamp appeared, often set in immoral chronotopes (or socio-timespaces; Bakhtin 1981) such as nightclubs or gangster dens (Iyer 2020). In the late 1980s and 1990s, with a changing moral economy (arguably, more permissive) and shifting audience demographics (an increase in young men, as I discuss later in the chapter), the vamp and heroine increasingly blurred as narrative figures (Ganti 2004, 2012; Chowdhury 2010), and heroine roles became both increasingly sexualized and marginal to the narrative.[3] This period saw the emergence of the raunchy and fleshy item number as a standard "commercial" element of Indian films (sometimes danced by heroine-stars, unlike the vamp-danced "cabaret" songs of yesteryear, which heroines did not generally dance).

As commentators have observed, item numbers "interrupt" the films into which they are inserted (Gopalan 2002), breaking into discontinuous locations and featuring unnamed, non-characters (the so-called item girl and her accompanists), often with little to no apparent narrative relationship to anything that came before or after. There is a sense that such sequences take over the film and its viewers. Music envelops and drowns out the film's world of speech, replacing dialogue with melody, just as it disarticulates the present body of the dancing item girl from the dubbed voice of the playback singer (Nakassis and Weidman 2018). Heavily accented rhythms inhabit the bodies onscreen, whose movements are (re)synchronized to its often foreign-sounding, or alternatively folk, cadence. Item numbers also take over the space of exhibition, causing the embarrassed to exit, the enthusiastic to whistle, and the uninterested to steal away for a cigarette or snack. And yet, such moments of separation are only ever temporary: the narrative always returns, bookending these seemingly self-contained sequences of eroticism and movement.[4]

Of course, to conceptualize such moments as "interruptions" is to presume that mainstream commercial film is, essentially, its narrative, the diegetic world that it symbolically represents to us in its textual form, that which we are called on to receive, interpret, and identify with. It is relative to this ideology – one not unfamiliar to film studies (Metz 1991[1971]:144)[5] – that the "item" is a caesura, a gap in some other, otherwise constituted continuity, an interruption of some more important and more reasoned (and often male) authorial voice (Silverman 1988). This way of thinking is certainly how many Tamil film directors see item numbers and other so-called commercial elements (such as heroes' "entry" scenes, introductory songs, and spectacular fight scenes; see Chapters 1, 4). For such directors, commercial elements like item numbers are impositions from outside; they are forced on directors and their films by producers and pressures to cater to "mass" audiences – which, in the context of item numbers, means young, male audiences.[6] Such items have to be worked around, controlled, integrated. And indeed, the realist-oriented directors in the Tamil film industry whom I interviewed and interacted with (almost all male) prided themselves on (or lamented) their (in)ability to incorporate such commercial elements into the narrative, to recuperate them to their stories by giving them a narrative function, to contain them by weaving elements of the filmic world (plot lines, characters, locations) into them rather than, as is the case with many films, have the item number be a complete stand-alone sequence, filmed on a separate film schedule and directed by someone else (the choreographer, or as it is called in the Tamil film industry, "dance master"), only to be jarringly inserted into the film later (Pandian 2015:167–79; Iyer 2020:200–2).[7] It is the item's discontinuity and narrative unreason that many directors and writers on Indian film most often bemoan as indexes of a failure of the industry to make, and the audience to appreciate, "good" cinema (Pandian 1996; Ganti 2012).

Such metadiscourses about song-and-dance sequences, however, do more than simply delineate a hierarchy of distinction and taste among directors, critics, and audiences. They are also an ontological politics of the image that manage an ambivalence, an irritation that the item provokes.[8] Filmmakers' textual strategies confront this provocation – sometimes by attempting to salvage the item and reconstitute narrative form and function from her substantial body, sometimes by abjecting her from it (*7/G Rainbow Colony* does both, as we see below) – just as their metadiscursive laments and deflections disavow the interruption of their representation by her presence. But what is this disturbance to the sovereignty of the narrative that the anti-cinephilistines feel they must repair or disavow?

The Item's Titillation

The problem of the item number isn't simply its perceived illogical discontinuity relative to the film's narrative.[9] There remains a disturbing power of the image itself, a power that not only cannot seemingly be contained by the narrative but also exceeds the image's status as a representation. In a word, the item number "titillates." This word, *titillation*, proliferates in accounts of item numbers, its dismissive articulation invoking a historically long-standing elitist social imaginary of cinematic reception (Gopalan 2002:19; Ganti 2004:82, 2012:83–7; Srinivas 2009:157–88): namely, that it is susceptible, or morally indecent, low-class young men – those "front benchers" who are manipulated, or pandered to, by greedy producers (Mazzarella 2013 calls these the "pissing men") – who are "titillated" by graphic depictions of barely clothed "glamour dolls" (the same men imagined, perhaps, to have been incensed by Vaibhav's slaps in Chapter 1).[10] The journalist Saibal Chatterjee (2003:17) writes, for example:

> [The item number is] a raunchy, rambunctious song performed by a lead actress, usually in a special appearance, and inserted in a film with the undisguised intention of exploiting her sex appeal. The item number is generally independent of the main narrative, for titillation is the name of the game in an age when filmgoers are difficult to please and hits are even harder to come by. (See also Govindan and Dutta 2008:194; Lakshmi 2008:27; Pinto 2006:86; Roy 2010:42.)

In such critiques, the sexual allure of the "item girl" and the libido of the male filmgoer are naturalized by the imputed inherent performativity of the explicit image. Titillation describes – it fantastically imagines – a seemingly direct relation of (female) image to (male) affect, an immediated moment of *seeing* the body of the "item," her absent presence converted into a pressing libidinal urge.

While such explanations are problematic as accounts of the performativity of the image, as ideologies of the image they force us to recognize that filmic images are indeed, as an empirical and ontological fact, irreducible to their representationality, their narrative function, their autonomous self-contained textuality (Doane 1988; Kasbekar 2001:286; Pinney 2004). That is, "titillation" makes for terrible film theory, but it is, as ideology and affect, a primary datum to be explained and not, as it were, explained away, for example, by appeal to narrative function, the inherent power of the image or whom it presents, or the supposedly natural or cultural susceptibility of heterosexual, male viewers.

The Item's Spectacle

To broach this performativity and its relationship to narrative, we might begin with Laura Mulvey's critical observation in her classic 1975 essay "Visual Pleasure and Narrative Cinema": that the spectacular "to-be-looked-at-ness" of the Hollywood actress – in particular, in song-and-dance sequences – bears a power to divert and freeze the image, as well as the narrative, which is, ultimately, propelled through her appearance and its containment. As Mulvey (2009[1975]:19) notes, while most Hollywood narrative cinema integrates the "alien presence" of the female form within its male-driven narrative, "musical song-and-dance numbers interrupt the flow of the diegesis," opening up a timespace of exception to it. Writing about the "showgirl" whose dance has been partially integrated into the diegesis (her comments applying equally to the item girl), Mulvey (2009[1975]:20) observes:

> For a moment the sexual impact of the performing woman takes the film into a no man's land outside of its own time and space ... Similarly, conventional close-ups ... integrate into the narrative a different mode of eroticism. One part of a fragmented body destroys the Renaissance space, the illusion of depth demanded by the narrative; it gives flatness, the quality of a cut-out or icon, rather than verisimilitude, to the screen.

Here, Mulvey makes three important points about the semiotics of spectacle and its eroticism that apply to the performativity of the item girl and film heroine (as well as to the mass hero discussed in Chapter 1). First, there is a productive, pragmatic and ideological tension, indeed an open-ended (that is, non-determined) problem space, instated by the "to-be-looked-at-ness" of bodies onscreen: between the realist representationality of narrative and the erotic performativity of its images. While the spectacle of the mass hero – as we saw in Chapter 1 – instates and encompasses the narrative within his substantial star image, the spectacle of the item girl unsettles the narrative by externalizing her from it (see Iyer 2020:198).

Second, the spectacle of the dancer and her "deictic," exhibitionist addressivity (Casetti 1998[1986]) has an aesthetic "flatness." Mulvey provocatively compares this flatness to the quality of an icon and contrasts it to the linear perspective ("Renaissance space") of realist painting (Panofsky 1991[1927]). With this comparison, she invokes an opposition between Byzantine modes of religious spectatorship (if she were an Indologist, Mulvey might have invoked *darśan* with Hindu idols[11]) and secular, modern verisimilitude, which she analogizes to the illusion of narrative realism. This is an opposition between an image that is divine and transcendent, present and performative – indeed, that looks back at us (Belting 1994[1990]; Mondzain 2005) – and an image that is secular, representational, sealed off from and blind to us. Yet while Mulvey characterizes this flatness as lacking depth – vis-à-vis the side of the screen that opens *into* the narrative world (that which is behind it, as it were) – this flatness is, I would also suggest, echoing Christopher Pinney's (2004:179–80) observations about "corpothetic" photographs in India, a spatiotemporal extension *into* the world of the image's screening. It is a forward-facing depth, a projection that spills out of the screen. Here, the "impact of the performing woman" lands not just outside of the diegesis but outside of the film text itself (Willemen 1994) in the timespace of the event of her appearance[12] – hence the deictic quality, or more precisely, reflexive calibration (see note 32 in Chapter 1), of her image. Something of her is present with her audiences in the dark public space of the theatre, the domestic space of the television room at home, the quasi-public/private space of the college screening room, or on the pixels on one's computer or phone screen. Indeed, as we'll see, what Mulvey (2009[1975]:22) calls the "sadistic" side of scopophilia – the way in which films punish the (image of) woman for her visual presence – doesn't just happen in a film's story; it also takes place in the offscreen stigma, violence, and exclusion that film actresses have historically been subject to in Tamil Nadu (Seizer 2005) and elsewhere.

Third, this pragmatic potency of the image – while affectively manifest as eroticism, while textually embodied in and as the showgirl or item girl, while actualized in an event of theatrical uptake or its blockage (as in the opening vignettes of the chapter) – is more wide-ranging than any of these entextualizations; it suffuses the cinema as a general potentiality that can be exploited, and institutionalized, to various effect: for example, in the realm of cine-politics and the (erotic) presence of the mass hero (as discussed in Chapter 1) or, as Tom Gunning (1986:68) points out – himself drawing the parallel to Mulvey's essay[13] – in the "attractions" of spectacle in early silent cinema (see also Hughes 1996).

To each of these points, however, we need to ask *how*: How is the item girl, and the film heroine-actress more generally, rendered *present* in particular empirical events of filmic apprehension (rather than only re-presented), disrobed and unveiled, projected out of the narrative and its world into the timespace of her exhibition? (Or vice versa – represented rather than presenced?) What makes such performative presence stigmatizing rather than positively valorized?[14] (Or vice versa – as with the mass hero discussed in Chapter 1?) How is the performativity of such female presence dealt with by filmic texts and the institution of cinema more generally? How is it cultivated or defeased, exploited or disavowed, anticipated or responded to? In particular, how is the stigma of this performativity expiated? Does it happen in the narrative text – as with the 1960s vamp who must be summarily, and often cruelly, disposed of from the plot with a stray bullet or some other ad hoc contrivance (Pinto 2006) or with a fetishistic poetics of "looks" – or does it surpass the text, requiring clean-up in extratexts like interviews (Ganti 2012:137–51), press releases, celebrity star images, or even academic apologies? In short, how might we theorize not just the textual or technological but the *social* apparatus, as Linda Williams (1989:45) has called it, of this performative presencing and the absences it depends upon and leaves in its wake?

Formulating such an account requires more than attending to film as a representational surface (for example, of looks, of narrative form), or as a text whose spectatorship we contextualize and multiply through studying events of cinematic "production" or "reception," or as an additive combination of all of the above. Rather, as I argued in the Introduction, it requires us to theorize the image as an entextualized act and event interdiscursively thread across its variegated contexts. Such an approach, thus, requires us to be clear that such performativity is *not* "in" the image or its affects. Rather, this performativity is the achieved, that is, contingent but systematic effect of a whole set of relations that are distributed across audiences, actors, filmmakers, and film itself as they come to be mediated in particular events by particular claims on what an image *is* and what it is to *see* an image, in particular, of women.

Ontological Politics of Sexual Difference

Mulvey's provocations – like the larger debates within feminist film criticism that Mulvey was responding to and which she opened space for – are, at one and the same time, a feminist politics of the sexual difference of the image (and the image of sexual difference) *and* an ontological politics of the image.[15] Such film theory is not simply a mode of critical reading but also an account and example of the ontological politics of the image at issue in this book. (Highlighting this ontological politics, however, is not to displace feminist readings of the filmic image but to draw out their critical interventions for my arguments here regarding ontologies of the image.) Such debates about sexual difference and the nature of images are not peculiar to Western film theory or practice, of course. We find similar contestations in Tamil cinema.

At issue in such debates in the Tamil industry are a set of widespread ideological assumptions – which I discuss in more detail in the sections that follow – about filmic images and actresses: in short, that actresses are disreputable, improper women, both because of what they do onscreen (kiss, hug, dance; indeed, simply appear) and because of what they are assumed to have had to do to end up onscreen (work on predominantly male film sets and fraternize – and, it is often assumed, have sexual relations – with actors, directors, producers, and other male industry personnel).[16]

While such assumptions were commonplace during my fieldwork and, for many, a kind of common sense – I observed and elicited them from many of the people with whom I interacted, male and female (though predominantly male), lower- and upper-class, rural and urban, inside and outside the film industry – they were also deeply contested. Many viewers with whom I spoke about such issues – male and female (but predominantly female), lower- and upper-class, rural and urban – claimed that they did *not* evaluate actresses' moral personhood based on their onscreen performance, saying, for example, that they only focus on the characters and the acting. As many noted, you can't say whether a woman is a good person or a bad person based on how she acts onscreen, or even from the fact that she appears onscreen; in any case, they reasoned, today all actresses do "glamour," and you can't say that all actresses are "bad." Problematizing the conflation of onscreen and offscreen, and rejecting its masculinization of spectatorship, this counter-discourse insists that the screen image is (or should be) mere fictional representation and no more.[17]

Many educated, urban young women in particular rejected the long-standing stereotype that actresses are necessarily fallen women, or "prostitutes," as actresses are commonly dismissed (Ganti 2004:94; Chinniah 2008:40–1; Krishnan 2009:189–91; Rajendran 2018b; see also Hardgrave 1993[1975]:95; Hughes 1996:258), a stereotype inherited, as noted above, from both the historical presence of actresses from the *devadāsī* community as well as from contemporary, and not unrelated, assumptions about casting couches and the liberal attitude of unmarried actresses towards premarital sex.[18] Contesting the view that to be an actress means "lying down," as one young man in Chennai once put it to me, such young women argued that actresses are just like everyone else who works a job (a discourse that has its own historical antecedents within the Tamil film industry, Krishnan 2009:194; see note 70 in this chapter).[19]

For those who rejected and disavowed the scopic logic of the cinema's patriarchal gaze in favour of spectatorship predicated on narrative representation and fiction, it was, by contrast to themselves, less sophisticated filmgoers of the past, conservative older generations, those in rural areas, or the subaltern poor (the supposedly titillated "front benchers" discussed above) who see female characters onscreen as simply the actresses' bodies, who reason about film images not as narrative representations but as performative acts in the here and now of their appearance, who assume that to appear onscreen always already presupposes and entails moral/sexual transgression. A good friend's mother – a lower-middle-class Dalit woman in her mid-sixties at the time – figured her own parents, born in the late 1920s, in precisely this way, betraying the generationally shifting and relational nature of this politics of the image. Such acts of alterity (Hastings and Manning 2004) attempt to recentre the moral community of proper film spectatorship; and they do so by refiguring what kind of a thing an image *is*.

Important for us here, then, is the way in which this politics of sexual difference (and age and generation, class and taste) and the politics of the image's being are two sides of the same coin; for claims as to whether an actress (or actor) is simply playing a character or is as (s)he appears, whether her (or his) screen appearance is an immoral (or cine-political) act or "just" acting, or whether actresses are fallen women (or actors, leaders in potentia) or just like anyone else, and so on all turn on assumptions and claims about what an image is or should be. Is it a performative presence or a fictional representation? A titillating act of exhibition or a voyeuristic/realist narrative text? An act of mere animation (that is, acting) or something more? As we see in the sections that follow, answers to these questions are not only about differing interpretations or modes of spectatorship. They are also a politics that is immanent to, because it manifests in and as, images.

The Actness of the Image

M. Madhava Prasad's (1998:88–113) discussion of the long-standing, if informal, cinematic prohibition of the onscreen kiss in post-Independence Indian film provides one entry into these issues.[20] Prasad observes that the taboo of the kiss was never an issue of the diegetic fact of the kiss – indeed, heroes and heroines kiss all the time in post-Independence Indian films; we usually just don't see it on-screen. Nor was it simply an issue of seeing a kiss onscreen, since foreign actors were not censored from kissing in Indian films. The issue, rather, was a particular configuration of image and ideology: it was *seeing* the *Indian* heroine kissing onscreen that was problematic.

Prasad (1998) argues that the onscreen kiss stands in for a whole ideological enclosure, a realm of "privacy" (between romantic lovers) that recognizes only the authority of the modern state and bypasses the traditional patriarchal authority of kinship and caste (which refuses such modern conjugality and privacy). It is this privacy that must be opposed through banning the kiss, a fetish metonym whose policing reaffirms the "compound authority" of and "alliance" between "feudal" (traditional) and "modern" elites, an alliance that Prasad argues organizes the production and reception of Indian cinemas (and of the nation) more generally (see also Jain 2007:269–314). On this account, the voyeurism of the cinema – its presumably intrinsic desire for a doubly displaced scopophilia (Metz 1986[1975]) – is subordinated to public norms of appearance, precisely because the private threatens a "real" subsumption (rather than the simulacrum of formal subsumption) that would open up a truly modern, liberal space of conjugal privacy (and state power). This, then, is why the kiss was banned for so long but *not* the "cabaret" dance (and later, the item number): namely, the kiss threatens to undermine a particular social organization of patriarchal power that the cabaret song and item number do not. Indeed, the cabaret and the item affirm that order in their public spectacle and moral, sexual discrimination.

Prasad's (1998) reading of the representational relationship between the kiss and the inauguration of a "private" outside of feudal authority is subtle and insightful. The line of thinking I want to follow, however, stays closer to the pragmatic surface of the item girl's body, the hero's and heroine's lips, and the dilated (male) pupils who watch them. Subtending questions of the "alliance" that cinema mediates through what it represents, kissing onscreen – like bearing flesh in a dance or hugging a hero – is also transgressive because, as observed by James Naremore in the chapter's epigraph, to kiss onscreen is to have presumably kissed offscreen, on set, in front of the camera, and thus, in the theatre (Krishnan 2009:181–4, 202–3; see also Naficy 1994:145–6; Mulvey 2015:24). And further, as an act of acting, it is to have offered oneself up to being seen publicly kissing onscreen (see Pinto 2006:110; Metz 1982[1975]:94). Not simply doing the profilmic act (itself already normatively improper), it is to have seemingly chosen and even desired, at some level, to do and to show that act, and to do so while standing on, to adapt a phrase from William Mazzarella (2013), the open edge of mass visibility, as if inviting the public gaze of anonymous others (also normatively improper).[21]

I say "presumably," "seeming," and "as if," of course, because each of these presumptions – "felicity conditions" of a sort (Austin 1962) for the performativity of the act of female appearance (and by extension, the kiss and the item number) – are just that.[22] They are, in their general form, the ideological basis of the politics of sexual difference and the ontological politics of the image discussed above. For while in the Tamil context, such acts of appearance and visibility are part of male respectability (Mines 1994) – indeed, they are claims to a certain status and recognition (Dickey 2013; Nakassis 2013b), as we saw in Chapter 1 – they are transgressive of patriarchal norms about respectable femininity, because, as evinced in the first vignette of the chapter, upper-caste/middle-class norms of male respectability and honour (*gauravam*) are predicated on men's control of the sexuality of "their" women. Visibility and the perceived desire to be seen, thus, risk a woman's chastity and reputation.

Vadivukkarasi (b. 1952), a veteran actress and former heroine in the Tamil film industry, explained this (meta)pragmatics of visibility to me as we drove in her car from the shooting spot of the mega-serial *Thirumathi Selvam*, in which she was acting, back to Chennai in 2011. Explaining that actresses have to constantly be careful to stave off the forms of talk that adhere to them, she ruefully but defiantly noted that some section of society will never respect you. Her voice dropped in pitch and changed in quality as she acted out in Tamil the gossiping voices that badmouth actresses: 'What is this? That girl's come half-naked wearing a glamorous dress … standing there in a transparent sari. She's [literally, 'it' (*atu*), a deictically distal, neuter singular pronoun] dancing with everyone.' 'Talk like that circulates,' Vadivukkarasi concluded, returning to her own default voice. Or, as one relatively conservative friend and his wife rhetorically put it, what kind of 'family girl' (*kuṭumba poṇṇu*) would *choose* to attract people with her body, would let *anyone* (read: low-caste, lower-class men) see her doing such "glamour" on set and onscreen, let them whistle, leer, and covet her (see also Krishnan 2009:196; Ganti 2012:123–33)?

By this conservative and circular logic of spectatorship, in short, to appear is itself a morally implicating act (in fact, it is two twinned acts: an act of appearing and an act of desiring to be seen). This logic is an inversion (and reiteration) of the sociological realism discussed in Chapter 1, where evaluation of the screen image is based on the presupposed sociological reality of its animators. Here, the reality of the image's animators is evaluated based on – is *entailed* by – the image's emanations from the screen. Under such conditions, by the actress's act of appearance the image itself becomes an act, one whose pragmatics proleptically organizes the filmic surface of the screen and the various stances that filmmakers, actresses, and film publics are willy-nilly forced to take with respect to it (compare Goffman 1974:70–2).

Politics of Vision

This actness of the film image, as is evident from our discussion above, turns on the question of what it is, and does, to *see*; which is to say, on the politics of vision – who can see and look at what, when, and where, with what effects and with what stakes. In South Asia, as Christopher Pinney (2002, 2004) and Kajri Jain (2007) have demonstrated, vision is not just visual, as ideologically construed in post-Enlightenment Western traditions at least. It is a tactile modality, a vector of action and exchange, force and embrace. It is the modality through which devotee and divinity, subject and sovereign transact (Babb 1981; Eck 1997; Pinney 1997:109–11). It is a vector of envy and destructive desire that can cause material harm (as in so-called evil eye or *kaṇ tiruṣṭi*; Dean 2013), just as it is also a medium of romantic love and intimate caress (Taylor 2003). Or, as we saw in Chapter 1, it is a combination of these, as in the erotic and adulatory tactility of the mass hero's and his male fans' locked gazes.

Vision can also be, as noted above, a medium of female sexual objectification and male desire, and given the tactility of vision in the South Indian context, a form of literal bodily violation of women. Young Tamil men and women refer to this type of vision as "*sight aṭikkiṟatu*." This slang phrase combines the English word "sight" with the Tamil verbalizer *aṭi*, which on its own means 'hit' or 'beat' and, as a verbalizer, generally connotes both a relation of pejoration/inappropriateness and haptic contact (Schiffman 1999:110). Arguably, the use of the English term "sight" similarly indexes this improprietous and non-traditional mode of seeing (Nakassis 2016a:89–123). While women may and certainly do *sight aṭi*, the prototypical subject is male, its object female. In short, *sight aṭikkiṟatu* denotes a quality, a scene or chronotope, an intent of masculinized vision, of publicly if furtively ogling a young woman as a sexual body or, for those more romantically inclined, as a *kanavu kanni*, a 'dream girl' (*kanni* meaning 'unmarried girl,' 'virgin,' 'freshness'). Such a gaze contrasts not just with the unmarked quality of everyday, non-sexualized vision but also with its complement – the normative, averted gazes of feminine modesty and male politeness, which refuse to look as they visibly perform not-seeing.

This mode of vision is carried over into the cinema. As many young men noted matter of factly, and as many female and older filmgoers conceded in lament (echoing Mulvey *sans la lettre*), today, women in film are simply there to be looked at. *Sight aṭikkiṟatu* was the whole "attraction" of the cinema (Gunning 1986) for many of its eager male spectators. As an older male interlocutor, and former assistant director, explained, reminiscing on his school days, the transgressive thrill of the cinema was/is that you can *see* women in a way that is difficult, if not impossible, outside the cinema (compare Metz 1986[1975]:266; Hansen 1991:35–6). (Difficult because, offscreen, women – and their family – don't just look but may hit back as well!) You can *see* the *actress*, not just as a character in a fiction, but beyond this, as a presenced body.[23]

It is this "*sight*" and the presence it affords that the rural husband and the college women discussed in the opening vignettes refused by blocking the violating visibility/vision of the filmic image. It is this *sight* that is rejected and disavowed by those who argue that they simply watch for the acting, who allow their own gaze to be voyeuristically contained by the narrative and its characters. And it is this *sight* that activates the "titillating" performativity of women's acts of appearing, threatening the chastity of and communicating stigma to the actress who is its object. Such *sight* transgresses – passes beyond – the screen with an indexical link that is not simply a trace of the profilmic past but an ongoing, present mark on the actress herself.[24]

The Explicitness of Performativity

Two dimensions intersect in these performative, tactile moments of presence and vision that can be teased out. The first is the perceived explicitness, or self-evidence, of the performative act (and the performativity of that explicitness); that is, how is the image offered up to us? Is it figured as a sign to be apprehended as an instance of that which it represents – and that, because to represent indexically presupposes having done the act – as with so-called lip-to-lip kissing scenes, where we see the kiss happen? Or is it figured as a disavowed sign-of-a-sign, displaced into song sequences (Gopal 2011) or figured through

Figure 2.1. The hidden kiss: Sivaji Ganesan and Saroja Devi in the song sequence "*Chittu Kuruvi Mutham*" (The Sparrow's Kiss), from *Puthiya Paravai* (New Bird; 1964, dir. Dada Mirasi); top left – Saroja Devi pulls Sivaji Ganesan in for a kiss; top middle – Sivaji's surprise/shock; middle – the hidden kiss (the static camera continuing to shoot the space where Sivaji was, reluctant to follow the action); bottom middle – Sivaji stands back up, licks his lips in satisfaction, and then, in the bottom right, wipes his mouth

conventionalized tropes such as the kiss hidden behind a tree or a bouquet of flowers that pops up at the last moment to hide the putatively profilmic and theatrical moment of indexical contact (Prasad 1998:90–1; Gopalan 2002:37; Figure 2.1)? How does the image seem to give itself over to us? What does it allow us to see or not see beyond the screen?

By "explicitness," I am drawing on J.L. Austin's (1962) notion of the "explicit performative," those sentence types that seemingly, by virtue of their mere utterance, constitute some action and thereby potentially bring certain social facts into being. As linguistic anthropologists have noted (Silverstein 1979:207–16; Lee 1997:16–94; Agha 2007a:55–8; Nakassis 2013a), such linguistic performatives are explicit in the sense that what they describe in their denotational text ("what is said") is carried out in and by the moment of utterance ("what is done," the interactional text; Silverstein 1993); as such, performatives provide reflexive sketches of themselves, often metapragmatically naming the act-type they attempt to enact, describing their very event of enunciation in and by their enunciation. (Hence, as per Benveniste [1971:228–30], the importance of the reflexively calibrated deictics, "I" and "you," which anchor participants in the act to its denotational textuality, as well as the simple-present indicative of the telic performative verb [in English], figurating and calling out to an ever-presence – a nomic calibration – of what is enacted.) Performatives, thus, present themselves as self-ratifying acts and in that way appear to be self-evident. To say, for example, "I say X" is to *say X*, just as to utter "I promise to come tomorrow" is to promise (to come tomorrow); it is to metapragmatically instantiate and offer evidence of what it represents itself as pragmatically doing. (Explicit performatives in English, after all, are all construable as hyponyms of the metapragmatic verb "to say.")

There is a similar seeming self-evidence to the spectatorial logic at issue in this chapter: to appear is not simply to have been (in front of a camera), but it is to *be* (at the moment of the image's happening); it is to instantiate what is depicted in the event of its filmic enunciation/exhibition. The heroine's kiss, like the item's flesh or her dancing 'with everyone' in a 'transparent' sari (as Vadivukkarasi put it above), betrays an ideologically mediated self-evidence that manifests not simply in/as a representation (as an image-text within a narrative) but as an act (an interactional text) unto itself in the ever-present of its exhibition.

The second dimension is *whose* act is it? To whom does the act's performative entailments return and from whom do they seem to emanate? Who is the *principal* of the act, the one responsible for it (Goffman 1979)? Is it the *animator* of the act, the person who performs the act, the person who appears before us on the screen, that is, the actress? Or its putative *author*, the person who orchestrated the actress's scene of appearance (for example, the director or dance choreographer)? Or is it some other party besides, the producer or even the audience? As I suggest below, different fractions of film may distribute these roles differently and thus exploit/expiate the transgressive performativity of filmic depictions of sexuality in different ways. To explore these questions, I look in more detail at the lodge scene and item number of *7/G Rainbow Colony*, discussed above, to show how performative responsibility and self-evidence are managed in and out of the narrative text, to show how this performativity and mode of being of the image – and its politics of (in)visibility and responsibility – registers its trace in the film text and in various responses to the film by its audiences and director.

Voyeurism and Exhibitionism in *7/G Rainbow Colony*

7/G Rainbow Colony was a big hit among urban youth audiences – in particular, young men – for its realistic portrayal of youth romance (Nakassis and Dean 2007; see Chapter 4). It was both popular and controversial, viewers opined, because it didn't pull its punches, didn't cover anything up, and thus, for its fans, was unlike other "commercial" films that sugarcoat romance, using narrative twists and turns to resolve the contradictions between loyalty to one's lover and one's kin that many youth acutely felt in their own lives. It was this contradiction that came to a head in the lodge scene discussed at the outset of the chapter, a scene whose explicit dialogues sealed the realist deal for many (male) viewers and was the major basis upon which almost all viewers ultimately evaluated the film, whether they loved or hated it, accepted or rejected it.

In this scene, the lovers – the middle-class North Indian Anitha and the lower-middle-class Tamilian Kathir – have escaped to the mountain resort town of Ooty, Anitha's arranged marriage to another (Kishore) impending. Having arrived at the lodge, Anitha begins to change into a nightgown in front of a shocked Kathir in a series of alternating medium and full shots.[25] In a dark and shadowy, half-lit, frontal full shot, Kathir expresses his feeling of awkwardness, announcing that he'll go and sleep on the balcony. The camera cuts to a forty-five-degree, medium close-up of a brightly lit, incandescent Anitha, who says that if he has confidence/trust in himself (*nambikkai*) they can sleep in the same bed.[26] In protest, Kathir, in a slightly off-axis frontal medium close-up, states that he might not be able to control himself, that something bad might happen. The camera cuts to a wide, full shot of Anitha (Figure 2.2 – top) as she says in Tamil: 'Fine. What if something improper/unexpected happens? What then? I've given you my heart. Won't I give you myself?' Dumbstruck, Kathir merely replies: "Anitha" (Figure 2.2 – bottom).[27]

The camera cuts back to Anitha, and then to Kathir, as she asks if what she says shocks him. From Kathir, the camera again cuts back to Anitha: a long, sixty second tracking shot of Anitha slowly moves from a full shot (slightly closer than the screen grab pictured in Figure 2.2 – top) to a medium shot (as pictured in Figure 2.3). During this shot, Anitha explains that she knows what they are doing is wrong but she

Tamil	English
A: *Sari.* (.6)	A: Fine. (.6)
Ēṭākūṭam nnā enna?	What if something improper/ unexpected happens?
(.2)	(.2)
Enna ippō?	What then?
(.4) *Manaseyē koṭuttuṭṭēn.*	(.4) I've given you my heart.
Enne koṭukkamāṭṭēnā enna?	Won't I give you myself?
{Audience goes silent}	{Audience goes silent}
K: <Shocked:> *Anitā.*	K: <Shocked:> Anitha.
{Men in audience clap, whistle; some laugh}	{Men in audience clap, whistle; some laugh}

Figure 2.2. Anitha (A) and Kathir (K) in the Ooty lodge in *7/G Rainbow Colony*

Tamil	English
Veṭkatte viṭṭu sollaṭṭā? (1)	Can I leave aside my modesty and say (it)? (1)
Oru nimiṣamāvatu (.5) *unakku* wife-*ā irukkaṇum nnu āseppaṭṟēn.*	For at least one minute (.5) I desire to be a wife to you.
(.9)	(.9)
Real wife. (1.2) *Manasāleyum,* <whispering, looking down (1.3)> *u- uṭampāleyum.* (.3) *Mmm.*	Real wife. (1.2) By heart, and <whispering, looking down (1.3)> b- by body. (.3) Mmm.
{Clapping by some male audience members.} (.7)	{Clapping by some male audience members.} (.7)
Ivvaḷavu nāḷum (.5) *nī maṭṭum tānē ippaṭi ellām* feel *paṇṇiṭṭu irunte.*(.8)	For all these days (.5) only you have been feeling this way. (.8)
But first time (.7) *nān* feel *paṇṟēn.*	But (for the) first time (.7) I feel (this way).

Figure 2.3. Anitha and Kathir in the Ooty lodge in *7/G Rainbow Colony*, continued

can't control herself, and she feels drawn by some "force." The medium shot holds as she continues, saying with a heartfelt, quasi-confessional delivery (notice the pause structure in Figure 2.3): 'Can I leave aside my modesty and say it? For at least one minute I desire to be a wife to you. A real wife. By heart, and by body. Mmm. For all these days only you have been feeling this way. But for the first time I feel this way.'

Across a series of medium shots (over-the-shoulder shots of Kathir and Anitha, shots of Kathir and Anitha sitting together on the bed in profile), Anitha offers more explanation to Kathir, and the audience, about why she feels this way now after being so harsh with him for so long; and further, why there is nothing wrong with her sexual desire. She explicitly declares the deliberateness with which she has contemplated this act and its ramifications; how while she may end up marrying Kishore, at least they can be together for one night, so that when

Tamil	English
Please (.5) *itukku mēlē etuvum pēsātē*. (.4) I feel like doing it! (.3) *Unakku iṣṭam ille nnā pō*. (.7) *Etō nān keñcuṟa mātiri irukku. Che!*	Please (.5) don't talk about it anymore. (.4) I feel like doing it! (.3) If you don't, then go. (.7) It's like I am begging or something. Che!

Tamil	English
<turns away (.8)> *Ite solṟatukku munnāle nān evvaḷavu yōsiccu iruppēn teriyumā?* <K moves closer to A (1.6)> Life full-*ā un ñābakatte vaccukkaṇum nnu āseppaṭṭēn*. <K touches A's shoulder, she bats his hand away> *Unakku puriyale nnā viṭṭiru*.	<turns away (.8)> Do you know how much I've thought about this before saying it? <K moves closer to A (1.6)> I just wanted to keep your memory with me all my life. <K touches A's shoulder, she bats his hand away> If you don't understand, just forget it.

Figure 2.4. Anitha and Kathir in the Ooty lodge in *7/G Rainbow Colony*, continued

Kishore touches her, Kathir's memory will come to her instead. She then interrupts herself (Figure 2.4), saying: 'Please don't talk about it anymore. I feel like doing it! If you don't, then go. It's like I am begging or something. Che!' She turns away from Kathir and continues: 'Do you know how much I've thought about this before saying it? I just wanted to keep your memory with me all my life.' Kathir touches Anitha's shoulder (Figure 2.4 – bottom). She bats away his hand and says: 'If you don't understand, just forget it.' Kathir says: 'No, Anitha,' and tries to touch her shoulder again.

After Anitha bats Kathir's hand away again, Kathir puts his head down on her lap, saying: 'It's all like a dream, Anitha. I can't believe any of it' (*Ellā kanavu mātiri irukku Anitha. Nambavē muṭiyale*). From this position of maternal comfort (indeed, throughout the scene, and film, Kathir is depicted as sexually immature and child-like; see note 26 in this chapter), Anitha then grabs Kathir by the hair on the back of his head and pulls him up, out of his dream and into the reality of her desire (Figure 2.5 – left). There is an abrupt cut to the first image of the item number, "January Madham" (The Month of January; Figure 2.5 – right), in a radical discontinuity of space (we shift from the lodge to a night club), colour (from browns and white to reds and blues), and angle of address (from a voyeuristic shot of the protagonists' backs to a frontal shot of anonymous dancers).

With this cut, music kicks in, Western electronic drums and later distorted rock guitars and synthesizers, as the lyrics of the song – visually voiced by the dancers and not by the characters, Anitha or Kathir – go on to describe the pleasures and ambivalences of the sexual act. Unlike

Figure 2.5. The cut from the diegesis (left) to the item number in "January Madham" (right)

Figure 2.6. Gangster and items in the dark nightclub in "January Madham"

other typical item numbers that don't integrate the item into the narrative (or vice versa), the item number in *7/G* – comprising a slew of semi-clad women gyrating in unison on the wet stage of a dark nightclub, as well as a pistol-brandishing man decked out in a trench coat and three-piece suit (the choreographer, Kalyan Kumar) and accompanying male dancers in suits (Figures 2.6 and 2.9) – is cut in parallel with a depiction of the heroine performing her own seductive dance for the protagonist in the diegesis (Figures 2.7 and 2.8).[28] The nightclub item number thus serves as a meta-text for the narrative (dance/sex) scene between Kathir and Anitha, framing and regimenting it even as it also, in certain ways, substitutes for it.

In the first shots of Anitha during the song, the camera follows her walking in profile behind a set of windows (Figure 2.7 – top). She turns and opens one of them in a frontal shot exposing her torso (Figure 2.7 – middle). This shot is followed by a cut-away to an awestruck Kathir in close-up (Figure 2.7 – bottom).

After a cut back to the dancers in the night club, who sing to the audience and for the lovers, Anitha begins her dance for Kathir. The looking structure, amenable to Mulvey's analysis of classical Hollywood cinema, juxtaposes shots of a "to-be-looked-at" Anitha with shots of Kathir's gaze (as in Figure 2.7) and shots of Kathir looking at Anitha

Figure 2.7. The opening of Anitha's (diegetic) dance for a gazing Kathir in "January Madham"

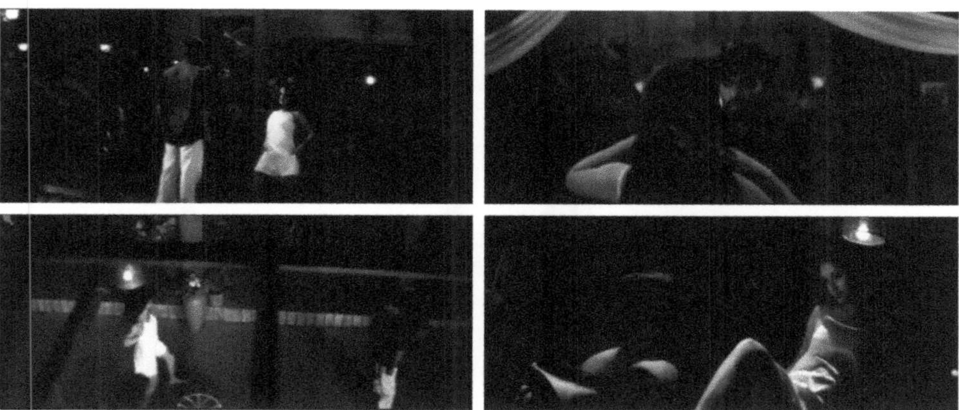

Figure 2.8. Shots of Anitha dancing for Kathir in "January Madham"; recruited as voyeurs (note the rafters between us and them in the bottom-left still; Metz 2016[1991]:101), we see him looking at her, as we see her as seen by him, looking at him in turn

with both in the same frame (Figure 2.8). Through these co-textual juxtapositions, Anitha's frontal exhibition for Kathir (note how they face each other in the stills in Figure 2.8) is anchored in the diegesis, set into the reportive, voyeuristic frame of Kathir's look, and from there to the look of the camera itself; the shots in Figure 2.8, for example, show Kathir and Anitha in off-axis angles, over-the-shoulder objective shots (top right, bottom right), and from vantages behind other physical structures (bottom left; also Figure 2.7 – top).

This poetics contrasts with the full-tilt, direct (that is, unshifted "deictic") frontal address of the female item dancers in the nightclub who, in a number of shots, look right at the camera as they sing and dance (Figure 2.9). Their exhibition is for the spectator/audience – it has no clear relationship to any spatial position or subject in the nightclub – just as Anitha's exhibition is for Kathir and, arguably, only then, through a relay of voyeuristic looks, to the spectator (Williams 1984:83).[29] While the former interpellates the (masculinized) spectator, the latter opens up a space of identification with both characters, though with particular focus on Kathir, himself interpellated (and desired) by Anitha.

As the song progresses, and the item-number dancers in the club become more and more undressed, the parallel cuts show Anitha and Kathir under the covers in sexual activity. These parallel cuts explicitly depict Anitha's agency and pleasure in the sexual act – she pushes

Figure 2.9. Full-tilt frontal address of the item number dancers in "January Madham," looking at us as we look at them

Kathir over and gets on top of him – as well as her (and tellingly not his) ambivalences. Here, the film shifts the spectator's identification with Kathir to an empathetic stance to Anitha, whom the poetics of the shots depict less as an object to be seen than as a subject of desire and emotion. (Importantly, a number of such shots are unmotivated by shots of Kathir's gaze.) We see closely framed shots of her face, in tears and wincing in pain (Figure 2.10 – left). We see their lips brush each other, and brushing over the body of the other, in close-up. The intercutting accelerates as the sex act nears completion, the poetics of the editing speed and its jittery jump-cuts and camera work iconically mirroring the intensity of the scene's affect and the transgressiveness of the act denoted by it. The scene ends with the lovers' hands intertwined, palms pressed flat against a steamed glass window in a visual citation to the 1997 super-hit, romantic epic *Titanic* (dir. James Cameron; Figure 2.10 – right).

In this internally split song-and-dance sequence, we find operative precisely the opposition Mulvey (2009[1975]) and others have pointed to: between spectacle and its performative stillness and narrative movement; between an exhibitionist mode of direct address and a voyeuristic play of gazes that sutures the spectator within the diegetic, reportively/nomically calibrated film world (Metz 1986[1975]; Williams 1989); between presence and representation. Item number and narrative scene stand juxtaposed in a "parallel syntagma" (Metz 1991[1971]:125), one next to the other in relations of difference and mimesis, interruption and continuity. In addition to the contrasts that we've noted (by mode of address, lighting style, colouring, locale and mise en scène, personnel, relation to the diegesis, and so on), there are also poetic echoes between the two: the parallels of the dancing; the way in which the lyrics of the song, sung by the dancers, describe the intimate acts engaged by the characters; the gradual darkening of the image of Kathir and Anitha as the sex act progresses, its colouring shifting from browns and whites

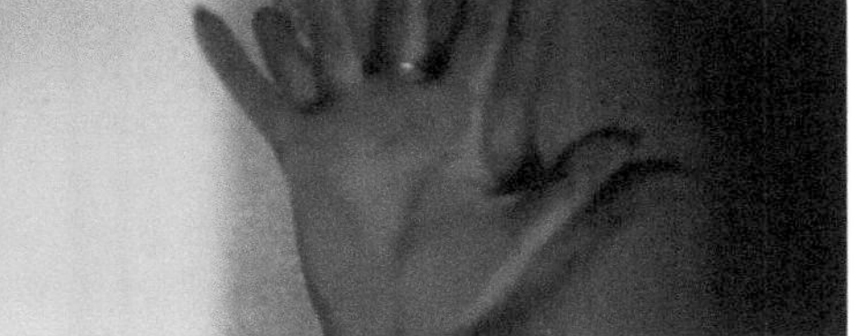

Figure 2.10. The affects of sex in "January Madham": left – Anitha's ambivalence at her "mistake"; right – Anitha and Kathir's hands intertwined in passionate climax, the last shot of the song sequence

to blues and blacks as they move from dance to sex (that is, the narrative sequence approximates the colour and brightness of the nightclub scene); as well as the quickening pace/tempo of the editing in both halves of the sequence as the song progresses.

But if they are entangled, these two halves are never quite integrated, and the identity of Anitha and the item dancer is only ever loose and temporary. In this juxtaposition, the item dancer is always kept to the side, sequestered from the narrative and suspended in the song, entwined in (theatrical, entextualizing) time but excluded in (represented) space. This differentiation and embedding replays the ontological tension at the heart of the image – between its representationality and its performativity, its status as narrative and as act. And it does so in a dialogic anticipation and response to the fact that both sequences – Anitha and Kathir's and the anonymous item dancers' – and their denotata (the transgressive affect of female desire and the acts of sex and sexual display) are part of a moral economy that entextualizes both as image-acts of a problematical sort (namely, obscenity), if in different ways. In other words, this tension in the image registers and attempts to manage the transgressive performativity of explicitly representing female sexuality and desire through the (conventionalized) transgressive performativity of the item's presence. In short, sex, female desire, and sexuality appear but only by being narrativized and auto-amputated at once, wrapped in the narrative motivations and needs of *7/G Rainbow Colony*'s male-authored and male-centred story, while also simultaneously sequestered from it, divided into dialogue and song, heroine and item, narrative and spectacle, a division that the film's item song metonymizes in its split form.

Indeed, while *7/G Rainbow Colony*, on the whole, was considered a controversial film, it was not really for its item number. Rather, for many of those with whom I spoke about the film, it was for the denotational explicitness of the heroine's verbal utterances that preceded the song sequence and for the premarital sex act that was denoted through and then enacted in it. Most of the people with whom I talked about the film – young men and women – empathized with the character Anitha, even if they were deeply ambivalent about the "mistake" that she made and the realism of the pre–item-number scene. For many viewers, whether they disliked the film for what they felt was its vulgarity or whether they liked it for showing things as they "really" are, the very fact of the heroine's explicit articulation of sexual desire and her acting on it generated a performative force precisely because (1) its utterance onscreen was seen to affirm the acceptability of publicly articulating female desire (that is, to say it onscreen was to assert it offscreen); (2) the narrative positioned her as a character to be empathized with and justified her decision;[30] and (3) the film's representationally realist framing asserted the sociological accuracy of such a portrayal – that is, as the male director, Selvaraghavan (b. 1977), insisted to me, young women today do have, express, and act on their sexual desires (Selvaraghavan 2005).

For those who rejected the film and its assertion/performance of female desire as obscene, it was explicitly because the *film* – and by extension, its director – condoned Anitha's "indecent" and "wrong" actions (see Lakshmi 2008:25).[31] While it was the actress Sonia Agrawal who animated the act (or rather, partially animated the act, for as a non-Tamil speaker, Anitha's voice was not provided by Sonia Agrawal but by an offscreen dubbing artist), for those viewers who took exception to the film's intervention into the cultural politics of public sexuality, it was the film's putative author, the *director* Selvaraghavan, who was denounced as "vulgar" and antipathetic to "Tamil culture."[32] This denouncing was partially due to his reputation for already having made edgy and, as some critics said, "pornographic" films that focus on youth sexuality (*Thulluvadho Ilamai* [2002], *Kadhal Kondein* [2003]). It was also due to the fact that Selvaraghavan, though relatively new to the industry at the time, already had a (largely male) fan following and that *7/G Rainbow Colony* was "his story" – both as the film's self-styled auteur-director and because, as widely advertised, the film was partly autobiographical (see note 53 in Chapter 4). By contrast, in general, Sonia Agrawal was not castigated for her actions, even if her character was.[33] Rather, she and her unnamed dubbing artist were commended for the realism that they brought to the screen, shielded, we might say, by the representational enclosure of the film and the director who was taken as its author and principal.[34] Here, the director's representational realism mitigated the sociological realism of the actress, putting the viewer in the space of representation, not presence, realism, not reality.

This repudiation and criticism of the film's linguistic and narrative transgressions – that is, such entextualizations of the film *as* performative – were not only located outside of the film (for example, as a criticism of the film and its director). They were also anticipated within the film as part of its narrative; for example, through the ambivalences expressed by the characters themselves about their "mistake" or through Anitha's fated, yet totally unexpected demise – we might even say punishment (Mulvey 2009[1975]; Williams 1984) – at the end of the film. (After the lovers argue in the street about their fate, Anitha is shockingly hit by a truck and then run over by a car; see Nakassis and Dean 2007 for discussion.)

Tellingly, in defending himself against such critiques and explaining how and why the film was structured as it was, Selvaraghavan (2005) drew on two bases of narrative representation: that of the story and of the reality it depicts. As he explained to me in an interview, without depicting the heroine's sexual desire and the lovers' sexual encounter, the story wouldn't make sense. The story needed both; and the story needed them because that is what today's young men and women themselves feel and do in real life.[35] (Notably, many young women that I spoke with found precisely *this* point to be the site of the film's *un*realism.) What is important here is how Selvaraghavan attempts to manage the linguistic and narrative transgression of the film's avowal of middle-class female sexuality and desire by deflecting responsibility (or principalship) for it by embedding it within a logic of the narrative and its ability to accurately capture how the world "really" is, not as the performative reality of the profilmic event or of its communicative exhibition but of its representationalist, referential veracity.[36]

And yet, the performative excess of representing desire and sexuality continually spills out of the realist narrative's bracketing quotation marks, and it is this excess – registered as the denouncement of the film's director as "vulgar" and "obscene" – that Selvaraghavan framed in our interview as "orthodox" hypocrisy, as a backward attempt to "pretend," as he put it. Such a defence is also implicitly, of course, a claim to a particular *kind* of image – an image whose appearance is justified if it is, in some sense, "true." But is the pretence not perhaps also Selvaraghavan's, that is, that film texts can (or should) simply represent "reality" and do/be no more? That if they are true, it is their reality that bears responsibility for their appearance (and no one else)?

Ironically, it was precisely the "orthodox" attitude towards public representation that required Selvaraghavan, as he told me, to verbally dress up this section of the film. As Selvaraghavan (2005) narrated it to me, the "dialogues" that drew negative attention were included so as to justify and narratively motivate the sex act in the film. (They also contribute to the characters' ambivalences in the act, as discussed above.) If it were up to him, he said, he would have shown the scene "simply," with little, if any talk. He would have just shown the sex act, as it actually would have happened in real life, rather than belabour the scene with the heroine's prefatory explanation, the hero and heroine's tentativeness, and a song sequence. Obscenity and controversy, here, hover between image and word, as two media of explicit performative transgression, the scene's split textual form registering in anticipation the performativity of the film's representation through its added dialogues (which themselves, ironically, became contentious among viewers) and its racy item number (itself performative, if with a distinct textual structure from the film's narrative transgressions, as noted below).

Yet if the controversy surrounding *7/G Rainbow Colony* turned on whether the director was the Goffmanian principal (that is, the one responsible) for the film dialogues and narrative he authored, what of the item number and its transgressions? After all, wasn't it he and the dance choreographer who orchestrated the scene of our sight? That made us *see* Sonia Agrawal as Anitha dancing, that made us see the bare supple flesh of the items, put into our presence? Indeed, what of the item dancers' and Sonia Agrawal's gyrating semi-nude bodies? In and beyond the shadow of the director's (narrative) transgressions – and, in Sonia Agrawal's case, partially cloaked in his narrative – their dances received little to no comment by viewers or in the press. Were their transgressive bodies mentioned, however, it would likely be *they* who bore responsibility for their fleshy presencing, not the male "dance master" (Kalyan Kumar) or the director (Selvaraghavan). In this way, we might say that the item song – with its partially interruptive, diegetic discontinuity – consolidates and contains the principalship of *its* performative presence within itself, consigning its transgression and stigma to its onscreen animators rather than to the director or choreographer (its authors), the former of whom bore responsibility for the performativity of the film's narrative representationality (including in the song sequence "January Madham" – namely, the represented sex act between Anitha and Kathir). (Similarly, the director's disowning of the interruption of the unnamed item dancer – that he didn't want to have such a sequence – serves to relegate the responsibility for her presence to her.) The chronotopic and ontological blending in *7/G Rainbow Colony*'s item number – part narrative, part spectacle; part representation, part performative presencing – thus evinces an exception within the film that suggests the rule.[37]

By being disconnected from (even if, as in a "realist" film like *7/G Rainbow Colony*, also partially integrated into) the voyeuristic narrative, the item girl and her exhibitionist number are disavowed by the film, just as she, and the heroine more generally, are devoiced, rendered agentively mute subjects, both by the offscreen dubbing artists and playback singers who speak as and sing for them and by the male authors who speak through them. Through this dual disconnection, the item dancer and the heroine – those textual sites of the open edge of mass visibility – are kept at an arm's length, always on the edge, cordoned off by the narrative and its authors, even as they are deployed as repudiated exteriorities *within* the text, carried along with it (as an entextualized/excretable fraction of it) even as they seem to stand outside it. And yet, like the performative force of the linguistic expression of sexual desire, such foreclosures and expiations are not complete, the immanent/imminent performativity of the heroine's and item's presenced bodies not rendered completely inert by the film text. For while it was not the film's item number that attracted controversy in the press and among those I interviewed but parts of its dialogue and plot, it was not when the dialogue started up that the middle-class college women fled or averted their gaze or that my male hostel mates turned up the volume to its distorted maximum, as discussed at the beginning of the chapter. It was when the song-and-dance sequence began, precisely the stretch of the film that some circulating VCDs of the film – pirated copies made to be watched in the domestic space of the home, often with one's family – had cut out from the film.

Kinship Chronotopes and Sociological Traces of the Performativity of Presence

While above I noted traces of filmic performativity in the fraught textual management of the item dancer and heroine and their uptakes, here I turn to the offscreen traces that this performative economy leaves on the sociological statuses of the artists who animate them. In particular, I focus on two observations about the heroine-actresses who inhabited sites of performative presence during the period of my research: first, they were almost never married; second, they were almost never seen as authentically ethnolinguistically Tamil. Both of these correlations, while not exclusive to the time of my research, took on a particular robustness in the post-liberalization, post-television period, beginning in the 1980s and 1990s, even as they perhaps are on their wane, as I discuss in the chapter's epilogue.

Marriage and Not-to-Be-Looked-at-Ness

After marriage, actresses in the Tamil film industry generally cannot act as heroines in commercial cinema – that is, as the object of *sight aṭikkiṟatu* or as a *kanavu kanni* (dream girl). Immediately after marriage, actresses generally shift away from being heroines: they begin to act as older sisters, sisters-in-law, or mothers, that is, they become character actors whose bodies are enveloped and shielded by the narrative; alternatively, some actresses move to women-centred genres such as devotional *Amman* (Goddess) films (as with, for example, Ramya Krishnan, Soundarya, Bhanupriya) or to the less glamorous small screen to act in women-centred serials or work as reality television personalities. Just as commonly, they simply disappear from the screen altogether.[38] Such dynamics do not apply to hero-stars (Chapter 1), who remain visible onscreen *as* heroes well after their marriages and into old age. This difference is precisely the result of the politics of vision and appearance at issue in this chapter (whereby appearance is not a threat to male respectability), the masculinized spectatorship it entextualizes (which invites forms of identification rather than sexual objectification), as well as filmmakers' presumptions about (male) audiences and the "business" of heroes (that neither will necessarily wane with marriage or age, as I discuss below).

It was not always the case, however, that actresses ceased to act as heroines after marriage. While from the inception of South Indian cinemas we can detect this post-martial tendency (Hardgrave 1993[1975]:95), up until the 1970s and 1980s many actresses – by my rough estimates, upwards of 40 to 50 per cent[39] – consistently and successfully acted as heroines while married.[40] From the 1980s onwards, however, the number of actresses who have continued on as heroines after marriage increasingly drops to a smaller and smaller and, at the time of my fieldwork, practically non-existent minority (Nakassis 2015; Karupiah 2017).

Important in this context is how the semiotics of female visibility discussed in this chapter took on a particular acuity and intensity in the 1980s and 1990s. The advent of television, associated home-theatre technologies, and widespread media piracy in the 1980s and 1990s enabled the easy circulation of film and other entertainment programming into the domestic – and in the Tamil case, often largely female – space of the home. One result was the (perceived) decrease in theatre attendance of the so-called family (that is, women's) audience.[41] And given that into the 2000s filmmakers' profits still derived primarily from theatres' ticket sales (due to the industry's difficulty in controlling piracy, creating a viable market for ancillary products, maximizing profits from television rights, or capitalizing on its diaspora markets), the increasingly absent family audience was of decreasing importance to commercial films' mode of address.[42] In its stead was a theatre audience imagined by filmmakers to be dominated by young men and their desirous eyes (Ganti 2012:9, 25, 84–7). This estimation is reflected in the emergence of a host of recurrent textual features in this time period, as Sathiavathi Chinniah (2008) has noted: the "rape scene" of the 1980s, the "item number" of the 1990s, the collapse of the vamp and heroine figures, the increasing marginality of (older) female characters to the narrative, the decrease in age of the heroine character (and the decreasing longevity, or "staying power," of heroine-actresses in the industry),[43] and her shift from a figure narratively embedded in multiple sentimental kinship relations (as sister, daughter, wife, mother) to simply being the unmarried love interest of the hero (what came to be parodied in the 2010s as the "*loosu poṇṇu*," 'crazy girl').[44]

It is in this context that actresses at the time of my fieldwork confronted a series of obstacles, economic and patriarchal, to their onscreen appearance after marriage.[45] After marriage, as one popular director explained to me over email, a heroine loses her "market," that is, her value-add to the film production's "business." This loss is because, he explained, "Now they [the male audience] know that she (i)s not there's [*sic*] anymore," that is, she is not there onscreen precisely because her image is no longer theirs to scopically possess, a point I elaborate below.

Here, filmmakers' reflexive orientation to a market of yearning male eyes embedded within a conservative public culture inscribes itself not simply in the textuality of cinema but also in casting decisions (recruitment to filmic role inhabitance, as it were), in the ways in which the image anticipates and presupposes a particular patriarchal logic: namely, for a heroine to be presenced onscreen the *actress* who animates her must be seen by male audiences as (sociologically, fantastically) available *offscreen*. Marriage introduces a blockage in the male spectator's sight line (and vice versa, as noted below). Hence, consider how one gossip website reported the heroine-actress Hansika Motwani's response to rumours of her impending marriage to the film hero Simbu: "These reports of marriage have made my movie producers really worried. I would like to clarify that I will not be getting married in anytime soon and I will only marry the guy my family chooses" (*SS Music Blog* 2013; see also TNN 2017). Here, voiced at one and the same time, is the economic logic of filmmakers (Hansika's producers fretting about her availability in their films and the box office impact of her being taken off the market, as it were) and the actress's claim to homely purity and traditional virtue (she will only marry who her family chooses), a polyphonic speech act that simultaneously distances herself from her screen image and the stigma of being scopically available while working to secure that very image/availability.

Even Simran Bagga (b. 1976), *the* sex symbol and reigning heroine-star in the mid-1990s and early 2000s, found herself unable to find heroine roles after her marriage. As she told me in 2011, after her marriage in 2003 and the subsequent birth of her child, she simply couldn't get any offers, even though she was actively trying (Simran Bagga 2011). Producers were unwilling to cast her as a heroine, she said, instead approaching her to play mother or older sister roles (at which she balked).[46] As she put it, revealing her own understanding of the conservative nature of the male-dominated industry (and its assumptions about actresses), "it's only the mindset of these filmmakers. They feel 'Oh my God, she's married. She will not do this. Oh my God.' It's just the filmmakers."

Important here is how the cinematic regime of *sight aṭikkiṟatu* is not only masculinized in its spectatorship but also anchored by a particular "kinship chronotope" (Dent 2009; Ball and Harkness 2015), that is, by a particular projection of (non-)kin relationality, of consanguinity and affinity, onto the timespace of the event of seeing the film heroine-actress onscreen (as well as onto the profilmic moment of acting), a projection that regiments and (de)activates such masculinized vision, rendering it experientially palpable and pragmatically efficacious. In particular, there is a discomfort for many male viewers with seeing a heroine onscreen who is married offscreen, precisely because to see her character is to see the actress and thus to be ogling and enjoying the *sight* of someone else's wife. (For some female viewers, the imputed shamelessness of a married woman making herself available to such male vision was the source of discomfort.)

Marriage interferes in and, in some cases, amplifies (as with sexualized "aunty" figures[47]) this filmic visual regime, generating a performative effect that makes a heterosexual, male spectator's act of *sight*ing the married actress taboo, just as it also thereby makes a married woman's act of acting as a commercial heroine problematic. As one lower-middle-class male friend from Chennai noted in Tamil, echoing the director quoted above, 'when you are *sight*ing a girl you are thinking about some possible future with her [that is, love, sex, or marriage], and if she is married how can you do that? Her future has already been decided.' As this sociological realism implies, such *sight* – and the presence it presupposes and entails – has a temporality; it must be emplotted in an open-ended present with its projectable future not closed off by the ritual transformation of having been wed. As one young male director, more exaggeratedly and cynically, put it, "heroines are like dolls, they are there to be sighted." He continued: "To be crass, in Tamil Nadu for most guys, there are no relationships with women that are not as a sister or a mother. Other women are barely even human as far as most guys are concerned. One can look at them however one wants. *Except* if they are married."[48]

Or, as he also implied, except if they are already kin. Just as marriage introduces a blockage in the male spectator's *sight* line, so too does consanguinity.[49] As a male Chennai friend from a lower-middle-class background noted, there is nothing morally wrong with women acting or with actresses per se, that is, as long as they aren't kin, as long as they aren't 'our women.' 'It's like *sight aṭi*-ing girls,' he explained in Tamil. 'When they aren't our sisters or mothers, we enjoy it. But if others are looking at them [our sisters and mothers] like that, we get upset.'[50] To be seen, then, the actress must be, in a sense, perpetually available to her male audiences (as a lover or wife in potentia) and thus, we might also suggest, *unrelated*, that is, as this friend indicated and as I elaborate below, not one of 'our women.'

An Alien Presence

If we take a longer historical view at who has inhabited these filmic spaces of stigmatic performativity, in addition to unmarried women, we notice an extremely high frequency of actresses figured as exterior, as foreign. The early decades of film exhibition in India, as Stephen Hughes (1996) has shown, almost exclusively screened Euro-American silent films, and Caucasian actresses and their sexualized presence before putatively aroused, native male eyes was a continual colonial anxiety.[51] Similarly, in the early years of Indian cinema, both silent films and talkies featured a predominance of Anglo-Indian, Eurasian, and white (-like) women acting as heroines,[52] and later – with the rise in the 1940s and 1950s of nationalist themes requiring chaste Hindu heroines – as vamps.[53] As noted earlier, this exteriority, sexual stigma, and its politics of visibility and respectability were also linked in the transition to sound cinema to questions of caste and community, in the Tamil case, to the stigmatized and socially marginal *devadāsī* or "dancing girl."[54]

With the ideological and political consolidation of an ethnolinguistically defined notion of cultural identity and regional sovereignty in the 1950s – namely, the Dravidian movement (see Introduction) – the numbers of ethnolinguistically Tamil heroine-actresses falls to a minority (roughly, by my estimates, from around half before Independence to 20 to 30 per cent from the 1950s to the 1980s).[55] As C.S. Lakshmi (1990,

2008) and others have noted, this ethnolinguistic identity politics and its articulation of the Tamil ethnopolity employed new rhetorics of language, community, and belonging that turned on tropes of female chastity and purity (Ramaswamy 1997; compare Chatterjee 1993) – deified as *Tamil̲ Tāy* (Mother Tamil) – as set against, and in need of protection from, a series of foreign others: the nationalist Congress Party, the Aryan North Indian, Hindi, Sanskrit, and English, and the extimate Tamil Brahmin (Pandian 2007).[56] Here, ethnolinguistic identity, kinship, and caste and class respectability – and the control over women's sexuality (and stigma) – were scaled to the (sub)national level, making the chaste Tamil woman an emblem of the honour of the ethnopolity. By the 1990s, in a period of liberalization and its shifting audience demographics and modes of spectatorial address (that is, its masculinization, as described above), the number of actresses coded as Tamil further declined to a little over 10 per cent or so.

At the time of my fieldwork, few heroines in the contemporary industry were considered Tamil, part of either the Tamil language or speech community (*sensu* Silverstein 1998; see note 14 in the Introduction).[57] As was often narrated to me by both film viewers and industry insiders (male and female), film actresses today come from everywhere but here: from Kerala (a state associated by many Tamils with relative female autonomy and "blue" movies), from Andhra Pradesh (where people, so say some Tamils, are even "crazier" about cinema than Tamils), or from North India (where the "culture" is more permissive and the cinema more "glamorous"). It is noteworthy that at the time of my research, most of the few heroines who were considered ethnically and linguistically Tamil – for example, Trisha Krishnan (b. 1983), Priyamani (b. 1984), Sruthi Haasan (b. 1986) – were urban, elite, and English-fluent Brahmins, a demographic confluence that, given the longer history of non-Brahmin Tamil identity politics noted above, already placed them on the ideological margins of the language community.

But more important than the putative demographic absence of "Tamil" heroines is the *use* that this fact was put to by contemporary viewers and industry insiders:[58] that is, how the visibility of the actress's hyper-present body, how the stigmatic performativity of her spectacle was linked to and justified by her foreignness, her unrelatedness, her putative status as non-Tamil, as not part of the "culture," as not kin; and further, how her extimacy – her close distance to the language community and film industry – was central to managing the respectability of cinema itself (Ganti 2009:112, 2012:119–51).[59]

When I brought up in interviews that almost no heroines were Tamil, producers, directors, actors, and other industry insiders (largely but not only men) echoed my observation by lamenting it. It makes it difficult to find actresses who can understand scripts, emote appropriately, and do their own dubbing, they said. It is a detriment to the industry and to the language, they would state. This absence was almost always explained by the lingering historical and seemingly irrepressible stigma of cinema, a stigma that industry insiders would often, but not always, say was unwarranted, as something of the past.

And yet, underwriting and implied by such laments and explanations is also an ambivalence, an implicit and simultaneous laudation: namely, that the alien presence of the non-Tamil actress is proof that "our" Tamil women have a seemingly inherent reluctance to be seen onscreen, to enter into the visual economy of the cinema (hence the slippage in this discourse, which self-evidently and seamlessly moves from the onscreen absence of Tamil heroines to the stigma of cinema as its explanation). As I was often told, Tamil women are (that is, should be) too shy, too modest (*veṭkam*), too chaste, and too concerned about chastity (*kaṟpu*) to act.[60] The actor Sriman Reddy (2008), for example, noted that a "*kuṭumba peṇ*" (family girl) will always think twice about entering cinema. Animating the internal voice of this homely family girl, he rhetorically asked: 'After hugging four different people and dancing around onscreen, after acting in a rape scene, after putting on revealing, glamorous dress, will anyone marry us?' (Not only blockable by marriage, note here how *sight* and the work of acting are figured as blocking marriageability for women.) Scaling up from the hypothetical family girl ("our girl," we might say along with my Chennai friend quoted above) to the ethnopolity itself, Sriman continued (not unproblematically, as noted at the outset of the chapter), saying that young women in Tamil Nadu today don't believe that cinema is an industry, that acting is an art.[61] This modesty and fear (*bayam*), as the veteran Tamil actress Vadivukkarasi similarity noted to me, was something in the "blood." An unchangeable primordial fact, it was the "culture" of Tamil (*Iṅkē Tamiḻukku nnu oru* culture *oṇṇu irukku*), this "culture" tellingly attributed by Vadivukkarasi to the language itself.

Here, the kinship chronotope of *sight*ing actresses onscreen implies and presupposes another timespace, an elsewhere where "good" "family girls" follow the "culture" of Tamil Nadu and stay off the screen. The screen, as a conduit to male vision and female presence, simultaneously presents a blockage, veiling ("good") Tamil women offscreen precisely by offering up an alien presence onscreen, one whose own respectability and cultural authenticity is effaced at the service of the former's. Indeed, in this culturalist discourse, it's not just that Tamil women don't act, but that they shouldn't; if they did, they would cease to be, in some sense, Tamil (Nakassis 2015), a conclusion already implied by the ideological figures that people this ideological chronotope of sight, sexuality, kinship, and (dis)respectability: the family girl and the prostitute, (consanguineal) sisters and mothers and (affinal) dream girls, those hidden from the screen and those on it. Here, echoing Teresa de Lauretis's (1984) argument about Euro-American cinema, the signification of Tamil woman turns on a discourse that would constitutively erase, while lamenting the absence of, historical Tamil women as able to appear on the screen as *Tamil* women (or at all).

Like the intratextual containment and marginalization of the item number and the extratextual denouncement or applauding of particular directors or actresses as "vulgar" or "bold," such ambivalent laudations/laments manage the cinematic excess of female sexuality by exteriorizing it. Taken together, such laments and disavowals confirm *and* expiate the stigma of cinema (and cinema itself perhaps), relocating it in the putatively non-Tamil status of its actresses, themselves kept at the edge of the narrative text. But not simply propping up and asserting a form of cultural identity and authenticity through forms of exclusion and stigma, such confirmations and disavowals also enable and turn on a visual regime that allows aspects of the image to come that much closer, allows desiring eyes to see that much further and to see differently, not just to the diegetic referents of narrative representations but to the tactilely proximal, animating bodies of image-acts pragmatically unfolding in their presence. Indeed, the anxiety about a particular kind of performative affect generated from seeing an unrelated female body is not simply about shoring up the sanctity of "Tamil culture" or the respectability of the film industry. It is also about generating or contesting forms of male patriarchal desire and pleasure, of enabling or disabling a performative and economic potency that can be harnessed by the film text itself and its stakeholders to various effect.

Like the scapegoat of ancient Greece, the often kinless *pharmakos*, treated as if a royal celebrity and then expelled from the city in its annual purifying ritual, brought into celebratory contact with the community only to be later stoned and have his genitals beaten (Burket 1985:82–4), *through* the film and its screen, the performative force generated by the social mediation of (im)proper femininity and female sexuality is concentrated in the act of seeing the actress and her body, a moment of tactile visuality requiring that she/her body is prepared and presented correctly for eventual renunciation: as unmarried and sexually available, mute and visible, desiring and desirous, base and alien. It requires her and her desire/sexuality to be only ever loosely stitched into the narrative and the ethnolinguistic community (and when too interwoven into their fabric, generating considerable risk and danger), and thus always detachable from and disavowable by both. She must be brought intimately close to the narrative and community but always already abjected, so that the performativity of the cinema can be kept as both public secret – public (in sight) and secret (out of mind) – and private revelation – private (personally consigned to her) and revealed (for all to see).

Conclusion

This chapter and the previous one have concerned themselves with the production of presence, the ways in which presence enables the performativity of images, and the emanation of the pragmatics of such image-acts through the texture of film and beyond. Such image-acts inscribe themselves in the personae and bodies of images' animators and authors; in forms of spectatorial uptake in theatres and other spaces of exhibition; in the metadiscourses of viewers, film artists, and filmmakers; and in the institutionality and sociology of cinema. Underwriting and at stake in the dynamics of both chapters has been an ontological politics of the image – those contestations, claims, and counterclaims about what an image is or should be: liberal representation or illiberal presence, truthful reflection or titillating/adulating touch, shadowy fiction or substantial action.

But if the chapters of Part I have pursued similar issues, equally important have been the differences. As we've seen, the mass hero and the heroine and item do not presence themselves in the same ways or with the same effects. The presupposed and generally entailed kinds of spectatorship that are involved are different – sacral, homoerotic adulation versus profane, heterosexist titillation. So too are the forms of social value (cine-political charisma versus sexual stigma); economic value (heroes are paid much more than heroines and item dancers, and their careers tend to last much longer); and narrative value (commercial films generally revolve around the hero while they marginalize female characters and actors).[62] Nor is the social apparatus – those mediations through which such presence is achieved – the same, with distinct (inter)textual structures, political economies, scopic logics, and social norms and types of controversies and debates. Comparing Chapters 1 and 2 shows how sexual difference, as well as the politics of class and taste, age and generation, and caste, decisively mediate and distribute the possibilities and effectivities of the presence and the actness of the image – and its representationality.[63]

The chapters of Part I have also shown how questions of performativity and being/ontology are always articulated, if variously, to questions of the production format and participation framework of image-acts, to questions of responsibility and agency, that is, to the question of *whose* act the image is. In *Mankatha* and *7/G Rainbow Colony*, we saw multiple kinds of performativity and representationality intersect with each other, amplifying and partially undoing each other in turn. In *Mankatha*, narrative logic and vérité style – the "touch" of the filmmakers – attempted to undermine the auratic presence of the hero-star while rendering the presence of the filmmakers visible in, and responsible for, the text. Yet in doing so, such representational realism curiously amplified the hero-star's presence, actualizing the performativity of Vaibhav's slaps for fans who entextualized such narrative logic and vérité style as image-acts of profaning the mass hero. Yet, as we also saw, responsibility for the slaps remained with the junior actor, Vaibhav. *7/G Rainbow Colony*, by comparison, illustrated how the narratively embedded performative act of linguistically expressing, and justifying, sexual desire and the theatrically anchored image-act of female appearance work with and against each other in a complex semiotic economy, with responsibility contested and distributed between the director (and his account of "reality") and the animating female artist, the former attributed responsibility for the narrative and its controversial representations of female desire and the latter held accountable for her own act of appearing. The actress/item's presence is stoked only to be disavowed, partially integrated only to be abjected.[64] In both cases, narrative and presence, representation and performativity appear both in opposition and as two sides of the same filmic coin, as two potentialities worked out in various ratios and yet to pragmatic and political effects that work in concert (if still unevenly distributed). And in both cases, it is the transgression of the nomic sacrality of male sovereignty – be it his body or his control over her body – that is at issue in triggering the performative image-acts in question.

But if presence is a central problematic in these cases, cultivated as the basis for performative effect or undermined through structures of representational fiction (or both), this tension between presence and representation simultaneously, and perhaps always already, turns on a series of absences – or rather, processes of *absenting*, of rendering invisible, of excluding. In this chapter, for example, consider the married woman who is forbidden to appear in front of the camera or the young women who look away from the screen, leave the room, or never even come to watch. Such women refuse to come too close to the cinema's images of woman, refuse to become voyeurs or addressees or objects of the text's gaze, to identify with the sexualized subject or object of that gaze; or – most importantly, perhaps – refuse to even be co-present with/in the image itself in the space of its exhibition/recording, thereby avoiding exposure to the possible and actual surveilling gazes of others (Russell 2020). Consider the narrative that marginalizes or effaces the heroine – in *7/G Rainbow Colony*, by killing her off – so that the hero may complete his course, or that excludes the item from its diegetic timespace, refusing to even give her a character or a name. Consider an industry that, in its early decades, effaced or marginalized lower-caste *devadāsī* actresses from the screen to make it respectable for upper-caste actresses to appear; and that, in more recent years, has largely failed to have women significantly involved in filmmaking except in the smallest of ways, most visibly and powerfully as actresses,[65] but even then, laments their lack of cultural authenticity as full members of the Tamil ethnolinguistic community precisely to laud the absence of "Tamil" women from the screen.

Each of these moments of absenting – while heterogeneous in their dynamics – stands in a relationship to the pragmatics of presencing: as a precondition, a prophylactic, a response, a contestation, a haunting. And while Chapter 1 affords comparable examples – the actor who refuses to act or the director who hesitates to write or direct (and then is made to), the actor veiled by his character (but then exposed by the mass hero's presence), and so on – it is no coincidence that the question of absence and exclusion more insistently hovers before, around, and after the question of women's presence. Returning to Teresa de Lauretis's (1984) arguments, we can say that this is because the absenting of women – from the industry, from the screen, from the audience, from respectable society – is itself the very condition for the presence and representation of male subjects (which is not to say, of course, that hierarchies among men and women – by caste, age, seniority, and so on – do not fractally turn on similar dynamics of excluded, marked subjectivities). The examples from this chapter support such an argument.[66]

But if, for de Lauretis, absence is problematic (signalling women's exclusion and subordination), just as, for Mulvey (2009[1975]), the frozen presence of the showgirl holds out a space against the voyeuristic, patriarchal pleasure of narrative representation, the Tamil case discussed here renders things more ambivalent. It does not displace de Lauretis's and Mulvey's critical arguments; rather, it multiplies the pragmatic possibilities that absence (and presence) afford. Absence and invisibility can themselves be modes of agency and protection from a patriarchal politics of vision and presence that threatens stigma and sexual violence to actresses (Naficy 1994). It is in this light we can extend de Lauretis's (1984) argument that the absenting of women (and ultimately, woman) from cinema is a condition of possibility for its regime of narrative representation by arguing that in the Tamil case – but more generally as well – representationality may also serve as a mode of prophylaxis against, yet also within, the pragmatics of presence, may itself be a mode of absenting that guards against as much as inflicts violence, may be a tool for and against a progressive gender politics, and thus is itself the terrain of an ontological politics.

As we've seen, the narrative realism of *7/G Rainbow Colony*, in participating in a patriarchal regime of representation, veils and protects the heroine-actress in ways it denies to the presenced item dancer. Indeed, the film does the latter – presences the item – in order to prop up the former – the representationality of the heroine. Recall, for example, and in contrast to the item dancers, the praise given to Sonia Agrawal's contribution to the realism of Selvaraghavan's film, a discourse that bracketed her presence precisely by allowing his representationalist image to stand in for her. Having become an/his image of woman, Sonia Agrawal's responsibility for the performativity of the narrative image – and arguably, her act of appearance – was relatively exempt, her personage protected, her presence diminished. My argument, of course, is not that *7/G Rainbow Colony* was or is a politically progressive film per se.[67] Rather, it is that voyeuristic representation is a strategy; it is itself an ontological politics haunted by the performativity of presence. And further, that in this case, this strategy is in contestation with an orthodox politics of sexual difference (which it also replicates in key aspects) and, in so being, opens up a variety of possible positionalities (indeed, absences and presences) within a structure of hierarchy and difference.

In short, in this South Indian case, representation and realism function as a kind of shield and mode of invisibility, attempting to (partially) absent the body and personage of the actress from her screen image, to insert a representational bracket instating a gap between the sign and its referent/animator (into which the authorial director may then enter; see also Chapter 4). And it is this variably diaphanous yet opaque screen that affords the possibility of a form of positive visibility for the heroine-actress that mitigates the stigma of her presence, that allows for fame and stardom as a respectable film artist rather than a mere "glamour doll" or "item girl," she who is left out of the narrative, left presented, exhibited, anonymous, and solely responsible for her "own" act of appearance. These two possibilities – these fates of the heroine-actress and the item girl – are not logically independent of each other, of course. They imply each other. As we saw, in *7/G Rainbow Colony* they are textually juxtaposed, cheek and jowl, even if in other moments they are otherwise distributed (for example, embodied in one and the same person or complementarily distributed and kept apart).

This play of visibility and invisibility echoes Lotte Hoek's (2013) argument about the preference of actresses in Bangladeshi cinema for close-ups of their body parts rather than shots that show their body as a whole, as well as Hamid Naficy's (1994) argument about Iranian cinema's dispreference for close-ups of women at all (Mulvey 2002); in both cases, as in the Tamil case discussed in this chapter, the question is how to manage the problem of presence, how to absent the actress from her image *through* the image's representationality and fiction. In all such cases, dialectical relations between presence, absence, and representation are differently configured; they are institutionalized and aesthetically entextualized in different ways, just as they afford different pragmatic possibilities – where forms of erasure and absence, at one level, entail and make possible forms of visibility and presence at another; and vice versa, where the presencing of the actress is a mode of effacing her at one and the same moment.

These ontological politics also echo, and call on us to reconsider, André Bazin's (2005[1951]b) and Christian Metz's (1986[1975]) attempts to characterize the specificity of the film image – in distinction from theatre, striptease, and cabaret – by its particular configuration of presence and absence. Metz suggested, for example, that the medium specificity of film – in contrast to the live co-presence of stage performer and audience – is characterized by the way in which the viewer is absent from profilmic space when the actors are present, while in the space of exhibition film actors are absent when viewers are present. Through this doubled absence, the cinema opens up whole new worlds on the screen that substitute, for a time, for the spectators' world. While for Bazin, as we saw in Chapter 1, such worlds are emanations of reality (presencings of it), for Metz, this sense of presence is an illusion, a voyeuristic "impression" afforded by the cinema's apparatus. But if, as Metz (1986[1975]:256) argued, Bazin's "cosmophanic" account, while an "excellent description" of viewers' experiences, is fundamentally misguided because it effaces the cinematic production of presence, we can say the same of Metz's own metapsychology, which ultimately effaces the production of cinema itself – and its regimes of absence and presence – as a culturally variable social institution (see note 3 in the book's Introduction).

The issue, as Miriam Hansen (1991:36) points out, is not whether cinema is intrinsically a medium of presence/exhibitionism or absence/representation. The film image is not intrinsically defined by *either* its presence or its absence, or by its exhibitionism or its voyeurism; nor are presence or absence, or exhibitionism or voyeurism, homogeneous, singular categories particular or unique to certain media. Rather, presence, absence, exhibitionism, and voyeurism are complex, multifunctional semiotic *achievements* by social projects of various sorts that actualize and thereby also conserve otherwise heterogeneous ontic possibilities of images. As such, they are the terrain of contested ontological politics that materialize in and as images. While voyeurism and its doubled absence is an ontological politics of the image that has been institutionalized in and deeply naturalized by classical Hollywood film and theories of it, voyeurism and its doubled absence are, as we've seen, fraught and fought for in the Tamil cinema, as they were, at a time, in nineteenth-century European theatre and early American cinema.[68] As achievements, we should add, they are thus always subject to revision, contestation, and change and reproduction. This is the nature of images, as I have suggested, even when (and perhaps especially when) it doesn't seem so.

Epilogue

When I conducted the core research for this book from 2004 to 2014, the prospects for a more gender-progressive Tamil cinema appeared grim (see also Eswaran Pillai 2015:248–51). Yet by 2016, things seemingly began to change. The leading lady Nayanthara (b. 1984), for example, had quit acting after her controversial marriage to then-married director and hero-star Prabhu Deva (b. 1973) in the late 2000s (at his behest, it is said; see Garoo 2016). She divorced him in 2012 and launched a comeback, by the second half of the 2010s earning the sobriquet "Lady Superstar" – an allusion to both the "Superstar" Rajinikanth, the reigning mass hero of his generation, and to "The Lady Superstar" Vijayashanti (b. 1966), the popular 1980s and 1990s South Indian heroine – indicating her ability to narratively and commercially anchor films on her own (that is, without a male star or a famous director). While still doing conventional heroine roles in "commercial" films, Nayanthara was also increasingly choosing to do hero-less, story-driven genre films that centred on "deglamourized" (Sreedhar Pillai 2018a) female lead characters; or, as one commentator put it, films where she is the hero (Rao 2018).[69] Around the same time, another leading lady of her day, Jyothika (b. 1977), returned to the screen after a hiatus of marriage and raising children, acting as a heroine in a string of successful women-centred, hero-less films.[70] In 2018, the recently married, popular heroine Samantha Akkineni (b. 1987) publicly announced that, like her peers in Bollywood who got married and kept acting, she too wanted "to prove that a married actress can be successful in the film industry … (and) set the precedence for the future heroines" (Moviebuzz 2018). And even Simran, long out of the industry after her marriage, made a minor comeback and scored a role as a heroine alongside Rajinikanth in the 2019 film *Petta* (dir. Karthik Subbaraj).

The year 2018 also saw the emergence of a #MeToo movement across South India, moving in solidarity from Hollywood to Malayalam cinema, and then later, if with some hesitation and much resistance, into Tamil cinema (Rajendran 2018c). The emergence of these commercial films alongside protests about the offscreen treatment of women in the industry point to a politics of gender (in)equity articulated through a purposive and explicit ontological politics of the image put into filmic practice and attempted industry reform (Rajendran 2018b). Interestingly, such films do so by displacing, if not totally erasing, the hero function (see Chapter 4), putting in his place female characters that far outstrip the one-dimensionality of the standard commercial heroine: for example, a feisty newspaper journalist in *U-Turn* (2018, dir. Pawan Kumar), an aspiring radio jockey mother in *Kaatrin Mozhi* (Wind's Language; 2018, dir. Radha Mohan), a documentary maker in *Magalir Mattum* (Ladies Only; 2017, dir. Bramma), a streetwise cocaine peddler in *Kolamaavu Kokila* (Kolam-powder Kokila; 2018, dir. Nelson Dilipkumar), an idealist district collector in *Aram* (Good Deed; 2017, dir. Gopi Nainar) (Sreedhar Pillai 2019b).

But more than these changes, and to the point of this chapter, the shift in the representation of women is a shift in the performative economy of the image, one that cloaks the heroine-star in a representationalist veil by putting her *into* a narrative.[71] Despite her sobriquet, "Lady Superstar," the films that Nayanthara helms (like those of Jyothika or Samantha) are story-driven, character-anchored narratives, not films designed specifically to build up either her "glamourous" star image or the cine-politics of the actress.[72] As Nelson Dilipkumar tellingly said of his directorial debut, Nayanthara's 2018 *Kolamaavu Kokila*, "all I can assure you is that you won't see Nayanthara anywhere in the film. You'll just see her character. I wanted to make an honest film – one that is about Kolamaavu Kokila [the heroine's name]!" (quoted in Subhakeerthana 2018b). Rather than presencing the star actress so as to encompass the film and its narrative, she is absented from it, effaced so that her *character* may appear in it and – we might add – so that her stardom may then, and only then, come into full visibility, not as a glamorous body but as a skillful actress, not as a co-present (mute) object but as a representing (speaking) subject.[73]

Symptomatic of this larger shift, it is in this context that a 2019 news story asked, in a hopeful interrogative mood, whether the item song was "on its way out" (Rajendran 2019; see also Kunapulli 2021:152;

Weidman 2021:198–9). Quoting heavily from "young, promising filmmakers who are not interested in forcing songs into the screenplay" and instead favour narrative-advancing acousmatic montage songs (rather than stand-alone song-and-dance sequences where the heroine/item is given voice by a playback singer), the article frames the item song as a relic of an earlier era of cinema dominated by the vulgar, filthy lucre of "commercial elements," which has now given way, instead, to the story and its director, appreciated by audiences who "are becoming very different now" (see also Chapters 3 and 4).[74] In this aspirational interrogative, in the hope of historical change and the disappearance of the item and her titillating presence, do we not again detect the ontological politics of the image that is at issue in this book, a response to the quivering performativity of the image and the bridling promise of narrative, of the animation of capital (and the actress) and the responsibility of authorship (and the director)? Do we not detect a new configuration of representation and performativity, presence and absence, onscreen and offscreen?

PART TWO

Representation/Presence

Chapter Three

The Politics of Parody

The primary carnivalistic act is the *mock crowning and subsequent decrowning of the carnival king* ... And through it [the ritual of decrowning], a new crowning already glimmers.

– Mikhail Bakhtin, *Problems of Dostoevsky's Poetics*, 1984[1963]

Pastiche is not only cathartic for its author; it is also sterilizing to its victim, who is condemned to rehash stereotypes endlessly or to abandon them altogether, and thus become someone else.

– Gerard Genette, *Palimpsests*, 1997[1982]

Introduction

Commercial Tamil cinema has long woven its texts from so many citational allusions, homages, and self-reflexive satires. However, until recently there was no such recognized genre of the spoof film, only so-called comedy tracks trailing in the shadows of the grandiose hero and his (relatively) more serious narrative, parodying him here and there, most often through narratively disjointed scenes of comically inverted or failed heroism (Nakassis 2010:209–21).

In 2010, this changed. On 29 January, "the first full-length spoof of Tamil movies" was released (Dhananjayan 2011, 2:320). It was aptly titled *Thamizh Padam*, or 'Tamil Film.'[1] A resounding success at the box office, *Thamizh Padam* was declared the first "super-hit" of 2010 in the Tamil film industry, an outcome that was not quite expected by many in the industry, including its makers.[2]

Thamizh Padam's executive producer, S. Sashikanth (2011), recounted to me that from the moment he and the film's director, C.S. Amudhan (b. 1974), got together to conceptualize the film, it was about "taking on the industry." Directed and produced by self-described "rank outsiders,"[3] and lauded in the English-language press as "a breath of fresh air" to the stuffy airs put on by the film establishment (Kamath 2010, 2014), from its first to last frame *Thamizh Padam* cannibalized nearly every recognizable feature of commercial Tamil cinema. From its nonsense, romantic song lyrics and over-the-top fight scenes to its formulaic plot and unbelievable twists, *Thamizh Padam* was intentionally oversaturated with spoof. Pushed to an "intertextual overkill" (Waugh 1984), the film featured "as much (of Tamil cinema) as you could cram into one movie," as C.S. Amudhan put it to me in 2014, with nearly every scene, dialogue, character (and actor; with parodied characters played by actors who animated them in previous films), song, dance, lyric, shot, location, set, and prop a reference to some or another Tamil film.[4] For its audiences and makers, however, what was most important was the way *Thamizh Padam* ruthlessly satirized the so-called mass heroes of Tamil cinema – those bombastic, larger-than-life celebrity star actors whom South India is (in)famous for producing, whose fantastical screen lives bleed into their public offscreen personages (and vice versa) and from there into populist political life (see Introduction and Chapter 1 for discussion).

For these filmmakers, "taking on the industry," then, was about taking the piss out of these heroes, revealing their celebrity and screen images to be ridiculous, cliché, and artificial. (Indeed, *Thamizh Padam* figured commercial Tamil cinema as metonymically reducible to the mass hero and his image.) The film attempted to show that the mass hero's perforation of the diaphanous membrane of the screen (that is, his excessive presence and cine-political potency) was simply, as it were, the emperor's new clothes. But the film was more than a lampoon of textual conventions of filmic "heroism" (as it is called in Tamil Nadu). It was also a critique of the production culture and political economy that is grounded by and emanates from such hero-stars. In other words, *Thamizh Padam* took as its object of parody the total cinematic fact of the mass hero; not simply a parody of particular texts, pastiche of particular genres, or satire of particular persons – or rather, through a combination of each of these textual strategies and more – as a "ludic image-event" (Strassler 2020:61), the film travestied and caricatured, and thus constituted an explicit attempt to decentre, a particular "regime of imageness" (Rancière 2007, 2009): in a word, a particular mode of being of the image.[5]

In this chapter, I use the case of *Thamizh Padam* to show the work of parody in producing the real, the way in which through a certain kind of (inter)textual and extratextual excess some images are made to appear unrealistic (including those of the parody itself) so as to open the space for a putatively proper representation of reality. This case reveals the way in which parody always already presupposes a certain conception of what reality is, a realist epistemology that is itself an ontological politics of the image. As Bakhtin (1981, 1984[1965]) showed in his discussion of the novel, parody and realism are twinned genres (or enregistered styles, as I call them in Chapter 4), the former denaturalizing one regime of representation (for example, the monologic epic) so as to open up the possibility for (the naturalization of) the heterogeneity and ambiguity that characterizes the latter.[6]

Not just a call for a different kind of image and a different kind of presence, however, *Thamizh Padam* was also a call for a different kind of production format – one based on directors, scripts, and stories rather than on hero-stars and their spectacular, powerful personages – and participation framework (Goffman 1979) – one with liberal spectators who maintain a critical distance and see the image for what it "is" (a representation and no more) rather than credulous spectators absorbed into the performative image of the mass hero. This politics yearns for an image that emanates *not* from the performative mass of the hero-star but from the representationalist relationship of a director to a (realist) fiction to a (real) world to a (liberal) public, aiming to replace one kind of (male) subject – that of the commercial hero-star – with another – that of the auteur-director. And yet, as I show, this politics *of* the image is shot through with ironies regarding the politics *for* its image. The success of *Thamizh Padam* turned on performative image-acts it would have us disavow, as well as on an illiberal form of kin-based, party politics that sat uncomfortably with its liberal politics of representation.

One aim of this chapter is to foreground this relationship between the politics *of* and *for* images as critical to the study of cinema (though the distinction has more general applicability). By "politics *of* images," I refer to those claims and contestations made through and by particular images. These claims and contestations can, obviously, be wide in scope, including anything from the nature of the social realities that such images represent and what can (or cannot) be imaged to questions of what an image is (and is not), what constitutes (im)proper spectatorship and uptake, and so on. By "politics *for* images," I refer to that semiotic work by various stakeholders (directors, producers, actors, industry unions, state organizations, film critics, fan clubs, film theorists, and the like) involved in bringing images into being (or blocking them from becoming), keeping them in circulation (or taking them out), and regimenting their exhibition and experience, interpretation and uptake, theorization, and so on. (My point in Part I, as the reader will recall, is that film theory – in Chapter 1, Bazin's writings; in Chapter 2, feminist film criticism – is such a politics for images, which has had its own effects on the shape of the politics of images.) Such work often takes place offscreen; but it also takes place onscreen in and through images, indeed, as the politics *of* certain images, as in *Thamizh Padam*, a film whose parodic excess also makes a sober plea for a different kind of image (and type of realism: namely, representational realism rather than sociological realism), form of spectatorship, production culture, and so on. The politics of and for images are two interlocking and sometimes overlapping dimensions of cinematic semiosis, of a process that stretches across film texts and across the screen but manifests in and as particular images. Every politics of an image presupposes some politics for images that takes place before or alongside or after the filmic image; but every politics of an image also consists, at least in part, in some politics for images that is immanent to it, that makes its own claims on its own and other images, on future images.

The Anti–Cine-Politics of *Thamizh Padam*

By taking up the tangled conjunction between star actor and film hero as its object of derision and disaggregation, *Thamizh Padam* attempted to alienate and "make strange" (Shklovsky 1965[1917]) the mass hero or, as elitist discourses on Tamil cinema typically disparage it, the "idol" that is "worshipped" by those putatively devoted and credulous subaltern subjects who can't see that "it's just a movie," as Kalyan Kumar (2011), the choreographer of *Thamizh Padam*'s opening song, put it to me. The executive producer of *Thamizh Padam*, Sashikanth (2011), voiced this discourse, saying of *Thamizh Padam*'s spoofing:

> These guys [mass heroes and their fans] deserve it [being made fun of]. If at all we put down anything, they deserve this [spoofing] ... But they're not gonna like it. That's for sure. You're bringing down their- this idol worship kind of scenario, where you're putting milk on that guys' thing [image/cut-out]. I mean, it's rubbish. It's real stupidity. I mean, if you look at it from a common man's perspective, what's happening is real stupidity.

Here, Sashikanth references religious Hindu rituals of *pāl abiṣēkam* wherein a divine image or idol – the deity him/herself (Davis 1999) – is sanctified by having milk, or other substances, poured over it. Such rites are also performed by fans on large images of hero-stars, sometimes with milk, other times with beer or soda (see Chapter 1). Here, Sashikanth iconoclastically typifies such practices as a false idolatry, a "real stupidity" that deserves to be made fun of and revealed for what it is (as he understands it at least, since such fan rites, while serious business involving fan-club rivalries, are not necessarily conceived of by fans as religious in any way – hence the use of soda or beer instead of milk; see Nakassis 2016a:271n4).

In a context where mass heroes are invested with electoral potential and where large sums of capital are invested in them, spoofing such powerful figures is risky, even sacrilegious, as Sashikanth suggested. Indeed, many spoofs elicit strongly negative reactions from fans and their heroes. A forerunner of *Thamizh Padam*, the popular television show *Lollu Sabha* (Star Vijay, on air from 2001 to 2010), for example, provoked the ire of the hero-star Vijay (b. 1974) and his fans with its spoofs of him, eliciting threats by the actor, attacks on the station's office by upset fans (Rambala 2011a, 2011b), and even jury-rigged bombs sent to the homes of the show's actors and director (Behindwoods 2008; compare Cody 2015; Yamunan 2017; Nathan 2018).[7] There were real stakes, then, in making and releasing such a film.[8]

These stakes were planted in multiple domains: in the textual economy of commercial films, wherein the hero dominates the diegesis and narrative; in the film industry's sociological organization and "heterogeneous" mode of production (Staiger 1985:87–95; Prasad 1998; Ganti 2012:177, 215–41), wherein mass heroes and their stakeholders wield enormous influence and authority over the image (at the expense of producers, directors, other actors, and technicians); and finally, in electoral democratic politics, wherein mass heroes' populist appeal provides them with political power. *Thamizh Padam*'s spoof intervened at all of these levels, linking them together in its attempt to displace one mode of being with another.

A Politics of (Im/possible) Worlds

Consider the narrative premise and diegetic world of *Thamizh Padam*. The film begins with the birth of a male child, Shiva, in a village hut. When his sex is discovered, it is decided that he will have to be killed, as required by village law (a parodic twist of Bharathiraja's 1994 film *Karuthamma*). In a flashback, we learn why the village *nāṭṭāmai* (headman, played by Ponnabalam, who starred as the villain of the popular film *Nattamai* [1994, dir. K.S. Ravikumar]) had decreed it to be so. Male children from the village of Cinemappaṭṭi (Cinemaville) all grow up and go to the metropolis of Madras, he intones under a banyan tree during a panchayat meeting (Figure 3.1 – left). Once in Madras, they start 'speaking "punch dialogues" [bombastic, poetic

Figure 3.1. Spoofed headman at the panchayat meeting in *Thamizh Padam* (2010, dir. C.S. Amudhan), under the banyan tree (left) spoofing the *stylish* gestures of the would-be mass hero (right)

dialogues delivered by action heroes], dancing "kuttu" songs [energetic folk songs], and then, if that's not bad enough, giving television interviews, even before their first film is released, proclaiming that they'll be the next chief minister!' All this, he gravely concludes to a crowd of villagers nodding along in assent, gives the village a bad name and causes it trouble with the government. Any family that allows a male baby to be born, the *nāṭṭāmai* pronounces, will be cast out of Tamil Nadu; and further, he declares to an audibly aghast crowd, if any family disobeys his order and maintains contact with such people, 'they will have to watch the films of that finger-twisting little brother [a reference to the aspiring mass hero Simbu] one hundred times on the panchayat television' (*Appaṭi pal̲uṅkunīṅka nnā anta viral āṭṭi naṭikkir̲a anta tambi paṭatte nūr̲u mur̲ai namma pañcayattin* TV-*le pākkaṇum ṭōy!*; Figure 3.1 – right).

When Shiva's character is born, his fate, then, is death by branded tetrapack (!) of spurge milk.[9] Before it can happen and minutes after his birth, however, he gets the attention of his grandmother, who is to administer the poison. When she confusedly asks: 'Who's that talking?' he replies: 'It's me, the Mini Superstar speaking' (*Nān tān Mini Superstar tān pēsur̲ēn*), another lampoon of Simbu (b. 1983), who anointed himself with the epithet "Little Superstar" (a citation to the "Superstar" Rajinikanth, the most massive of the mass heroes since the 1990s). Shiva asks his grandmother to put him on a train to Madras (where all trains stereotypically go in the "nativity" films of the late 1970s and 1980s), where he will become a "*periya hero*" (big hero).[10] He then delivers one of *Iḷaiya Taḷapati* (Young General) Vijay's punch dialogues from the action film *Pokkiri* (2007, dir. Prabhu Deva): "*Oru muṭivu eṭuttā nānē en pēccu kēṭkamāṭṭēn*" (Once I make a decision, even I won't listen to what I say). The old woman responds in amazement: 'You really *are* going to become a big hero,' and decides to take him to Madras where Shiva (played by the adult, comic actor Shiva) grows up to become a "hero."

Of interest here is not simply the satire of the uppity actor, Simbu, who baptizes himself a star when he is metaphorically, and in baby Shiva's case literally, still wet behind the ears with afterbirth; nor the ludicrousness of an infant giving punch dialogues like an adult mass hero. What is most salient is that in this and subsequent scenes, the character frames himself, and is framed by others, as a film hero, even though he does not act in any films. Shiva's character, Shiva, while treated as a film hero by the narrative, is not an actor in the diegesis. (Nor is the actor Shiva a mass hero in real life.[11]) Rather, the character Shiva is simply a mass hero living in the (non-cinematic) world of the film. The mediating membrane of the screen is dispensed with in the diegesis of *Thamizh Padam*; or rather, the film enacts its dispensing for us so that we may see it all the more clearly. This self-reflexively doubled/collapsed timespace lampoons, with each absurdity that unfolds, the idea that the hero-star exists on and off the screen at once *as a mass hero* without slippage.

Narrativizing this slippage at its outset, *Thamizh Padam*'s parody focuses on precisely those generic aspects of the mass hero's image that cultivate this onscreen/offscreen entanglement, in particular, those aspects that frame and "build up" the hero-star as a political leader to his fan audiences.[12] Take, for example, the opening song in *Thamizh Padam*, a spoof on the formulaic genre convention for presencing the hero in all his prowess and *style* (Nakassis 2016a:161–7). As the song begins, we see large cut-outs of Shiva. Milk is poured over one as the crowd screams 'Long live our leader!' (Figure 3.2), while another is ritually protected against the "evil eye" (Figure 3.3 – left). As the latter act is performed, the cardboard cut-out morphs into Shiva's physical body as he *stylishly* salutes the audience (Figure 3.3 – right).

As we see these images, a chorus of voices sings praise to Shiva, addressing him as the 'lift [elevator] of the poor,' 'the leader of the world, the god who can topple even [then-US president] Obama' (*Ulagattukku talaivan nī, Obama-vai vīḻtta vanta iṟaivan nī*), among other caricatured superlatives. Shiva himself sings: 'I am a god to save the world' (*Ulaga raṭcikka kaṭavuḷ nān tān*); 'I am the adored child of our [INCL.] community of mothers [a reference to the first mass hero and former chief minister, M.G. Ramachandran]' (*Namma tāykkulattukku nān tān cellappiḷḷai*); and, looking directly at the camera: 'I am the single man who has touched heaven, who has risen to the pinnacle of history. I am both the head/leader [a reference to *Thala* Ajith] and the general [a reference to 'Young General' Vijay]' (*Tani āḷā siṅkaram tōṭṭēn, sarittiramā uyarntuppōṭṭēn, Thalaiyum nān tānē Taḷapatiyum nān tān*).

Figure 3.2. Performing *pāl abiṣēkam* on Shiva's image; in the background, flags fly with Shiva's face on them as crowds of people hold their hands up in respectful supplication

Figure 3.3. Neutralizing the "evil eye" accrued to Shiva's image (left) as it comes alive and *stylishly* salutes us (right)

Shiva makes various references to his political ascendency in 2011 (Figure 3.4) and, at one point, even tells the audience, deictically pointing directly at the camera, 'praise me and your life will flourish; worship me and you'll receive *moksha* [that is, be freed from the cycle of rebirths]' (*Ennai vāḻttippāru vāḻkkai seḻikkum, ennai vaṇaṅkippāru moṭcam kiṭaikkum*). And when Shiva is giving an inane philosophical aphorism – a parody of the *tattuvap pāṭṭu* (philosophical song) of M.G. Ramachandran and other mass heroes who therein offer sage advice and wisdom to the audience (in *Thamizh Padam*, Shiva advocates the necessity for unity through a metaphor of different types of *vadai*, or fried lentil cakes) – a drunken fan, voicing the director's mockery, asks Shiva to stop, saying: 'We can't stand your philosophy, older brother!' (*Un tattuvam taṅkātu-[a]ṇṇā*).

Figure 3.4. Shiva telling us that 2011 will be 'our' year in politics

These jokes each turn on how the image of the mass hero represents less a narrative world than indexically points beyond the screen to the offscreen status and identity of the actor in relation to his fan-spectators/cadres – hence, the caricature of all those deictic gestures (frontal shots, looking to the camera, saluting the audience, use of second-person grammatical forms) that break the so-called fourth wall – suggesting that the problem at stake is the failure of the mass-hero film to be transformed from what Benveniste (1971:206) called *discours*, dialogic communication between co-present interlocutors (here, the hero-star and his fan viewers), into a self-contained narrative, what Benveniste called *histoire* (see also Metz 2016[1991]), a failure to abstract from indexical co-presence into symbolic representation (or, as linguistic anthropologists would put it, from a reflexively calibrated interactional text, anchored in the personage of the hero-star, to a nomically calibrated denotational text, anchored in the seemingly impersonal enunciation of the film).

In this light, consider how *Thamizh Padam* lampooned the "titles" that name and adorn the mass hero's personage (compare Munn 1986; Roth 2008). Such titles – such as Superstar (Rajinikanth), *Ulaga Nayakan* (World Hero; Kamal Haasan), Ultimate Star *Thala* (Ajith), *Iḷaiya Taḷapati* (Young General; Vijay), Little Superstar (Simbu), Action King (Arjun), Powerstar (Srinivasan) – are what Saul Kripke (1980) called *rigid designators*, indexical signs that (extensionally) refer to the object to which they are baptismally attached "rigidly" across all possible worlds (that is, semantic/intensional counterfactuals). Exploiting this semiotic function, such superlative sobriquets traverse and collapse onscreen and offscreen in acts of adulatory nomination, their reference cutting across the screen to both the star actor *and* the narrative heroes he animates, that is to say, to the transcendent star persona that interdiscursively unites them (see also Chapter 1).[13]

As the film's producer, S. Sashikanth (2011), put it, *Thamizh Padam* "was intended to make fun of people having these titles for themselves" (compare Genette 1997[1982]:134). He continued: "It's stupid. I mean, I really don't understand what makes them think they can have titles for themselves. It's just-, it's ridiculous. It's just really ridiculous."[14] Satirizing the way such titles blur the reel and the real into the "worshipped" celebrity of the hero-star, Shiva in *Thamizh Padam* has a number of hypertrophic names: "Mini Superstar" as a neophyte and then "*Akila Ulaga* Superstar" and "*Periya Taḷapati*" in his adulthood. These are reflexively marked as caricature not simply by their citationality or by the surfeit of titles that Shiva has, but also in their semantic and morphological excess. Shiva's titles feature a greater number of terms (not Superstar but *Akila Ulaga* Superstar) and denotationally more expansive modifiers, such as *akila* (whole, all) and *periya* (big, older).[15] Most interesting to note in this regard, and perhaps to the point, is that after the release of *Thamizh Padam*, *Akila Ulaga* Superstar (Superstar of the World in Its Entirety) – a blend and augmentation of the titles of Kamal Haasan and Rajinikanth, the two most eminent hero-stars of their generation – stuck to Shiva, the actor, trailing him across and outside his film texts, tongue-in-cheek, as part of his name, parodying and conforming at one and the same time the performative semiotics that *Thamizh Padam* tells us is problematic.

Chronopolitics

Thamizh Padam's satire of the mass hero, however, was not simply a representationalist attack on the way in which real and reel spaces/worlds are warped and blurred in/by signs of his excessive presence. Nor is it simply an attack on the cine-political mode of social relations that his auratic image and its rigid designators of identity figurate – namely, the cinematic adulation of the hero-leader and the figuration of his audiences as devout fan-cadres. It is also a *chrono*politics, an attack on the temporality of the mass hero. It is the anachrony of the mass hero that *Thamizh Padam* hopes to show us, that he is *out of time*, both in the sense that his chronotope is absurd and unrealistic, and that it is untimely in this modern day and age.[16]

Consider the scene that bridges the film's opening flashback and its first song. After Shiva has moved to Chennai and become a young boy, he bears witness to a number of rowdies terrorizing the local bazaar and extracting protection money. Frustrated in his impotence,

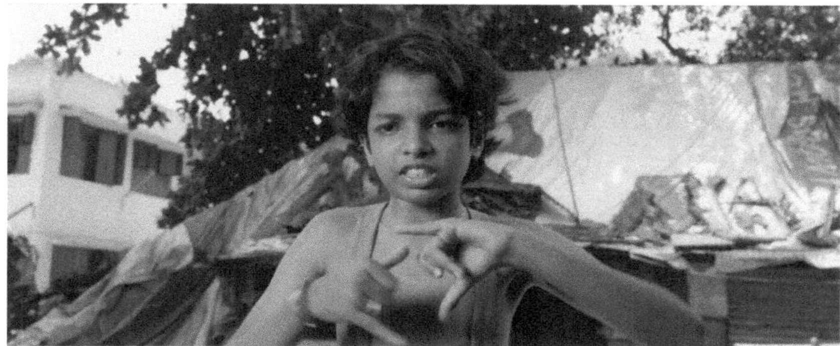

Figure 3.5. A young Shiva delivers a punch dialogue to his grandmother: 'It's been ten years since I've been born, but I'm still only ten. When will I become a hero so I can raise my voice against this atrocity?' (*Nān poṟantu pattu varuṣam āyiccu, ānā pattu vayasu āvatu. Nān eppa hero āyi nānē galāṭṭā tatti kēṭkuṟatu?*)

Figure 3.6. Shiva riding a stationary bicycle and transforming from a child (left) to an adult hero (right) in five seconds time

our young Shiva runs home to his grandmother to deliver a series of finger-twirling, swoosh sound-effected punch dialogues (Figure 3.5).

In response, his grandmother simply tells him to peddle on a nearby parked bicycle. When the young Shiva protests in disbelief (another trace of the filmmaker's satirizing voice), she insists. And indeed, as depicted through a five second time-lapse shot, when Shiva begins pedalling on the stationary bicycle his young, pantless legs (Figure 3.6 – left) age into adult panted legs (Figure 3.6 – right). Now a college-age hero, he returns to the market just in time to beat up the rowdies in a fight scene (parodying Rajinikanth's *Baashaa* [1995, dir. Suresh Krissna]) that leads into the opening song of the film.[17]

Similarly, consider *Thamizh Padam*'s climax sequence, a parody of the hit film *Kaakha Kaakha* (2004, dir. Gautham Menon). The villain, D.'s henchmen have captured Shiva's fiancée and taken her to an empty warehouse. She screams his name: "SHIVA!" (Figure 3.7 – top left), and the head henchman shoots a bullet at her from across the room (Figure 3.7 – top right). Shiva – who is in the hospital after receiving a beating from the bad guys while in a deep, alcohol-induced slumber from their recent Pondicherry road trip – awakens when he hears her call (Figure 3.7 – second row, left). He gets out of bed and does one hundred push-ups as the theme music kicks in (we hear him count them: "45 … 68 … 100"; Figure 3.7 – second row, right). Cut to the bullet in mid-air, flying in slow motion. Cut to Shiva grabbing his gun. (The lyrics of the song here mockingly sing: "Too much! *Muṭiyale*! *Kaṭavuḷē! Taṅkale*! *Itu* over-*u*!" [Can't take it! Oh God! Can't bear it! It's too much!]) Shiva gets into an autorickshaw. He haggles with the auto-driver (third row, left). He stops for tea. He checks this watch (third row, right). He grabs a newspaper. Cut again to the bullet in mid-air (fourth row, left). Shiva gets on a city bus and casually flirts with the woman next to him as if he had not a care in the world (fourth row, right). Cut to the bullet in mid-air. He goes to his dry cleaner to get his jacket cleaned. He checks his watch (fifth row, left). Cut to the bullet in mid-air (fifth row, right). Cut to Shiva urinating on the roadside (sixth row, left) and, again, checking his watch. Finally, he arrives at the warehouse and enters. The bullet is still flying in slow motion, ever closer to the heroine. At the predestined last second, Shiva leaps and saves her (sixth row, right).

In these examples, the joke is to play up the disjuncture between the narrative time of the hero and the expectable duration of the represented diegetic events he is involved in, the latter presumably conforming to linear Newtonian time (Aumont et al. 1992[1983]:93–4). Within the temporal envelope of a bazaar shakedown, Shiva has run home, talked with his grandmother, gone through puberty and aged a decade (and simply through a montage of bicycling), and run back to the bazaar! Within the time it takes a bullet to travel across a room, Shiva was able to exercise, haggle, have a tea, flirt on the bus, pick up his dry cleaning, relieve himself on the roadside, and save the damsel in distress!

But if, as a small child, our hero Shiva has not yet internalized this epic/heroic time (hence his initial disbelief in the wisdom of his grandmother), now into the age of heroism he knows his time. Checking his watch confidently, he is sure that he has all the time in the/his world. Such a parody, of course, is a joke about the form(ulaicness) of fictional film, invoking a more general point about filmic temporality and its irreality. But key here is that such jokes figurativize this formal parody as a parody of the hero-star himself, metonymizing "cinema" in the absurdity of the mass hero. Moreover, the reflexive sensibility of the hero

Figure 3.7. Shiva, our hero who knows he has all the time in his world

to his own temporality serves not simply as the film's enunciated wink to the viewer about how heroes exist in a fantasy time (which if read literally are impossible)[18] but also to suggest, again, that the hero has come to take seriously his own absurd temporality, that he himself has confused (what the film figures as) the artificial temporality of cinema for "real" time (in contrast, by implication, to a properly realist cinema, which would render reel and real time as coincident as possible).[19] Like the example of the drunk fan discussed above, which depicts a character – an internal fan-spectator – for whom the hero-star's antics are already excessive (even his fans think he is too much!), here the suggestion is that the only one who takes the hero-star's inanity and absurdity seriously is he himself.[20]

This asynchrony is also figured by *Thamizh Padam* as a kind of anachrony: that the hero's time is not (and *should* not be) our time is framed by the film as a sign of his untimeliness, of the fact that mass heroes are something of the present that should go into the past and perish. The film's executive producer, S. Sashikanth (2011), gave explicit voice to this idea, commenting about yesteryear mass heroes like M.G. Ramachandran:

> They come from a different era, right? They were *gods* then. They were gods. Uh that kind-, that was their kind of thing. The celluloid was a way of looking into the gods. They [the film audience] didn't get them on television. They don't get to see them on roads. Today, [the hero-star] Suriya is accessible when you're buying a (bar of) soap. He is there. So, it's no big deal. You can get to *see* them. It's not the same (at that time), "I don't know where to see these people." You know, that's- that completely, this connect of seeing god onscreen is great [that is, was greater] then, I think. Imagine you don't get to see these people otherwise in real life. But today, internet, you- it'll come, but you get to see his *face*. But then, unless you cut somebody's photo, and keep them in your house and then look through them, you don't even know, you can't, that visual connection of wanting to see somebody you like is, was non-existent ... But I think that we're on the threshold, that cusp of leaving behind a lot of baggage and then moving forward. I think in the next five years, ten years, I think that's gonna happen. You look at the old filmmakers, they've pretty much died. They've all gone, like out of the industry.

Here, a religious ontology of the image – as immanent presence, as "god" – is figured as a thing of the past ("They come from a different era," as Sashikanth put it), which hasn't quite but will soon go away, as part of a generational shift, both of the audience – who, in urban areas at least (where *Thamizh Padam* ran the most successfully), have become "updated," as one of *Thamizh Padam*'s screenwriters K. Chandru (2010) opined (see also Kurai 2012:44) – and of filmmakers. As *Thamizh Padam*'s director, C.S. Amudhan (2010), averred, "many of the young people who are making films today are taking themselves lighter, are not treating the whole thing with, how do you call it?, with devotion that the last generation did, you know? We're not taking ourselves that seriously."

This is a familiar and long-standing iconoclastic narrative about popular Indian cinemas: that they are developmentally stunted but (always) in the process of maturing out of a(n almost) past era of rural subaltern credulity, idol worship, fetishism, and fantasy (Vasudevan 2010; Ganti 2012; Mazzarella 2013), what Sashikanth typified above as "real stupidity."[21] The desired, if continually deferred, telos of this narrative is a modern realistic cinema patronized by liberal, cosmopolitan (middle-class) subjects who can take a joke, who know that the hero's time is not their time (in fact, not anyone's time), who know that it's "just a movie" and no more – which is to say, that it is not a performatively potent image-act of real presence or cine-politicking.[22] *Thamizh Padam* situates itself in and through this narrative, marking off a (present-)past from a (present-)future, performative presence from representation, fantasy from realism.[23] *Thamizh Padam*, of course, is *not* a representationally realist image of the world but a hypertrophied, absurd representation of the bloated irreality of the mass hero (that is, a caricature of his sociological realism).[24] Yet animating this satirically unreal and performative image *is* a yearning for a representationally realist image that is a transparent window, not to the mass of the hero but to the world itself, as narrativized by a film director and his story.

For Another Kind of Image

In reflecting back on *Thamizh Padam* four years after its release, C.S. Amudhan (2014) noted to me that, whatever flaws or critiques there were of the film, "I went out and said all the things that I wanted to say." When I asked him what that was, he said that he wanted to make the "definitive spoof," "a comprehensive Tamil cinema mirror." But there was more than that, he indicated. He continued by describing a later scene in the film where Shiva returns to his rural hometown of Cinemappaṭṭi (Cinemaville) to locate his family:

> Well see, the thing, the dialogue that is spoken in *Thamizh Padam* when Shiva spends his first night there (in Cinemappaṭṭi). He says: "What

> happened to this village? And there is nobody here anymore." And the dialogue that the guy [an older villager, acting as Shiva's guide] says is actually, was something that I wanted to say, you know. He said … "*Vāl̲ntukkiṭṭa kuṭumbam ṅkur̲a mātiri itu vāl̲ntukkiṭṭa ūr ((???)).*" Which means, he's saying, like a family that's lived well and then gone down, this is a town that has lived well and then gone down to ruins. "*Oru kālattule Bharathiraja, Gangai Amaran inta mātiri āṭkaḷ ellām vantu iṅkē panniṭṭuppāṅka. Appō orē* shooting *nallā irukkum. Ippa inta pakkam yārumē varutu illai* <mouth click> *((???))*" [Once upon a time, directors like Bharathiraja and Gangai Amaran shot films here. There was a lot of shooting then. It was good. But now no one comes this way anymore]. That's the reason the town is desolate, because there is no shooting happening there. But in a sense, that was the golden age of cinema for Tamil cinema, you know, when Bharathiraja and Gangai Amaran and Sundarajan were at their peaks and making original, cultural-based cinema, unique cinema from Tamil Nadu. That was actually the golden age. And what he is saying was actually a reflection of what we thought.

Here, we may recall Linda Hutcheon's (2000[1985]) observation that parody always harbours within its heart conservative nostalgias; or adapt Gerard Genette's (1997[1982]) observation regarding parodic satire and caricature in European literature, that there is always a particular normative semiotic ideology that underwrites satire. While parodic satire ideologically frames itself, and is often framed by scholars, as transformative, romantic, and liberatory (for example, Bakhtin 1984[1965], López 1990; compare Harries 2000:120–34), caricature, Genette points out, abides a slightly different, if related referentialist ideology: that what is being caricatured should be expressed in some other, more referentially accurate, simple, or plain style. Caricatures often frame their targets, Genette (1997[1982]:96) notes, as "artificial language," as unnecessarily stylized nonsense.

Both these ideologies are united in *Thamizh Padam*, whose implicit framing of the image holds out for a representationalism that it hopes to make possible, arguing that in the place of the mass hero Tamil cinema might generate something approximating the "original, cultural-based," "unique" cinema of Tamil cinema's "golden age," the realist nativity film of the late 1970s and 1980s. This desire is evident in the quote above, as Amudhan laments the loss of such narrative-centred cinema and its generation of auteur-directors who brought unadorned, naturalistic representations of village life to the screen. In this sense, *Thamizh Padam*'s parodic image is a means to a representationally realist end, to a cinema that rearticulates image and referent as authentic and truthful by replacing one subject – the hero – with that of another – the auteur-director.

But while in the above quote Amudhan framed this concept as a turn inwards, to "nativity" and the "culture" of the Tamil people, it faces outwards as well. Like many of the directors whom I have interviewed in over a decade of research on Tamil cinema, Amudhan continually framed his own aspirations and efforts, and his own critiques of Tamil cinema, against a recognizable cosmopolitan canon of Hollywood and "world cinema" auteur-directors (for example, Scorsese, Kubrick, Tarantino, Kurosawa) and their narratively driven and (comparatively) realist films (Pandian 2011:200; see also Vasudevan 2010:7; Ganti 2012). Amudhan's invocation of the realist nativity films of the 1970s, then, should not be read as a simple call for a nostalgic return to a "golden age" but as a provocation for a continually different – that is, non-formulaic and "original" – cinema, in the way that the director-led realist films of the late 1970s offered a fresh break with the hero-driven commercial cinema of their time.

In the wake of *Thamizh Padam*, a spate of such "different" films were, indeed, released (for example, *Aaranya Kaandam* [2011], *Pizza* [2012], *Kadhalil Sodhapuvadhu Yeppadi* [2012], *Soodhu Kavvum* [2013], *Jigarthanda* [2014]). Such films have since been variously called by critics and scholars of Tamil cinema as "new wave," "experimental realism," and "neo-noir" (Gopalan 2008, 2021:209–59; K. Hariharan 2013; Kailasam 2017; Kunapulli 2021).[25] As Vasuki Kailasam (2017:7) has put it, *Thamizh Padam* was a "signpost" for these small-budget films that broke from the hero-driven commercial fare that dominates mainstream Tamil cinema *and* from the neonativity films that proliferated in the 2000s (Chapter 4) and had themselves become something of a "formula" by the end of the decade (Gopinath n.d.-a; Damodaran and Gorringe 2017).[26] Like *Thamizh Padam*, this new crop of films were directed by new "outsider" directors without film industry backgrounds (for example, Thiagarajan Kumararaja, Karthik Subbaraj, Balajimohan, Nalam Kumarasamy) and produced by new producers with (arguably) equally outsider credentials (for example, C.V. Kumar, S.P.B. Charan, and S. Sashikanth, *Thamizh Padam*'s producer). And like *Thamizh Padam*, such commercially successful films were self-reflexively quirky and experimental ("not taking themselves too seriously," as Amudhan said above, of the "young people … making films today"), violent and absurdist, lacking both substantial hero figures – indeed, articulating a deep crisis of masculinity, as Kailasam (2017) argues – and a strong moral and emotional core (what in Tamil Nadu is called "sentiment" and is strongly linked with female kin relations). Registering at one and the same time an enthusiastic cinephilic relation to the Tamil cinema of the past[27] and, as K. Hariharan (2013) has argued, a deep disaffection with and yet intimate investment in Tamil identity (cine-)politics (Eswaran Pillai 2015:272–88; Kunapulli 2021:103–4), such films can be seen as actualizing precisely the sensibility of *Thamizh Padam*, not as a negative parodic form but as a positive aesthetic claim on the image, one that breaks with Tamil cinema's existing conventions (indeed, its very being, I would argue) by revealing, through its markedly reflexive, enunciative gestures, its own filmic apparatus (Metz 2016[1991]:64–71).[28]

But if the parody of *Thamizh Padam* attempted to break with convention and usher in a different kind of image, it did so by leaving certain things in place – in particular, a certain narrative economy of sexual difference, something also true of the "neo-noir" films discussed above, which often lack any significant female characters.[29] This is not to say that *Thamizh Padam* didn't parody clichés of femininity (it did), but – as some commentators noted (Gopinath n.d.-b) – it failed to challenge certain conventions of the industry and thereby reproduced some of its dynamics; in particular, in its focus on heroism, *Thamizh Padam* replicated the secondary status of female protagonists as effaceable means to the hero's (as well as the male director's) ends (see Chapter 2).[30]

Amudhan's plea was not just about textual aesthetics, however. It was also a plea for a different production culture. Below, I turn to a marketing stunt between C.S. Amudhan and the director Venkat Prabhu, which took place three months after *Thamizh Padam*'s release. This stunt was itself a spoof, an offscreen prank that aimed to demonstrate and make fun of the self-seriousness of the film industry. This prank echoed critiques articulated by *Thamizh Padam* and its makers – that the uptight and hierarchical sociality and sociology of the industry deleteriously impacts how films are made – even as it too left certain things in place (such as gender politics in the industry).

For a Less Serious Industry

In March 2010, at an engagement party for *Thamizh Padam*'s producer, Dayanidhi Alagiri, S. Sashikanth, C.S. Amudhan, and Venkat Prabhu found themselves deep in their drink. Amudhan had recently released an ad spoofing Venkat Prabhu's ad campaign for his own film *Goa*, a comedy film that came out on the same day as *Thamizh Padam* and which also featured a significant amount of hero-parodying humour. The print ad took *Goa*'s tagline "A Venkat Prabhu Holiday" (and typeface; Figure 3.8 – left) and transformed it into "A C.S. Amudhan Working Day" (Figure 3.8 – right). In doing so, Amudhan mockingly

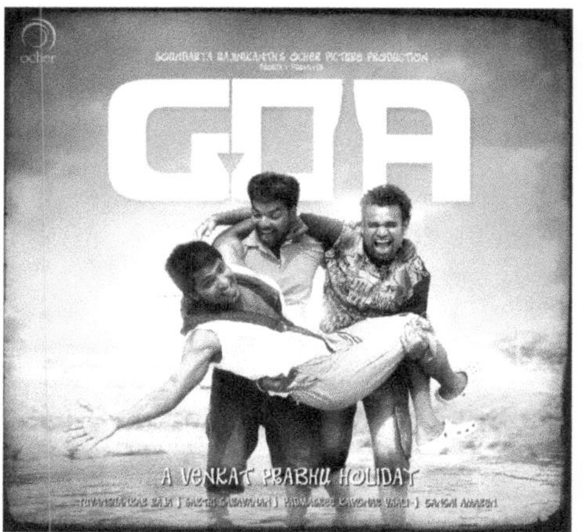

Figure 3.8. Left – *Goa* ad ("A Venkat Prabhu Holiday"); right – *Thamizh Padam* ad spoofing *Goa*'s ads ("A C.S. Amudhan Working Day")

contrasted himself – as an outsider to the film world who had to work for his chance in the industry – to Venkat Prabhu – as an insider who comes from a famous film family who, by implication, had his film career (his "holiday") handed to him (see note 33 in this chapter). As Amudhan (2010) told it, he showed the ad to Venkat Prabhu, who said in faux protest and anger, "the nerve of you!"

Over drinks, they decided that Prabhu should make an ad that "pulls the leg" of *Thamizh Padam* in return. Venkat Prabhu subsequently released an ad that spoofed a recently published *Thamizh Padam* fiftieth-day celebration ad that featured the headline "*Ēn? Etaṟku? Eppaṭi? Ena eṅkaḷukkē puriyāmal ōṭikkoṇṭirukkum 50-āvatu nāḷ*" (Without our understanding why, for what reason, or how, *Thamizh Padam* is running for its 50th day [in the theatres]; Figure 3.9 – left). *Goa*'s ad had the headline: "*Itanāltān … Itaṟkākatān … ena eṅkaḷukkum makkaḷukkum purintu veṟṟikaramāka ōṭikkoṇṭirukkum 50-āvatu nāḷ*" (Both the people and we understand why and for what reason *Goa* is running successfully for its 50th day [in the theatres]; Figure 3.9 – right). The idea of the ads, Venkat Prabhu and Amudhan both told me, was "cheap publicity," a fun way to keep people talking about the films as they wrapped up their theatrical runs.[31]

After a series of such spoof print-ads went back and forth, "everyone was getting heated about it," Venkat Prabhu told me in July 2010. He and Amudhan started getting calls from their producers, from

Figure 3.9. Left – *Thamizh Padam* ad celebrating fifty days in the theatres; right – *Goa* ad, also celebrating fifty days in the theatres, spoofing the *Thamizh Padam* ad

the producers' council, from eminent senior actors, and from worried friends. All warned that these kinds of public fights were bad for everyone involved. They were counselled to stop their feud and bury the hatchet.

Around the same time, Amudhan and Shiva were invited for the second episode of the recently begun NDTV television talk show *Hands Up* (2010–11), hosted by journalist, film critic, and parallel cinema filmmaker Sudhish Kamath. Kamath was an ideological ally and friend of both Amudhan and Venkat Prabhu, having written a favourable review of both films in the English-language press as examples of a possible future for a new and "different" Tamil cinema (Kamath 2010). *Hands Up*, as Kamath put it to me in 2014, was an attempt at a new kind of show, one that didn't have any of the conventional "rules" for a talk show. Central to this attempt was the sociality of the show itself: egalitarian, irreverent, and playful – the exact opposite of the stereotype of how the sociality of the Tamil film and television industries works: hierarchical, reverent, and self-serious (compare Ganti 2012:202–7).

To make light of this stereotype, *Hands Up* featured a bit called "Mocktales," where guests had to humorously redub some scene from a film they were a part of. In early March 2010, Amudhan and Shiva redubbed, and spoofed, a scene from Venkat Prabhu's *Chennai 600028* (2007), in which Shiva had acted. As Kamath (2014) reasoned in an interview with me, "I made them spoof up for a segment from Venkat Prabhu's film, because, I mean, he's the only guy (in the film industry) who's not going to take offence if we make fun of him."[32] In late March, Venkat Prabhu and his brother, the comedian Premji Amaren, were invited to the show. In collusion with Amudhan, they decided to use their Mocktale (in this case, a scene from Rajinikanth's *Chandiramukhi* [2005, dir. P. Vasu], which Premji had already famously parodied in Venkat Prabhu's previous films) to make fun of *Thamizh Padam*. What followed was a series of Facebook posts by Amudhan and Prabhu that played up the faux feud. Each comment framed the other director as an ego-sensitive megalomaniac (for example, Amudhan's comments that *Thamizh Padam* is "an epoch defining movie" or that he had been hurt by Venkat Prabhu's Mocktale). The posts sparked a series of ad hominem attacks online by their respective social networks against the opposing director.

Given the decidedly serious response to their prank, Amudhan, Prabhu, and Kamath decided to turn up the volume. Playing it up through a series of public communiqués – Kamath taking responsibility for the feud on-air, issuing a public apology online, re-editing comments from the *Hands Up* episodes for televised teasers to make it seem that Prabhu was really upset with Amudhan, and vice versa – the fight was made to seem genuine. Alongside such staged drama, *Hands Up* elicited sincere sound bites from industry personnel (for example, the journalist Shakti, from the industry magazine *Galatta*; the director Gautham Menon) weighing in on how the two directors should resolve their differences.

On the first of April, Venkat Prabhu and Amudhan came together on *Hands Up* to allegedly clear the air and patch things up. Instead, they staged an even more emotionally charged drama where each traded jabs and puffed up their egos, Venkat Prabhu even storming off stage at one point. Towards the end of the episode, with emotions seemingly running high, they revealed the whole thing to be an April Fools' prank on the audience by two close friends.

The prank they staged turned on the idea that what one director simply meant as a joke to be taken "lightly" was taken too seriously by the other, who was thereby figured as having too much "ego," prompting a serious attack in return. The moral, as the show framed it, was that the industry shouldn't take itself as seriously as it does. As given voice by S.P.B. Charan, Venkat Prabhu's friend and *Chennai 600028* producer, in a link segment of *Hands Up* that aired after the prank was revealed: "The seniors in the industry, lighten up! There are a lot of new directors and actors, new fresh blood coming in who have a great sense of humour. So, learn something from them. We are learning a lot from you guys. But you have to take a page out of our books as well. So, lighten up people."

The prank, in short, played on the ease by which people assumed that even those who are known to be easygoing and always joking (Venkat Prabhu and Amudhan) were in a serious battle of egos, that underneath the veneer of humour was ultimately and always an industry sociologically organized around sensitive individuals who just can't take a joke. As Kamath put it to the directors on-air before revealing the prank: "Is there a thing called a sense of humour for the Tamil film industry? Because you guys are the funny guys, and if you guys can't take a joke, then I don't know who can." That one couldn't intuit that it was a joke, then, was the basis of the joke (Boyer and Yurchak 2010). Through its deception, the stunt positioned its onlookers as credulous subjects – indeed, as that founding subject of the cinema, the rube – who mistook fictional representation for reality, as unable to conceive that film personalities could, in fact, simply be joking around when it came to their own public images. In other words, the prank elicited the belief that images of film personalities are never mere representations but are always residually performative image-acts, be they of the mass hero's presence on the big screen or of a joke between directors on the small screen.[33] It was a lesson, the prank suggested, that younger directors – the "new fresh blooding coming in with a sense of humour," as Charan put it – had to convey to both the "seniors" of the industry and to audiences. In the end, after all, it was the youngish directors Amudhan and Venkat Prabhu who had flipped the script, who had controlled the narrative of the prank to show the audience what was illusion and what was real, what is a performative act and what is a mere representation of it.

While this difference was most clearly framed as a politics of age and generation, it was also, of course, a politics of masculinity, of male homosociality and privilege – one that echoes *Thamizh Padam*'s (and *Goa*'s) onscreen privileging of the (lampooned) hero and his (lampooning) director noted above[34] – for, indeed, the forms of sociality and public presentations of self through which all this unfolded – casual drinking and jocular ribbing, cool irreverence and indignant outrage – are not available in the same way to women (in particular, in public or in the context of men), except with potentially much more acute and punitive stakes, a fact reflected in the general absence of women from this prank and its associated social contexts.[35]

A Politics of Production

The offscreen "feud" between Amudhan and Venkat Prabhu underscores that *Thamizh Padam*'s critical bite was as much about the sociology and political economy of the film industry as it was about questions of aesthetics or audience uptake. In this faux feud, in my interviews with the film's makers, and in *Thamizh Padam* itself, we can detect a call for a different mode of image production and, in particular, a different locus of authority over the image: that of the director and not of the hero-star.

In this light, consider again Shiva's introductory song in *Thamizh Padam*. About three minutes into the song, a caption appears when Shiva is singing about how he's the dream boy of all the college girls (Figure 3.10 – top). The text reads "*Inta pāṭalai pāṭiyavar uṅkaḷ Shiva*" (Your Shiva is the singer [+HON.] of this song) – a reference to how some of the films of the hero-star Vijay in the 1990s provided a caption onscreen telling the viewer that he, the hero-star, was singing the song that the viewer was hearing his character sing in the diegesis (rather than, as is typically the case, the song being sung by a professional playback singer).[36] About seven seconds later, the caption changes (Figure 3.10 – bottom). A matrix clause (and a sentence-final period) has been added, framing the now subordinate clause and adding another voice into the mix: "*Inta pāṭalai pāṭiyavar uṅkaḷ Shiva enṟu pōṭumāṟu kēṭṭuk koṇṭār*" (He [Shiva] asked [+HON.] (s.one) to put "Your Shiva is the singer of this song").

In the first image-text, the linguistic and cinematic deictics (the proximal demonstrative, the second-person possessive pronoun, Shiva's look to camera) interpellate the fan viewer, yet are not explicitly enunciated by Shiva (who is referred to in the third person by his proper name). This is, to borrow a phrase from Christian Metz (2016[1991]), a figuration of an impersonal enunciation, as if the film itself is addressing us in a simple act of presentative reference.[37] In the second, by contrast, we see a representation of a previous speech act of metapragmatic direction, one that embeds the first captioned image-text within a request, namely, to put 'Your Shiva is the singer of this song' onscreen. The implicit object of this indirect reported-speech construction is the enunciator itself, an embedded addressee in the linguistic text of the caption that is not impersonal at all: it is the very director of the film, he

Figure 3.10. A politics of production format; top – 'Your Shiva is the singer of this song'; bottom – 'He asked (s.one) to put "Your Shiva is the singer of this song"'

who was asked (pragmatically ordered, I would argue) to put the first caption onscreen by the singing hero-star. And while the first caption parodies a practice of aligning and blurring onscreen and offscreen, the second puts that first performative act into bracketing quotation marks (that is, into a reportive calibration), and in doing so lampoons the division of labour it implies: namely, the widely held belief (and in some cases reality) that it is not the director but the film's hero-star who controls and directs the film (Pandian 1992:95–6; Ganti 2012:211; see discussion in Chapter 1), who tells the audience what he wants them to know. Hence the necessity to have the caption twice, first to enact the hero-star's intervention into the image's production format (cloaked in a quasi-impersonal construction) and second, to suggest that it is at the expense of the will of the filmmaker – who is no longer the author or principal of the film text but merely a toiling animator of it (though, ironically, he is the author of the caption that would inform you of this fact) – and his story.[38]

In interviews with me, Amudhan consistently invoked "the story" as the basic, foundational element guiding his filmmaking (see also Selvaraghavan's framing of the "story" in Chapter 2 as guiding his filmmaking).[39] As Amudhan (2010) said of his process, "I let the story, the narrative rule the process. I don't cast until I finish my script. I wait until I'm sure what the product is before doing anything else." This process is in contrast to a film built around a "bankable star," as Amudhan (2014) later put it to me, with other elements filled in by simply following a standard "formula" (see note 1 in this chapter).[40] In doing so, Amudhan voiced a common criticism of commercial Tamil cinema: that instead of a sensible story and a coherent narrative, its films are made up of a jumbled mix (a *masala*) of disjointed "tracks" (comedy, romance) and spectacles (fights, item songs) loosely woven around the hero (see also Vasudevan 2010:4–7; Mitry 1997[1963]:5–8; Ganti 2012:207–13). Commenting on how the rise of hero-star–oriented cinema in the 1950s and 1960s (and again in the 1980s and 1990s) displaced an earlier mode of story-driven cinema, Amudhan (2010) noted:

> And I think it [hero-star–centred cinema] started to take away the sheen of storytelling … I don't mind ten movies a year coming out like that … but it became completely topsy turvy, we had *only* movies of this kind coming out. And I think we have an inherent- as a people, as Tamil people we have a very rich ethos out of which to make stories. And we are very good storytellers. I think we lost that … because this [heroism] was hogging all the space.

As Amudhan put it, the problem is that the hero-star has eclipsed the story and its teller. Again, this is not just a critique of a kind of image or textual aesthetics but of a mode of production and political economy. Amudhan's appeal is both a plea for the story (and not the hero-star's image) to guide the filmmaking process and for the authority of the director – as storyteller/author – to subordinate actors as mere performers animating *his* story.

Similarly, for S. Sashikanth (2011), who conceived his production house, YNOT Studios, as a source for "alternative" commercial productions, choosing a film was not just about "content" (or story) but also about the "script" (Ganti 2012:223). Emphasizing that he chooses films solely based on their scripts, Sashikanth distinguished himself from producers who choose their projects based on the "market value" of the hero-star or the director. As he further emphasized, he never listens to oral "narrations" of stories (the typical way that films are pitched in the industry) but only will *read* scripts, by which he meant a detailed production script that transparently lays out – scene by scene, shot by shot – all aspects of the filmmaking process (from découpage to properties to dialogues).

This appeal to the text-artifact of the written script was a criticism of an industry that has long worked independently of production scripts (even when they exist) and has preferred a more improvisational style of filmmaking (Ganti 2012:155–74, 225–32; Pandian 2015). Invoking the script, then, was a way of framing the rest of the industry as backward (even illiterate), ad hoc and disorganized, inefficient and economically opaque.[41] As Sashikanth lamented, the economics of the industry feeds on black money, bloated budgets, and non-transparent accounting and operates with, as he estimated, ninety-five failures kept afloat by five mega-hits (see also Ganti 2012:9, 11, 27). He said, outlining his own business "model" in comparison:

> Our [YNOT's] model, again, is very clearly we don't work on this exponential kind of looking at profits and things like that. I think you should be able to create a value chain right across to the distributor, the theatre guy. The producer should understand that if he creates a product, he- his return should be clearly 15, 18 per cent market standard when you're creating as a kind of thing- You shouldn't suddenly build- make a film for 8 crores [80 million] and try to sell it for 20 crores [200 million]. It's stupidity, actually. (my underlining)

For Sashikanth, the heterogeneous mode of production built up around the mass hero turns on huge windfalls from a few films rather than a serial, rationalized mode of script-dictated production that is efficient and that calculates and thus manages risk. Note, in particular, the corporate register of Sashikanth's discourse and the business imaginaries it invokes and opposes: "making" and "selling" films in order to collect "exponential profits and things like that" (which is "stupidity") in contrast to a "value chain" where "a product" (note, not a "film") is "clearly" and reliably able to give a "return" according to some "market standard."[42] Akin to Llerena Searle's (2016) discussion of the enregistered contrasts between the figures of the liberal, cosmopolitan corporate "professional" and the vernacular, corrupt "businessman" in Indian real estate – another suspect, stigmatized industry in the Indian context; recall, Sashikanth is originally an architect (and C.S. Amudhan a corporate ad director) – here, Sashikanth invokes a contrast between the (self-)educated, corporate executive producer (himself) and the unlettered, slapdash film producer (compare Ganti 2012:7, 215–41). (Sashikanth emphasized in our interview that he had studied scriptwriting classes for how films are supposed to be made in a proper, corporate manner.)

In short, *Thamizh Padam*, both as a film text and the outcome of a mode of production, rejected both a *kind of film image* and *a kind of cinema*, from the level of the film text and its chronotopic organization (mainstream, fantasy "mass" films for untimely, credulous subaltern crowds versus alternative, realist "class" films for modern, liberal publics) to the social organization of the industry (hierarchical versus egalitarian, older versus younger generation, hero-stars versus directors/producers), its modes of sociality (uptight versus laid-back), and economic organization (black versus white, irrational versus rationalized). But with economic and political stakes so high, in an industry so putatively hierarchical, self-serious, and thin-skinned, how did such a film ever even get released, let alone made? What was the politics *for* the image that made it possible for such a politics *of* the image to come to light?

The Politics for an Image

Making a film like *Thamizh Padam*, as industry insiders, audiences, film critics, and its makers all noted, was gutsy (*tairiyam*), even unthinkable. When I asked the former director and producer, and current comedian, Manobala (2010) – who played one of Shiva's sidekicks in *Thamizh Padam* – if most producers would have opted to take on a project like *Thamizh Padam*, he noted dramatically in Tamil:

Eṭukka māṭṭāṅka sār! *Veḷi āka muṭiyātu.* *Tamiḻ Nāṭṭai poṟutta varaikkum* Thamizh Padam *nān* *eṭuttiruntā ennai kai kālai veṭṭi* *pōṭṭiruppāṅka.*	They'd never take it on, sir! It would never come out. As far as Tamil Nadu is concerned, if I'd made *Thamizh Padam* they [the ones spoofed by the film] would've chopped off my legs and arms.

Less sensationally, Sashikanth (2011) noted: "There was an existing rule in the industry that any movie that makes fun of movies doesn't work in the box office ... It's just like a psychological thing that people [filmmakers, producers, actors, and so on] used to carry, that whenever movies made fun of (other) movies they didn't work in the industry" (compare Harries 2000:18).

While ultimately Amudhan and Sashikanth found a production house (Cloud 9 Movies) to bring the film to theatres (see note 3 in this chapter), the film did face setbacks along the way.[43] There was resistance from the Tamil Film Producers Council, which tried to stop the film's production at the outset. There were problems at shooting spots, as when fans got upset at seeing huge cut-outs of Shiva in the opening song trolling their favourite heroes. It was difficult to cast actors and hire technicians ("Nobody would want to be part of a spoof, unless it's a rank newcomer who says 'I've got nothing to lose,'" Amudhan said to me in 2014).[44] And once cast, actors often felt uncomfortable with their lines, asking Amudhan to change them or tone them down for fear of "hurting" the parodied person (and suffering the fallout personally).[45] Once completed, the film faced resistance from distributors, who were initially unwilling to buy it, requiring the production house to take on the task of distribution.

In the end, however, the film got made. It was released. It was a hit. Audiences, in general, found it hilarious, knowingly laughing with the film at their heroes (and perhaps at themselves). Contrary to what might have been expected, there were no fan mobs ripping out the seats in theatres, no threats or bombs sent to the director, no publicly outraged film personalities. Indeed, what was more surprising was the conspicuous absence of any kind of public, widespread negative reaction to the film upon its release, from either the industry or its publics (even if certain film stars' feelings were reputed to be hurt – such as the "Little Superstar" Simbu – and some persons' careers affected from the satire they endured).[46]

Was the lack of negative reaction following *Thamizh Padam*'s release indicative that its interventions were a *fait accompli*, its politics a foregone conclusion? Was *Thamizh Padam* simply the telltale sign, as Rajan Kurai (2012) has argued, that the mass hero was already dead, his rotting corpse ripe for parody? That, as English-language journalist Sudhish Kamath (2014) suggested, Tamil cinema had (finally) "come of age" (compare Eswaran Pillai 2015:266; Ganti 2012:19)? That, as one of *Thamizh Padam*'s screenwriters, K. Chandru (2010), said, audiences and filmmakers today are "updated" and matured by world cinema, rejecting the "formula," as Sashikanth (2011) put it, instead demanding "alternative," sensible "content"? Or perhaps that, as Amudhan said to me, the filmmaking team knew the limits of good fun and, with a couple of exceptions (for example, the hero-star Simbu), avoided *personally* insulting anyone (see note 45 in this chapter)? Or maybe Amudhan and colleagues got away with it simply because, as Amudhan and Sashikanth also noted about themselves, they were "rank outsiders" to the industry who never assistanted with anyone and thus who didn't know better, who had nothing to lose and owed nothing to anyone in the industry?

Perhaps. Many of these reasons make sense given changes in post-millennium Tamil cinema,[47] and they fit with the familiar (ideologically charged) narrative of the maturation and modernization of the Tamil film industry discussed above, just as they fit neatly with *Thamizh Padam*'s makers' own narrative of triumphing against the odds (itself perhaps elicited by the interview frame of some of my research). But rather than rehash these stories, I'd like to draw attention elsewhere: to a particular politics *for* the image that underwrote *Thamizh Padam*'s politics *of* the image, one based on kinship ties, political muscle, and the counter-threat of physical violence and state force.

Consider how Sashikanth, an elite corporate architect, got into films. Central to Sashikanth's story is that his father is a politician, at the time, a member of the legislative assembly from the Dravida Munnetra Kazhagam (DMK) political party.[48] Around the same time that Sashikanth decided to get into film production and "take on the industry," so too did his close friends Dayanidhi Alagiri (forming Cloud 9 Movies) and Udhayanidhi Stalin (forming Red Giant Movies), two grandsons of *Kalaiñar* (the Artist) M. Karunanidhi (1924–2018), then chief minister of the state and leader of the DMK, a political party that rose to prominence, in part, through its connection (first, positive, and later, antipathetic) with M.G. Ramachandran, the first mass hero to move from cinema to Secretariat (see Introduction). Sashikanth (2011) put it to me this way:

> So, what happened was that from being a complete outsider in the industry I was suddenly associated with people who were suddenly looked upon as the big guys in the industry … And we wanted Cloud 9 to back the movie because we were facing political issues, political not in terms of politicians, but in terms of the industry guy(s) trying to politicize *Thamizh Padam* (because it was a spoof).

In other words, Cloud 9 was able to leverage its kinship connections to powerful politicians to become "big guys in the industry," a fact that allowed Sashikanth to deal with the internal "political issues" of the film industry. Amudhan (2014) said regarding their difficulties with making the film: "The thing that made it happen was that the production house was a big political entity at that time … So that kind of calmed the fears." Or as K. Chandru (2010), one of the film"s screenwriters noted to me, the implicit backing of the DMK allowed them to be more "bold" in what they wrote.

The consensus, in fact, among the industry persons with whom I spoke, once I queried them on this issue, was that this film was possible *only because* of the fact that the son of the notorious politician/rowdy, Mu. Ka. Alagiri – Karunanidhi's son, who at the time had an iron grip on the southern city of Madurai and held a cabinet position in the central government – was producing the film. As one actor opined in Tamil (with the caveat that he didn't want his frank speech about politics to be associated with him), 'with that kind of political support, there wouldn't be any kinds of problems. With Alagiri behind his son, anyone who was upset with the film would just have to shut their mouths and their assholes and sit quietly' (*sūttaiyum vāyaiyum pottīṭu tān pōkaṇum*). This backing involved not simply the threat of intimidation. Indeed, with its producer's family in a position of influence vis-à-vis the police and other non-state agents, *Thamizh Padam* didn't have to contend with one of the main impediments to producer and distributor's profits: piracy.[49]

During this same time, Karunanidhi's grand-nephews and Dayanidhi Alagiri's cousins, Kalanithi and Dayanidhi Maran, were also increasingly monopolizing film production and distribution, integrating it into their expansive media empire, which included Sun Television and Kalaignar TV, among a number of major newspapers and radio stations. As one film producer pointed out to me, at the time of our interview (late July 2010) all of the box office hits of 2009–10 with the exception of one, *Kalavani* (2010, dir. A. Sargunam), were produced or distributed by family members of the DMK party's higher echelon. And that success, he noted, was precisely because of their ability to both avail free publicity and to easily sell the television rights of their films through family-controlled media. One of the keys to the success of *Thamizh Padam*, according to Sashikanth (2011), was that it had a well-thought-out and clever marketing campaign that was able to generate a lot of buzz (Dhananjayan 2011, 2:321). While the content of the campaign may have been clever, the ability to continually blast the public with it at virtually no cost was surely important as well.

Conclusion

If image politics concern the contestation, but also distribution, of images and what they represent (and the entailments therein), they also critically involve not just *what* is imaged but what *is* an image, what it can be or become (or should not be or become); such a politics involves a redistribution and transformation, as Jacques Rancière (2007, 2009) has put it, of the sensible and intelligible, a particular "regime of imageness."[50] Such redistributions and transformations are mediated by and afford particular political projects. Yet such projects do not simply aim to open up new spectatorial sensibilities or intelligibilities or textual aesthetics, as Rancière suggests, but also, as I have argued across these chapters, to actualize and institutionalize new modes of the being of images.

Such projects take place through both a politics *of* and a politics *for* images. In my usage, this distinction is meant to highlight the fact that political questions surrounding film images are not confined to questions about representational content or form – who or what is represented onscreen or not, how images bolster particular offscreen structures of power and privilege, and so on – but also the pragmatic claims that are made for and against images, the multiple kinds of complex semiotic work that are necessary for images to exist – to be conceived, made, circulated, exhibited, experienced, interpreted, written about and theorized, and so on. Such work takes place on and off the screen – indeed, as is evident in *Thamizh Padam*, the politics of its images are claims for and against other kinds of images.

This distinction is also meant to highlight the dynamic relationship between these two dimensions of cinematic semiosis, the non-synthesizing, mutually constituting dialectical relationship between them; the way in which one gives rise to the other, and vice versa: how claims and contestations for and against images give rise to images, images that make claims for other images (and themselves) but also for particular modes of production, political economies, and social relationalities that themselves are the matrix for further contestations and claims by, on, and for images. This intertwined relation between the ontological politics of and for the image is particularly clear in parody; in *Thamizh Padam*, as we've seen, its parodic texture (its mockery of the populist mass hero and his "worship," its chronopolitics, and so on) is enabled by particular contestations, exertions of power, modes of social interaction and relationality, and semiotic labour for the image (its kinship-based political backing, its corporatization, publicity stunts, its crony capitalism, male homosociality, among other politics still),[51] with the hope that this politics of/for might, in fact, bring into being a different kind of image and production culture; that it might defang the cine-political performativity and insistent presence of the mass hero and replace it with a representationalist image, one driven by a story and script in the control of directors and their producers.

But if so, this points to a curious performative contradiction and ideological erasure immanent in this parodic image politics. Part of the moral of *Thamizh Padam* was that it – like any and every film – is "just a movie." The film and its stakeholders ask us *not* to see the hero-star's image, and in fact all images, including its own, as what they otherwise are: performatively potent image-acts that affect and presence themselves in the scenes of their appearance. Instead, they ask us to simply see them as mere re-presentations. And yet, the spoof image cannot, by the very fact that it clashes with and partially becomes what it excessively mimes, help but be an image that traverses, and consubstantiates, onscreen and offscreen in precisely the ways that the mass hero's image does.[52] Its double-voiced citationality (Bakhtin 1981; Nakassis 2013a) harnesses an unstable alchemy, the representationality of its parody reversing itself into performativities that it itself would deny and yet needs at one and the same time. What else, after all, is a parodic act if not a performative enunciation that "masquerades" as a representation (compare Austin 1962:4), a "mirror" as C.S. Amudhan put it, whose bite and bark ask us to disregard what it is so that it – or some other, future image – might become otherwise? To take *Thamizh Padam*'s intervention seriously, then, is to inhabit a subjectivity that doesn't, and yet then does, take its images (too) seriously; it is to cut a Gordian knot through an image that, in ironic inversion, traces the lines of the onscreen and offscreen in precisely those ways it says it doesn't and advises against. Could, after all, *Thamizh Padam* simply be "just a movie," even as it asks us to simply see movies as "just" that?

Such an ontological politics of the image, thus, is not straightforwardly made up of opposing tendencies, of presence/representation, performativity/diegesis-narrative. Rather, each such potential is embedded in and erupts out of and into the other. This internal tension that is a fold upon itself, this volatility is, as I have argued in this book, the general condition of all filmic images. This condition is the very problem space of ontology/being, one that parody lays reflexively bare and (re)produces precisely by its excesses, precisely by staging and diagramming this tension, by making the textual surface of its enunciation this unstable terrain.

Yet if, as I have argued, the being of images is internally heterogeneous and dynamic – indeed, is a problem space of multiple claims on and for images – it is also because the mutual relationship between the politics of and for images, through which modes of being thicken (or dissolve) and are rendered by-degrees (un)stable, does not unfold in any straightforward or reflective way, if it happens at all. (Any such politics, after all, is always an open-ended gambit, liable to failure.) As we noted, there is an ironic, even contradictory, relationship between the politics of *Thamizh Padam* and (some of) the politics for it. Indeed, there is no reason to think that the liberal politics of *Thamizh Padam* (say, in attempting to shift genre conventions or production processes) need have any implications regarding the crony-capitalist networks of circulation that made the former possible (though there is no in-principle reason why they couldn't).

The question of interest for this chapter is under what conditions could a politics *of* an image itself serve as a politics *for* an image, and vice versa (even if those politics *for* don't necessarily "take")? What is important to ask, thus, is how and when these politics of/for the image come to be linked to each other (and what kinds of projects aim to and do accomplish such linkage), sutured together in and as the image itself, in and as its mode of production, social relations, and being – in the case of *Thamizh Padam* so as to shut up the assholes while putting the rest of us in stitches.

Chapter Four

The Politics of the Real

(Today,) nobody wants to see a hero flying.

– Selvaraghavan (2005), director

I don't believe in fantasy. I believe in truth. I think I'll fall in(to) truth. *Enakku vantu varavē illai nnā* [And if it stops coming to me] I won't make films … *Oru nāḷ-le maṟaiñciṭuvēn nān* [I'll just disappear one day].

– Balaji Sakthivel (2008), director

Yatārttam enṟāl enna?, evaruṭaiya pārvaiyil ivai etārttam? … etārttattaic citta-rikkiṟēn enṟu colvatu cātiya etārttattai appaṭiyē tirumpa colvatu enṟākiviṭātā? Attakaiya etārttappaṭaṅkaḷ cātiyin camūka uṇmaiyai pēcukiṟatā? Allatu kaṭṭamai-kkiṟatā? [What is reality, and from whose point of view? … In saying, "I am representing reality" isn't one simply reiterating a caste reality? Do such realist films really speak the social truth of caste? Or do they instead construct it?]

– Stalin Rajangam, *Tamil Cinimā*, 2016

Introduction

Each chapter of *Onscreen/Offscreen* has taken up some aspect of the ontological politics of the Tamil film image, focusing on how the image is both the object and site (or medium, we might say) of contestation about what an image *is, could,* or *should be.* Evinced in these cases are tensions between the potentialities of performativity and representationality, between presentist hero and realist story, actors and directors and producers, animators and authors and principals. But if in the previous chapters I explored how realism – or more specifically, *representational realism* (distinct from the analytic term *sociological realism* discussed in previous chapters) – lurked in and erupted out of filmic images dominated by some other aesthetics and pragmatics (be it of the spectacular mass hero, his parodic satire, or the "titillating" heroine/ item dancer), in this chapter I turn to those Tamil image-texts that reflexively frame themselves and are framed by their makers and viewers *as* 'realist' (*etārttam*), 'true' (*uṇmai*), or 'natural' (*iyalpu*).[1] I focus, in particular, on two films: *Kaadhal* (2004, dir. Balaji Sakthivel), a small-budget film that became an unexpected box office hit in a period of crisis for the Tamil film industry, and *Subramaniyapuram* (2008, dir. Sasikumar), a critically acclaimed and popular film noted for its period realism and gritty violence. I am particularly interested in how performative effects of various sorts emerge within and through such realist films, often in unanticipated ways. In the chapter's conclusion, I mobilize these materials to return once more to André Bazin as an uncanny theorist of the Tamil film image. Affirming Bazin's account of realism as characterized by a respect for the film image's being (Morgan 2006), I suggest that realist image-texts such as *Kaadhal* do indeed reflexively orient themselves to the nature of images. Yet that nature is not fundamentally, as Bazin might suggest, a function of the medium's capacity to embalm its object, reveal the intrinsic ambiguity and openness of the world, present its facticity, enable the spectator's freedom, or satisfy their desire to (existentially) tame time and inscribe their (historical) participation in it (see Chapter 1). Rather, as I have argued, it is, and is a function of, those ontological politics that images bear and are constituted by (which may comprise the above, but need not). Realist image-texts register and orient themselves to – indeed, intervene in and exemplify – this ontological politics (though they are not the only ones); they take a stance towards it, if always from a particular ideological position, in a particular way, and cloaked in a particular aesthetic style. In this sense, realist films like *Kaadhal* do indeed respect the being of the image, not because of their capacity to enable an ethical openness to the pregiven ambiguity of the world that they (re-)presence but because of their capacity to *ambiguate* the world in which they intervene, to render that world – and in the process, its images – polyphonic and unfinalized/ unfinalizable (Bakhtin 1984[1963]:58–9).[2]

Questions of Realism

As noted in the book's Introduction and in Chapter 1, questions of representational realism are foundational to film studies.[3] They are also central to the global history of cinema, given both the early framing and circulation of cinematic technologies as indexical record and spectacular simulacrum of the real (Rosen 2001; Doane 2002; Bhrugubanda 2018) and as an aesthetic style within classed and raced hierarchies of value. Such questions are as contentious and slippery as they are foundational and central, perhaps accounting for the topic's continued interest or, as Joel Snyder (1980) suggests with regards to photography, its place in an axiological structure of thinking about images in Western discourse.

Part of the complexity of the topic is that both the extensions (instances of) and intensions (predicable properties) of the term *realism* and its cognates (in Tamil, *etārttavātam*) are highly variable (Jakobson 1971[1921]; Snyder 1980; Dickey 2009), differing by historical period, genre and mode of production, sociologically and institutionally, by medium and across media cultures. What counts and is describable as "realism" is not the same in literature as in cinema; nor is it the same within cinema in the early twentieth century as in the early twenty-first century. Nor is the realism of a "classical" Hollywood film the same as the realism of an art house Indie film or a Tamil "experimental" or "commercial" film. Similarly, what film critics or directors take to be realism is not the same as what the general public (whatever that might mean) construes as realism, just as critics, directors, audience members, or academics do not agree among themselves – nor may they, individually, from moment to moment, or even in a single moment. *Realism* bears the properties of what is called within linguistics a *shifter* (Jespersen 1922:123–4; Jakobson 1990[1957]; Silverstein 1976; Gal 2002), a term whose referent shifts and slips across contexts of occurrence.

This shiftiness has not stopped anyone, of course, from offering accounts for what realism *is*. If anything, it has abetted it. But rather than trying to pin down the term and answer the question, What is realism?, I want to focus on this very question – and the messy diversity of answers to it – as a problem space to be interrogated as such (Mitchell 1986, 1994). What would happen if we broached realism, thus, not simply as a property of film form or of the filmic apparatus/medium but as an open, empirical question? To do this is not simply to ask after the "context" – historical or cultural – of something called realism (or of particular so-typified realist texts) in order to chart its variations and differences (though that too is necessary). Rather, it is to ask *how* the very posing of the question by stakeholders in the image (its critics, theorists, makers, audiences, distributors, exhibitors, and so on) – and, critically, their contestations over that question – does work, socially, politically, and aesthetically. One can offer an adequate account of realism and what it is, I argue, only by taking this approach; for, if realism "is" anything, it is precisely as a function of this shifting, uneven space of contestation that plays out on and off the screen. In short, realism is the site of an ontological politics: of what is real; of what an image is, or should be, such that it could characterize that reality; and of the quality of that characterization.

The Register of Realism

To treat realism as an empirical object and a site of ontological politics is to treat it as both perspectival and multiple (Jakobson 1971[1921]) – and thus subject to contestation – and conventional (Aumont et al. 1992[1983]:109) – and thus subject to stabilization and transformation; in other words, both relative to some situated positionality yet also tenuously normalized (and seemingly objective) *across* a set of positions within some social domain.

To capture this dynamic, it is productive to think of realism as a kind of *register* (Silverstein 2003a; Agha 2007a), along the lines of how linguistic anthropologists have analysed speech registers – specifically, as *an enregistered style of representation*. The concept of register is useful for thinking about realism in cinema because, first, it analytically links together realism as a formal, filmic style and realism as an ideology, or metafilmic stance; and second, because the concept highlights how such linkages are the outcome of historical processes of conventionalization (or *enregisterment*) that are open-ended and subject to contestation and transformation in and by the events in which they are drawn.

As discussed by linguistic anthropologists, a speech register is a repertoire of linguistic forms united by their common non-referential indexical values, often characterized by speakers as "different ways of saying the same thing." For example, "legalese," youth "slang," thieves' "cant," and the like denote repertoires of speech forms that in their use contrastively invoke and enact particular stereotyped contexts of use, kinds of speakers and their characterological qualities, and cultural values, among other things, and in so doing, point to (or typify) their own contexts of use and users vis-à-vis those very stereotypes.[4]

As Asif Agha (2007a, 2011, 2017) has shown, all register phenomena – no matter what their modality or medium (they need not be linguistic) – are duplex in this way. A register is the historically structured conjunction of (1) a set of signs that are contrastively assembled (vis-à-vis other such assemblages) by their conventionalized, stereotypic indexical values relative to (2) some ideology that construes the social indexicality of such signs, indeed, that serves as a metasemiotic model or frame

(Goffman 1974:68–9, 82) regimenting their contextualized use, construal, and pragmatic values.

Realism, from this perspective, is a repertoire of film forms (though always including other non-filmic elements as well, insofar as all registers bleed across media) linked together by a semiotic ideology (or set of ideologies) that construes and typifies such repertoire forms with a set of convergent, and conventionalized, non-referential indexical values or, what we might call, *metafilmic stereotypes*. As noted above, these are historically and culturally variable, though in general, realist texts as we find them indexically presuppose a referentialist ideology of some sort or another, reflexively stipulating a *referential-denotational* (or truth-functional) fidelity between filmic text and reality, sign and object. (Contrast this with the sociological realism of the actor, where the semiotic ground is not between sign and object but between sign and animator; and where the issue isn't "truth" but "appropriateness.") As claims on the real (Bucholtz and Hall 2005; Aumont et al. 1992[1983]:114), however, realist texts implicate an ontological politics whose pragmatics and aesthetics always outstrip questions of reference or denotation, whatever form this realism takes (metaphysical, perceptual, psychological, and so on).[5] That such texts often efface this fact and direct our attention to their putative referential fidelity is, of course, part of the pragmatics of such claims. Indeed, as Nelson Goodman (1976) argued, in-principle grounds to judge such referential relationships (namely, "fidelity" to the real, truth-functionality) are necessarily problematical, and thus political, since "reality" itself isn't singular at any one time, just as our impressions of what feels realistic (including so-called natural perception) are always already historically and culturally conditioned (see also Metz 1991[1971]:111).[6] Both reality and our sense and image of it, thus, are the outcome of, among other things, processes of semiotic mediation and conventionalization.

This, of course, is not to say that realisms are not referential or even true in some way in some cases; rather, to the extent that they are so is the outcome of a particular kind of semiotic process, of a gambit played by realist texts themselves. Indeed, the basic presupposition of such texts and the discourses that typify them(selves) as "realist" is that they are to be evaluated as – and, indeed, *are* – true, real, authentic, believable, the thing itself, and so on.

What the concept of register brings to this discussion is that by reflexively indexing (a stance to) their own semiotic ground (their "first-order" indexicality, as it were), realist signs also thereby come to be ideologically associated (or enregistered) with "second-order" indexical values (Silverstein 2003a). Such second-order indexicalities run orthogonally to, and typify and construe, the first-order values that they build upon and from which they emerge. Notice, for example, how realist film styles inevitably also invoke – as a function of their referentialist stance – socio-historically particular, stereotyped kinds of personhood in particular, stereotyped kinds of relationality vis-à-vis the image-text: for example, a particular kind of (auteur-)director engaged in a particular mode of (often non-"commercial") production (Bordwell 2009[1979]), a particular kind of (liberal) spectator in a particular mode of (silent) reception, with all the characterological qualities implied therein. They also come to be stereotypically associated with particular types of content, themes, locales (Aumont et al. 1992[1983]:108) – in the Tamil case, "serious" and tragic subject matter, often centring on love and sexuality, and caste and class inequality in rural settings – as well as particular modes of exhibition ("art" house cinemas, film festivals; in India, multiplexes and film clubs), particular political programs or even political parties (think, for example, of state-sanctioned Soviet social realism); and so on and so forth. Relative to the (film text–focused) referentialist ideologies that animate registers of realism, such (context-anchored/projecting) indexical values are typically considered extraneous to what constitutes the register (the referential indexicality of the film text) and are often erased from ideological reflection (instead, technique and aesthetic form are often privileged and naturalized as the basis of what "counts as" realist). Socially, however, such non-referential indexicalities are perhaps the most important part of realisms and are often criterial to what counts as realist. Recall, for example, Bazin's own refusal of certain kinds of content and contexts – such as pornography, executions, authoritarian propaganda – as constituting "bad" realism (see Chapter 1).

As Bazin's refusal indicates, the typification and framing of some text as realist always proceeds contrastively. Realisms, like all registers, are *relational* (Gal 2018; Gal and Irvine 2019). Something is realist relative to something else (Jakobson 1971[1921]; Goodman 1976:37; Carroll 1988:142; Aumont et al. 1992[1983]:116–17; Mitchell 1994:345–70; Nakassis 2009); in the Tamil case discussed further below, realism is most obviously relative to non-realist "commercial" cinema and, in particular, to its mass heroes. This relativity means that realism, as with all registers, is not an autonomous style (plus some ideologically mediated stereotypes). Rather, it is the structuring of a number of contrastive styles (and with them, contrastive figures of personhood, types of content/themes, modes of production, distribution and exhibition circuits, production formats and participant frameworks, and so on).[7] When we contemplate realism or any other such style, we tend to focus on *part* of that contrast set rather than the diagrammatic whole. In this reduction is a particular ideological operation that narrows our attention to realism *as if* it could be treated on its own terms as a sui generis phenomenon independent of other aesthetic styles, despite the empirical observation that realisms are patently not so. And while this reduction is typical of all registers, it is particularly acute with realisms (contra, for example, deeply and explicitly dialogic styles such as parody; see Chapter 3), given that their operative claim is often that they serve as a representational mirror and thus are determined by their objects in some relatively immediated or direct way, irrespective of other (conventional) styles.

Such contrast relations do not only hold across styles or texts, however. They are also internal to them. As Mikhail Bakhtin (1981) observed about the heteroglossia of everyday life and the polyphony of literature (and, in particular, realism in the novel), registers of language interpenetrate and interanimate each other and, in doing so, enter into unstable and potentially transformative relations with each other. Registers – of language or of cinema – live (and die) through the signs whose indexical values they mediate (as we saw through our discussion of caricature and satire in the last chapter). As indexical signs, however, the elements of a register's repertoire do not signify outside of any particular situation. They are always contextualized in particular ways in particular events of entextualization, relative to any number of other indexical signs, indeed, cheek and jowl with other enregistered styles as well as with non-cinematic genres and chronotopes (or genred timespaces) of everyday life.[8] This contextualization is precisely why the default normative values of any enregistered sign, including realist ones, are always recontextualizable in by-degrees tropic ways with variable pragmatic effects. Such recontextualizations may amplify or undermine the enregistered values of particular signs – such as those of a realist style or those of the mass hero; or those associated with particular caste groups or those that would contest them – or, as we have seen in this book and explore more in this chapter, do *both*.

Another way of saying this is that register phenomena, including realism, are *scalar phenomena*, worked out at various scales, from media to genres, from whole films down to fractions or aspects of them (dialogue, mise en scène, acting style, camera movement, editing style, narrative structure, and so on). Not all the elements of some stretch of a "realist" film text (shots, scenes, and the like) need be construed *as* realist. And while film texts are often typified (that is, entextualized) in an all or nothing way, from the point of view of the *texture* of an image-text, realism is a gradable phenomenon. There can be more or less of it at different moments in a text, or across texts. Similarly, the scale and textual locus of realism (dialogue, camera work, mise en scène, editing, narrative structure, and so on) may shift across historical periods.[9]

Take, for example, Christopher Ball's (2017) discussion of lens flare as an enregistered index of realist co-presence with the profilmic. Lens flare occurs when light is scattered ("flared") in a lens or camera, either by internal reflection or by imperfections in the lens, creating a streak or patch of bright light in the image. Lens flare, like any other so-enregistered realist sign, can be deployed in image-texts that are patently not realist – that is, co-occur with signs that do not index, or partake of, the real – such as digitally animated sequences (where no lenses are used), as in *The Lego Movie* (2014, dirs. Chris Miller, Phil Lord), which Ball discusses, just as they can become detached from their realist origins and re-enregistered in new ways (as lens flare had, in Hollywood for a time, come to stand as an indexical sign of J.J. Abrams's cinematographic style). Similarly, commercial cinema in many film industries, including "classical" Hollywood but also commercial Tamil film, utilize realist techniques, such as continuity editing, spatially coherent mise en scène, denotationally coherent emplotment, and so on, even as such elements are set alongside or embedded within non-realist elements, such as parallel star-texts (for example, of a mass hero; Chapter 1), song sequences (Chapter 2), or an epistolary letter addressed to the audience (see below). This is why realist texts are not simply shifty and relative, but gradable and characterized by relative densities, as well as by breaks and disjunctures vis-à-vis other differently enregistered indexicalities (of the not quite real, or differently real). Every such break or disjuncture is a dynamic moment of potential change and transformation or reiteration and reproduction of the register in question, precisely because the process of enregisterment, and the social life of a register, unfolds through such events of (co-)textual juxtaposition.

With this discussion in mind, in what follows I pursue the following questions: What is the ontological politics of the image born by the ongoing, dynamic enregisterment of realism circa the mid-to-late 2000s in Tamil Nadu, during which time I was conducting ethnographic fieldwork? In what ways has the enregisterment of realism and its others also entailed – that is, consisted in and created – ontological contestations of the image?[10] And in what ways do the precipitates of these processes – recognizable, named styles and the image-texts they typify – also harbour, by necessity, a panoply of ontic potentials? How do realist texts bear, at one and the same time, those modes of being of the image and styles of representation and performativity that they would bracket, negate, and even deny to exist in the name of the real? As we'll see, realist texts exacerbate even as they attempt to mediate tensions between presence and representation, animation, authorship, and responsibility. This is the uneasy terrain that I have explored throughout *Onscreen/Offscreen*. In such image-texts, representation and performativity intertwine with and repulse each other, sitting in uneasy configurations on and off the screen.

Enregistering Realism in Tamil Cinema

As noted in the Introduction, the emergence of a discourse about realism in South India is coterminous with sound cinema, with the emergence of a "Tamil" cinema, the consolidation of a Tamil people, and, later, the figure of the mass hero who would represent the latter through the former. As we saw, realism as an aesthetic style at this moment was articulated in and by a reticulated diagram of metafilmic contrasts (Table 4.1): between the figure of the excited, illiberal subaltern viewer (as sourced from popular theatre; Hughes 1996, 2018; Dickey 2009; Mazzarella 2013) and the calm elite aesthete (and reluctant viewer of cinema);[11] the non-modern and the modern; the theatrical and the cinematic (modern cinema repeatedly being called on to sever itself from its theatrical pasts); the aural and the visual (first, in the lament that Tamil films had too many songs, and later on, too much theatrical oratorical dialogue); the "mythological" and the "social" (the former genre depicting mythic pasts, the latter contemporary society); as well as the fractally analogic distinction between Indian (read: less realist, less modern, less cinematic, less visual) cinema and Western (read: more realist, more modern, more visual) cinema (see Metz 1974[1971]:38, 40–1).[12]

This ideological discourse has had a remarkable longevity, easily elicited from filmmakers as well as from film viewers in my own ethnographic research in the 2000s (see, for example, discussion in Chapters 1 and 2). While realism as an aesthetic style (that is, repertoire) has certainly changed since the 1930s, this enregistered set of stereotyped contrasts – realist films as "different" from "commercial" films, as "class" cinema and not "mass" cinema, as "serious" and not "escapist," as sophisticated (and upper-class) and not vulgar (and lower-class), as properly cinematic and not excessively theatrical, and so on – has persisted with remarkable continuity.

In the 1950s and 1960s, this assemblage was swept up into a transformed star system with the rise of the dominant stars of their generation:

Table 4.1. The ideological diagram of realism in Tamil cinema: Some metafilmic stereotypes

Realism	"Cinema"
Cinematic, visual	Theatrical, aural
"Social" genre (present, secular)	"Mythological" genre (non-present, divine)
Modern	Folk, pre-modern
Art	Commercial
"Class" (subtle acting, sophisticated directing)	"Mass" (vulgar heroism, titillating spectacle)
Serious	Escapist
Western	Indian
Interpellating a calm, elite aesthete	Patronized by an excited, subaltern crowd

the mass hero M.G. Ramachandran (or MGR) and the thespian extraordinaire, Sivaji Ganesan, an ideological division of star labour that fractally recursed these enregistered contrasts (namely, the "mass" and "class" films in which they acted; compare Krishnan 2009:222; Srinivas 2009:78). By the mid-1970s, this star system began to wane, and with its passing, the once-monumental studios of Madras collapsed.[13] This period also saw the adoption of new technology (in particular the lighter Arriflex 35-2c camera that allowed directors to do without the infrastructure of the studios and shoot outdoors with relative ease) and the graduation of the first generation of film-school students who cut their teeth on global realist and art cinemas outside of the industry establishment.[14] It was also a time, as noted in the Introduction, of increasing public cynicism towards the modernist dreams of both Nehruvian nationalism (any remaining idealism eroded by the autocratic declaration of National Emergency by Indira Gandhi in 1975) and Dravidianist cine-politics (Kurai 2012; K. Hariharan 2013), which appeared less and less a social movement of uplift and instead an empty, kleptocratic shell of its former revolutionary self. In this moment, Tamil cinema turned away from its known hero-driven formulas towards new, experimental modes and styles of representation.

The films that emerged into prominence at this time were marked as "different" from both the "mass" and the (then-perceived-as-realist) "class" films of the previous decade by their location shooting, minimal lighting with high-intensity key lights and soft filler lights (rather than the studio-style three-point lighting; Eswaran Pillai 2012:83), long takes and improvisation in performance, a preference for visual methods of narration and laconic dialogues in colloquial dialectal speech (rather than the use of elaborate and flowery, high-register, and caste-neutralized dialogue to convey narrative), an influx of "new faces" (rather than established heroes), narratives that played down the hero function and/or featured "anti-heroes," and a penchant for rural ("nativity") settings (rather than urban milieus) replete with signs of cultural and pastoral authenticity (rather than elite modernity), including, as we see below, explicit markers of, and at times valorization of, particular "dominant" non-Brahmin castes linked to the southern regions of the state (not coincidentally, the ones from which a number of key directors of this moment hailed).[15] It was this period, the reader will recall from Chapter 3, that C.S. Amudhan, the director of the hero-spoofing film *Thamizh Padam* (2010), cited as the "golden era" of Tamil cinema, one driven by auteur-directors – such as K. Balachander (1930–2014), Balu Mahendra (1939–2014), Mahendran (1939–2019), and Bharathiraja (b. 1941) – and their (relatively) realist stories.

In this flash of commercially successful "experimental" films arose two new stars, Rajinikanth (b. 1950) and Kamal Haasan (b. 1954). By the 1980s and 1990s, these two actors came to dominate the Tamil industry and were seen as taking on the mantle – and replicating the classed (and casted) distinctions (compare Krishnan 2009:222) – that united and distinguished MGR and Sivaji Ganesan, respectively. While both began as character actors in realist, small-budget "nativity" films of the late 1970s, by the 1990s Rajinikanth's image had "trapped" him as *the* populist, cine-political hero of the "masses," while Kamal Haasan came to be seen as the consummate "class" actor.[16]

By the turn of the twenty-first century, cracks began to show in this configuration. In 1999, at the apotheosis of his popularity, Rajinikanth's blockbuster *Padaiyappa* (dir. K.S. Ravikumar), a record-setting hit that was rife with political intimations, was released (Nakassis 2017, 2019). Rajini's next film, *Baba* (2002, dir. Suresh Krissna), written and produced by the star himself, was even more politically explicit, culminating in an open-ended last scene that implied that Rajinikanth was ready to move directly from the screen into electoral politics.[17] The film was a stunning flop. Rajini did not enter politics (see the book's Conclusions). And he didn't make another film until 2005's *Chandiramukhi* (dir. P. Vasu), a comeback film after a significant gap of three years (particularly long if one considers that Rajinikanth released nearly sixty Tamil films in the 1980s, an average of five or six per year, and sixteen films in the 1990s, an average of one or two per year).

With *Baba*'s failure, technical advances requiring larger budgets and longer shooting schedules (and thus increased financial risk), increasing competition with television, home-viewing, and piracy (first on VHS then on VCD and DVD), and a shift in audience demographics (from "family" audiences to young men; see Chapter 2), the early 2000s appeared to many to be a crisis moment and, hence, a moment of transformation. Producers, many of them new to the industry, began financing small-budget films made by a fresh generation of filmmakers, technicians, and actors. These directors, raised on the realist cinema of the late 1970s – some of whom (for example, Bala, Ameer, Vetrimaaran, Selvaraghavan, Mysskin, Venkat Prabhu) were former assistants or kin of the directors of that period (Balu Mahendra, K. Balachander, Kasturi Raja, Gangai Amaran) – were hailed as a "new wave" of Tamil cinema.

One prominent trend in this new wave was a return to the "nativity" themes of the 1970s and 1980s, a return that was itself an antipathetic turn away from the increasingly sclerotic yet still hegemonic Dravidian discourse on Tamil identity (Leonard 2015) and the glossy, MTV-style and urban, national (right-wing) focus of the big-budget directors of the 1990s (such as Mani Ratnam and S. Shankar), whose films also reflected their own (upper-class and upper-caste) dissatisfaction with the Dravidianist dispensation (Chakravarthy 2018). In addition to deploying long-standing enregistered signs of realism and "nativity" – such as the use of non-professional actors, continuity editing, avoidance of special effects, handheld cameras, long takes in deep focus, shaky camerawork, natural lighting, outdoor locations, a focus on the details of the everyday, colloquial laconic dialogue, coherent and plausible narratives (with a lack of comedy "tracks" and narratively integrated song sequences) – such films were characterized by deeply negative ("nihilistic" and "Byronic," as cinematographer-director Rajiv Menon [2009] put it to me) and conflicted, yet otherwise decidedly average, male protagonists in tragic stories that featured increasingly explicit representations of caste, violence, and sexuality (Eswaran Pillai 2015:272–88; Eswaran 2021). By the end of the 2000s, one commentator derisively noted that the narrowing (re)enregisterment of realism in Tamil cinema had resulted in a "formulaic realism" (Gopinath n.d.-a; compare Aumont et al. 1992[1983]:114), one now predictably centred on the "reality" of violent, rural male youth, cynical and disillusioned with the utopias of Tamil nationalism and the post-liberalization Indian nation.

In that moment of uncertainty in the early 2000s, however, what struck many commentators as notable – even "unprecedented" (Krishnan 2008:139; Kurai 2012) – was the way in which realist films, such as *Kaadhal* (2004, dir. Balaji Sakthivel), *Autograph* (2004, dir. Cheran), and

7/G Rainbow Colony (2004, dir. Selvaraghavan), surpassed at the box office the hero-oriented films alongside which they were released. Many in and out of the industry deemed the success of these films a watershed moment, heralding the coming of age of Tamil cinema, its turning the corner towards the telos of a modern realist cinema (compare Vasudevan 2010; Ganti 2012:19). More interesting than this claim (after all, it isn't the first time this heralding has been sounded; see Introduction) is the ontological politics it presumes upon. Below, I focus on the film *Kaadhal* to explore this politics.

Kaadhal (Love)

A small-budget film featuring new faces and non-professional actors (*Ananda Vikadan* 2005b), Balaji Sakthivel's (b. 1964) *Kaadhal* (2004) performed unexpectedly well with audiences and critics, running for 150 days in theatres and turning a large profit ("Film News" Anandan 2008).

Kaadhal is a love story that begins in Madurai, a southern city in Tamil Nadu ideologically associated in the public and cinematic imaginary with a pre-modern and violent caste-linked feudal order (Krishnan 2008; Leonard 2015; Damodaran and Gorringe 2017). In the film, Aiswarya, the school-age daughter of a dominant-caste (and implied Thevar) family, and Murugan, a poor, slum-dwelling (and implied Dalit, or formerly "untouchable") mechanic, fall in love.[18] Knowing that Aiswarya's family won't accept the union, they elope to Chennai, where they attempt to establish a household. Consensual love and (pre)marital sexuality, however, are rendered impossible in the film by the "realities" of caste. After much searching, the girl's paternal uncle discovers where the couple (now husband and wife) have moved. He convinces them to come back, promising that all will be well back in Madurai. Aiswarya and Murugan return only to be violently separated, each savagely beaten and cursed with calls from Aiswarya's frenzied family members to kill them both. While questions of caste in the rest of the film run just under its surface, in this wrenching climax sequence they erupt into relative explicitness. Earlier interrogated by Aiswarya's uncle as to his caste – 'Are you a lion [that is, Thevar like us],' he asks, 'or a dog or pig [that is, Dalit]?' – Murugan is later viciously insulted as a 'low-caste dog' (*kīḻ jāti nāy payale*), arrogant enough to touch 'our girl.' As her father repeatedly smashes Murugan's head onto a large rock, Aiswarya cries out that she'll do whatever her father says (Figure 4.1). He demands that she rip off her *tāli* (the necklace tied by the groom around the neck of the bride during the wedding to effectuate marriage) and repudiate

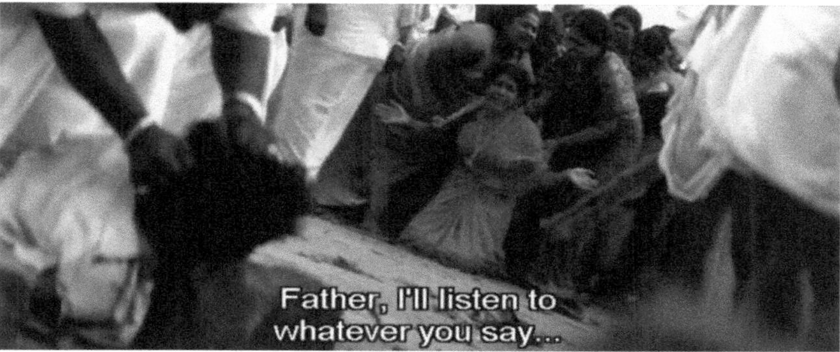

Figure 4.1. Aiswarya yielding to her father as he savagely beats her husband, Murugan, in *Kaadhal* (2004, dir. Balaji Sakthivel)

Figure 4.2. Denouement of *Kaadhal*: Aiswarya (right) recognizing a crazy beggar, her ex-husband Murugan (left)

the union. As her father is about to crush Murugan's head with a large stone, she acquiesces.

Years later, in the neighbouring town of Dindigul, we see Aiswarya riding on the back of a motorcycle with her new husband (of the same caste, it is implied) and a small child. At an intersection, she looks over and sees a crazy beggar: Murugan (Figure 4.2).

She recognizes the tattoo of her name on his chest and her wedding *tāli*, filthy and wrapped around his fist. She faints. Awakens in a hospital, crying. She walks out as her husband sleeps at the foot of the bed. Wildly yelling Murugan's name in the street, she looks for him. She finds him, wandering aimlessly. She falls to the ground, wailing and hitting her head in lament: 'I made a mistake, I thought you'd forget about me; I lost you to protect you; you've become crazy because of my mistake! I'll never leave you again!' (Figure 4.3 – left). Murugan

Figure 4.3. Denouement of *Kaadhal*, continued: Aiswarya falling at Murugan's feet (left), as her husband finds her in the street (right)

doesn't recognize her. Behind her, the husband has come outside with their baby (Figure 4.3 – right).

Aiswarya hears the baby and cries out, recognizing the irreversibility of her fate. The stoic husband betrays no anger. He walks towards her and pats the baby on the back, pointing to it, that it needs her. He hands the baby to her, then softly touches her head. He turns to Murugan and brings him around, and with both of them on his arms begins to walk down the street. Rolling text appears over a high-angle full shot (Figure 4.4). It explains that this story was relayed to the director, Balaji Sakthivel, by a man (Aiswarya's second husband in the film) while on a train ride, which Balaji Sakthivel has put into cinematic form for the viewer. This man, it tells us, admitted Murugan to a mental hospital where they are helping him to recover.

Realism's ~~Heroism~~

The public reception of *Kaadhal* lauded it for its 'realism' (*etārttam*) and 'naturalness' (*iyalpu*), focusing not only on those hallmark stylist features of realism discussed above but also on an affective receptivity and phenomenological recognition and identification with the screen that the film prompted (*Ananda Vikadan* 2005a; Kanchibhotia n.d.; Krishnan 2008; Kurai 2012). Viewers described *Kaadhal* and similar films of this period to me as 'showing my life,' 'putting what is in our hearts onscreen,' or 'rewinding our life before our eyes' (*namma* life rewind *paṇṇina mātiri irukku*).

Just as important, and just as often invoked in my conversations, was that *Kaadhal* was "different," a statement that pointed to the film's lack of "heroism" and associated "commercial" elements (spectacular fight sequences, separate comedy "tracks," and the like). A statement like we want "reality" in our films today, as one assistant film director

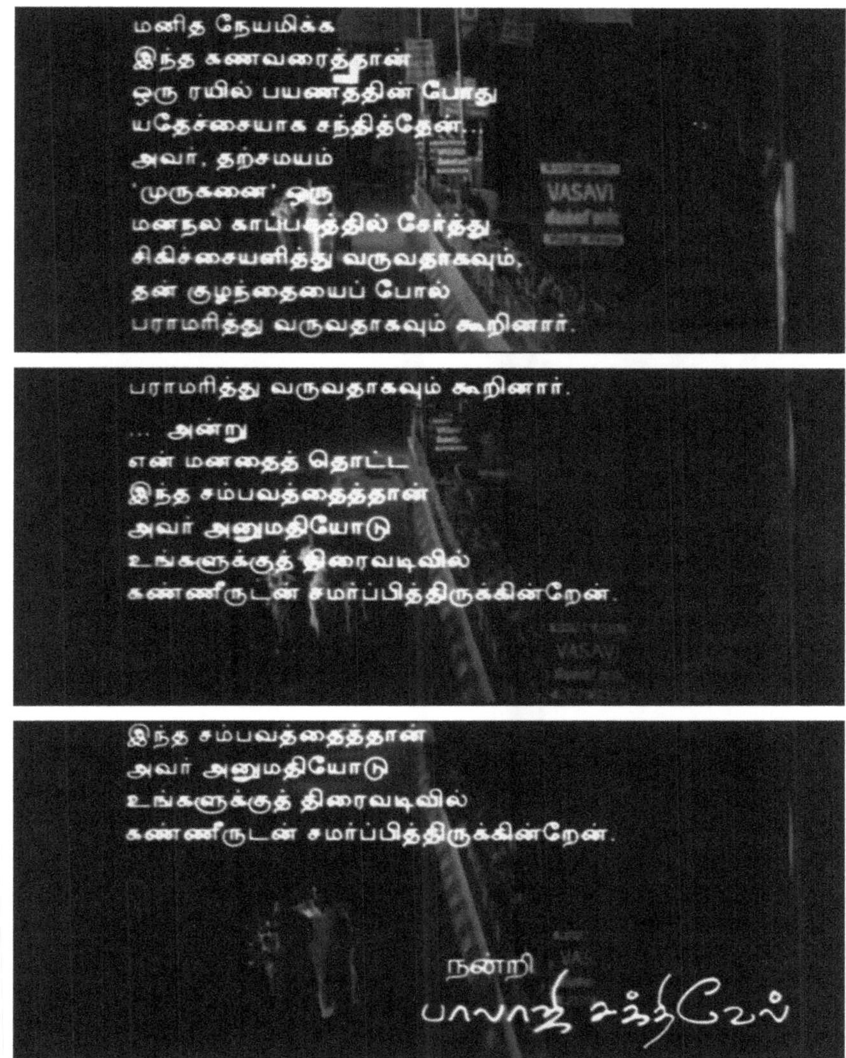

Figure 4.4. The rolling text in the final frames of *Kaadhal*

Figure 4.5. *Kaadhal*'s embedding of the mass-hero film: Rajinikanth's title sequence from *Baashaa* (1995, dir. Suresh Krissna)

said to me in 2009, also meant 'we're tired of heroism in our films,' as one Madurai college student commented to me in 2008. The realism of *Kaadhal* and its popularity signalled, as anthropologist and film critic Rajan Kurai (2012) put it, the 'death of the (mass) hero' (*katānāyakanin maraṇam*) and his presentist, performative image, revealing the extent to which, within this Tamil context, mass heroism and realism are ideologically pitted as diametric opposites. (Of course, as we see in Chapter 1 and the book's Conclusions, it is not an either/or zero-sum game, even if these ontological politics reveal deep and not always resolvable tensions.)

Yet if realism supposedly emerges in the absenting of the hero, this is not simply a replacement of one kind of film or image-type by another on the screen, at the box office, or in audiences' or critics' preferences. Rather, the absenting and negating of the hero and his performative image is an active semiotic operation *within* realist films. In such films, the mass hero appears, not as a presenced personage but as a decentred representation screened within a storied diegesis (Leonard 2015:160).[19] In *Kaadhal*, for example, the lovers escape from Madurai to Chennai on a bus. Cutting from the previous scene – where Aiswarya's mother and aunt are watching the climax of the 1997 Vijay melodrama *Kaadhalukku Mariyadai* (Respect for Love, dir. Faizal) – this scene begins with the iconic 1990s-era title sequence of the "Superstar" Rajinikanth (Figure 4.5).

From this embedded filmic image, the camera cuts to shots of the inside and outside of the bus as we hear Rajini's title sequence continue on in the diegetic space. The image cuts back to the bus's television screen, whose frame and curvature we can clearly discern.[20] On it we see Rajinikanth's "entry" in his super-hit 1995 film *Baashaa* (Nakassis 2017). The camera cuts to a nervous Murugan and then to a recently married couple sitting across the aisle from Aiswarya and Murugan. Intercut with shots from *Baashaa*, we see with Murugan as he observes the groom with his expensive, if gauche, wedding dress and tobacco-stained teeth, ignoring the attempts by his newlywed wife to get his romantic attention. Enraptured by the screen image, the groom brushes her off, telling her to watch the film, smiling at the screen and saying to her (but really to himself): 'Look [-HON.] at how amazing *Talaivar* is [+HON.]!' (*Talaivaru* super-*ā pinṟāru, pāru*!).

Here, the embedded appearance of the auratic mass hero is put under erasure as a contrastive sign of realism. This embedding provides a particular stance for the spectator to take up vis-à-vis the mass hero and his fans. Consider the structure of looks in the scene (Figure 4.6): from a frontal shot of Rajinikanth deictically greeting the audience of *Baashaa* (1), the camera cuts to an image of Murugan casually looking at the television screen and then to his right (2).[21] It then cuts to what Murugan sees: the couple across the row, the groom eagerly looking at the screen while his bride looks at him, the camera's rack focus shifting from the groom to the bride (3). The camera then cuts back to another frontal shot of Rajinikanth from *Baashaa* (4), then to a shot of the groom shifting his gaze from the film to his bride (5), and then back to the film (with the rack focus now shifting from the bride to the groom).[22] The camera cuts back to Murugan (6), with the camera now positioned where the couple is (though it is not their gaze). Murugan evaluates the groom negatively in comparison to himself, brushing his facial hair in an act of machismo as a self-addressed voice-over provides a gloss on his judgmental look: 'I'm so much better than him' (*Nāma evvaḷavō tēvale*). The camera cuts back again to the newlywed couple as the groom dismisses his amorous bride in favour of the pleasures of the mass hero, the rack focus shifting from the bride to the groom as he tells her to watch the television (7); and finally, to a shot where we see both couples, though only Murugan is in focus (8). In this final shot, in contrast to the bridegroom who looks away from his bride and to the screen, Murugan turns away from what he was gazing upon and turns towards his wife-to-be, Aiswarya, and smiles in self-satisfaction.[23]

Here, the poetics of looks figurate a set of contrasts between a vulgar fan who can't see what is really in front of him (his wife) and a critically aware subject (Murugan) who can. This diagram of difference

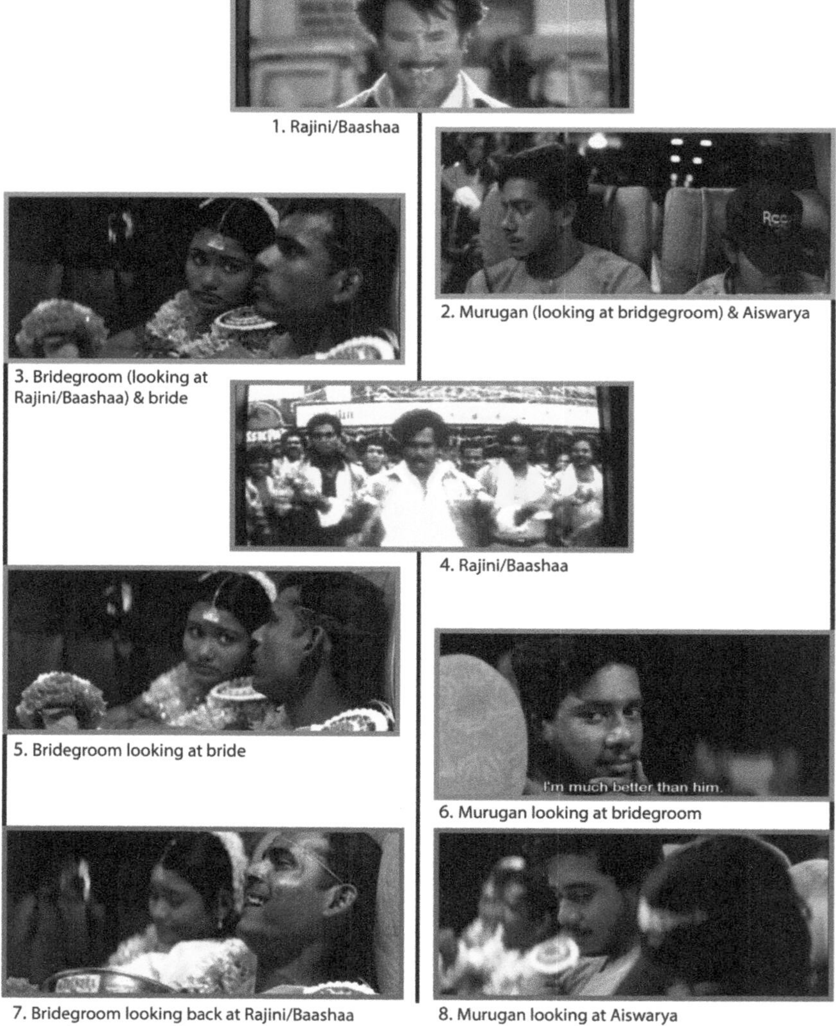

Figure 4.6. Structure of looks in the bus scene in *Kaadhal*, figurating a diagram of contrast; note the parallelism and chiasmus of the first and second phrases ([1–3: Rajini – Murugan/bridegroom] × [4–6: Rajini – bridegroom/Murugan]), followed by the parallel 45-degree-angle shots of the bridegroom (7) and Murugan (8), each seated next to each other but across the bus aisle, flanked by their (out-of-focus) partners

effectively turns the presence of the mass hero into a sign of misrecognition and illusion. A voyeuristic gap is inserted between the exhibitionist mass hero and the audience as a way of opening up the world of the realist diegesis. It is this gap that Murugan inhabits, both as a site for our realist identification and as a metapragmatic commentary on the relationship of commercial Tamil cinema to its putatively credulous audiences (compare Hansen 1991:25–8; Sundar Kaali 2000:186–7), a doubled space that we, as viewers, are invited to inhabit by seeing *with* Murugan.[24] (Indeed, the fan-groom never looks back at Murugan.)

Realism in such moments is not simply contrastive with other enregistered filmic styles; it is internally constituted, in its textuality, by this diagram of contrast. *Kaadhal*'s realism *needs* the mass hero in order to anchor and open up its own representationalist image, just as it needs that illiberal figure of the fan and his mode of spectatorship so as to interpellate its own liberal spectator. Here, the performativity of the image is bracketed by a narrative frame that models our own uptake of the image *as* realist representation; and it does so by diegetically showing us someone (Murugan) seeing someone else (the enraptured fan) take up the image as performative.

This Is a True Story

Yet this hold on the real is tenuous, uncertain. There is something symptomatically anxious about the image of cinema within *Kaadhal*: namely, that its realism always risks devolving into, and being rejected as, fantasy and untruth, of becoming mere "cinema." This operation of bracketing and embedding the performativity of the filmic image so as to open up a space of representationality, thus, does not simply stage its opposite; it dialogically anticipates it and prophylactically attempts to hold it at bay (compare the marginalization of the "item dancer/number" discussed in Chapter 2).

Consider the metafilmic enunciation at the paratextual edges of *Kaadhal* that it is a true story. After the film's requisite thanks, *Kaadhal* opens with Tamil writing on the screen: "*Itu … uṇmaic cambavattai ātāramākakkoṇṭu uruvākkappāṭṭa tiraikkatai*" (This … is a screenplay that was created based on a true incident; Figure 4.7 – left; a frame that is also deployed in *7/G Rainbow Colony*, also discussed below; Figure 4.7 – right).[25]

Yet the claim does not simply open the film; recall, as mentioned above, that *Kaadhal* also ends by framing the film's story as a historical truth (Casetti 1998[1986]:97). Consider this transliteration and translation of the text that rolls on the screen's final image (see Figure 4.4):

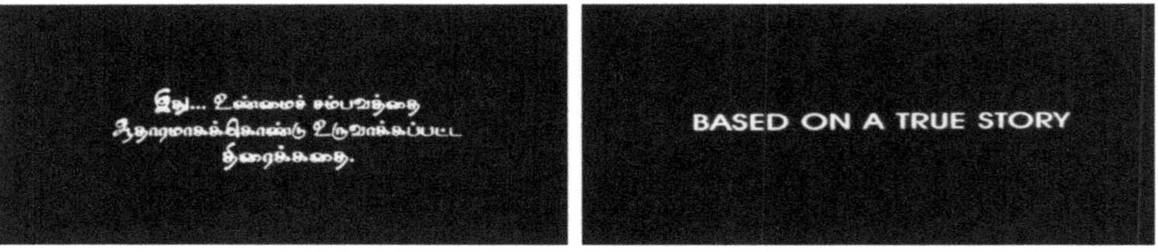

Figure 4.7. Framing the real, "This is a true story": the opening frames of *Kaadhal* (left) and *7/G Rainbow Colony* (right)

Manita nēyamikka
inta kaṇavaraittān
oru rayil payaṇattin pōtu
yatēccaiyāka cantittēn …
[I accidentally met this humanitarian husband on a railway journey …]

Avar, taṟcamayam
"Murukanai" oru mananala kāppakattil cērttu
cikiccaiyaḷittu varuvatākavum,
tan kuḻantaiyaip pōl
parāmarittu varuvatākavum kūrinār.
[He said he had admitted this "Murugan" to a mental hospital for treatment and was looking after him like his own child.]

… anṟu
en manatait toṭṭa
inta campavattaittān
avar anumatiyōṭu
uṅkaḷukkut tiraivaṭivil
kaṇṇīruṭan camarppittirukkinṟēn.
[… I tearfully submit to you in cinematic form, with his permission, this story that touched my heart on that day.]

Nanṟi
<signature:> *Pālāji Caktivēl*
[Thank you, Balaji Sakthivel]

What are the pragmatics of these framing devices? And why does the historical reality of the event need to be asserted, not just once but twice?

In the latter enunciation, the film's putative historical truth is entextualized in a kind of epistolary letter, narrating a "found manuscript"-esque story told to the director on a railway journey. Importantly, in South India, chatting and exchanging stories with strangers on a long train ride (versus, for example, a bus, where people typically watch films or listen to songs) is a recognizable genre of everyday discourse.[26] The cinematic frame of the rolling text, thus, offers up a plausible, already conventionalized narrative frame, authenticating its own evidentiary realism even as it enunciates the narrative realism of what it frames. Here, we see how realism works itself not only through a poetics (or metapragmatic function; Silverstein 1993) of enregistered qualia of the real (reflexively framing/entextualizing the image *as* realist) but also as an explicit metapragmatic discourse that sits on the edges of the film and its diegesis, one that harkens to viewers' own experiences of non-cinematic narratives through the *effet de réel* (Barthes 1986[1968]) of the (reportive) framing device.[27]

What is important, further, is how this discourse intercedes into the film as if to combat and anticipate a spectatorial voice that would typify the film as fantasy, unbelievable, untruth; a voice, as discussed above, that echoes from the origins of cinema in South India, that would utter "cinema" and unreality in one and the same breath (Dickey 2009).[28] Such a frame, thus, is a negation of cinema in the cinematic name of the real (see Prasad 1998:100).

But this framing is doing something more than just asserting the film as a statement of historical fact ("dicentizing" it, as Ball [2014] would put it[29]), inducting the viewer into an interdiscursive chain running from the moment of viewing to the director's encounter at the train station (and the viewer's own similar experiences) to the represented events themselves (in effect rendering contiguous each of these events as part of one and the same timespace; Silverstein 2005a). It is also the recognition of, and prophylactic hedging on, the fact that the edge of *Kaadhal*'s realism runs against an intersecting set of taboos – of caste and female sexuality – whose imaging onscreen risks forms of illiberal, negative performativities offscreen. As I show below, the metapragmatics that would dicentize – indeed, naturalize – *Kaadhal*'s story as historical fact is itself an *argument* about the reality of caste patriarchy. Yet it is one that trembles at the taboos of caste and sexuality that it attempts to represent in their putative bare truth, ultimately representing the reality of one (caste) only by effacing the other (sexuality) in fantasy (or, in *7/G Rainbow Colony*, as we'll see, vice versa). This double strategy, I show, is an attempt to bracket such performativity by reconfiguring the production format of the film text (Goffman 1979): such a framing hedges on the authorship of the film and abdicates the responsibility (or principalship) for its arguments by deferring them to a reality that it simply relays to us 'tearfully in cinematic form.' In doing so, *Kaadhal*'s realism is rendered ambivalent and split by the performativities of the image it confronts yet cannot ultimately control.

Representing Taboo

As discussed in Chapter 2, in *The Ideology of the Hindi Cinema*, M. Madhava Prasad (1998) argues that twentieth-century Hindi cinema, like the Indian nation-state it imaged, engaged in an implicit pact with India's "feudal" patriarchal casteist order, recognizing that order's authority over the family and its representation in exchange for the cinema's own representational sovereignty. The result, evident in Tamil cinema as well, was an implicit prohibition on representations of conjugality and the private beyond the patriarchal family and its "genealogical formation," to borrow K. Ravi Srinivas and Sundar Kaali's (1998:212) phrase. This prohibition was most evident in the long-standing (if unofficial) ban in various Indian cinemas on the hero and heroine kissing onscreen. Such a taboo act, Prasad (1998) argues, would represent/instate a space of modernity, a space of voyeuristic spectatorship, the very subject position from which fictional realism is situated: where we can see the kiss, but the lovers cannot see us, where they (the characters) are alone, unaware of our surveilling gaze (see the looking structure discussed in Figure 4.6). The ban, in effect, demanded that the image remain residually "deictic" (Casetti 1998[1986]), that is, that the screen always face out in an act of exhibition whereby acts represented onscreen are always evaluable as acts in the timespace of their exhibition.

While Prasad gives much consideration to the kiss, here I focus on his off-hand observation that it wasn't just the kiss that was banned in twentieth-century Hindi cinema but also uttering onscreen the word "Shudra" (a term denoting the lowest caste rank in the *varṇa* system; Prasad 1998:93). Why should uttering "Shudra" – or "Dalit" or equivalent terms, in Tamil or other Indian film industries – be banned so as to recognize feudal authority, an authority vested in Brahmin and upper-caste non-Brahmin domination of Dalits and other low-caste groups?[30]

I don't think there is one cause for both bans, though they evince similar semiotic dynamics and intersect at key sites, namely, the upper-caste management of women's sexuality. By generalizing Prasad's focus on the kiss and the proper caste name (Shudra, Dalit) to valorized depictions of female sexual desire and identifiable caste groups (the former pair being fetishized prototypes of the latter), an analysis of *Kaadhal* shows how these taboos interact with each other in a single semiotic economy.[31] Critical here is what Luke Fleming (2011, 2014, 2018) has theorized as the "rigid" performativity instated by taboos; under contexts of taboo and the avoidances they entail, tabooed acts, Fleming observes, come to be invested with a recalcitrant, powerful performativity that is difficult to defease or bracket (as for example, by quoting or otherwise reportively framing them; Nakassis 2013a). This difficulty, as we'll see, is compounded when taboos combine; in the cases we discuss, while each filmic taboo – depicting female desire and identifiable castes – has its own performative force and potential, and either one is representationally manageable, their intersection is qualitatively different and explosive in perlocutionary effect, precisely because one – female sexuality – is foundational to the other – caste (dis)honour (see discussion in Chapter 2).

Critical is that the claims to realism of films like *Kaadhal* and *7/G Rainbow Colony* turn on representing that which others refuse to show as it is, that is, to *reproducing reality* rather than how the "closet society, who say that everything is in order" – as *7/G*'s director, Selvaraghavan (2005), said to me in an interview – would *represent society* as it should be.[32] Yet doing so is difficult – "walking on the knife's edge," as Selvaraghavan put it – precisely because, as we saw in Chapter 2, representations of the real risk being taken as directorial avowals of what is depicted, that is, as performative image-acts themselves. In such moments, realism warps to the performativity of its own semiotic form, variously contorting itself to stave off such performative effects so that its filmic image might be (taken up as) a representation and no more. At stake, then, is the question of how, and when, filmic representations – of caste and sexuality – are taken to be or prevented from becoming performative image-acts. How and to what extent can the representational frame of realism bracket the seemingly unbracketable performativity of the reality of taboo? And when does it fail?

Caste and Sexuality in *Kaadhal*

As a number of film scholars have noted (Srinivas and Sundar Kaali 1998; Sundar Kaali 2000; Rajangam 2016; Leonard 2015; Damodaran and Gorringe 2017; Chakravarthy 2018), the changing landscape of caste politics in the decades leading up to the new millennium shaped and was shaped by Tamil cinema. The 1980s and 1990s were a period of political consolidation and ascension of so-called dominant ("backward") castes, such as Thevars, that had failed to be fully integrated into the Dravidian movement. In this period, such castes both moved into the film industry in increasing numbers and began to wield more formal political power (in electoral positions, the state bureaucracy, the police, and so on). This political power was used as much to promote the social mobility of their own castes as to actively and violently suppress formerly "untouchable" Dalit (or "scheduled") castes, who in the 1970s and 1980s through government reservations and other policies had also begun to reap the benefits of social mobility. The 1990s saw Dalit groups begin to mobilize in protest against such violence as well as a number of caste riots.

This politics carried over into cinema. Through the idiom of "nativity" films of the 1970s, in the 1980s and 1990s enregistered signs of caste identity – and caste and regional essentializations, such as dominant castes like Thevars being valorous and violent, and Madurai being a space of "murder and mayhem" (Damodaran and Gorringe 2017:§26) – became increasingly naturalized in the name of realism (compare the casteless figure of the fantastical mass hero; Rajangam 2016), what Damodaran and Gorringe (2017) call "3M" films (Madurai, Murder, Mayhem). It is in this fraught context – where a particular image of caste itself had become enregistered as a sign of the real – that *Kaadhal* was made and released.

For his part, Balaji Sakthivel's stated intention in *Kaadhal* – as he articulated in interviews with me (first in December 2008 and then a decade later in September 2018 and October 2018) – was to articulate a *critique* of caste, to "raise questions" among the audience about the hypocrisy of caste identity and female sexuality.

Balaji Sakthivel recounted to me in 2008 (and again in September 2018) how *Kaadhal* came to him, citing an incident that happened when he was a teenager in the 1970s, living "down south" in the town of Dindigul, near Madurai. (My account below combines the details from his two narrations.) He heard a "dialogue," he said, vividly narrating walking past a house where, through a window, he overheard a Thevar girl speaking with her mother. The girl – having gotten married, unbeknown to her family, to a boy from a different caste – hesitantly and jokingly asks her mother: 'Hey Mom, if I liked (and married) someone, what would you do?' 'He's one of us [that is, our caste], right?' (*Namma āḷ, illa?*). When the girl responded: 'No, Mom,' the mother simply said, in all seriousness: 'I'd chop you up and kill you' (*Unne veṭṭi konnē pōṭṭuruvēn*). He'd never heard such 'cruel' (*mūkkamāna*) words in his life, Balaji Sakthivel said, horrified. Later, he found out that the girl was beaten by her family, and the boy disappeared. That's how fanatical Thevars are about caste (*jāti veṟi*), he said.

Based on a true story. Yet this incident was not the story that *Kaadhal* cites in its conclusion. In our 2008 interview, immediately after narrating this "dialogue," Balaji Sakthivel dropped a bombshell: the rolling text at the end of the film – the one that claims the film is the true story of another, Aiswarya's second husband – was made up. He never met such a man. It was simply another "script," a 'lie' (*poy*) as Balaji Sakthivel put it, one he was publicly revealing for the first time in our interview.[33] Telling here is Balaji Sakthivel's equivalence of "script" – the text-artifact used here as an emblem of cinema – and lying. This equivalence draws on the widely circulated opposition among film directors (and more widely), as we noted above and in Chapter 1, between "cinema" and reality/truth. This equivalence – and its use to distinguish different kinds of film images (the one that lies versus the one that tells the truth; the unrealistic versus the realistic image; see Bazin 2005[1946]:19) – diagrams the ambivalence, and perhaps performative contradiction, at the heart of realism: a truth that lies (but shouldn't), a reality cloaked in the unreal, cinema that is not "cinema."

But why lie, given the horribly common, and instantly recognizable, nature of such events (Srinivasan 2016)? As we'll see, this 'lie' reveals the performativity that animates realism and the amount of work necessary to hold off that performativity so as to represent (something of) the real.

Consider an early scene in the film, mentioned above. In a directly frontal shot, Aiswarya's mother and sister-in-law sit and watch television, ignoring their elderly, blind mother-in-law in the next room. Ghostly images from the climax of *Kaadhalukku Mariyadai* (Respect for Love) flicker over the shot (Figure 4.8), as if we are in the television, its images projected from/onto our eyes as Aiswarya's mother and aunt sit engaged by the melodrama. While the grandmother is yelling at her daughters-in-law about their lack of concern for where their daughter is (she is eloping with Murugan on the bus, recall), they cry, worrying whether the lovers in the film will reunite, in horror that they might not (echoing Balaji Sakthivel's horror noted above).

"What does it mean?" Balaji Sakthivel rhetorically asked me in 2008. 'I'm asking a question,' he answered. 'You [the characters in the film, the audience members in the theatre] accept all of this in a film [inter-caste love marriage], but you won't accept it when it comes to your own daughter?'

Figure 4.8. Aiswarya's mother and aunt watching *Kaadhalukku Mariyadai* (1997) in *Kaadhal* (2004), the televisualized film image spectrally framed within the screen's frame

Balaji Sakthivel's aim in the film, however, was not simply to critique caste patriarchy and show the cruel realities of caste. He also wanted to show people's humanity, that out of something terrible something good can come, to show that violence was not the only response to challenges to caste purity. So while the film begins with the hypocritical sisters-in-law, it ends with a 'wonderful soul' (as Balaji Sakthivel put it in the Tamil magazine *Ananda Vikadan* [2005b]), Aiswarya's (second) 'humanitarian' husband. Here, the film models a transformation of the viewing subject, ending with a site of spectatorial identification (embodied by the husband's character) that *accepts* the heroine's past, that accepts that his wife had loved, and even married, across lines of caste.

Why the rolling text at the end of the film, though? It wasn't part of the original script, only added after the film was shot, just a week before its release. As Balaji Sakthivel put it to me, he was afraid. He wasn't courageous (*tairiyam*) enough. Would the audience accept the film's ending as written? Would they have felt that he botched the climax (climax-*le sotappiṭṭān ṭā*), dismissing the film as ending with a fantasy, with a totally unbelievable character (compare Aumont et al. 1992[1983]:114–15)? Would the "male chauvinistic mind" of the audience, he said, a mindset consumed by caste (*jāti*) and race (*inam*) and the purity of its women, hate the film, asking in disgusted disbelief: 'What man would do that?' Such a viewer, he ventriloquated, would not: 'I would never eat the half-eaten leftovers [literally, 'spit food'] of someone else' (*Innoruttan sāppiṭṭa ecci sāppāṭu sāppiṭamāṭṭēn*). Such a viewer would reject the film and its ending despite, or perhaps because of, the fact that, Balaji Sakthivel suggested, such things are common.

Habituated to caste, its seed planted in our minds by our parents, the director recounted that he himself felt uneasy (*neruṭal*) when he watched the first cut of the film. His years of immersion in a casteist society raised a resistant voice in him that he worried would be there for other viewers. To maintain identification with the film, and to prevent it being rejected – indeed, to force the viewer to accept the reality of such things – he had to frame it with a fictional story (*kaṟpanai katai*), a 'lie' about a "real" story told to him by the husband, by a 'wonderful soul' actually out there. 'It's always the case,' he reasoned, that 'while we won't sacrifice ourselves, we will accept someone else who makes the sacrifice (we can't/won't)' (*Eppavum tiyāki ākamāṭṭōm namma, ānā tiyākam paṇṟavanai ēttukkuvōm*). With that mindset, encouraged by the rolling text, when the husband accepts Aiswarya, the (male) audience member would think: 'Wow, what a great man that guy is, look at him. We're not like that. He accepted her. He's a really unique/different person' (*Che, appaṭi oru peruntanmaiyāna oru āḷ irukkāru pāruṅka. Atu namma kiṭaiyātu. Avar ēttukkiṭṭāru. Avar vantu romba vittiyāsamānavaru appaṭi nnu ninaippān* audience).

At the same time, Balaji Sakthivel said, the rolling title was a "disclaimer," akin to the fine print at the end of a newspaper/magazine put to avoid defamation suits (*māna naṣṭa vaḻakku*; literally, 'honour-loss/destruction case'). But disclaiming what? And defaming whose honour?

The disclaimer was, of course, his own: that the opinion of the film was *not his*. It was someone else's story. This really happened. This really happens.[34] And the defamation being disclaimed was that of the film's dominant-caste audience members. That is, it is not *me* showing *you*, a man from *your* caste (or a caste like yours), accepting 'half-eaten, saliva-drenched food [that is, a spoiled woman] from someone else [that is, a Dalit man].' It is not *me* preaching to *you*; it is not *me* criticizing *you*, defaming *you*.

At play here, as noted above, is the patriarchal casteist discourse that would make the sexual purity of its women a sign – indeed, the very embodiment – of caste honour and respectability, and of its men in particular. While the husband's acceptance of Aiswarya may be entextualized by the film and its director as an act of "sacrifice," the very notion of sacrifice already presumes upon a competing entextualization: that accepting a soiled wife – and from a Dalit, no less – is a humiliating dishonour to the character, his (represented but real-world) caste, and the viewer who would identify with either. What is being disclaimed through the veil of the real, then, is a representation that would cinematically cuckold the Thevar caste and castes like it, that is, a performative image-act of insult by the director to a dominant-caste, non-Brahmin male viewer who feels himself negatively interpellated by the film. Such an interpellation would, the director feared, undermine his political message to abandon caste fanaticism and its patriarchal hypocrisies by eliciting both.[35] The film's framing as historical truth (what Benveniste [1971:206] called *histoire*), then, attempts to elicit from viewers sympathy and emotional identification with the narrative and its characters – indeed, to take it up as an authorless, impersonal representation *for* them (Metz 2016[1991]) – rather than a personal act of offence (*discours*) directed *at* them *by* the director.[36]

In order to tell the truth, then, Balaji Sakthivel had to engage in "a kind of storytelling," one that "made it [the film] more realistic!," as he exclaimed in October 2018. To insist that someone could indeed be humane like this, to insist on a deeper truth about humanity in a society that is cruel and cannot believe in the humanity of others, one had to lie. One had to insist, beyond all prejudiced disbelief, on it being a "true story."[37]

Frustrated Textuality and Sexual Reference

This performative excess of the realist image – this fear of an uptake of the film *as* an image-act of caste insult – didn't just necessitate the (re)framing of the film and its last scene, however. It infused the very thread of the film's narrative, insinuating itself as an effaced, yet present logic working against and through its realist structure and politics.

Consider again the film's treatment of Aiswarya's sexuality. When Aiswarya and Murugan reach Chennai, they have nowhere to go. So Murugan goes to where his close friend, Stephen, lives: a "mansion" (or hostel) for bachelors, where Stephen stays in a room with six other men struggling in various ways to make ends meet in the city. While they cannot stay with Stephen – women are not allowed in such mansions – they manage to use his room and the public bathroom to shower when his roommates are out for the day. In the room, Aiswarya begins to undress but feels embarrassed, under siege by the gaze of looking others; the room is filled with eyes on its walls that see her: cardboard demon masks, pictures of children, pin-up girls, and, especially troubling to her, a photograph of the roommates at the beach drinking beers and smoking cigarettes. At her request, Murugan comes inside, covers the eyes of all the pictures he can, and, with his back to her, shields her with a blanket from the rest. He asks: 'So no one can see you now, right?' She responds, demurely smiling: 'Only *sāmi* (god) can see me,' referring to

Figure 4.9. Seeing Aiswarya see the god Murugan seeing her in *Kaadhal*

a picture of the god Murugan whose eyes have remained uncovered. She says this in a frontal shot of her face reflecting in, and superposed on top of, the deity's image, each looking at the other as they look at the camera while it subtly tracks in (Figure 4.9; compare Pinney 2004:197). 'So, only god is able to see you, it seems,' the protagonist Murugan flirtatiously responds. 'It's Murugan *sāmi* after all,' she coyly replies, revealing the god's identity to him.

At hearing his divine namesake, Murugan turns around, smiling in joy, and hugs Aiswarya from behind. What follows Murugan's blockage of the public (male) gaze of Aiswarya (what I discussed in Chapter 2 as *sight aṭikkiṟatu*) and its inauguration of a private, and divinely sanctioned, conjugal space is a conventional, symbolic song-and-dance sequence, "Kiru Kiru," that depicts the lovers' sexual desire – the lyrics describing their trembling bodies wracked with intense yearning and hesitant fear as they dance across a series of extra-diegetic locations).[38] The song ends with a mansion resident discovering Aiswarya's bindi stuck to the wall of the bathroom stall where she had showered. Realizing there's a girl in the mansion, he gathers other residents in the mansion to investigate. The camera cuts to a shot of Aiswarya and Murugan in the room, just about to kiss on the mouth yet interrupted by a knock at the door. With the diegetic world and its narrative returns male publicity, interrupting the lovers' private sexual encounter.

Later, the lovers attempt to get a registered marriage but are unable to because they lack a place of residence, and so try to find an apartment to rent. By the end of the day they have failed to secure their own private space of conjugality. To pass the night, Stephen recommends that they go to a local theatre to watch the last two films of the night, and then take a bus to Tindivanam (a town about 130 kilometres south of Chennai) and back. As it turns out, Aiswarya is having her menstrual period, as we learn from seeing Murugan buying her sanitary pads, which she goes to put on when they are at the theatre. After a night riding the bus, the next day the couple manages to rent an apartment of their own and conduct their marriage. On the morning of the first day in their new conjugal space, Murugan goes off to work. Before he returns home, however, Aiswarya's uncle has discovered their whereabouts and arrives to take them back to Madurai.

While in 2018, Balaji Sakthivel explained the purpose of his "disclaimer" as securing spectatorial identification, in 2008, when he admitted to me his "script," he framed it as a problem of filmic reference, saying, in a stretch of discourse wracked with hesitations, hedges, codeswitches, and ellipses:

> The first time I'm admitting, in this interview, but uh, it's a kind of script I think, because nobody, no male- it's a male-dominated society, nobody will admit it. ((No one)) touch *paṇṇinā- avaḷe vantu* touch *paṇṇ((inā))* they won't ((release)) it. *Nān vantu anta paṭattule avaṅkaḷukku* sex *varṟā mātiri, appaṭiyē atilē* <mouth click> some limit was there. So, that's also not such a reality *Kaadhal*, as far as my humble knowledge is concerned.

> The first time I'm admitting, in this interview, but uh, it's a kind of script I think, because nobody, no male- it's a male-dominated society, nobody will admit it. If ((no one)) touched- if he touched her, they won't ((release)) it [the movie]. In the film, it was like they were about to have sex (but didn't), in that way in that <mouth click> some limit was there. So, that's also not such a reality (in) *Kaadhal*, as far as my humble knowledge is concerned.

Here, the issue is not just one of spectatorial identification, nor even about the director's capacity to *represent* the act of sex between a Dalit boy and a virginal Thevar girl (be it directly or through euphemism). It is the capacity to narratively emplot such a sexual union as part of the story, that is, to serve as a referent in the fabula. "Some limit was there" on the realism of the film at this juncture of caste and sexuality; in real life, he admitted, they would have had sex. But in reel life, they couldn't.

Note how the performativity emanating from the very thing that is the basis of the realist conceit of the film – that it will reveal the truth of the nexus of caste and sexuality – infects the representationality of the filmic image and its narrative structure, breathing life into both *as* the avoidance of that very performative force. *"Nān tavirttuṭṭēn"*

(I excluded/avoided it), Balaji Sakthivel said in 2008. The semantic range of the verb he used here, *tavir*, includes the English senses of to expel, exclude, interrupt, prevent, frustrate, control, restrain. The interruption of the kiss, the bureaucratic hurdles to their registration, the inability to rent a home, Aiswarya's menstrual period – the narrative structure of the second half of the film blocks, frustrates, expels, and restrains Aiswarya's sexuality (Anand 2005; Rajangam 2016).[39] While, as we saw in Chapter 2, the representation of female sexuality harbours a performative force, here its intersection with caste renders this performativity unmanageable and, in the end, effaced from the diegesis itself.

A comparison to Selvaraghavan's *7/G Rainbow Colony* (discussed in Chapter 2), which was released the same year as *Kaadhal*, is helpful. *7/G Rainbow Colony* is situated almost exclusively in the metropolis of Chennai and completely avoids any discussion of caste.[40] The major division is class and ethnicity – the protagonist, Kathir, is a lower-middle-class Tamilian, and the heroine, Anitha, an upper-class Punjabi. By contrast, *Kaadhal* splits itself – as Rajan (Kurai) Krishnan (Krishnan 2008; Kurai 2012) has pointed out – between a "down south" Madurai and an up-north Chennai, the former of which is framed as feudal and thoroughly casteist and the latter as modern and absent of caste. While *7/G Rainbow Colony* took its charge to show the realities of middle-class female sexuality (as imagined by its male director, at least) and had its couple have sex, Balaji Sakthivel – as we saw – felt himself unable or unwilling to do so. "They won't release the film," as he said above. Or, as he said in October 2018, in recognition of the semiotic economy in which he was caught: 'I didn't base (my film) around sex like Selvaraghavan' (*Itu nāṉ Selvaraghavan mātiri anta* sex base *paṇṇi nāṉ paṇṇale*)[41] – which is to say, he based it around caste but only at the expense of the reality of sex, just as, by implication, Selvaraghavan based his film on sex but only by avoiding the reality of caste. At the intersection of these two sites of taboo performativity – caste and sexuality, and in the very configuration that is most problematic and performative: the sexual relationship between a Dalit man and a dominant-caste woman – the representation of consensual, conjugal inter-caste sexuality is rendered so problematic that it never appeared either onscreen or in the plot of either film.[42]

The repercussions of such a performative representation are not imagined. Cheran's 1997 *Bharathi Kannamma*, for example, a story about a Dalit (Pallar) man in love with his Thevar landlord employer's daughter, triggered protests and attacks on movie theatres and buses from Thevar groups for the way in which it was taken to dishonour their caste (Nambath 2003; Rajangam 2016; Damodaran and Gorringe 2017; Chakravarthy 2018:166; see also Pandian 2008:136–7).[43] *Kaadhal* avoided such violent protests by, in the end, protecting the chastity of the dominant castes that it attempted to critique for their patriarchal hypocrisy and casteist violence.[44] As Stalin Rajangam (2016) points out in an important critique, despite its anti-caste politics, by cloaking the narrative in the veil of realism the film ultimately justifies a Thevar self-understanding of caste valour, violence, and purity, naturalizing a Thevar identity that it constructs in the name of "reflecting reality."[45] In other words, despite, and perhaps because of, its caste critique, *Kaadhal* participated in the twinned process of enregistering caste and enregistering realism.

To Rajangam's critique, I would also underline the way in which this casteing of realism follows from the long-standing contrastive structure of realism vis-à-vis the "commercial" cinema and its casteless mass hero. Among the viewers that I spoke with (across a range of castes), the realism of both *Kaadhal* and *7/G Rainbow Colony* turned, among other things, on the way in which such films bucked the "usual" love story, with its fantastical happy endings, instead showing the "reality" of love as difficult and tragic, a sentiment that resonated with many I knew who in their own lives faced resistance and violence from their own and their lovers' kin. The tragic endings of both films, indeed, were evaluated by many viewers as *necessary* for their realism, since a "happy" ending – like that of an idealist film like *Kaadhalukku Mariyadai*, where the hero and his love triumphs over all – would be the "normal" ending of a "commercial" film, and hence unrealistic (Nakassis and Dean 2007).[46] In reaching, thus, for a space outside of the mainstream, in differentiating themselves from a cinema of the past and present, and in attempting to bring a liberal critique (of caste or heterodox sexual morality), these films ironically played into an equally long-standing caste politics with its own investments in the interdiction of inter-caste marriage.

This contingent yet necessary confluence, or "bundling" – to borrow a term from Webb Keane (2003) – is not only the result of the tangling of caste politics and ontological politics as they play out in the fraught textuality of film. Such bundling also enables such politics, opening the text up as a resource for political action. Consider, for example, the not unexceptional uptake of *Kaadhal* in the south of Tamil Nadu, as reported by the journalist and author S. Anand (2005).[47] When Murugan was being beaten during the climax of the film, S. Anand relays:

> An aspiring filmmaker friend who watched *Kaadhal* in a Madurai cinema talked of how Thevars – the dominant "backward caste" of the southern districts – in the hall shouted aloud: "Fuckers, this will be your fate if you

> think you can get our girl." Dalits watching the movie in the southern districts were intimidated both by the depiction of the hero and by the participative enthusiasm of the Thevars among the audience.

And later, in the final scene, when Aiswarya "spots Murugan as a mad man at a traffic signal," he reports: "This is where some young Thevars in the audience shout in Madurai's cinemas: 'Keep off our women.'" In such moments, notice how part of the film – a scene of dominant castes beating the Dalit protagonist – is entextualized not as realist representation critical of caste violence but *as* an act of caste violence. Framed by these metapragmatic utterances ("Fuckers, this will be your fate if you think you can get our girl"; "Keep off our women"), the film image is projected/mapped from the screen *into* the timespace of screening and onto the bodies of Dalit viewers.[48] In this violent act of uptake, an impersonal realist representation is ontically transformed into – indeed, has already given itself over to becoming – a personal, performative act of intimidation and threat, precisely against but also through the simultaneous entextualization of caste critique and realist aesthetics that the film attempted to articulate.

Acts of uptake such as these, needless to say, render ambivalent any investment in realism as a telos of modernity emerging out of pre-modern feudal structures and aesthetics of caste patriarchy (see also Dickey 2009; Damodaran and Gorringe 2017:§65), since at the heart of early twenty-first-century Tamil realism and its images lurks precisely those presumably "feudal" yet decidedly modern forms of caste violence and illiberality that have been disavowed but remain present across this history of enregisterment. The point, however, is not simply whether a film like *Kaadhal* contests or naturalizes caste, as if it were one or the other. *Kaadhal* represents neither a liberal, urban critique of caste or commercial cinema (issued by filmmakers and critics) nor an illiberal naturalization of caste through acts of uptake (by "down south" filmgoers) but both, depending on one's point of view. Both sides of such split antinomies – urban/rural, Chennai/Madurai, elite/subaltern, filmmakers/audiences, text/uptake – are simultaneously inscribed in their others as the very problem space of realism. Recall Balaji Sakthivel's narration of why he put the "disclaimer": he himself, as someone raised within the prejudices of caste, felt uneasy as a viewer of his own film; he felt an 'irritation' in his own split subjectivity that crept in from his own casteist mofussil past to his liberal metropolitan present, an irritation that called for its own textual strategies, that inscribed within the film a simultaneous liberal and illiberal potential, that split and entangled the text's realist and performative moorings, one to and in the other.

Here, the semiotic thread of this process of enregisterment is precisely the tension between the representationality and performativity of the image, the very ontological politics of the image that has been at issue in this book. This tension is what is at stake in Thevar youth intimidating Dalit youth through their uptake of realist critiques of caste; but also in film criticism, such as Rajangam's (2016) and Damodaran and Gorringe's (2017), which would read such realist films for their performative effects and rightly demand an alternate politics, and semiotics, of realism that would work not to reflect but foster and bring about different possible realities. The tragic irony is that, in his 'lie,' this is precisely what Balaji Sakthivel was attempting to do, yet in the eyes of some, failed to achieve.

At the same time, it is also important to see that the co-enregisterment of realism and forms of caste identity are not total or finalized. Despite, and as a function of, their deep conventionalization, like all enregistered styles, realisms give themselves over to their own transformation and unfinalizability (Bakhtin 1984[1963]:58). It is the loose linkage of enregistered styles and the ways in which they are always inevitably contextualized in by-degrees deviant ways from the norms and past iterations governing their present intelligibility that allows for flight from those norms, for their tropic reappropriation and re-enregisterment (Agha 2007a). We might look, for example, to the ongoing struggle to resignify realism and its relationship to caste in the crop of Dalit-directed, realist films released in the 2010s – such as Pa. Ranjith's *Attakatti* (2012) and *Madras* (2014), and Mari Selvaraj's *Pariyerum Perumal* (2018; produced by Pa. Ranjith) – which have featured explicitly Dalit protagonists and spaces, and challenged the stereotyped, casted enregisterment of realism in Tamil cinema (Damodaran and Gorringe 2021; see also the book's Conclusions).

The Production Format of Realism

The ontological politics of realism is not only a class politics of distinction; a liberal critique of caste, patriarchy, or subaltern populism; or a caste-based identity politics. It is also, as we have seen in previous chapters, an industry politics of production format (Goffman 1979), a politics of who stands in what relationship (or "footing") to the image (for example, as its author, animator, principal, and so on).

Consider, once again, Balaji Sakthivel's "disclaimer," the non-fictional "script" in which he wrapped his fictional yet very real story, in particular, the presence of the director in the disclaimer: the first-person 'I' (the first-person possessive *en*, the first-person verb ending -*ēn*) and his name/signature. The rolling text breaks with the voyeuristic/impersonal participation framework of the film right at its edge, in a moment of direct address where the 'I' of the director speaks to the 'you' of the audience (the plural second-person dative, *uṅkaḷukku*, and the conative 'thanks,' *nanṟi*).[49] What is the semiotic function of this deictic mode of address and, in particular, the director's signature? What is he signing exactly? And with what footing?

The genre of the rolling text, as noted above, is akin to an epistolary letter, with the 'I' and the signature naming the letter's author. But if it instates the letter's author, it does so by hedging on the authorship and principalship of the film within which the letter occurs. In effect, as we saw, the letter retroactively reframes the film's production format, moving into a mode of personal address at the end of the film precisely to prevent the entextualization of what came *before* its break *as* a personal address (that is, an insult) rather than an impersonal narration.[50] The indexicality of the signature and the rigid designation of its name, in short, have an enunciative, performative function of undersigning the reality of the story by displacing the film away from its director, who becomes, instead, a mere relay or animator of another's "true story."

But we can say more, since the signature is a citational allusion that echoes, and differs from, the auterist trademark of the director Bharathiraja – the fount of the "nativity" films of the 1970s and 1980s (Chakravarthy 2018) – who often ends his films with his identifiable voice conveying a message for the audience, followed by his signature onscreen. As Balaji Sakthivel told me in September 2018, he initially thought to dub this section over the rolling credits but, in the end, felt that it would be *too much* like Bharathiraja; hence, he opted for the written text. In and by its effacing of the authorship and subjectivity of the director, in and by opening up the space of objectivity through his signature, the signature thus also acted as a claim to an auterial footing to the film precisely by a (crossed-out) gesture to another realist director and paragon of auteur style. This "I" of discourse (Urban 1989), thus, instates the subjectivity of the director vis-à-vis his encounter with his audience precisely by integrating his name into a citational chain of other, absent names (Derrida 1988; Butler 1993), becoming an auteur precisely by negating his own authorship, making a claim on the image precisely by disavowing it being his image at all. And in so doing, Balaji Sakthivel attempted to hedge on *Kaadhal*'s uptake as caste critique while in fact articulating a caste critique, to accrue positive value from the film (and gather a name in the industry) while avoiding responsibility for its negative value.

As I have suggested, this dynamic is the double gesture of realism more generally, which immediates through mediation; which entails the real by contrasting with and integrating into its textual fabric its opposite, its negation; which makes its own performative entailments by framing itself as mere representation. Here, the realism of the image is not a function of indexical "traces" of the profilmic emanating to us but is a function of a much more complex and circuitous indexicality, mediated by a complex poetics of enunciation, a history of enregisterment, and by the intertextual webs that the rigid designation of the director's signature and name cite.[51]

We might contrast the function of the director's name with the function of the hero-star's name discussed in Chapter 1. As we saw, a film starring a hero-star ultimately circulates in his name. He stands as the film's principle/principal of authorization, if not authorship. By contrast, while the reportage about *Kaadhal*, but also of films like *7/G Rainbow Colony*, noted the performances of its actors, the quality of the music directors' songs, the camerawork, and the like, all such films interdiscursively travel in the names of their directors, as grammatically possessed by them or modified by their proper name: Balaji Sakthivel's film, a Selvaraghavan film, and so on (and *not* Bharat's film, a Ravikrishnan film, and so on). Ultimately, this possessive claim is, I would argue, one of the primary functions of the disclaimer – namely, to disclaim *and thus lay claim on* what is already assumed to be the case: that it is the director who is responsible for the image, that it is the director and director alone who speaks through his films (for it is he who has the right to disclaim in the first place).[52] Hence, the ironic need for "this is a true story" – to enable this double gesture of disavowal and avowal at one and the same time. This doubling strategy inserts the director as the rightful mediator between the real and the audience, as the mediating screen between the world and the theatre. It is *he* who shows us what is real, not the hero (see also Chapter 3).[53]

New Faces and the Director's Image

This tension between the hero('s spectacle) and the director('s story) is a central reason why such realist films feature so-called new faces so prominently. Part of such casting is economic, as producers and big stars in the Tamil industry are hesitant to produce or act in such films.[54] Part of it is aesthetic: as Balaji Sakthivel averred, non-professional actors act more naturally (see also Kuleshov 1974[1929]:57; Bazin 2005[1948]:22–4, 2005[1951]a).[55]

But it is also about directorial control (Ganti 2012:211–13). The bigger the hero-star, the more "compromises" are demanded on the film by the producer, the hero-star, and his fan audiences. The presence of the hero-star distorts the script. It changes production choices. As we saw in Chapter 1, the director often has to consult with and ask for permission from the film's hero for what is depicted. By contrast, the new face can be controlled. He makes no demands. He needs no "commercial" elements: a special "entry" song, four to five fights, "punch dialogues," an attractive heroine on his arm.[56] He is a blank slate, and the audience expects nothing of him (see Metz 2016[1991]:69), seeing only what the director wants them to see, his character, rather than his previous roles or offscreen persona.

In short, the use of new faces allows the director to take a footing to the film as the main (if not sole) author and principal (even partial animator) of its images.[57] And further, it allows the film to circulate in the director's name, just as it thereby allows fame and value to return to it (and him) in turn (Munn 1986).[58] The presence of a hero-star, on set and onscreen, threatens to transform this production format, the narrative world that it anchors, and the political economy that it enables.[59] This threat is also ontological – transforming the image from realist representation of a diegetic world into a presentist fantasy glorifying the hero in the world of his theatrical appearance – and political – dulling the critical potential of (the director's) realist images by routing them through the star value and cine-politics of the hero's image.

Consider, again, Balaji Sakthivel's liberal political aim in *Kaadhal*: to raise questions among the audience about caste patriarchy. The presence of a big hero would make this goal impossible, he argued:

They [heroes] say: "*Ṭēy appaṭilām vēṣam pōṭuṟāṅka ṭā, nān tān paṇṇuvēn, nān tān ippaṭi paṇṇuvēn,*" *ippaṭi etirttu kēṭṭā, kēṭṭuṭṭu paṭam ōṭirum, ānā oṇṇum paṇṇa māṭṭāṅka … Anta* heroes-*lām … pōrāṭṭam-lām* <laughing> *paṇṇa māṭṭāṅka.*	Heroes say: "Hey, they [politicians] put on a mask and pretend, but I'll do it, only I will get it done." They'll speak up against some issue, and the film will run (well in theatres), but they won't do anything. Protesting and all that <laughing>, they'll never do it.
But in *Kaadhal*, I'm saying: "*Atu kiṭaiyātu. Itu tān* real. *Inta* hero, *pāvam aṭipaṭṭu settān. Pāruṅka, paittiyam ānān. Pāttīṅkaḷā?* *Atān* real. *Avanāl etuvum paṇṇa muṭiyātu.* *Jāti iruKKU!*"	But in *Kaadhal*, I'm saying: "It's [how heroes show it] not like that. *This* is real. This hero [Murugan], poor guy, he's beaten to death. Look, he became crazy. Did you see? That's what's real. And he can't do anything about it. Caste EXISTS!"

You can convey the same political message as *Kaadhal* with a hero-star in the film, Balaji Sakthivel conceded, but the realism of the film will be converted into a kind of fantasy, recentred around the personage of the hero-star rather than the issue at hand. When I pushed him to elaborate, he narrated an alternate "commercial climax" to *Kaadhal* as he had pitched it to the legendary production house, AVM Studios, and the actor Dhanush (the younger brother of Selvaraghavan who, at that time, was beginning his ascent from a character actor to becoming a commercial hero). In this hero-centred version, Aiswarya's family won't smash Murugan's head on a stone, but push his face into a mound of sand. 'What will the hero do?' Balaji Sakthivel asked dramatically. Continuing his re-enactment of his pitch to AVM and Dhanush, he said: 'Sand stuffed into his mouth, when they start to drag him he'll spit it out in a plume of sand. When they grab his shirt, BOOM! He'll hit them and grab a huge knife. Right when we are wondering if he will live or die, that's when his heroism (*vīram*) will come out. Immediately after the girl says that she won't take off her *tāli*, then "Aha!" he knows she's for us [INCL.] (*nammakkāṇṭi avaḷ*). Then he'll rip the bad guys to shreds in a ten-minute fight. When the fight is over, he grabs the girl by the hand.' At this point, Balaji Sakthivel snapped his finger, and delivered the heroic dialogue that would clinch the scene: 'What was it you [-HON.] asked me, am I a dog or a pig? I'm a lion, man!' (*Enna ṭā kēṭṭe? Nāyā panniyā? Nān siṅkam ṭā!" appaṭi nnu pōyiṭṭē iruppān*!) With that, the film would end, he concluded his re-enacted narrative pitch. Parodically imitating the enthusiastic response of the producer and actor in lapping up such a treatment, he began clapping: '"Amazing!" they'd say, "this is super, it's just what we want!"' (Claps, *piccu-* super *itu tān vēṇum-nbāṅka*!).[60]

In this narrative re-enactment, Balaji Sakthivel lampoons what he would have to do to his film to make it palatable to a commercial producer and aspiring commercial hero-star: "punch dialogues" (heroic one-liners), spectacular fights, the hero triumphing over the bad guys, the lovers uniting, and, perhaps most importantly, the erasure of caste conflict. Not a dog or a pig – that is, a Dalit – the hero would be a lion – that is, a Thevar – the twist of the film now being that the lion (that is, caste valour) was hidden inside the hero until he had to rise to the occasion to defend *his* – and, to the dominant-caste spectator, *our* – girl (hence Balaji Sakthivel's use of the inclusive, first-person plural benefactive, "*nammakkāṇṭi*," reportively embedded to align his addressee's point of view in the narrative – the producer and actor to whom he was pitching the film – with that of the caste hero and his imagined spectator). "I can do::: (a climax like this)," he concluded, "but I wo::::n't," poetically elongating the vowels of the modalized predicates to give emphasis to his refusal. 'Because real life isn't like that,' he said, and 'I wanted to make a reflection of real life' (*Ēnnā nijam appaṭi kiṭaiyātu. Nijattai tān nil̲al paṇṇa virumbinēn*).

Realism's Illiberal Extimacy and the Suspension of Belief

In late September of 2008, I met with Sasikumar (b. 1974), the director, producer, and one of the main actors in *Subramaniyapuram* (2008). *Subramaniyapuram*, like *Kaadhal*, is an example of what Karthikeyan Damodaran and Hugo Gorringe (2017) refer to as the "Madurai Formula" or "3M" films discussed above.[61] The film is a realist period film about the 1980s, taking as its backdrop the political shift in Tamil Nadu when, as the director put it to me, politics became about "rowdyism" and youth became objects of manipulation and pawns in political plays of violence.[62]

Briefly, the film depicts two lower-class youth, Azhagar and Paraman, who along with their friends get involved with a family of local, upper-caste Pillaimar politicians (as indexed by a fleeting visual reference to V.O. Chidambaram Pillai, a nationalist leader from the caste). As the family manipulates the youth to enact violence in their attempts to maintain a hold on their waning power, the young men get increasingly involved in a world of crime, eventually turning against the family (and trying to kill them) after the family hangs them out to dry in prison. Azhagar, however, is in love with the daughter of the older brother of the family. In the end, she betrays Azhagar to protect her family, just as in the climax one of the young men's close friends, Kasi (played by the comedian-actor, Ganja Karuppu), betrays Paraman (played by Sasikumar) for money, resulting in Paraman's murder by the family's henchmen.[63]

As I exited my interview with Sasikumar, I ran into Ganja Karuppu in the lobby of the office. This serendipitous run-in with the man who played the lynchpin of *Subramaniyapuram*'s tragic climax was a moment out of frame, both in the sense of being outside of the frame of my research – we chatted only briefly in the space of the waiting room, he going in and me going out of the office – and in the sense of being outside the frame of the film. The oddness of our encounter was also because it had been anticipated in my conversation with Sasikumar only minutes before. In describing the level of emotional attachment that people had to the film and its tragic protagonists, Sasikumar referenced Kasi's betrayal in the film's climax, a beautiful and disturbing scene that includes a long two-minute Steadicam shot of Kasi walking away from the riverbed where Paraman is being hacked to pieces. In the shot, we see Kasi hurriedly move away from the river (Figure 4.10 – top left),

Figure 4.10. Steadicam shot in *Subramaniyapuram* (2008, dir. Sasikumar) revealing Kasi's/Ganja Karuppu's betrayal of Paraman

anxiously looking back now and again at Paraman's murder as it recedes into the background (Figure 4.10 – top right). He finally arrives at the main road, where a turquoise ambassador car waits for him. He walks up to it and takes some money (Figure 4.10 – bottom left). He sits down on a mile marker. His body deflates. He pants, and his body expands as he lights up a cigarette, taking a long puff that seems both nonchalant and remorseful, as if in his exhalation he expelled both his sin and stress (Figure 4.10 – bottom right).

The long single shot was designed, Sasikumar said in our interview, to force the viewer not to focus on Paraman's murder as such, but on Kasi and his act of betrayal, to contemplate with Kasi what he had done in the real time of his walk; doing so, the director suggested, would stoke the viewers' emotional response at his wretched betrayal (compare Chapter 1).[64]

In theatres, the scene elicited yelling and insults from audience members. At this moment of betrayal, audience members condemned Kasi as he condemned Paraman. Angry, viewers cathartically expiated the evil of Kasi's betrayal by cursing him. It is this scene, and the crowds' reaction to it, that Sasikumar cited in our interview to demonstrate his point that the film affected the audience at a deep, emotional level. It was evidence of the film's realism.

But it was also its opposite. Immediately after making this point, as a joking aside, Sasikumar noted that Ganja Karuppu, the actor who played Kasi, still refused to come to the theatre to watch the film. Indeed, it was also at *him* that they were yelling in the theatre, not just at Kasi. If he dared to show his face at the scene of the crime, audience members would scold him, curse him with "vulgar" words, and even threaten to hack him to pieces with a machete! Sasikumar said:

Inta paṭatte patti nān teriñcukkiṭṭatu ennenna	What I learned about this film is that
avaṅka atai paṭamā pākkale.	they don't/didn't see it as a film.
Atu tān enakku bayamā <light laugh> *((eppaṭi)) iruntatu, paṭamā ((pākka/ pāruṅka)) appaṭiṅkṟa mātiri ennennā*	That's what scared me <light laugh>, how they were looking at it, because
avaṅka atai paṭamā pākkale.	they didn't see it as a film.
Atukkuḷḷe pōyiṭṭāṅka avaṅka.	They went so deep inside it.
So *appa ennennā anta reṇṭu* character-*um Aḻagar* character-*um konnuṭṭān, Paraman* character-*um kollum pōtu*	So, when the two characters, Azhagar is killed and when Paraman is killed,
romba emotional *ākiṭṭāṅka.*	they became really emotional.
...	...
Atanāle tān anta Kāsiyai tiṭṭuṟāṅka.	That's why they scold that Kasi (character).
Innum kūṭa avarē payappaṭuṟāru.	He's [+HON., Ganja Karuppu] still afraid.
Theatre-*ukkē varamāṭṭāru.*	He won't come to the theatre.
Kāsiyā naṭicca comedian *vantu varamāṭṟāru.*	The comedian who acted as Kasi won't come.
Tiṭṭuṟāṅka.	They curse him.
Ellārumē tiṭṟāṅka.	Everyone curses him.
Atuvum Maṭurai-le bayaṅkaramā keṭṭa vārttaile vulgar-*ā tiṭṭuṟāṅka.*	In Madurai in particular, they vulgarly curse him with really bad words.
"Nī ūrukku vantā unnai veṭṭuvēn!"	"If you [-HON.] come here, I'm gonna chop you to pieces!"
ṅkiṟa mātiriyellām solṟāṅka.	They say like that.

When I ran into Ganja Karuppu, I couldn't help but ask if it were true. He confirmed it, humorously but gloomily describing how people would try to hit him, attack him, and insult him, Ganja Karuppu the actor, for betraying Paraman, the character. With each word of his comically exaggerated report of abuse, his body recoiled from an imagined blow. We laughed. Ganja Karuppu entered Sasikumar's office. I went back to the college hostel where I was staying at the time.

Here, I dwell on Sasikumar's bemused narrative of audience uptake to highlight the uncomfortable intermingling of representational and sociological realisms, of impersonal image-text and performative image-act, and how they confront each other in Sasikumar's narrative of spectator affect. In this somewhat genred (perhaps clichéd) narrative, this affect is both an ambivalent sign of the film's realism (the film is so realistic that it "disturbed" the viewer, Sasikumar claimed) and an illiberal performative excess that problematizes and undermines that realism (they didn't see Kasi/Ganja Karuppu's actions as part of a film at all). In our interview, Sasikumar (SK) continued his narrative, after I (CN) expressed my surprise, by focusing on a particular incident with two elderly women:

CN: *Appaṭiyā? Anta aḷavukku pōyiccā?*	CN: Really, it's really gone that far?
SK: *Anta aḷavukku pōyiruccu. Nān Dindigul-le* shooting *naṭanta iṭattukkellām pōyi ellāttukkum* thanks *solr̲atukku pōnēn. Appa avaraiyum kūṭṭiṭṭu pōyiruntēn. Nān anta kōyil-le* scene-*e kūṭṭiṭṭu pōkum pōtu avar toḷ mēl kaiyōdu kūṭṭiṭṭu pōnēn. Kūṭṭiṭṭu pōkum pōtu oru* ladies-*lām uṭkārntu iruntāṅka.*	SK: It's gone that far. I'd gone to all the places in Dindigul where shooting had happened to say thanks to everyone. I took him [+HON., Ganja Karuppu] along. When I took him to the scene at that temple, I brought him with my arm on his shoulder and holding his hand. When I took him, some women were sitting there.
<subtle change in voice quality, drawl:>	<subtle change in voice quality, drawl:>
"Avanōṭa nī ēnppā sērr̲e?	"Son, why're you hanging out with him.
Avan tān turōgi, <breaking into laughter> *l(h)e?"*	He's the traitor, <breaking into laughter> isn't he?"
<CN & SK laughing heavily>	<CN & SK laughing heavily>
<higher pitch:> *"Avan tān turōgi, le?*	<higher pitch:> "He's the traitor, right?
Innum avanōṭa ēn sērur̲e(h)?!"	Why are you still hanging out with him?!"
<SK laughing>	<SK laughing>
"Why are you going with him?	"Why are you going with him?

He's a-" uh (1) ((???)) <default voice quality:> "*Illa-mmā avaru en* friend *tān. Paṭattukkāka, paṭattukkāka," appaṭi nnu sonnēn.*	He's a-" uh (1) ((???)) <default voice quality:> "No ma'am, he's my friend. It's just for the film, for the film." I said like that.
"*Summā* movie, *paṭam tān*." <raised pitch and volume, more clearly articulated:> "*Paṭattukkāka irukkaṭṭum-ppā. Atukkāka paṇam vāṅkiṭṭu appaṭi paṇṟatā?*"	"It's just a movie, just a film." <raised pitch and volume, more clearly articulated:> "Fine, it's for a film, son. But to take money and do all that?!"
So, they involve so much.	So, they involve so much.
"*Paṇam vāṅkiṭṭu paṭattukku irukkaṭṭum-ppā, at(h)ellām irukkaṭṭum-ppā.*"	"He took the money, fine, it's for a film, let all that be, son."
"We are not deciding. *Paṭattukkāka vēṇāmā?*"	"We [actors] are not deciding. You can't do that [act as a villain] for a film?"
"*Paṭattukkāka irukkaṭṭum-ppā. Ate paṇam vāṅkiṭṭu paṇṇ(h)a muṭiyum(h)ā?*"	"Fine, it's for a movie, son. But can you do that for money?"
appaṭi nnu.	They were saying like that.
So, they'll (be) that much involved.	So, they'll (be) that much involved.
Nērle pākkum pōtum avanai anta anta appaṭiyē tān ((āyiṭṭāṅka/pākkuṟatu)).	When they see him in person, that, that, they ((see him/become)) just like that.

'Hey son, why are you hanging out with him? He's the traitor, right?' In this joking narrative filled with laughter Sasikumar animates these older, rural women as exemplars of the familiar, haunting figure of the illiberal spectator, the rube (Kuleshov 1974[1929]:45; Mitchell 1986, 1994; Hansen 1991; Jain 2007:299; Mazzarella 2013): confused, blinded by emotion, their faith irrationally born away by realism and unable to see that it's "just a movie," instead seeing through the film and imputing to its fictive shadows the substantive reality that it merely depicts.

Like the Metzian or Barthesian spectator who indulges but ultimately disavows his own credulity by projecting it onto someone else (Metz 1986[1975]), who can temporarily immerse himself in the image only to safely leave the theatre (Barthes 1986[1975]), Sasikumar invokes the realism of his film – the world it immerses you in – precisely by pointing to what he takes to be the excessive affect of the rural audience, they who *fail* to withdraw, who fail to limit the boundaries of the screen to the fiction, who fail to suspend their disbelief, indeed, who *believe.*[65] Realist effect, here, depends on and recruits the credulity of the viewer – it presupposes and entails viewers' "confusion" between film and reality, onscreen and offscreen (hence the illiberal extimacy of the liberal, realist image).[66] More specifically, Sasikumar's animation of these elderly ladies recalls the subject who craves and "worships" the mass hero (recall the bridegroom next to Murugan in *Kaadhal* enthralled by Rajinikanth's image), an idolator who is believed, by Sasikumar, to believe in the truth of what, to Sasikumar, is mere fiction, "just a movie." Here, we find ourselves, again, squarely caught in the ontological cine-politics of the image, that gravity whose mass we find perturbating Sasikumar's narrative and his realist film. But if in Chapter 1, the performativity of the image turned on the transgression of the sacral stardom of the mass hero, here, as in Chapter 2, what is transgressed is the public moral order of the social ('Can you do that for money?').

With these stakes in mind, we can read Sasikumar's narrative against itself, to recover a different interactional text (Silverstein 1996), one Sasikumar relayed but couldn't (or refused to) hear. Note the repetition in Sasikumar's narrative of the women's speech: 'Fine son, it's a film, but ...' (*irukkaṭṭum-ppā*), an utterance that Sasikumar takes as a sign of these women's stubborn confusion. Yet we can hear, across Sasikumar's unfolding entextualization, that it is also a sign of the director's own stubborn confusion (and the women's recognition of it), his refusal to acknowledge – and thus, in fact, his implicit acknowledging of – their voices and the performative potential of the image he made (compare Jain 2007:7–10). 'Fine, it's a film, but ...' How could Kasi do that for money? Or, which amounts to the same, how could Ganja Karuppu, the actor, act in such a horrific role? What kind of person must *he* be to do so?, the women asked.[67] 'It's just for the film ... It's just a movie,' Sasikumar countered. And yet that was the exact point of these women: it was for a film (not "just" for a film). That it was a film raised their very question, a question of moral culpability for *choosing* to be part of, and enactively and publicly showing, the betrayal, the transgression of the social, that the film created for viewers. For these elderly women, this question, this betrayal is indifferent to Sasikumar's presumed division of onscreen and offscreen, his "just."[68]

This indifference or openness is the exact opposite of what Samuel Taylor Coleridge (1817) famously called the "suspension of disbelief," that mode of audience engagement that characterizes how audiences (should) engage with fiction by willingly bracketing the unreality of the image. The suspension of disbelief implies that in our more rational moments, were we to see the film as it really is, as a mere re-presentation, as a fiction and a fantasy, we *would* and *should* disbelieve cinema's fiction, that it is "real" (Metz 1986[1975]:270; Aumont et al. 1992[1983]:77). Yet these women's uptake reveals that what is suspended in the normative liberal spectatorship that makes Sasikumar deaf to their point is precisely *this* belief, a belief in the patent reality that cinema is part and parcel of a world in which it acts, that the screen dwells in its surroundings as much as any other act or event does, never extricable from them, stubbornly insisting without respite: 'Fine, it's a film, *but* …' (compare Metz 1982[1975]:94; 2016[1991]:147). Who, after all, then, is credulous?

And indeed, we might ask, what does this credulity – suspended or otherwise, in belief or disbelief – reveal about the subject who takes it on, or projects it onto an other in an act of alterity (Hastings and Manning 2004)? Footings to fiction, in other words, are political and ethical stances. If so, the issue isn't simply credulity but the forms that it may take and the entailments generated therein. The credulity of the suspension of disbelief (and its imputation of credulity to others; which is to say, the very contrast of representational and sociological realism that has threaded the various chapters of this book) reveals not only an imaginary of reception (by class, age, gender, urbanity/ruralness, and so on – as we have had occasion to see across the book) but also a stance towards mediation itself. It reveals a rationalist semiotic ideology (Keane 2003; Strassler 2020:154–65) that desires to know the image as simply shadows – whether iconophobic or iconophilic (Mitchell 1986) – and no more (Kulick and Willson 1994:11). Such a stance disavows the patently social context of the image, its evident actness and potent performativity; it disavows and allows for the shirking of responsibility for the image, for its inevitable and necessary entanglements with the worlds of its making and uptake, even as it lays its own claims on them. It too, as an ontological politics, is a politics of footing.

Conclusion

In this chapter, as in this book, my aim has to been to outline the ways in which the potentialities of the image – as representation and act, as realist representation and performative presence – are entangled with and confront each other; and yet, at the same time, how each gives way to the other, and even amplifies the other, in and as the polyphonic texture of the image. As we have seen, the structure of realism in these films is marked by a confrontation with forms of performativity that such image-texts attempt to bracket and yet can never fully control, because, in fact, they constitutively need them. Realisms are entextualized by a gesture that inscribes their own limits, the tracing of a contrastive boundary within their instantiations' own textual bodies, a boundary that both authorizes the reality of their representationality while precisely falling into their opposites. This is manifest in the Tamil case in the figure of the illiberal spectator and the figure of the mass hero as they appear within realist films. It is manifest in the avoidance of taboo performativities of caste and sexuality, in those attempts to show them as they "really" are while pulling away from and effacing them at once. It is manifest in the complex forms of uptake by viewers in events of exhibition and in the metadiscourses about such films by filmmakers and viewers. This ambivalence is part of the ideological structuration and political economy of cinema in Tamil Nadu, of the fact that realism and its dreams of immediation are always already enregistered against the mediation of "cinema" (even as and *because* realism is an enregistered cinematic aesthetic style), of the fact that director and hero find themselves in conflict in/over the production format of the image-text, and so on.

Such dynamics and the ontological politics they bear, however, are not peculiar to Tamil cinema – even if they manifest in a particular way in it – but are more generally found among registers of representational realism, as and where we find them. Indeed, the close links between the ontological politics of the image and realisms in different contexts – from classical Hollywood to contemporary Kollywood, post-war Italy to post-revolution Iran – reveal the way in which the former is often worked out through and within the latter; that is, they reveal how contestations over what an image is or should be often take the vestments of realism and play out through the question of the real. If so, perhaps it is because, in these contexts at least, it is relative to the "real" that images (and signs more generally) are relationally defined (Mitchell 1986:43; Keane 2003). Realism, in other words, lurks within the metaphysics of the sign, though how this works itself out can take rather different forms in different times and places (see, for example, Shulman 2012). An empirical account of realism is precisely a study of this working out (or enregisterment, as we've termed it in in this chapter) and the political stakes, social relations, semiotic processes, and modes of being by which it proceeds.

In conclusion, I'd like to return to Bazin's own take on cinematic realism, affirming it and differing from it at once. For Bazin, cinema is precisely that representational medium that, because of its being (or, rather, what Bazin takes to be its being), reserves some part of itself to that which goes beyond representation to presence itself (see Chapter 1). The style that recognizes that reservation is, as Daniel Morgan (2006) argues, what Bazin calls *realism*. Realism, thus, is an aesthetic style and ethical stance that respects and takes into account the being of the filmic image.

Here, we affirm Bazin's conception of realism. Realist films do indeed respect the being of the filmic image. But not because film is inherently connected to reality in its continuity or contingency, but because what it means to be connected to the real *is always a political issue*, because *the politics of and for the image is (the basis of) its being*. Realist films explicitly orient their textuality and their politics precisely to this fact. If this point is particularly clear in the Tamil case – insofar as the centre of gravity of Tamil cinema is the presentist mass hero, such that all realist Tamil films find themselves, of necessity, attempting to carve out a representationalist space for themselves *out of* and by contesting his cine-political performative image – it is not peculiar to it. The point is more general: all realisms participate in an ontological politics that they bear in the filmic and cinematic forms they manifest.[69]

Conclusions: Ends and Openings

Plus ça change, plus c'est la même chose.
– Jean-Baptiste Alphonse Karr, *Les Guèpes*, 1862[1848]

Plus c'est la même chose, plus ça change.
– Michael Silverstein, "Language Structure and Linguistic Ideology," 1979
– Marshall Sahlins, *Historical Metaphors and Mythical Realities*, 1981

I warn you that the bull is about to charge.
– J.L. Austin, *How to Do Things with Words*, 1962

We must say of the cinema that its existence precedes its essence; even in his most adventurous extrapolations, it is this existence from which the critic must take his point of departure.
– André Bazin, "In Defense of Mixed Cinema," 2005[1952]

An End of an Era

On 5 December 2016, J. Jayalalitha, the chief minister of Tamil Nadu and leader of the AIADMK party died. Jayalalitha was a former film heroine, the onscreen and offscreen romantic companion of M.G. Ramachandran (or MGR), the founder of the AIADMK and the first and biggest "mass hero" of the Tamil cinema. In her time, Jayalalitha was a popular, glamorous actress. She rose to political power through her association with MGR, joining his party after retiring from film and winning control of his party after his death in 1987. In the years following, Jayalalitha transformed into a mass leader and cultivated her own cult of personality – though, tellingly and as an exception that proves the cine-political rule, not by leveraging her screen image but by explicitly disavowing it, desexualizing her heroine image and instead becoming *Ammā* (Mother), as she came to be called, the Mother of the Tamil polity.[1] With Jayalalitha's death, fissures in the AIADMK began to appear, first by caste (between O. Panneerselvam's Thevar faction and Edappadi K. Palaniswami's Gounder faction) and then by (fictive) kinship, with the former two factions opposed to Jayalalitha's companion, V.K. Sasikala, and her relatives. Meanwhile, Jayalalitha's rival, *Kalaiñar* Mu. Karunanidhi, the leader of the DMK party from which MGR split to form the AIADMK in the 1970s, was in his nineties, infirm and out of active politics. (He died under two years later, on 7 August 2018.) He had passed the baton to his son, Mu. Ka. Stalin, a dynastic transfer of leadership that confirmed the feeling of some that the DMK (like the AIADMK) had turned its back on a coherent ideology of social justice, having become an empty, dynastic shadow of its former revolutionary self.

After Jayalalitha's death, political demonstrations rocked the state – many of which were seemingly spontaneous, acephalous mass protests. Not only were they apparently leaderless, but they actively excluded – indeed, forced away – political leaders of mainstream parties from participating in them. By all accounts, there was a vast political vacuum in the state, with holes left by the utopian ideology of the Dravidianist parties and the great leaders (*periya talaivarkaḷ*) who had brought that ideology to the masses through film and other media.

For many, this political moment felt like the end of an era, an end to cine-politics, an end to the Dravidian movement, an end to mass heroes. Already in 2012, anthropologist and film critic Rajan Kurai (2012) had declared that the mass hero was dead – citing the release of the films *Kaadhal* (2004, dir. Balaji Sakthivel; see Chapter 4) and *Thamizh Padam* (2010, dir. C.S. Amudhan; see Chapter 3) as his death knell – even if he (the mass hero) and the film industry that orbited him had yet to realize it. Could there ever be another MGR? Jayalalitha? Annadurai or Karunanidhi?

And yet, neither Dravidianism nor cine-politics have faded from view. If anything, they have taken on a new, intensified if also unexpected – and sometimes tragic and farcical – form. In October 2017, *Ulaga Nayagan* (World Hero) Kamal Haasan – the cinematic heir to Sivaji Ganesan's mantle as thespian extraordinaire and "class" actor of the Tamil industry – declared his intention to form a political party (as had Sivaji, in failure ultimately, decades before) and began the work of contesting elections (to no success in the 2019 and 2021 elections). And on 31 December 2017, Superstar Rajinikanth, the heir to MGR's cinematic crown, after decades of speculation and fan demand, declared – to everyone's and no one's surprise – his intention to enter formal politics. (In late 2020, perhaps also to everyone's and no one's surprise, he walked back this intention.[2]) Neither embraced the hegemonic Dravidian political ideology – Kamal declaring his to be a "middle" way and Rajini declaring a "spiritual" politics that many feared was the harbinger of a Bharatiya Janata Party (BJP)–backed, right-wing Hindutva politics. Other would-be contenders, such as Seeman, the former film director and leader of the Naam Thamizhar Kadchi (We, the Tamilian's Party), captured the attention of the Tamil public by espousing chauvinistic views that have amplified, if also deeply criticized, Dravidianist rhetoric of the past but with a decidedly pro-ethnically Tamil bent.[3] And if that wasn't enough political drama, the next major hero-star in the wings, *Taḷapati* (General) Vijay, was gathering headlines as the next to enter the fray, following "MGR's path," as his father, director and producer S.A. Chandrasekhar (2010), put it to me in an interview nearly a decade before.[4]

The mass hero is dead, long live the mass hero ... Cine-politics has passed, yet there it is. But certainly not in the same form as it was. Technological changes in the Indian media ecology and film industry, changes in the political economy of Tamil cinema and other media (for example, the emergence of widespread telephony and media platforms like WhatsApp and YouTube; Cody 2018, 2019; Devadas and Velayutham 2021), changes in the narrative forms and tropes of mainstream cinema, changes in the political landscape of the region and the nation (the retrenching of a centrist, anti-regionalist Hindutva politics in Delhi, the dismal national performance by the Indian National Congress, and the weakening of previously strong, regional parties in Kerala, Bengal, and elsewhere), deep political cynicism among the Tamil public about national and regional modernism, and the very fact of the long, winding history of cine-politics – all these conspired to make it such that this cine-politics could never be a simple continuation of what came before. Yet, from the perspective of the ontological politics that have concerned *Onscreen/Offscreen*, *plus ça change, plus c'est la même chose*, and vice versa ... struggles over the nature of images continue on.

Killing the Mass Hero

In 2016, before Jayalalitha's or Karunanidhi's death, before Kamal's, Rajini's, or Vijay's declarations of entering (and leaving) politics, something rather unexpected and, from the perspective of the ontological politics that have concerned this book, telling happened. Rajinikanth teamed up for his next film with the relatively new director Pa. Ranjith

(b. 1982). After working as an assistant director and then associate director under Venkat Prabhu (see Chapters 1 and 3), Ranjith made two relatively small-budget but critically acclaimed and popular films – *Attakkathi* (Cardboard Knife, 2012) and *Madras* (2014). Both films operated in a familiar mode of director-helmed, story-driven realism. What made them stand out was their explicit Dalit politics, something – as we noted in Chapter 4 – that had been until then avoided, even prohibited, in the Tamil film industry. Rajinikanth's decision to team up with Ranjith came after the release of the former's lukewarmly received *Lingaa* (2014), a film directed by K.S. Ravikumar, who had directed a number of blockbuster Rajinikanth films from the 1990s. *Lingaa* was an unsuccessful return to the tropes and narrative organization of Rajini's 1990s films, films made at the height of his cine-political potential; to some, *Lingaa* verged on unintentional self-parody – a sign of the times (Chapter 3).

The first film that Ranjith and Rajini made together was *Kabali* (2016), a gangster drama that highlighted the plight of low-caste Tamils in Malaysia. The film made huge business, enabled by the producer S. Thanu's ability to leverage Rajinikanth's star value to draw in (middle-class) urban multiplex audiences in Tamil Nadu, in other regions of India, and even in overseas markets, as well as to draw in capital, pre-release, through various marketing tie-ups that cashed in on Rajini's star image (Chakravarthy 2018:286; Gerritsen 2021:152–5). Yet despite its financial success, many fans and critics were dissatisfied with the film, some (Rajini fans) averring that it was not enough of a "Rajini film" and too much of a "Ranjith film," while others (Ranjith fans and film critics) claiming the opposite, that it was a compromise on Ranjith's part. Some said that it was both, that the film couldn't decide if it was one or the other (Rangan 2016).

With Rajini acting his age (retaining his naturally white hair), with subdued "*style*" (Nakassis 2016a) and, moreover, as a character limited by the diegetic world (see Chapter 1), many fans reported not feeling the star's presence. He was missing, as it were, from his own image. It was telling, indeed, that before the film's release Ranjith described Rajini's character in the film to the press by saying that he wanted to bring out the great *actor*, the Rajini of *Mullum Malarum* (Thorn and Flower), a realist nativity film directed by the realist auteur extraordinaire, Mahendran.[5] Released in 1978, *Mullum Malarum* dated to the emergence of Rajini into a film industry that, for a short time, lacked mass heroes. The unresolved problematic raised by *Kabali* was, how can one put a star like Rajini *back* into a realist story, into a director's world, into a world without mass heroes without losing out on the star's presence and power? Could the Rajini of *Mullum Malarum* act in the auratic force field, the "image trap" (Pandian 1992) of the "Superstar"?

It was something of a bigger surprise, then, that following the seemingly negative answer to this question, Rajini declared his very next venture to *again* be a film directed by Pa. Ranjith: *Kaala* (2018). This announcement was only eclipsed by Rajini's later proclamation during the post-production of the film that he would be forming a political party.[6] Even more than *Kabali*, *Kaala* disappointed Rajini fans and divided its public. Focusing on the lives of low-caste Tamils in the slums of Bombay, and with an explicitly political story about gentrification within the city's and the nation's right-wing Hindutva dispensation, Rajini again acted his age, as an elder local big man and gangster in the slum, and with subdued heroism and *style*.

If fans and critics characterized *Kabali* as a film split between Ranjith and Rajini, *Kaala* left viewers with no doubt that it was a "Ranjith film," one wherein their *talaivar* (leader) had become a narrative tool within the director's own politics of and for the image (Kumar 2018). *Kaala*, as many commentators noted, attempted to break many of the conventions of commercial film, to open up a different cinematic space of representation, a different "regime of imageness" (Rancière 2007, 2009).[7] Critics lauded the strong, substantial female characters who were not just "eye candy," as well as Ranjith's casting of dubbing artists with low-pitch voices and actresses with dark skin.[8] They noted the strong social message of the film, its strongly opposed stance to nationalist Hindutva politics, its ambivalence to the Dravidianist dispensation and its (casteist) hegemonic articulation of Tamil identity, and its explicit championing of Dalit rights (compare Ram Manoharan 2021). They praised its sophisticated visual, aesthetic qualities.

But most of all, beyond all this, what critics and the viewers that I spoke with commented on was what Ranjith's film *did* to Rajini, the mass hero, and his image. Critics and viewers noted how in *Kaala*, like *Kabali*, the hero was unabashedly located by his low caste: *Kaala*'s hero is surrounded by, and mobilizes, radical political images (of Ambedkar, Periyar, Che Guevara, Nelson Mandela, and others) and emblems of Dalit identity (the colour blue, references to the colour black, eating of beef, and so on), as well as bears the long negatively stereotyped names of the oppressed rather than the names of Hindu gods (as in Rajini's past films from the 1990s).[9] Critics also highlighted how *Kaala* and *Kabali* put Rajini *into* a story, made him become his character, dimmed his star, and slowed his celebrity.

Kaala and *Kabali*, in short, broke stereotypes. But they didn't just re-enregister the mass hero – they dismembered him. Indeed, what was most radical was how both films narratively *attempted to kill the hero*, something absolutely unthinkable (and yet, of course, thought and dreaded) by fans of such invincible mass heroes.[10] Right before the interval of *Kabali*, Rajini's character is shot and lays still on the pavement, the intermission turned into a period of dread as the audience wondered whether and how Rajini could be dead onscreen. What was suggested at *Kabali*'s interval took on narrative reality in *Kaala*'s climax. The upper-caste (Brahmin) villain and Hindutva politician has set fire to the hero's slum in a sequence that masterfully alternates between the villain sitting for a recitation of the *Ramayana* (the epic story where the high-caste Ram defeats the evil Lankan demon Ravana) and the conflagration in the slum (Rajangam 2018).[11] In the slum, the hero Kaala (played by Rajini) says to the scared residents who want him to wait out the fight rather than join the fray: 'What if I, only a single person, die? You all are here too.'[12] His mouth clenched, he intones: 'Everyone here is a Kaala,' and walks out for the final confrontation. He fights, but is shot and falls, his body seemingly burned up in the fire like Ravana in the *Ramayana*.[13]

The denouement shows the victorious villain return to the slum to raze it and rebuild it for his development project to "purify" the city. Yet the people rise. As the villainous politician smells the soil, a small slum girl throws a fistful of black dirt at him, sullying his immaculate white dress (Chakrabarty 2001). As he looks up, he sees Kaala, in his signature all black (*kālā* also means black in Hindi), walking in the crowd as a song kicks in, singing about Ravana and his legendary ten heads regrown. Kaala disappears only to reappear elsewhere in the crowd, an apparition to the villain, who is confused, disoriented. Following the courageous girl's lead, the rest of the crowd joins in, throwing black soil – the colour of the subaltern working class, as Kaala says earlier in the film – onto the villain (Figure C.1 – top left). As the music continues over the scene, the riotous protest fantastically transforms into a Holi-esque dance party, with black powder flung in every direction as the destruction of evil – here, the villainous politician – is celebrated (as in Holi, as in the *Ramayana*). In a beautiful sequence that fully alienates itself from the diegesis that came before it, the black is replaced with dusts/soils of various bright colours – red and blue, the colours of communism and Dalit uplift, prominent among them – as we see shots of the crowd with Rajinikanth/Kaala masks on (Figure C.1 – top right). The camera zooms out to an impossible, aerial shot where a rainbow of colours explodes – red, blue, purple, pink, yellow (recalling, again, the "Festival of Colour," Holi, but also perhaps a multiculturalist politics of diversity) enveloping both the crowd and the villain alike (Figure C.1 – bottom right).

Figure C.1. *Kaala*'s (2018, dir. Pa. Ranjith) climax: the villain enveloped in black (top left); confused, the villain surrounded by a red sea of Kaalas (top right); the mass hero's final gesture (bottom left); the pulverization of his body (bottom right)

In *Kaala*, then, the body of the hero-star is diegeticized (itself a kind of death) … shot and burned (a narrative death) … then revived as spectral figment … and finally dispersed as dust in the chromatically diverse body politic of the subaltern residents who, indeed, have all become Kaala to fight their oppressor, "mass heroes" – the "mass as hero" – in Eisenstein's (1977[1949]:16, 122) sense.[14] Here, the crowd and, by extension, the audience are interpellated, but not as fan-followers of their *talaivar* in a form of symbolic identification that would hold him up on a pedestal, as in the typical mass-hero film, which audiences had been socialized to for the last several decades. Rather, the insistent presence of his star body is representationally turned, *within* the narrative (rather than in the theatrical space), into the literal atmosphere of the crowd. He is vaporized into the air they breathe, inhaled by them, covering their skin, his substantial presence penetrating their being in a form of indexical, even Eucharistic, ontological identity. If the star's body in *Kaala* has been killed, his character's spirit has been transubstantiated; yet only by sundering spirit from body, actor from star, cinema from (cine-)"politics." (And here, we might say, voicing fans' chagrin, the last man standing was not Rajini but Ranjith, the director who had orchestrated this representational theatre for us.)

Much more detailed analysis – along the lines deployed in previous chapters – could be applied to *Kabali* and *Kaala*, though I won't do so here. What I want to underline, instead, is how these films – and *Kaala*, in particular – stage and summarize, without resolving, the complex ontological politics of and for the image that have been at issue across the two parts of this book, if in a way that pushes them to a kind of limit.[15] Consider some of the multiple, and multiply complex, ontological politics at play in *Kaala*:

- A mass hero is embedded into, and thereby diegetically negated by, a directorial "class" film, but one that reverses the latter's upper-class and upper-caste politics through its strong, subaltern Dalit voice. Not just contesting the image of the mass hero, here Ranjith's film contests the casted enregisterment of realism (Chapter 4), its simultaneous naturalization of non-Brahmin caste domination of Dalits, and its liberal critique of caste. Tellingly, many in and out of the industry were irked by the explicitness, and perhaps to their mind uppitiness, of this Dalit politics, ironically – if predictably and sadly – accusing Pa. Ranjith of caste divisiveness rather than working to bring all castes together (for example, under the identity label "Tamil").
- Many fans lamented that Ranjith had used Rajini's mass image for his own (to their mind, narrow) political agenda. Some Dalit friends and public commentators (*Dinamalar* 2018), by contrast, speculated that Rajini was using Ranjith to capture the otherwise deeply split Dalit vote (if united, upwards of 20 per cent of the population); of them, some worried that a second-coming of a mass hero like MGR would be a step backward for a socially progressive Dalit movement (a worry not unlike that of other caste-based electoral parties, such as the Vanniyar Pattali Makkal Katchi (PMK), who feared Rajini's popularity would split their own ranks; see note 29 in the Introduction).
- Yet what, then, to make of the fact that Rajini's own avowed "spiritual politics" was seen to be amenable to the right-wing, anti-Dalit Hindutva politics represented by the *villain* of *Kaala*?[16] Was it Rajini trying to de-saffronize his image? Or was it Rajini trying to delink his offscreen political position from his onscreen image? Was it the star struggling with his own "image trap" (Chapter 1), attempting to remake his own star image through collaborating with a new, young director with his own vision and aesthetic style (see, for example, *IndiaToday.in* 2018)? Things became even more confusing when, at precisely the time of the release of *Kaala*, Rajini spoke against a massive, bottom-up social protest in the city of Tutukudi and supported the BJP-friendly AIADMK government's

violent crackdown on protestors. In *Kaala*, however, Rajini's character calls for and incites protests uncannily similar to what unfolded in Tutukudi, creating a dissonance between his screen image and his offscreen politics that many did not know what to do with (see, for example, TNM Staff 2018a; Harikrishnan 2018; Sudhir 2018).[17] Was Rajini's onscreen incitements, thus, a contradiction (why, anyway, should the actor's and the character's politics align?) or just an actor acting out a script – which is to say, to *what subject* would this be a contradiction?

- For his part, Ranjith expressed his aim to use Rajini's image to bring social awareness of injustice to a wider audience and to "raise questions" in the society about the place of caste and inequality (not unlike Balaji Sakthivel's aims in *Kaadhal* discussed in Chapter 4).

All these are ontological claims on and for the image, claims that variably entextualize the image as an act or as a representation denuded of actness. They are claims that interdiscursively read the image onscreen and offscreen at once, with and against each side of the screen. They are claims that ideologically articulate the image to its stakeholders (that is, presuppose a particular production format and participation framework): as moral principals of it or as mere animators of it. They are claims that, avowedly or in disavowal, recognize the image as an enunciation in the political, communicative context of its exhibition, from the set to the theatre to the state to the nation. What is an image, indeed?

Perhaps *Kabali* and *Kaala* are just two of the thousand cuts necessary for the death of the hero (narratively, if not socially); or perhaps they are just passing (non-fatal) scrapes and scratches in the churning ontological cine-politics of the Tamil film image. Or both – as change and continuity; for even as *Kabali* and *Kaala* appear as, and are, instances of historical change, we can also see them as the bringing to the surface of a longer-standing set of forces and contestations of and for the image, a meta-filmic image that resonates with Marshall Sahlins's (1981) and Michael Silverstein's (1979) characterizations of the dialectical relationships of culture and history, structure and event, metapragmatics and pragmatics. It is these tensions and constitutive potentialities of the image that we see played out in the ontological politics for and of *Kabali* and *Kaala*, but also in all the films that I have taken up in this book: tensions between presence and representation, star and director, and most of all, between the ambiguity and interpenetration of realist image-text and performative image-act. Death, rebirth, continuation, change – these are the terms and coordinates of the dynamic modes of being and becoming of the image.

/ / /

In concluding *Onscreen/Offscreen*, I return to two issues raised in the Introduction concerning what I called there *a linguistic anthropology of the cinema*. Through a reflection on the question of the performative representation, I first unpack the methodological implications of such an approach to film and cinema. In the final section, I consider its invitation to rethink what linguistic anthropology is and might be as a field.

Performativity/Representation and the Method/Theory of a Linguistic Anthropology of Cinema

As we have had occasion to see across the book, questions of representation and performativity, like shards in a kaleidoscope, align or appear orthogonal to each other at different moments, in different textual configurations, to different viewers, in different contexts. They confront each other as ideological opposites just to then appear in close symbiosis, amplifying each other like chords struck on strings alternating in harmonious tension, cacophonous disharmony, or even cancelling each other out, 180 degrees out of phase.

As J.L. Austin (1962:55) long ago noted, the line between what he called the *performative* and the *constative* (truth-functional statements) is less than clear. One of his examples of how performatives are "infected" by the truth-functionality of their sense and reference is the speech act "I warn you that the bull is about to charge." As Austin and others – such as Émile Benveniste and Michael Silverstein – have suggested, and as we have seen in various chapters of this book, the performative act is characterized by the bringing to bear of some figuration or representation (be it an image-text or a denotational text) on the event of semiosis that serves as its interactional infrastructure and instance of occasion, indeed, enactment. Yet if canonical examples of performative speech acts involve the alignment of the representationality/aesthetic form and the actness of the utterance, such textual partials – as linguistic anthropologists have pointed out in their analysis of everyday interaction (Silverstein 2004) – are also always liable to complex forms of partial disalignment and destructive interference (Agha 2007a).

Austin (1962) ends his lectures on *How to Do Things with Words* by collapsing the distinction between performatives and constatives as *types* of linguistic constructions or acts, instead constituting them as aspects or tendencies of all acts, if in varying ratios. In many ways, my discussion of film images has followed Austin in doing so. Yet, as Benveniste (1971:231–8) argued, simply concluding that all speech acts are part performative, part constative is ultimately an unproductive gesture (although it is, in its way, a necessary gesture). Such a conclusion conflates and reverses what is, in fact, Austin's major advance: namely, that different types of acts (performative and constative acts, to use those simplified labels) have real differences in their semiotic (con)textures, in how they actualize/entextualize different capacities as contextualized achievements of semiotic functionality; and moreover, that these differences make a difference (Nakassis 2013a). They have observably distinct social effects and uptakes. They have distinct semiotic economies and ecologies. They are wrapped up in and disclose different ideological enclosures.

The point, then, isn't that all signs have a little bit of both spices in them but that these potentialities are actualized, or cooked up and institutionalized, in particular ways, to particular (political, pragmatic) ends and through particular (semiotic, aesthetic) means. And this matters. Rather than a metaphysical point about action (that it is a *masala*), my point has been empirical: how *are* such potentialities actualized? Institutionalized? Made habit? And what, indeed, are the potentialities of an image? Which is to say, could we know such potentialities if not through the study of actual processes and effects of semiosis as they take place in and across events – since, after all, what an image *is* and *can* do is unknowable independently of (even if it is not reducible to) what it *does* do? What would such a study look like? By what methodology must we pursue these issues, in particular, in the case of this book, as it bears on the theoretical question of the image's being?

This question has lain at the heart of the chapters of *Onscreen/Offscreen*, if as an undertone trembling its surface – namely, that there is an inextricable relationship between method and theory, that one implies the other, that in each is encompassed the other, and that, in the cases at hand, ontological questions about the being of film images are opened up or hamstrung as a function of the methodology of their inquiry. On the one hand, as we've seen, an adequate method must be finely attuned to the textual surface of film, to its poetics, its intertextualities, to the properties of its media. At the same time, however, as the various chapters of the book have also demonstrated, it is not enough to simply inspect the texture of a film, indeed, to bound off a film (or any fraction of it) as an internally contained sui genesis whole with features independent of its cinematic context of happening (be it production, distribution, exhibition, other texts, and so on). It is a mistake to treat "text" independently of *entextualization*, the multiply situated and perspectivally complex processes by which a text is carved out of its surround, *made* to stand apart from its context for some set of persons (Silverstein and Urban 1996). To assume text independently of such a process is to reify *one* perspective (most often, that of the methodologically individualist film analyst), while effacing the labour of that reification.

Which is to say, it is epistemologically indeterminate whether a film is or is not performative or representational, personally enunciative and deictic or impersonal and reflexive (*sensu* Metz 2016[1991]), or even a little bit of one or the other outside of some particular perspective on some particular event of semiosis. But more to the point, it is also *ontically* indeterminate since, as I have argued, such designations (performative, representation, deictic, reflexive, and the like) are themselves *achievements* of semiotic and metasemiotic labour of various sorts. To study such issues (ontology/being, performativity, textuality, enunciation, spectatorship) is to study such labour as it mediates and is mediated by such processes of entextualization.

What I have been arguing against, then, is any conceptualization of text that would rigidly and statically separate out an inside and an outside.[18] Such a conceptualization problematically cleaves off empirical investigation (which deals with the putative outside of the text) from textual analysis (which deals with its seemingly internal organization). From our perspective, one cannot exist without the other, because that putative outside is already *inside* the text insofar as text is always relationally defined by some dialectic of entextualization/contextualization (Silverstein 1992). The boundary of a text is already drawn inside of it, just as it projects itself beyond that boundary.[19] The point, of course, is not that texts and contexts don't exist, analytically or empirically; rather, it is to refuse to accept such a division as pregiven and obvious. It is to ask the question of *how* such a division comes about as a situated semiotic and political process amenable to – indeed, demanding of – empirical investigation.

This argument is not, then, as I suggested in the Introduction to the book, a plea for "reception studies" against "textual analysis" or even to add one to the other, for it is precisely this purification of text and context that, in abiding the ideology of text, makes it impossible to broach the issues that I have attempted to analyse in this book (Kulick and Willson 1994:1; Srinivas 2009:5; Nakassis 2016a). Such a move effaces precisely what our object of analysis is: semiosis as event, as process, as relation, as equally communication and political contestation. All such purifications are, of course, a politics for the image – as when they purify an image so as to ground a disciplinary project, associated methodology, and theoretical and filmic canon.[20] Indeed, such purifications project an image of being, an ontology (often taken as THE ontology), made in the image of its project, methodology, and canon.

If the methodology that we have followed, then, weaves a textual and an empirical analysis of cinema, it is not because there is a "text" waiting to be contextualized by empirical ("reception") study, or a spectator "position" waiting to be "activated" by an embodied viewer, or because any of these pairs (textual–empirical analysis, text–context/reception, spectator–viewer) are fundamentally different in kind. None of these are true.[21] Rather, it is because, dipping our toes into the river in media res, we work forward and backward to triangulate and provisionally reconstruct precisely the processes and relations through which any so-entextualized image-text comes into being, comes to be experienced, interpreted, contested, affirmed, circulated, and take on the qualities and relations and powers that we and others find it to manifest. To study all this is to historically and ethnographically attend to the situated events and processes through which such phenomena take textual form and are taken up in various moments; it means attention to how such phenomena become objects of reflection, contestation, and institutionalization (or not); it means attending to how they mediate and are mediated by such events and processes, on and off the screen; and further, it means tracing out how such events and processes dialectically constitute and come to be connected to each other. Text/context, onscreen/offscreen – the space we work to study is that backslash, that mediating relation and metasemiotic operator, the dialectical, diaphanous membrane of the ontological politics that has concerned this book.

Doing so, as we've seen, allows us to revisit anew and retheorize a number of topics that have concerned film studies and related fields. It also offers occasion to rethink what constitutes linguistic anthropology itself as a field.

For a Linguistic Anthropology of …

Let us return, in the end, to the claim embedded in the phrase *a linguistic anthropology of cinema*: that *Onscreen/Offscreen* is not simply a work that draws *on* linguistic anthropology but is a work *of* linguistic anthropology. At issue in this claim is the question of what are the centres and boundaries of our field.

If, historically, the phrase *linguistic anthropology* named, after the fact, the entangled space from which linguistics and sociocultural anthropology split in mid-twentieth-century North America – namely, the anthropological study of language in/and culture (Hymes 1964a) – one might wonder what, indeed, "a linguistic anthropology of *cinema*" might mean as *linguistic* anthropology? As has been clear, the phrase *a linguistic anthropology of cinema* denotes neither a study of speech or language in film or the cinema nor an account of "film language," at least not in the sense that drove the application of structuralist methods and concepts to the study of filmic "codes" (see Introduction, in particular note 7). Instead, as we've seen, a linguistic anthropology of cinema is an analysis of the pragmatics and metapragmatics of events and processes of cinematic semiosis. It is a study of the reflexive knot at the heart of the being of filmic and cinematic images, those mutually constitutive relations between the material and textual form of images, the pragmatic effects they occasion in the events of their happening, and those reflexive semiotic practices that take images – and the larger cinematic institution they orient – as their object, construing such images, making claims on them, and thus mediating their becoming, interpretation, use, circulation, and institutionalization.

But what makes this *linguistic* anthropology per se? Why not just simply call it "semiotic anthropology" (Mertz 2007) or "ethnographic semiotics" (Worth 1981:202), or just plain semiotics for that matter?

I insist on the phrase *a linguistic anthropology of cinema* because the expansion of linguistic anthropology's empirical purview beyond "language" – for example, to cinema or to any number of cultural forms – has been implied by linguistic anthropology's major interventions into the study of language and discourse for at least the last half century, if not since its origins. This fact necessitates that we shift, or better, *multiply* the centres of gravity of linguistic anthropology beyond the study of "language," not in a mode of self-negation, abandonment, or centrifugal dispersal but as a collective, centripetal process of positive self-differentiation. (The elliptical genitive construction "a linguistic anthropology of …" is meant to suggest any number of other possible linguistic anthropologies, with as many potential objects of analysis as possible modifiers of the noun phrase, all linked together *as* linguistic anthropology.) How so?

We might begin with the observation that linguistic anthropology has always argued against any concept of language that would excise social and cultural life from it and vice versa, that would not take into account the mediation of social and cultural life by linguistic discourse. This argument has led to the view that the linguistic is always shot through with, and characterizable by, precisely those semiotic grounds (iconicity and indexicality) and aspects (sensuousness, materiality, performative force) that the ideological focus on language as an abstract, symbolic representational "system" obscures or excises. The result of these arguments has been the erosion of the sui generis autonomy of that object "language" – what Saussure (1986[1916]) called *langue*, or semantico-grammatical structure – and a critique of such a conceptualization as sufficient in the holistic study of discourse, society, or culture (Hymes 1964a, 1964b; Silverstein 1976, 2005b; Keane 2003; Agha 2007b; Stasch 2014; Nakassis 2016b; Fleming 2020; Harkness 2021). This line of thought, in turn, has pushed the field towards a more expansive account of language: on the one hand, to the ways in which the linguistic is always entangled with and constituted by, even as it is ideologically purified from, the non-linguistic (in particular, through the mediation of indexical practice); and thus, on the other hand, to those semiotic functions that, while well evidenced by linguistic discourse, are at play in any number of other media and modalities of semiosis (Mertz 2007; Gal and Irvine 2019). Indeed, all of linguistic anthropology's analytics and theoretical innovations (indexicality, metapragmatics, ideology, entextualization, enregisterment, stance, mediatization, dicentization, rhematization, and so on), while developed out of the study of linguistic discourse and the insufficiency of a structuralist concept of "language" to account for it, are *necessarily* generalizable beyond language. Which is to say that linguistic anthropological inquiry has long attempted to base itself not on "language" as its foundational object of study but on articulating a space beyond but inclusive of language precisely through a study of it(s limits). If so, then linguistic anthropology's epistemological, methodological, analytic, and theoretical engagement with semiosis – as "language" or/in "culture" – necessarily troubles any notion of "language" that would define its study *based on* the purification of its putative uniqueness or medium specificity (namely, symbolic denotation; Harkness 2021). This is what I mean when I say that linguistic anthropologists do not study "language" even if, and especially when, they study what, from a formal, structuralist perspective, would be denoted by the lexeme *language* or even *langue*. To aver otherwise is to walk back on the critical purchase of linguistic anthropology. It is to yield the definition of the field's boundaries to an object and mode of analysis it fundamentally problematizes. For if we hold that the basis of our field is language ("in" discourse, "in" interaction, "in" social context, "in" culture), what indeed *is* language such that it could stand apart from discourse, interaction, context, culture, and so on, and thus be put "in" them? The catachresis of linguistic anthropology, thus, both pragmatically deconstructs and explodes the very concept of language while expansively reimagining what a linguistic anthropology of "it" could be. Might it include cinema? And if so, how would that help us rethink semiosis tout court, in any number of media, including "in" "language"?[22]

For these reasons, I insist that this project is a work of *linguistic* anthropology, precisely to hold on to the genealogy, sensibility, and training from which this project's arguments and position emerge (which include, of necessity, disciplinary linguistics, among other fields) while, at the same time, not conceding the definition of and zoning off of what language is and what it is to study it – namely, what constitutes linguistic anthropology – to precisely those accounts that linguistic anthropology refuses as its own, especially when it itself ambivalently voices them. The phrase *a linguistic anthropology of ...*, thus, issues an invitation to rethink and open up what linguistic anthropology is and could be within but also beyond its current, if ever-shifting bounds *as* linguistic anthropology, an invitation given over to those within its fold and those who have yet to recognize themselves as already welcome and at home within it, be they students of cinema or ...

Notes

Introduction: Ontological Politics of the Image

1 The complex linkages that I discuss in this book between ontological politics and the modes of being they presuppose and entail are pervasive far beyond the Tamil cinema. We can see them similarly evinced in medieval and (post)colonial Indic debates over Hindu idols and other godly representations (Davis 1999:44–9; Rajagopal 2001; Pinney 2004; Jain 2007), Byzantine contestations of religious icons (Belting 1994[1990]; Mondzain 2005), nineteenth-century European debates over theatrical representation and the presence of the stage (Power 2006:19, 47–8; see also Vega 1986[1607–08]; Evreinov 1927, 1973; Schechner 1988), debates about the permissibility of film images in (post)colonial Pakistan (Cooper 2018) and northern Nigeria (Larkin 2008:135–8, 209–13, 253), (anti)modernism in the plastic arts in Europe (Levaco 1974; Rancière 2007), the institutionalization of fictional narrative film in early twentieth-century Hollywood (Gunning 1991; Hansen 1991; Gaudreault 2009[1999]:101–12), and mid-century American pornography (Williams 1989), among many more examples, including André Bazin's own realist project, as I discuss in the main text below and in Chapter 1. Like weeds in the garden, when one begins to look for the ontological politics of images and the multiple ontologies and modes of being they engage and engender, they are all one finds, their leaves above and their roots below the fertile soil. A garden, after all, is a labour, and an aesthetic and political one at that, which is tenuous and unending, no matter how neat and clean it appears at the moment of well-cultivated and carefully curated exhibition and experience.

2 These questions are not meant to exhaust the wide and complex range of ways in which the being of the image has underwritten film studies. On some classic examples of how these questions have been articulated in film studies, see Benjamin 1968[1935]; Eisenstein 1943; Bazin 2005[1945],

1985[1950]; Kracauer 1960; Mitry 1997[1963]; Baudry 1986[1970], 1986[1975]; Metz 1986[1975], 2016[1986]; Mulvey 2009[1975], 1989, 2002:258–60; Cavell 1979; de Lauretis 1984; Doane et al. 1984. See Hollinger 2012:7–19 for a review of these questions in feminist film criticism. On current concerns about the being of the image in the era of the digital and the return to classical debates, see Prince 1996; Morgan 2006; Gunning 2008; Schoonover 2012; Lefebvre 2021. On issues of image ontology in art history and visual studies, see Mitchell 1986, 1994, 2015; Jain 2007; Elkins and Naef 2011; in visual and media anthropology, see Pinney 2004; MacDougall 2006; Larkin 2008; Mazzarella 2013; Pandian 2015; Strassler 2020.

3 Christian Metz (1991[1971]:111) notes, for example, that "the collective notions of what an image is" is a sociocultural variable that impinges on the intelligibility of filmic images (see also Worth and Adair 1972). What Metz does not pursue is how this is so, what the range of such variability is, how this variability impacts the way film studies must (methodologically) proceed and what it can (theoretically) explicate, and, perhaps most importantly, how such "collective notions" are ideological in nature – objects of political contestation and negotiation – and thereby function as regimenting metapragmatics on not just the intelligibility but the becoming and thus the being of images.

4 *Ontology* and *being* are tired, burdened terms, their interdiscursive histories – some connected, some disconnected – bearing much indexical baggage. This book doesn't aim to speak to all, even most, such discourses on (the study of) being. Instead, I am focused on one particular use, that of André Bazin and those who have taken him up. Colleagues in sociocultural anthropology may be disappointed that I do not directly engage the so-called ontological turn in anthropology or similar developments in related fields, though some of such work (for example, Latour 2005) finds expression in my uptake of Annemarie Mol's (1999) notion of "ontological politics." I hope, however, that those with such interests will find utility in my own formulation of the issues. As evident in the main text above, my aim is a kind of paleonymics that works itself through empirical and semiotic analysis, aiming to (de)provincialize film theory's engagement with ontology and images (see Chapter 1 for more discussion), as well as regions of the metaphysical enclosure within which being has taken on some of its baggage (what we might call with Whorf [1956(1939)] "S[tandard]A[verage]E[uropean] philosophy"). Some readers in film studies may feel that these arguments are not really about being or ontology but about other issues (efficacy, doing, worlding, epistemology). But aren't all such issues *also* ontological, and being at issue in each of them? Why concede being to a conception of it that would purify it from questions of efficacy (performativity), doing (pragmatics), worlding (cosmopolitics;

Cadena 2010), and epistemology (semiosis)? Not simply narrowing our theoretical discourse, such a purification also allows that central question of film theory – what *is* a film image? – to remain cordoned off and safe in its methodological space, confined to particular, familiar approaches and objects of exemplification (for example, a Euro-American canon of images) rather than fully open to the diversities of cinematic experience and manifestation, and the gamut of ways of studying both. The challenge, then, is to reconsider what ontology and being might mean in the context of film studies and linguistic anthropology through an ethnographic study of Tamil commercial cinema, or rather, what we might do and undo with these terms, engaged with, yet also outside of, such confinements.

5 Moreover, saying that modes of being are relative to situated positionalities, perspectives, ideologies, and the like is not to deny that images "have" a mode of being, as seemed to be implied, for example, by much 1970s film theory. Indeed, one cannot ask after the being of images without a focus on the politics of this very question (or vice versa), not because the former is a chimera of the latter but rather because the former is always already mediated by and manifested through the latter. (This point is clearly argued by Bazin [2005(1946)] himself, who suggests that the "myth" of realism historically precedes cinema and, indeed, has guided its becoming.) In broaching this argument, I follow the move in linguistic anthropology to problematize questions of semiosis (and by extension, the being of language) through appeal to the situated nature of semiotic ideologies of various sorts. (Throughout the book, I use the term *ideology* in the particular sense that linguistic anthropologists have developed; see, for example, Woolard 1998; Gal 2002, 2005, 2018; Keane 2003; Gal and Irvine 2019; for a comparable usage in visual studies, see Mitchell 1986; in media anthropology, see Larkin 2008:3–4; compare Branigan's 2006 use of "language games.") At the same time, I extend the focus on ideology by asking how ideologies of various sorts mediate the very being – the *what* (*is*) in "what is an image?" – of that which they rationalize, regiment, and construe: in the instance, film images. It is for this reason that I prefer to speak of ontologies here rather than ideologies of the image, even if they implicate each other. Finally, note that this shift to a pragmatist approach to the question of being helps avoid the problem of falling into either an easy nominalism, a naïve empiricism, or a metaphysical idealism, instead committing us to a *semiotic realism* (Silverstein 2004; Nakassis 2018) that recognizes and makes empirically investigable the reality of semiosis and the social. It is precisely this semiotic realism that forces us to take seriously both the fact of relativity (that is, semiotic mediation) – say, of the modes of being of the image – *and* the necessity of empirical inquiry (which is itself semioticaly mediated, of course) as the best mode of accounting for and exploring

their reality. Thanks to Jack Sidnell for pushing me to elaborate this productive tension between nominalism and realism that inheres in semiotic mediation, and thus in linguistic anthropology's accounts of it; see also note 6 in Chapter 4.

6 Here and throughout I use the terms *film* and *cinema* in Metz's (1974[1971]) sense to heuristically distinguish textual precipitate (what appears on a screen), *film*, from the wider social institution, *cinema*, though the distinction is neither firm nor absolute. See discussion in the main text below.

7 The supposition that film studies and linguistic anthropology need to, or even could, be in dialogue might strike some readers as unexpected ("out of left field," as one reviewer of an early draft of the manuscript put it). There are precedents, however, as in the passing connections between the work of Sol Worth and Christian Metz (Worth 1969; Worth and Adair 1972; Metz 1974[1971]:188, 2016[1986]:§18). Martin Lefebvre (personal communication, 2020) informs me that Metz had written a summary of Worth's work for his personal files. Steven Feld (personal communication, 2020) reports that Hymes's "ethnography of communication" (for example, Hymes 1973:70–1) was in dialogue with Worth's work at one level or other, and vice versa (as is clear from Worth and Adair 1972; Worth 1974; see Gross 1981:15n5, 16, 22n8 on this influence on Worth and his student/collaborator Richard Chalfen). In addition, the work of Steven Feld – trained in anthropological linguistics and the anthropology of music at Indiana University, as well as in professional filmmaking and photography – is another point of contact between film theory, visual anthropology, and linguistic anthropology, as reflected in his writings (for example, Feld and Williams 1975), filmmaking, and translations (for example, his translation of Metz 1980 – published in an issue dedicated to Sol Worth in *Studies in Visual Communication*, the successor journal to *Studies in the Anthropology of Visual Communication*, which Worth began – and Jean Rouch; see Feld et al. 2020). Nevertheless, there has never been much of a sustained interdisciplinary engagement between these fields.

There is, however, a common history – even a virtual, unwitting conversation around shared touchstones – that centres on both fields' fraught relationship to the object "language" and their attempts to develop a semiotic theory adequate to the complexity of their objects of analysis. Indeed, one way to characterize the history of academic film studies is by its struggles with the application and modification of linguistic theories and methods to film, be it formalist poetics (Eisenstein 1943; Kuleshov 1974[1929]; compare Jakobson 1981; see note 9 in this chapter), linguistic structuralism (Metz 1974[1971], 1991[1971], 2016[1986]; Lotman 1976; Bellour 2000[1979]), generative grammar (Branigan 1984; Colin 1995; compare Worth 1969:302–17; Worth and Adair 1972), enunciation theory (Casetti 1998[1986]; Metz 2016[1991]), linguistic pragmatics (Jost 1995; Odin 1995), functional linguistics (Bateman and Schmidt 2012), literary narrative theory (Gunning 1991; Gaudreault 2009[1999]), or, just as commonly today, a rejection of all such applications and analogies as inapt, misguided, and perhaps best left as a curiosity of the history of the field (Bordwell 1985; Tröhler 2018:20; Odin 2018:107). Tellingly, such linguistically inspired accounts of film have stood in a distant relationship to questions of the ontology of the image – either in distinction from them (for example, Bazin finishes his classic essay "Ontology of the Photographic Image" [2005(1945):16] by famously saying: "On the other hand, of course, cinema is also a language"; Morgan 2018:237), as critical of them (as epiphenomena of more basic semiological, psychoanalytic, ideological functions, as in so-called 1970s Screen theory), or as simply indifferent to them. In such works, a semiotic ontology of the film image is something of a contradiction in terms.

One can similarly characterize linguistic anthropology by its struggles against the narrow application of formalist linguistic theories and methods to language and, by extension, to "culture" more widely, as I discuss in the book's Conclusions.

Of course, as Christian Metz (1974[1971], 1991[1971], 2016[1986]:§30) and others quickly realized (Worth 1969:302–17; Worth and Adair 1972:138, 162), the analogy of "film language" fails because film is not like language insofar as language is like what Saussure (1986[1916]) called *langue* (that sui generis, autonomous denotational "system" that enables language's referential function), an argument that, as just noted, linguistic anthropologists were making at this time as well about language: namely, that linguistic discourse is not like language insofar as language is reduced to *langue*. If the project of film semiology failed, it was precisely because of the problematic, blinkered conceptualization of language and semiosis it was using (Bateman and Schmidt 2012:17, 27–33, 129), not because of the non-utility of semiotics per se nor because of the pre- or a-semiotic nature of film or other imagistic media. The semiotic baby need not go out with the structuralist bathwater.

This pragmatist deconstruction of "language" – the refusal to concede the object "language" to a structuralist conceptualization (as symbolic representation) but instead critically work through it – as part of the articulation of an empirically adequate and expansive semiotics that might enter into a dialogue with film theory also distinguishes the approach in this book from the dialogue of visual and sensory anthropology with film studies (centred around, in particular, ethnographic film). Both visual and sensory anthropology, like much contemporary film studies, have tended to argue that "semiotics" – by which is usually meant structuralist semiology (Keane 2003) – is inadequate given its overdependence on "representation" and "language." Ironically, such a view reproduces the structuralist fallacy in critiquing it, uncritically accepting the limited conceptualization of "language" – and thus semiotics – as handed down by structuralism itself (see also Hymes 1964b:9); in doing so, such a view fundamentally misunderstands both how discourse works and how semiotics might productively be part of a comprehensive understanding of film, cinema, and other imagistic media. See discussion in Ball et al. 2020.

8 For some recent examples of how linguistic anthropology can inform the study of film and cinema, see Lefkowitz 2005, 2019; Meek 2006; Nakassis and Dean 2007; Nakassis 2009, 2010, 2015, 2016a, 2017, 2019, 2020; Malitsky 2010; Bucholtz 2011; Gershon and Malitsky 2011; Hardy 2014; Peterson 2014; Kirk 2016; Nakassis and Weidman 2018; Caton 2021.

9 *Entextualization* denotes the emergently structured process by which co-occurring signs come – and are made – to cohere together (as "text") in dynamically unfolding events (Bauman and Briggs 1990; Silverstein and Urban 1996). It is akin to – indeed, has a common genealogy with – what Sergei Eisenstein (1943) described with his capacious notion of *montage*. Both terms describe those indexical juxtapositions of signs, of any type, that form iconic resonances and dissonances, poetically cumulating and gelling in ways that enable emergently structured congeries ("texts") to both *depict* and *act*, to narrate and performatively enunciate, to represent and presence. This adequation of *entextualization* and *montage* is not meant to suggest that all aspects of Eisenstein's notion of montage (see also Kuleshov 1974[1929]) are equivalent to linguistic anthropologists' notion of *entextualization* but instead to provoke an intertextual link between Russian Formalism – as expressed in Eisenstein's film theory – and linguistic anthropology – as mediated by Jakobson's (1987[1935], 1960[1958]) discussion of the aesthetic/poetic function and its uptake by Silverstein (1993) as metapragmatic function (Nakassis 2019, 2020). One difference, for example, is that Eisenstein (1943:36–7) opposes montage – as a dialogic, emergent property of textuality in its indexical juxtapositions – to "bare documentary information" or "representation" – as a monologic, denotational textuality, we might say – and thus (artistic, imagistic) experience to (referential) information. Linguistic anthropologists, by contrast, like Jakobson, have insisted on the poetic organization of even "bare documentary information" and the constant interaction of these two dimensions. Despite such differences, Eisenstein's notion of *montage* captures each of the important features of the concept of *entextualization*: as evenemential process, as token-type relation, as iconic indexicality, as non-modality specific, as perspectival and distributed, as emergent, and as the basis of eventhood and meaningful experience (see also Nakassis and Morgan's contributions in Ball et al. 2020). By zoning off swatches of semiosis as coherent units of social experience and action ("text"),

entextualization enables texts to reach beyond their contexts and circulate *between* events (Agha 2005; Silverstein 2005a), becoming the object of focus and action across disparate yet entangled social sites. Entextualization implies *interdiscursivity*, those indexical and iconic relations between events of entextualization. (Note that interdiscursivity is generally concerned with relations between distinct events of semiosis – say, the indexical links [drawn] between events of production on a film set and a theatre, or between script discussion and post-production colouring, and so on – and not simply cultural/literary texts, as canonically understood; in this, it differs from the narrower focus of intertextual relations between films.) Every event of engaging a film image – from imagining it in a script, to inscribing it with a camera, to watching it in a theatre, to talking or writing about it afterwards, and so on – is a process of entextualization and interdiscursivity, where the flux of experience is rendered coherent, metasemiotically cut out from its surround ("context"), attended to, interpreted, and thereby articulated to other possible or actual events (moments of production, other films and past experiences, other events of uptake, future images). A focus on entextualization and interdiscursivity points up the evenemential contingency and dynamic temporality of semiosis to form "text" vis-à-vis a co-constitutive surround, its "context" (at whatever scale). Critical for both concepts is that such relations and processes are understood as the basis of and as comprised by acts whose meaningfulness and relevance are constituted by their achieved *effects*, by those perturbations they have in and by their happening, relative to their concurrently produced context (Silverstein 1992). On such a view, context is not a static out-there within which texts are thus situated but is itself a dynamic *relational process and precipitate*. See main text for more discussion.

10 This approach makes *Onscreen/Offscreen* an ethnography of a particular kind with particular aims. Whereas an ethnography of reception (for example, Dickey 1993a, 1993b, 2001; Nakassis and Dean 2007; Pandian 2008; Krishnan 2009; Srinivas 2009; Nakassis 2016a; Gerritsen 2019) might dwell on the intimate lives, spaces, and routines of viewers and their engagements with the cinema; or an ethnography of film production (for example, Pandian 2011, 2015; Ganti 2012) might detail the modular processes of scriptwriting, shooting, post-production work, the social relations of the industry, its political economy, and the like (Rossoukh and Caton 2021) – all of which my research touched upon and some of which I reference as relevant to my arguments in this book – my goal in this book is different and more selective. I don't aim to offer a comprehensive picture of the Tamil industry or its worlds, nor do I cover all the aspects that go into the Tamil cinema or its images. Rather, I am pursuing particular theoretical

questions as prompted by my ethnographic research through a series of case studies.

11 My presentation of these terms as pairs is not to suggest that they are opposed per se; indeed, they each presuppose and necessitate each other. Rather, I am interested in how an ontological politics, and the ideological field it instates, figures such correlative pairs as oppositions. Which is to say, while the terms function as analytics for me, their oppositional conjunction indicates their ethnographic relation within the fields of activity that I take as my object of analysis.

12 However, even by 1928, 90 per cent of screened films were still foreign imports (Hughes 1996:12), and the biggest film stars were Western actors like Eddie Polo and Pearle White. Indian actors' names in the cinema, Baskaran (1996:7) notes, were not even publicized until the 1930s. While the 1920s saw an increase in Indian-produced films, as Stephen Hughes (1996) reports, they were continually outnumbered by the number of import feature films (for example, 63 Indian feature films versus 615 imported films in 1921–22; 108 Indian films versus 775 imported films in 1926–27), though the Indian films were screened at and circulated between theatres for longer.

13 As Stephen Hughes (2007:10) has suggested, in the 1920s such theatre-cum-recording stars were more popular than either Hollywood or Indian silent film stars.

14 The distinction of speech versus language community is Michael Silverstein's (1998). In contrast to a language community – a group reflexively constituted through orientation and loyalty to some named and often standardized denotational code (a "language") – a speech community is formed through networks of communicative activity regimented by shared norms of indexical value that almost always utilize multiple denotational codes, dialects, and registers. While, ideologically, Tamil Nadu is a state defined by the Tamil language community, as a speech community it is comprised of multiple "languages" (Tamil, Telugu, Malayalam, Hindi, Urdu, English, among others), numerous dialects and social registers (by caste, class, subculture), written scripts, and so on. See Nakassis and Annamalai 2020.

15 Reflective of this uncertainty, the first talkies had dialogue and songs in multiple languages. Consider, for example, *Kalidas* (1931, dir. H.M. Reddy), today considered the first "Tamil" talkie. Made in Bombay and directed by a native Telugu speaker, *Kalidas* had its hero speaking in Telugu, heroine singing in Tamil, as well as dialogues with Hindi and Sanskrit. The film was marketed as a "Tamil-Telugu talkie" or simply as a "south Indian talking film," indicating, Stephen Hughes (2011:215) suggests, that the very notion of a "Tamil" film had yet to come into circulation. Similarly,

consider Ellis R. Dungan's description of his 1937 film *Ambikapathi*, starring the Tamil stage actors M.R. Santanalakshmi and M.K.T. Bhagavathar and made in Calcutta for a Tamil producer: "Cinematographer Krishna Goap, a Hindu, was from Bombay; camera, Paul Briquet, was French; and Mr. Schulmeister, a German, was in charge of the laboratory processing. Arthur Bradburn, an Englishman, was the sound engineer. Then we had a Bengali art director and an Irish studio production manager, Bill Moylan. Lastly, there was me, the American director" (Dungan and Smik 2001:64). The film was written by the Tamil scholar Thanigachalam (under the pen name Elangovan), who translated a number of scenes from MGM's 1936 production of Shakespeare's *Romeo and Juliet*, which Dungan used as inspiration to adapt the Chola-era epic. All that said, exhibitors in the 1920s already had a sense that South Indian audiences preferred Telugu or Tamil subtitles and South Indian locales and content, though this sense didn't differentiate by language per se but by region. What was clear, however, among critics at least, was that the ethnolinguistic identity of films *should* matter, as reflected by their claims at the time that films of the day were not "Tamil" enough – for example, in who was producing them, where the locales were, what language the dialogues or songs were in, or what the quality of the Tamil therein was.

16 This differentiation of the Tamil film/industry from other film-types/industries was linguistic and infrastructural, but above all ideological. For while the use of language in films became (relatively) monolingualized across this period, and while production locales, distribution circuits, exhibition centres, and audiences became more centralized in the Madras Presidency, it is important to see that the "Tamil"ness of the Tamil film industry was (and is) an ideological overlay on top of a much more complex multicultural and multilingual community of cinematic practice. As they were in the silent era, the post-1930s regional film industries were and have continued to be multilingual and multicultural, with stories, technicians, character actors, heroines, and films themselves circulating across industries (see also Ganti 2012:156; Mukherjee and Mehta 2021:2–6; see note 15 in this chapter). For reasons that will become clear in the main text below, it is primarily heroes who are confined to their regional industries (see also note 32 in this chapter). Critically important, then, was the *sense* that films and the industries that produced them could (and should) be parcelled out by linguistically named communities.

17 It wasn't only the Dravidian movement that used theatre and cinema for political propaganda. The Indian National Congress's nationalist agitations found expression in theatre and cinema of the 1930s, though their use of such media waned during the Second World War as the Dravidianist use of theatre and cinema waxed. The Congress resigned its rule

in the Madras Presidency in protest at the advent of the Second World War, which led to more stringent censorship by the colonial state and decreased use of nationalist propaganda by the Congress. However, by and large, the cultural elites of the Congress Party in the Madras Presidency disparaged the cinema and saw it as a vulgar and dangerous medium (though, see Baskaran 1996:82), in contrast to the Dravidian movements' active use of and positive attitude towards the cinema as a medium of social uplift and education, political mobilization, and entertainment. While many South Indian artists were swept up into the nationalist movement and the Congress Party, with time (and the death of Satyamurthy, one of the few Congressmen who supported the Tamil cinema) many, including M.G. Ramachandran, shifted their support to the Dravidian movement.

18 Restrictions on the use of raw stock, petrol rationing, power cuts, and the destruction of South Indian film markets beyond the borders of India (for example, in Burma) all led to a reduction in film production during the Second World War (Baskaran 1996; Dungan and Smik 2001:75–6). Drama, in its stead, flourished in the 1940s, in particular, Dravidianist-themed plays with their didactic messages of social reform and critique.

19 As Eswaran Pillai (2015) points out, the studios that produced such canonical DMK films did not necessarily have strong Dravidianist leanings, even if the writers and actors did, but instead exploited the popularity of such plays as part of their risk-mitigation strategy.

20 We should underline that such directors and dialogue writers brought the politically powerful oratorical style characteristic of the Dravidian movement to their films, if only in key sites (as discussed in the main text below). As Harold Schiffman writes regarding the emergence of a non-Brahmin koiné (versus the Brahmin dialect that had previously so functioned as something of a spoken standard):

> In the mid-20th century, it is clear that the chief disseminator of this SST [standard spoken Tamil] has been the modern Tamil "social" film. There is remarkable uniformity of SST irrespective of whether the studios were dominated by the DMK political party or the Congress – that is, usage is similar in MGR films and Sivaji Ganesan films, to take only two examples. Despite the DMK's public oratorical style, which emphasizes a purified, archaized, and highly alliterative Tamil, their films used SST that varied hardly at all from the kind found in other studios' films, *except when the hero expatiates in the special DMK-preferred alliterative style.* (Schiffman 1998:376; my italics)

We can also point to song lyrics as another key site where the literary influence of politicized (Dravidianist) registers of high-register Tamil (*sentamiḻ*) flourished in the Tamil cinema.

21 At the same time, as a capital-intensive and profit-generating industry, filmmaking began to increasingly draw cultural elites to it, both as investors and technicians (Baskaran 1996:44). Cinema drew from the cultural elites, Pandian (1996) suggests, because a number of the skills associated with cinema – from writing and directing to technical labour and musical performance – were predominantly available to them. See discussion in Chapter 4.

22 Hughes (1996:193) notes that initially, however, the turn to mythologicals was (1) seen by exhibitors as being relatively more respectable and less morally objectionable in comparison to foreign film content; and (2) able to draw in higher proportions of women and family audiences, if among a wider (that is, lower) class and caste demographic.

23 The gentrification of Hollywood and the cultural politics of realism in South India at this time are linked. The institutionalization of Hollywood in the first decades of the twentieth century, through the political economic dominance of its films across the globe, entailed the emanation (Silverstein 2013) of its enregistered realist styles (and associated discourses, figures of classed personhood, even personnel) to elite South Indians (filmmakers and audiences alike; Pandian 1996:952; Hughes 1996:150–75; Eswaran Pillai 2015). As Stephen Hughes (1996) notes, elite South Indians in the first decades of twentieth-century Madras City followed changes in the global market of film, as did, with some time delay (given the physical movement of prints), provincial, working-class audiences – this temporal gap (for example, the ongoing popularity of action serials in the mofussil despite shifts in preference to full-length feature films in Madras City) itself constituting a site of social distinction. Here, we see how a global hierarchy of value and genre is inscribed and projected onto local class and caste hierarchies of filmgoing (compare Nakassis 2016a:33–88). See Eswaran Pillai 2015 on the influences of Hollywood cinema on the Tamil studio system and the films they produced from the 1930s to the 1950s (see also Dungan and Smik 2001 and the documentary *An American in Madras* [2013, dir. Kiran Bali] on Ellis Dungan's importation of certain techniques and aesthetics from American cinema to Tamil cinema in the mid-1930s and 1940s).

24 As I also discuss in Chapter 4, the genre of the "social" took on a mantle of realism in contrast to mythological films, even if such films do not appear to contemporary aesthetic consciousness (or film scholars) as instances of realism per se (see Pandian 1996 on this issue as well). Rajan Krishnan (2009:295) notes that Annadurai and other DMK leaders saw their own films as equivalent to Italian neorealist attempts to forge a political cinema. Baskaran (1996:31) also notes the deep influence of classical Hollywood on Annadurai.

25 One factor that abetted this shift, in addition to elite demands for fewer songs and more realism in their cinema (Pandian 1996), was the cap on raw stock during the Second World War at 11,000 feet (whereas films before then were generally made using between 18,000 and 20,000 feet), a reduction that required a tighter narrative structure and a reduction in the number of songs (Eswaran Pillai 2015).

26 This transformation was also the result of the spread of cinema that came with mass electrification across rural South India; pre-dating this electrification, the nationalist use of cinema in the 1930s and 1940s had a lesser penetration of the countryside, making it such that it could never achieve the level of mass popularity that the Dravidian cinema eventually received (Baskaran 1996).

27 While part of the condition of this shift in the star system was the emergence of a Dravidianist use of cinema – itself riding off of the language politics of the previous half-century – it also turned on a set of technological changes in the industry. Experiments with post-synchronization of sound and later with (female) "playback" (where songs were prerecorded in studios and then synced to visual recording), and then with dubbing in the 1940s (Eswaran Pillai 2015), made it possible to separate singing from acting. The new generation of DMK stars – MGR and Sivaji – did not sing. (In MGR's case, he couldn't sing well enough to break into the industry as a hero in the earlier dispensation.) This was in marked, and in some cases intentional, contrast to the stars from the past (Weidman 2015, 2021).

28 In contrast to MGR (who began with the Congress and came later to the DMK), Sivaji Ganesan began his career through a close affiliation to the DMK, eventually leaving and joining the Congress Party, even trying his hand (and resolutely failing) at a political career in the late 1980s (after MGR's death).

29 One finds this rhetoric expressed a generation later by caste-based parties such as the Vanniyar Pattali Makkal Katchi (Working People's Party; PMK for short) and the Dalit Viduthalai Chiruthaigal Katchi (Liberation Panther Party), who worried that, for example, Rajinikanth's entry into politics in the early 2000s would threaten to undermine their vote-banks (both caste-conglomerates including many stalwart supporters of MGR; Sivathamby 1981:44), the PMK going so far as to incite violent attacks on theatres screening Rajinikanth films as well as on Rajinikanth fan clubs (Chakravarthy 2018:6, 194).

30 Much scholarship has been dedicated to offering explanations that would de-exoticize this cine-politics, de-linking it from culturalist assumptions of the peculiarity of South Indian audiences or elitist arguments about the gullibility of credulous subalterns. Such work has, instead, emphasized the contingent, non-essential and non-deterministic nature of this phenomenon

(Pandian 1992; Dickey 1993a, 1993b; Krishnan 2009; Srinivas 2009; Prasad 2014; Gerritsen 2019). To this end, for example, M.S.S. Pandian (1992) showed how MGR's films and the offscreen metadiscourse about his star persona worked to insistently co-construct each as the image of the other, forming a kind of "common sense" that abetted his movement from screen to Secretariat. Sara Dickey (1993a) has pointed out that the narratives of mass heroes like MGR expressed real-life concerns of his fan audiences, just as S.V. Srinivas (2009) has suggested – in the case of the Telugu mass hero Chiranjeevi – that the form of such mass films stokes audiences' cinephilia. Rajan Krishnan (2009) illustrates the way in which modern ethnolinguistic subjectivities and identities came to be expressed in the linkage between the narrative figure of the speaking hero and the indexically relayed body (face, voice, gait, mannerisms) of the animating actor such that the former could be projected onto the latter and both sutured to a subject position to which so-interpellated citizen-spectators could align themselves. Prasad (2014), perhaps most forcefully, argues for the historically contingent nature of this phenomenon, as linked to the emergence of the federal Indian nation-state, as discussed in the main text above.

31 The formation of linguistically defined states came to pass, first, in the creation of Andhra Pradesh for Telugu speakers in 1953 (Mitchell 2009) and later, with the States Reorganisation Act of 1956, in the creation of Madras State for Tamil speakers (renamed Tamil Nadu in 1968), Kerala for Malayalam speakers, and Mysore State for Kannada speakers (renamed Karnataka in 1973). The linguistic division of the Madras Presidency further institutionalized filmic distribution channels by the boundaries of ideologically and electorally inscribed language communities.

32 As Prasad (2014) notes, while every aspect of the linguistically circumscribed regional film industries (heroines, comedians, villains, directors and other technical personnel, producers, stories, songs, films themselves, and so on) has widely circulated beyond their own borders, heroes generally have not, immobilized *within* and *by* the communities that they have, over this historical emergence, been taken – indeed, been demanded – to represent by their audiences. The opening up of film markets beyond Tamil Nadu, and the economic dependence of such heroes on those extra-regional markets, thus stands in tension with the status of such hero-stars *as* (regional) political figures. As Prasad (2014) and S.V. Srinivas (2009, 2016) have suggested, the capitalization of the star power of such heroes in such transregional markets dims their (regional) cine-political potential, precisely because it disarticulates the political community of their address from the film markets of their circulation.

33 As S.V. Srinivas (2009) has insisted, the structure of this relation is not a top-down one, orchestrated by the stars or by the industry. While the

narrative form of mass-hero films figurate the mass hero's political representation of "the people," its insistent character in film – what M.S.S. Pandian (1992) called the hero-star's "image trap" – and its literalization in electoral politics is the result, as Srinivas shows, of a *demand* made on the mass hero by his fan publics, who often insist against the very stated wishes of the heroes themselves – as we will see in Chapter 1 – that they take political stances and serve as political leaders for them, representing them offscreen as they have onscreen. That fans so demand is not to deny the canny interests of such actors, or even their manipulation of their screen images with the aim of political returns. Rather, it is to argue that these returns are not necessarily the final cause of this cine-politics and that the push into politics is also coming from the star's fans and other stakeholders (for example, directors; see Nakassis 2019).

34 This discussion shouldn't be taken to imply that the ontological politics of cine-politics and its discontents are peculiar to this era. Not only do the tensions that underwrite this ontological politics of the image – in particular, its capacity to be both/either representation and/or presence, narrative and/or spectacle, fantasy and/or reality, star-vehicle and/or story, and so on – have a longer vintage than the mass hero. We find them already in the silent and early sound eras (Hughes 1996; Pandian 1996; Prasad 2014:163–70); we also find them in industries far beyond India (as Srinivas 2009 and Prasad 2014 themselves both note). One might consider figures as diverse as Ronald Reagan, Donald Trump, Joseph Estrada, among others (though my suggestion, of course, is not that these diverse figures are all equivalent as to their image politics – they certainly are not – but simply that the ontological politics of the mass hero are not radically unique or peculiar to South India). In addition, we find them in South India in domains other than cinema (though, for reasons noted in Chapters 1 and 2, I share Srinivas's and Prasad's hesitations to too quickly reduce cine-politics to a culturalist account of other domains, such as religion, as if cine-politics were simply an epiphenomenon of something else). Finally, as we see in the book's various chapters, within contemporary Tamil cinema this politics of presence/representation and the performativity/representationality of the image is manifest in any number of filmic sites beyond the mass hero. As such, it is necessary to see the cine-politics of the mass hero as *one*, if central, part within a wider ontological politics of the Tamil cinema and thus as an entry point from which we can theorize a more expansive semiotics and politics of the image far beyond the Tamil case.

35 The emergence of this star system in the 1950s and 1960s was abetted by the studio system and its political economy, even if it ultimately undid the studios. By the 1960s, the industry's two major stars – the populist "mass"

hero MGR and the consummate thespian and "class" actor Sivaji Ganesan – controlled the fates of the industry, starring in nearly 28 per cent of the industry's output in the 1960s (Eswaran Pillai 2012:80). This centralization of star control was partly due to the influx of new sources of non-Brahmin capital as a result of the Second World War (Barnouw and Krishnaswamy 1980:120; Sivathamby 1981:51). This influx occasioned the entry of a new set of producers who began to book stars outside of their studio contracts for higher sums; and this rise in star salary resulted, in turn, in a shift of power from the previously all-powerful studios to the stars themselves, with heroes like MGR able to leverage their popularity (and the financial risk, and potential reward, of depending on it for profit) to control every aspect of film production, from dialogues, to fight choreography, to song lyrics, and so on. It was in relation to the stars, then, that studios, but also writers and directors (in particular, auteur-directors such as A. Bhimsingh and C.V. Sridhar) and other minor hero-stars (Gemini Ganesan, S. Jaishankar, S.S. Rajendran, and others), stood in relation, both in struggle and cooperation. This situation was largely a result of the fact that, in contrast to other Indian cinemas, parallel or art films have never had anything of a hold, or space, in Tamil cinema independently of commercial cinema, with so-inclined directors (and other technicians) working within the confines of the mainstream industry (compare Majumdar 2021). With the expansion of online Tamil publics in recent years, however, there has emerged a parallel space for short films that circulate online and outside of the mainstream commercial cinema. Note, then, that the tension of director and star discussed in the chapters that follow has a relatively recent vintage in Tamil cinema (which isn't to say that it didn't exist at all before), dateable to the rise in the 1970s of the auteur-director who wrote the story, the dialogues, and directed the film. Earlier, the primary site of tension would have been the relationship of the studio versus the star (Eswaran Pillai 2015) or the writer versus the star (Prasad 2014).

36 This pair – Rajinikanth and Kamal Haasan – was seen as replicating the division of star labour between MGR and Sivaji (and earlier, M.K.T. Bhagavathar and P.U. Chinnappa) as "mass" versus "class" actors. As Rajan Krishnan (2009) has pointed out, however, this division presumes a set of homologies that don't really work. For example, while MKT is often adequated to MGR, it was P.U. Chinnappa who was known as an action hero (like MGR) *and* a great actor (like Sivaji Ganesan). Similarly, the opposition of Vijay and Ajith Kumar, often compared to MGR and Sivaji, obscures that Ajith also acts in mass films. And both sets of stars are popular across class and caste lines, in contrast to stereotypes that mass heroes are more popular with lower-caste and lower-class audiences and class heroes with upper-class and upper-caste audiences. More important than how

sociologically accurate such a set of divisions are, however, is their status as local ideologies that understand the industry as, for example, split on class lines, star and image type, and so on. In other words, such a division is itself a construal and instance of the ontological politics that concerns us in this book.

37 The centralization of the Tamil film industry in the 1960s around its hero-stars – and thereby in tension with its other possible agents and authors (initially studio producers and writers, but later auteur-directors) – has persisted for the last half century (which isn't to say that many things haven't changed as well, of course). Similarly, the political implications of cinema have also persisted, if perhaps fundamentally altered in recent years (Kurai 2012; Rajanayagam 2015; Ranganathan 2021; see the book's Conclusions for more discussion). Indeed, since MGR, no mass hero has ascended to the Secretariat. What I am most interested in here, and what I take up in the chapters that follow, is the longevity of what I see as the immanent possibilities of the filmic image, which are rendered clear and institutionalized in this post-1960s organization of Tamil cinema and politics – namely, the tensions and complicities that emanate from the image of the mass hero between the performativity and realism of the image, between presence and representation, star animator and directorial author, hero and story, actor and character, and onscreen and offscreen. It is in these immanent possibilities of the image (that may or may not be actualized in formal politics) that my concern lies.

Chapter 1. The Hero's Mass

1 While known in the film industry and to audiences as Vaibhav Reddy, Vaibhav's given name is Sumanth Reddy, Sumanth also being the name of his character in *Mankatha.* Two other main actors (and members of the gang) lend their names to their characters: Prem and Mahat. This kind of complex play and slippage of onscreen/offscreen is not uncommon in Tamil cinema; see also Chapter 3 on *Thamizh Padam*'s Shiva.

2 The transcripts in Figures 1.1 and 1.2 are organized as follows: the leftmost column provides the length of each shot in seconds; the second column provides a second-by-second enumeration (each row representing one second), with the duration of the shot also indicated by colour blocking. Colour blocking extends across the columns so that onset and extent of shots can be correlated with camera movement, shot types, dialogue, and non-linguistic action. Shot distance, in the third column, is indicated as follows: F = full shot, M = medium shot, MC = medium close-up (mid-chest), MC+ = between MC and close-up, C = close-up.

(These designations are relative and rough, given that the fluid, handheld camera-work's framing and distance is affected by zooms and the physical movement of characters and the camera.) Zoom-in/movement-towards the profilmic space is indicated with solid arrows and zoom-out/movement-away with striped arrows (onset/cessation of movement corresponding with the end points of the line/arrow); pans (L, R = left, right) are in [square brackets]. Shot angles are rendered in parallel columns (for example, in Figure 1.1, shot and reverse shot; in Figure 1.2, angle 1 and angle 2), with screen shots placed at their time of occurrence. A small map in the bottom left indicates camera position and orientation in the profilmic space. Non-linguistic action and dialogue are in the right-most columns. V = Vinayak (played by Ajith Kumar), S = Sumanth (Vaibhav Reddy), G = Ganesh (Ashwin Kakumanu). Dialogue is spaced relative to the time elapsed so as to correspond with the shots with which they co-occur. Cuts within dialogue are indicated by the colour block of the shot during which they occur. In Figure 1.2, relative timing of non-linguistic action and dialogue are indicated by vertical placement within and across rows. English glosses of the Tamil original are provided to the right of the corresponding Tamil. These transcripts were designed by Emily Kuret and myself. Emily Kuret annotated the scene in ELAN (https://archive.mpi.nl/tla/elan) and prepared the transcripts in Adobe Illustrator.

3 This fan anger recalls a 1964 *Kumudam* article discussed by Prasad (2014:53; see also Srinivas 2009:63–4), where an imaginary subaltern fan, "Cycle Rickshaw Mallayya," protests about the heroine of *Padagotti* (1964, dir. T. Prakash Rao) slapping the hero, MGR: "I cannot accept this, the director has made a big mistake." Interestingly, it is not the actor who is imagined to be faulted but the director (as in the cases discussed in Chapter 2 and Chapter 4), in contrast to the case discussed in this chapter (see also Nakassis 2020). In ventriloquating the fictitious subaltern spectator Mallayya's anger, note how *Kumudan* presupposes a particular production format (Goffman 1974, 1979) – that it is directors, qua authors, who are responsible for the film image – and in so doing, arguably, reveals the magazine's own middle-class ideology of the image.

4 In another television special on Vijay TV entitled *Happy Birthday Ajith* (1 May 2012), dedicated to Ajith's forty-first birthday, Vaibhav was again called on to narrate Ajith fans' anger at him. Vaibhav laughingly recounts how he was going to go to see the late show of the film on the day of its release at Albert Theatre, a famous (and famously working-class) cinema hall located in the central Chennai neighbourhood of Egmore. Right before leaving for the theatre, however, Vaibhav (V) received a phone call from his friend and actor Shiva (Sh), warning him not to come to the theatre. (Shiva was also a guest on the Vijay TV special and, as the reader will

recall, the host of the Sun TV special discussed in the main text above; he is also the same Shiva of Chapter 3.)

V: <voicing Sh:> *"Hey maccān inta mātiri nānu Shalini madam ellām Albert Theatre-le pāttōm. Mēle vantuṭṭu pāttuṭṭu oru irupatu muppatu pēru vantāṅka* box-*kiṭṭe."*	V: <voicing Sh:> "Hey bro, me and Shalini madam [Ajith's wife] and everyone saw (the film) at Albert Theatre. (After the scene) about twenty or thirty people came up to our box seats."
<Affecting an impatient, agitated fan looking under the seats:> *"Avan eṅkē?!" ((appaṭi solliṭṭu))* Seat-*ukku kīḻē ellām tēṭināṅka!"*	<Affecting an impatient, agitated fan looking under the seats:> "'Where is he [-HON.]?!' They were looking under all the seats!"
{Audience laughs}	{Audience laughs}
Sh: *Uṇmaileyē!*	Sh: Seriously!
V: *Uṇmaileyē tēṭināṅka!*	V: Seriously, they were searching (for me)!
Sh: *Uṇmaileyē enne kēṭṭāṅka! "Vaibhav vantirukkānā?" appaṭi nnuṭṭu.*	Sh: They really asked me, "Has Vaibhav come [-HON.] here?!"

5 When Vaibhav finally saw the film at the famous upscale Chennai multiplex, Sathyam Cinemas, right after he slapped Ajith an uproar ripped through the thousand-seat theatre, he reported to me (Vaibhav Reddy 2016). As he said on the Sun TV special, voicing that chorus of angry, shocked viewers: "*'Tēy Thala aṭikkiṟap(ḷe)! Nī beep n-b- beep beep,*" his co-star and co-guest, Premji Amaren, laughing and saying the delocutive, expletive-censoring bleeping sound along with him "*beep beep beep beep beep*!" (Hey, he hit *Thala!* You [-HON.] y- b- beep beep beep beep beep beep!), 'If even at the (upper-middle-class) Sathyam this was the reaction, what would it be like at other (more working-class) theatres?' Vaibhav rhetorically asked. With this comparison, Vaibhav both confirmed the distinction of liberal subjects, who see images as mere representations, and illiberal subalterns, who fail to see images thusly, while at the same time undermining that very distinction as a demonstration (and icon) of the scene's (and Ajith's) power.

6 The only physical retribution Vaibhav reportedly received was from his friend, and aspiring mass hero and ardent Ajith fan, the "Little Superstar" Simbu, who, when he saw the scene, reportedly grabbed Vaibhav

and punched him in the arm while yelling "*ṭēy*!" (Vijay TV special, 1 May 2012).

7 There is some uncertainty as to whose idea this blooper was. Vaibhav Reddy (2016) indicated that it was the director Venkat Prabhu's idea for him to do it, while the cinematographer, Sakti Saravanan (2016), indicated that it was Vaibhav's. Venkat Prabhu (2016) equivocated, first saying it was Vaibhav's idea, then indicating that it might have been his own.

8 Note that this reframing is precisely the opposite function of a canonical blooper. While bloopers usually pierce the diegesis to reveal the film's profilmic making, here we see the blooper attempting to defuse the diegesis-transcending slaps that happen in the film, instead patching up that narrative breach by turning to another, different "real": that of the star (on which, more below in the main text). Thanks to E. Summerson Carr for pushing me to articulate this point. On the stage actor having to apologize for his image-act, see Krishnan 2009:174–80.

9 On the notion of an image-act, see Bakewell 1998; Bredekamp 2010[2018]; see Nakassis 2019 for discussion.

10 My aim here is to not to provide a comprehensive account of Bazin's complex and heterogeneous thought (see Henderson 1972; Staiger 1984). Rather, my use of Bazin is avowedly selective and pragmatically tailored, on the one hand, to elucidate and help theorize certain dynamics within South Indian commercial film while, on the other hand, engaging certain uptakes of Bazin within film studies. My own sense is that the heterogeneity of Bazin's account of the image reflects his own registering of the image's ontological and aesthetic heterogeneity. From this point of view, the project in taking up Bazin should not be to clarify the "true" Bazin or provide the "best" reading of him. Rather, it is to identify the tools and intuitions that Bazin gives over to us as part of our own projects to clarify the culturally and historically manifest ontologies and modes of being of the image as we find them, the social processes that entail them, and that they in turn entail.

11 For Mitchell (2004), the issue is less that pictures as such are agents than that there is a metadiscourse that prevails about the animacy of images, which leads to a double consciousness about images as both inert representations and lively agents (see also Mazzarella 2013). My concern is slightly different – namely, how are we to account for the performativity of images (an account that necessitates rigorously theorizing this "as if" -ness)? To do so requires that we resist letting a focus on Euro-American conceptions of images slip into an all-too-common universalizing tendency to simply talk about images per se, and in doing so naturalize Euro-American ideologies and desires that bear the marks of primitivism. Consider, for example, Barthes's (1981:7) admission in his discussion of

photography: of his desire "to be a primitive, without culture." This desire is, at heart, a desire for immediacy and a suspicion about "language"/ signification (Barthes 1981:51 on the punctum making one "a primitive, a child – or a maniac; I dismiss all knowledge, all culture, I refuse to inherit anything from another eye than my own"). See Gunning 1989 on this "primal scene"; Rancière 2007:15 on Barthes's "Romantic poetics"; and Stewart 2003:672 and Kulick and Willson 1994:11 on a certain kind of primitivist tendency in cinema and media studies.

12 The question of temporality and subjectivity is key here, and here there is ambiguity in Bazin's thought. On the one hand, as Philip Rosen (2001:29) has pointed out, Bazin's account of the indexicality of the image is of a temporal lag (for example, Bazin 2005[1951]b:97; see also Doane 2002:23): the image inscribes, and thus refers to, that which happened in the past (that is, it indexically presupposes a reportive calibration to its referent) and presences it with some kind of relative immediacy for the precarious, if active subject in their now-present (that is, it indexically entails it in a reflexive calibration vis-à-vis the viewer). Rosen reads Bazin's ontology as articulating the way in which cinema is seized upon by the modern liberal subject given that subject's supposed desire to arrest time, to control it and the threat of death and change that it portends; it is with respect to this desire that cinema becomes important to the subject. And yet, by embalming time and duration, by preserving the unity of temporality and re-presencing it for the subject, the finitude and fact of time reinscribes that very threat to the subject, if now in a controlled, aestheticized (that is, ritual) form. Cinema forces the subject, on this argument, to actively confront the very reality that they are threatened by (if in a safer way), which is why, Rosen argues, respect for reality is such a "cinematic value" for Bazin: the "genuine realist attitude" involves both exploiting and checking the "impulse to control time" (Rosen 2001:28). Realism forces the subject to confront their desire to stop time, makes them stop being defensive and controlling, and opens them back up to the nature of reality and its temporal flux. "Realism becomes an act of heroism," Rosen (2001:28) writes. Another way of stating Bazin's ontology, then, from Rosen's point of view, is that the specificity of cinema involves a conjunction of the time-less and time-filled (nomic and reportive/reflexive); it is outside of time but preserves time; entextualizes (that is, de-/re-contextualizes) duration. And this conjunction is what makes it appeal to the modern subject. See also note 14 in this chapter.

On the other hand, Daniel Morgan (2006, 2013, 2018) and Tom Gunning (2008) argue that the temporality of presence for Bazin is not simply, or always, one of delay or historical relay of some reality that the image is not; and thus, the image is not simply a representation of some other profilmic reality to which it stands in a correspondence relation of indexical reference. (Bazin didn't use the term indexicality; this gloss on Bazin's position comes from commentators such as, for example, Wollen 1969; Rosen 2001; Doane 2002.) Rather, there is an immanence or simultaneity between the cinematic object and its image, an *identity*, at some level of their consubstantial being; they are, for some subject at least, one and the same. Morgan takes this self-presence to show that Bazin is not bound to a semiotic analysis, that the being of his image is not based on a representationalist correspondence model of image and (past) reality. This argument, however, rests on a rather narrow notion of indexicality – as Morgan (2006:447–8n18) himself notes (see also Morgan in Ball et al. 2020:§7) – in contrast to the broad notion of indexicality as defined by Charles Sanders Peirce (for example, 1931–35:2:§92, 248, 254, 274, 283, 305) and those who have developed his semiotic (see Nakassis 2016b; Gershon and Malitsky 2011:47; Ball et al. 2020 and references therein; Lefebvre 2021). This argument also seems to be based on a particular (post-)Enlightenment semiotic ideology (Briggs and Bauman 2003; Keane 2003). Indeed, underwriting Bazin's writings and those writing about him rests an ontological presupposition, namely, that the world and semiosis are of different orders; on this aporia, photography and cinema appear of interest because they blur that distinction even as they thereby reinscribe it (Cavell 1979:16–17; Morgan 2006:452). W.J.T. Mitchell (1986:60–1) observes that this presupposition itself expresses the foundational ideological division in Western theory between nature and culture that informs the image/text divide. Hence, nature:culture :: world:sign :: idea:word (idea as the iconic reproduction of the world by causal impression, to which a word arbitrarily stands) :: iconic-indexical:symbolic :: photography:other plastic arts. On this quasi-structuralist analysis (whose object of critique is structuralism), semiology appears on the culture side of things and sets off signs from the world. Yet this ideological division makes the icon and index inherently ambivalent signs, since they stand in for nature *within* culture; in particular, it makes photographs, Mitchell suggests, appear as mystical signs: for example, as signs without a "code," as nature that is in culture (Barthes 1981), as emanations from reality, and so on; see note 11 in this chapter on primitivism in visual studies and cinema and media studies.

13 As Bazin (2005[1946]) elsewhere suggests, this realization caters to a particular kind of desire for history, for a participation in its present unfolding (Hassan 2017).

14 As these and other presencing media indicate (including pre-photographic portraiture), presence is an achievement that is neither automatic nor medium specific. But if not medium specific, the being of the image depends on a particular kind of (metasemiotic) externality; in Bazin's case,

a particular psychological desire and existential anxiety of the subject who projects his "mummy complex" (Bazin 2005[1945]:9) onto images (see note 12 in this chapter). As Philip Rosen (2001) and Mary Ann Doane (2002) have pointed out, this stipulated subject (and their putative desires and anxieties) are historically and culturally particular, linked both to long-standing Western semiotic ideologies about representation (Keane 2003) – what Bazin himself called the "guiding myth" of a "total cinema" that would offer "an integral realism, a recreation of the world in its own image" (Bazin 2005[1946]:21; what Sol Worth [1974:338] called "the ethnographic impulse") – and to a more particular historical context, and media ideology (Gershon 2010), inaugurated at the turn of the nineteenth century in Europe and the United States (namely, industrial modernity), one that is not independent, of course, of anthropology's own investments – intellectual and technological – in filmic/ethnographic documentation (Worth 1974:340; Pinney 1997:17–71; MacDougall 2006).

As this discussion suggests, questions of the being of the filmic image are already open and distributed beyond the image and its apparatus, open to other ideologies, other subjectivities, other desires, and other ontologies (and indexicalities; Pinney 1997; Nakassis 2017; Strassler 2020). The image's being – even in, perhaps especially in, Bazin's case – turns on the ways in which images are metasemiotically framed, which are culturally, historically, and contextually variable and multiple. As Rosen (2001:20–1) also points out, the phenomenology of cinema that Bazin describes – for example, its capacity to "bear away our faith" (Bazin 2005[1945]:14) – requires that viewers already be socialized to *how* the apparatus works (see also Lefebvre 2021:11), since without such collateral knowledge (a kind of media ideology; Gershon and Malitsky 2011), the capacity to address the subject's desire is unrealized. And, as Christopher Pinney (1997:111–12, 138–9, 200–7) points out in the Indian context regarding photography, such knowledge of how the apparatus works – while perhaps necessary – is not sufficient to produce any particular investment, or desire, for photographic indexicality per se.

It is worth noting, following Worth (1974) and MacDougall (2006), that anthropology's own ontological politics of the image, in particular its commitment to the ethnographically realist film image, is itself entangled with certain aspects of film studies through the writings and work of Bazin, Jean Rouch, and the French New Wave.

15 Translation is altered as per Staiger 1984:106 and Morgan 2006:450.

16 Bazin characterizes Chaplin's comedy as realist because of the way in which it stages subjects' encounter with a world of objects that resist and render precarious their existence. This observation draws on a paper by James Tweedie (2018), "The Genius of the System, or, André Bazin's Design Thinking,"

presented at the conference Bazin@100 (12 October 2018 at the University of Chicago; cited with permission), and comments by James Lastra.

17 We might say *de*-provincialize rather than provincialize – as Amanda Weidman pointed out to me after reading an earlier draft of this book – since film theory has traditionally based its universalist accounts of film from a narrow focus on a small range of (national) film cultures (American, German, French, and Italian, in particular), against which "regional" industries like the Tamil cinema are marginal and peculiar, if studied at all. The methodological nationalism implied here, of course, is fractally compounded by flattening the cinemas of South Asia into "Indian cinema," while taking the unmarked referent of that phrase to be Hindi cinema, thereby erasing or doubly marginalizing the "regional." For a lucid statement of this problematic, see Kunapulli 2021:1–9, 14–15, 25–7; see also Velayutham and Devdas 2021:2–3.

18 As I elaborate in the chapter's conclusion, decentring Bazin's ontology is not to dismiss it as epiphenomenal ideology. His own discourse has had tremendous effect, most importantly for us here, in championing certain aesthetics – in particular, neorealism – that have gone on to have important afterlives in filmmaking practices all over the world (Andrew 2011), including India (Majumdar 2021). No mere ideology, and yet ideology all the same, the Bazinian ontology of the image (in fact, any claim to *the* being of the image) is also a metapragmatics of filmmaking, criticism, and uptake with pragmatic entailments of various kinds. Consequently, to suggest that the Bazinian ontology is a culturally particular ideology of the image is not to say that it isn't itself still ontological (which is to say that ontology and epistemology are not opposed, but co-constitutive, logically and in empirical/processual fact) or that it is "mere" ideology to be dismissed or ignored (as in much 1970s film theory) – indeed, all such dismissals already harbour their own implicit claims on the nature of images (Rodowick 1994[1988]; Baumach 2019).

In that way, Bazin offers *an* ontology of the image, an *account* of the existence and being of the filmic image to a historical, social subject. To this ontology, we might compare other cases, such as those discussed in this book. The hope is that this comparative ontological project might help us (compare Whorf 1956[1939]; Silverstein 2000), in fact, theorize the being of the image without having to fall back into questions of medium specificity, essence/substance, spectator metapsychology, or the easy metaphysics of presence that Bazin's writings almost but never quite slip into. Such a project also allows us to lay bare the conflation of the ontological and the normative that inheres in many accounts of the filmic image's being (including Bazin's; Aumont et al. 1992[1983]:124). In this we echo, though to much different ends, Christian Metz's (1986[1975]:256) critique of Bazin, when he notes that the "cosmophanic conceptions" of Bazin "give us excellent descriptions of this feeling [of the spectator]." "These theories," Metz continues, "are still of great interest, but they have, so to speak, to be put the other way round"; in this case, such feelings, conceptions, and theories must be treated as empirical phenomena to be investigated rather than as accounts of a priori ontic properties of the image. But contra Metz, such feelings, conceptions, and theories are not reducible to textual organization of film or to the apparatus (that is, to that domain he called the cinematic, that residue that remains after all that is not unique or peculiar to film is removed), nor are they "in" the spectator (as empirical person or textual figure). Rather, they are to be found in the relations among them and more social sites still. Our critique, then, is not that presence is a mirage or illusion, "the quasi-real presence of that unreal itself," as Metz (1986[1975]:267) puts it. Rather, we ask how presence is achieved as such in all its mediated reality.

19 This distinction of the character actor's and hero-star's capacity to be presenced is not a hard distinction, as we see in this chapter, but a relative one (within a continuum of possibilities); indeed, character actors also, and often, come to transcend their films, just as every mass hero himself enters into a diegetic world as a character. However, the character actor is relatively more contained by the narrative than the hero-star, just as the vector of typecasting is different for character actors and hero-stars. The former are cast because their transtextual (or offscreen) persona fits a character in the narrative; the latter's star personage, by contrast, demands a type of hero-character.

20 Pandian (1992), Srinivas (2009), and Prasad (2014) have importantly pointed to the extra-narrative supplemental nature of this kind of filmic image – on the one hand, it presupposes a particular kind of star image; on the other hand, it entails the "build-up" of that star image by interdiscursively travelling back to it. Rajan Krishnan (2009) has most thoroughly theorized this supplementarity, importantly pointing out how the iconic and indexical dialectic of film images enables a cine-politics of representation, in particular, when embedded within a (symbolic) "consensual realism" that would link the actor and character in a common moral framework. I build on this work by asking: How is presence achieved as and in contingent events of semiosis? How does this presencing afford certain performative potentials? Indeed, what *is* a film image such that it could be, and do, this kind of work (the work of cine-politics)? In what follows, then, while I draw on each of these accounts, my aim is to put them into a more direct conversation about the modes of being of images, the question of presence and performativity, and the semiotics that underwrite both.

21 Prasad (1998) contrasts imaginary identification (where I become Him, my ideal object of desire) and symbolic identification (where I identify with

Him for the qualities that make him different from and superior to me). See also Žižek 1989:116–22; compare Stacey 1999[1991].

22 This issue recalls the Player's adage in *Rosencrantz and Guildenstern Are Dead*: "Audiences know what to expect, and that is all they are prepared to believe in" (Stoppard 1967:76), though here the question of expectation far exceeds realist immersion, the trope of life imitating art, or the mistaking of representation for referent, insofar as what is in question are these very binaries of life/art, representation/referent. On the suspension of (dis)belief, see Chapter 4 for more discussion. Thanks to Jack Sidnell for pointing me to this reference.

23 Ajith removed "Ultimate Star" from his title credit sequences starting with his previous film *Asal* (2010), directed by Saran, whose 1999 film with Ajith, *Amarkalam*, first featured the epithet. In a 2010 interview (*Dinathanti* 2010), Ajith gave the following reason for dropping this epithet: 'recently, Indian cinema is starting to travel in a new direction,' and 'I want to welcome such changes to tradition.' (Over a decade later, on 1 December 2021, Ajith released a press release that he did not want to be called by his title, *Thala*, any longer either, but simply by his personal name, Ajith Kumar [TNM Staff 2021].) We might read Ajith's struggles with his "image trap" as reflecting a number of the ongoing changes that scholars have noted about post-millennial Tamil cinema, including the transformation – and perhaps waning – of cine-politics in the state (Kurai 2012; Rajanayagam 2015; Kunapulli 2021; Ranganathan 2021; see the book's Conclusion for more discussion).

24 The reasons Ajith publicly gave for dissolving his fan clubs include the misuse of his name by fans for their own (political) ends and their not following the orders of the central fan-club leadership (that is, Ajith's wishes; on similar dynamics in Telugu cinema, see Srinivas 2009). For Ajith's original letter in Tamil to his fans, see http://www.ajithfans.com/news/2011/04/29/official-press-release-ajith-dissolves-his-fan-clubs/. For a loose English translation and reporting of the story, see *IndiaGlitz* 2011.

25 See, for example, a video of the first-day show at the Albert Theatre in Chennai, https://www.youtube.com/watch?v=ZEEXqMBveN0. (Other fan videos that I consulted in my analysis have since been taken down.) For descriptions of first-day first-show fan practices in South Indian cinema, see also Srinivas 2009; L. Srinivas 2016; Gerritsen 2019; see Gerritsen 2021 on the gentrification of fan activity beginning in the 2010s and concomitant changes in the figure of the fan (from ambivalence to nostalgia/loss). One can perhaps detect some of these dynamics in the middle-class televisual reception of Vaibhav's narrative of the slap sequence (as humorous, surprised, anxious) described in the main text above.

26 The use of "game" here is also a reference to Venkat Prabhu's recognizable way of captioning his films. A number of Venkat Prabhu films replace the

word *film* (in the conventional directorial attribution "A Venkat Prabhu film") with a noun a propos to the topic/name of the movie: for example, "A Venkat Prabhu Holiday" (*Goa*, 2010), "A Venkat Prabhu Diet" (*Biryani*, 2013), "A Venkat Prabhu Reunion" (*Chennai 600028 II*, 2016), and so on.

27 See Nakassis 2016a:166 on frontality in Tamil cinema; see Eswaran Pillai 2015:138–9 on its antecedents in drama and its relationship to modes of Indian filmic stardom. See Kapur 1987; Pinney 1997, 2002, 2004; MacDougall 2006:173 on frontality in various manifestations of visual culture in South Asia; compare Gunning 1989, 1991; Williams 1989; Hansen 1991; Casetti 1998[1986]; Dagrada 2014 on aesthetics of frontality in European and American film.

28 Such presence is often framed in popular and academic discourse by appeal to the Hindu concept and practice of *darśan* (for example, Jacob 2009; Rogers 2011; L. Srinivas 2016:198–9; Gerritsen 2019), that tactile visual modality through which devotee and God transact substance, where the idol-sign *is* its divine object. While fan subcultures in Tamil Nadu cite darśanic practices, I hesitate to reduce cinematic spectatorship to Hindu religious ontologies; indeed, this mode of vision is shared with non-religious figures (for example, political leaders, sexualized/stigmatized actresses, as we see in Chapter 2; Jain 2007:305), just as it is grounded in specific political histories and aesthetic conventions irreducible to "religion" (Srinivas 2009; Prasad 2014; compare Ram 2008 and Bhrugubanda 2018 on religious films and their devotional spectatorship). Rather than characterizing a peculiar "cultural" mode of vision, we might suggest that *darśan* is a particular manifestation of a general potential of the efficacy of visuality (Pinney 2004:193) – one that, in any case, can be found beyond Hinduism and South Asia (see, for example, Freedberg 1989; Belting 1994[1990]; Bredekamp 2018[2010]). Thanks to Kajri Jain for pushing me to articulate this point.

29 We can note the irony and tension here (which I return to towards the end of this chapter; see also Chapters 3 and 4, and the book's Conclusions) between director and hero as two authorizing principles/principals of the film text, between the film being Venkat Prabhu's or Ajith's. This tension, as we will see, runs throughout the film (and perhaps all such films), and it was an explicit concern of the director, who, this film being his first foray with an actor of such celebrity, wanted to make sure that his story and script wouldn't be overwhelmed by Ajith's larger-than-life star image (Venkat Prabhu 2016). While Venkat Prabhu talked to me about the "responsibility" he felt to make a film that catered to Ajith's fan audience and guaranteed the big box office openings expected by the producer, he also worried that his own story and directorial identity would be lost in the mix. He wanted to make sure that *Mankatha* was not just an *Ajith* film but also a *Venkat Prabhu* film. The last image of the film is Ajith and Venkat

Prabhu hugging (compare the blooper with Vaibhav). Venkat Prabhu is smiling, and Ajith is giving a thumbs up to the camera. Venkat Prabhu is holding a microphone (which the director uses to direct), and Ajith is in his police officer's uniform (indicating that this image was perhaps taken at the same time as the opening scene was shot). On top of this image is stamped "A Film by Venkat Prabhu," as if to reiterate that, in the end, it is still *his* film (or at least *by* him), if only with Ajith's approval (an issue of no small importance, as we see in the main text below).

30 *Kireedam*, we might hypothesize, was rejected as a whole because the narrative conspired, in the end, against the hero-star, while in *Mankatha*, the film as a whole – despite the slap sequence and a number of other scenes that irked fans – still built up Ajith's star image (if it also reconfigured it in a negative, villianish hue). Note how this difference in the relationship between narrative and star image entails a different scaling of the image-act: in *Kireedam*, the film as a whole is entextualized by fans as an act to be rejected, while in *Mankatha* particular scenes – and particular fractions of particular scenes (Vaibhav's slaps) – are entextualized as image-acts to be rejected. We might further wonder if the structure of responsibility – the production format (Goffman 1974, 1979) – also differs, with the director of *Kireedam* being held responsible for the act (versus the actor Vaibhav in *Mankatha*).

31 We might analytically distinguish, following Goffman (1974:524–31), the "natural figure" of Ajith Kumar (the biographical, named person) – who animates a number of "staged figures" (characters in narrative films) – and the star figure of *Thala*. This star figure is wrought out of the relation between the natural figure, Ajith Kumar, and the oeuvre of staged figures he animates (itself an emergently ordered intertextual series). This star figure is simultaneously embodied in both the natural figure Ajith Kumar and his staged figures *by* articulating one to the other. What is of interest to us here is the (partial) collapse and blurring of star figure, natural figure, and staged figures, and the attempts (and failures) to separate them; Pandian's (1992) "image trap" describes the way in which the star figure (*Thala*) "traps" the natural figure (the person, Ajith) in a kind of suspended animation: a repeated intertextual loop of "his" staged figures, made in the image of his stardom. Thanks to Jack Sidnell for encouraging me to articulate this point.

32 The phrases *nomic calibration* and *reflexive calibration* are Michael Silverstein's (1993, 2021). Silverstein distinguishes three ways – or "calibration types" – that some (narrating) semiotic event metapragmatically indexes, or frames, its (narrated) semiotic object: reflexively, reportively, and nomically. A reflexive calibration denotes the case wherein a metapragmatic indexical sign's value is determined relative to the event of its happening (and thus sign and object are spatiotemporally coincident), as when the referent of "I" is the animator of the utterance-token "I." (The poetic

function [Jakobson 1960(1958)] is a residual reflexive calibration of all discourse.) A reportive calibration denotes where narrating and narrated event are non-coincident but in the same spatiotemporal envelope, as in reported speech constructions, where "I" may denote not the quoting speaker but some quoted "I" in some other event of speech. A nomic calibration denotes where metapragmatic sign and object are not in any common spatiotemporal frame of reference, any indexical link between them seemingly effaced (that effacement, of course, being a kind of indexicality; Agha 2007a:43–5; compare Benveniste 1971:205–15 on *histoire* and *discourse*). Nomic calibrations are typical of expressions/enactments of axiological, divine, or transcendent normativities. Fictional texts present a border/blended case between reportively and nomically calibrated texts, bracketing the reflexive values of indexical signs (such that, for example, "I" typically indexes the character-speaker and not the actor). Some fictional texts, such as realist ones, purport to be reportively calibrated (where the diegesis appears as part of our historical world), though there are important ways in which the fictional frame – especially in fantasy – detaches the diegesis from any clear common spatiotemporal frame of reference and thus functions nomically. See Nakassis 2020.

33 Mitry (1997[1963]:15) writes, for example, of film as "a language in which an equivalence of the data of the perceptible world is no longer acquired through (more or less) abstract shapes but through the *reproduction of concrete reality*. Thus reality is no longer 'represented' … It is *presented* … [R]eality becomes employed as an element in its own narration" (italics in original; see also Panofsky 1959[1936]:31). On the "trace," see discussion in Ball et al. 2020. Such indexicality is, following Lefebvre's (2021) discussion of Peirce (1958:8:§368), a *reagent*, whose indexical ground is staked on our knowledge of the production of such photographic images. This type of indexicality contrasts to what Lefebvre, following Peirce, calls indexical *designations*, which function as pointers both to the characters (within the fictional universe of discourse) *and* to the actors. The latter (indexical designation) is particularly at issue in the way stardom (interdiscursively) anchors the sociological realism of the image, as discussed further in the main text.

34 The entrenchedness of certain forms of social hierarchy between industry personnel on and off the screen is also reflected in the use of honorifics when narrating and describing *Mankatha*'s slap sequence (even in acts of reference where neither Ajith, nor his fans, are present). Consistently in my interviews, Ajith and his character are referred to with honorific second-person pronouns (in reported speech) and third-person pronouns, often accompanied with honorific terms like "sir" or "*aṇṇan*" (older brother). By contrast, Vaibhav, the actor, and Sumanth, the character, were generally not accorded honorifics. Only on one occasion was Ajith referred to with

a non-honorific form (and in this case, it co-occurred with the kin term *aṇṇan*). On similar use of honorifics within the Hindi film industry, see Ganti 2012:202–3.

35 The analytic term, *sociological realism*, contrasts with what I call in this book *representational realism* (or sometimes, simply *realism*), a family of ideologies and styles that variously entextualizes/construes texts as standing in some referential-denotational relationship to their object ("reality"). See Chapter 4 for more discussion.

36 Instructive is how fans' anger extended not just to the slap sequence but also to scenes where other characters stood in important textual positions beyond their perceived offscreen qualifications. For example, after seeing the film together, Suresh expressed annoyance when the actor Mahat got a choice line. 'Who is he to get such a line in Ajith's film?' Suresh asked. Similarly, Vaibhav and Venkat Prabhu both described to me how fan audiences (and others) were irritated that Vaibhav had a song dedicated just to his character. This song sequence, which focuses on Sumanth's deep affection and love for his wife, sets up his betrayal of Vinayak and the gang. As Venkat Prabhu (2016) insisted, this song is necessary for the story, because if Sumanth's emotional bond with his wife isn't established, then his rage at Vinayak's insult to her honour won't be emotionally effective. Interestingly, the importance of the slap sequence is not only demanded by the "story," but, as such, it demands *prior* scenes. Here, a set of implicational narrative relations emerge from the emotional and dramatic nature of the slaps, which spin out requirements for other scenes. These narrative demands decentre the hero-star as the text's pre-eminent metafunction or "motivation" (Thompson 1988). And it is precisely this chain of scenes that fans took issue with as a sign of the audacity of 'little boys' in the presence of a big man. Why are these other minor guys taking up so much of the screen instead of Ajith? Vaibhav (2016) said to me (CN):

> And everybody were against my song (CN: in the beginning [of the film]), except for the director Venkat Prabhu … Lots of people, producer's side and other people and all, "You know, it is Ajith sir's fiftieth movie and uh why does this guy get a song?" *appaṭi nnu solliṭṭu* (they said like that). First day also there was a reaction. And the- when the song was onscreen, everybody started, you know::, they started talking *ēnnā "Enna ṭā, inta paṭattule ((enna)) ivanukku* song-*u*? *Enna, Venkat Prabhu* friend *tān, enna vēṇālum paṇṇuvāṅkaḷā, Thalaiyin* fiftieth?" *inta mātiri tān. Annaikki* night *((vantu))* phone *paṇṇi avare kēṭṭēn Ajith sir-e, uh uh "Aṇṇā inta mātiri tiṭṭuṟāṅka ellārum"* [because "What the hell man, why does he (-HON.) get a song in the film? What, because he's Venkat Prabhu's friend they think they can do whatever they want in *Thala*'s fiftieth film?" It was like that. That night I called up Ajith sir and said, "Older

brother, they're all scolding like this"] … He HE HE was one of the reason who didn't make people cut the song [that is, why they didn't cut the song] … People told them uh before release, that that producer's side and other people and all. Only Venkat Prabhu and uh Ajith sir, *reṇṭu pēr maṭṭum tān vantuṭṭu* [only the two of them] they were against it. "*Illelle ((itu vantu)) paṭamā pāruṅka* [No, no, just look at it as a film]. Don't see it as like, you know, uh- We should do something different." So that's what he liked also, Ajith sir liked also. So "*paṭamā pāruṅka* [see it as a film], it'll be perfect."

37 This anger is mixed with a form of pleasure. Villains – those who threaten the face of the hero – are both objects of anger and pleasure (see also the discussion of *Subramaniyapuram* in Chapter 4), not simply because the villain's arrogance presents an opportunity for the hero to fully display his mass (Nakassis 2010:143–225) and not simply to relish/abhor seeing someone transgress onscreen, but also because they enable the fan subject to take on the star's personage in stewardship, to protect the star's image through their joyful hate for the villain. Such negative figures are necessary, as indicated by the way in which Vaibhav was jokingly referred to on the set of *Mankatha* as a "*bāli āṭu*" (sacrificial lamb; Vijay TV special, 1 May 2012). As Naren, a friend and former ardent Rajinikanth fan noted of the famous villain Raghuvaran, 'we all like him,' 'we look for him (in the film),' even if fans are also angry with him for hitting/cursing Rajini. For the hate of the villain is in the service of a larger love; it is a hate that one can cherish. In this regard, Ajith playing a villainous protagonist in *Mankatha* is doubly interesting (and arguably, central to the film's success), as it collapses these ambivalences, one into the other.

38 Note, here, how Vaibhav also contrasts a cool, liberal voice and an emotional, illiberal voice through his codeswitching and quotative construction, distancing the latter while inhabiting the former by enveloping the Tamil quoted speech in English (compare Nakassis 2016a:89–155).

39 This avarice is brought out by the film's post-production colouring. (On colour grading in Tamil cinema, see Pandian 2015:128–33.) The film has a sickly greenish-yellowish tinge. "The psychology of green," Sakti explained, "denotes greediness." Designed by the filmmaking team in pre-production, this colouring, Sakti stressed, is in contrast to the "smooth" image and bright and glossy, "sophisticated" colour palette used in most of Ajith's films, and in certain scenes in *Mankatha* itself (such as the climactic fight sequence). The reference that they used to guide the colourist was the 2001 film *Swordfish* (dir. Dominic Sena). Having determined the colour palette in pre-production, the costumes of the film were selected and designed, with greys, blacks, and other dark colours used to complement the green/yellow tint of the film (Sakti Saravanan

2016; Venkat Prabhu 2016). In 2009 when I worked on the Venkat Prabhu film *Goa* (2010), Sakti Saravanan talked about his preference for handheld cameras and a darker image, in contrast to the incredibly bright, colourful image of mainstream Tamil cinema (that bright image itself was necessary, he suggested, to overcompensate for the old, dull projectors of most mofussil theatres). Early on (for example, in films like *Saroja* [2008, dir. Venkat Prabhu]), his choices in camera work and colouring, he said, were (wrongly, he implied) critiqued as indicating his lack of skill rather than a concerted aesthetic choice.

40 The shots in this train yard sequence are generally longer than the film overall (with a mean shot length of 3.18 seconds/shot, compared to 1.62 seconds/shot for the whole film and a mode of 0.92 seconds/shot), the introduction fight scene (whose average shot length was 0.91 seconds/shot), and the climactic fight scene (1.14 seconds/shot). (The average shot length of the fight scenes in the film as a whole is 1.01 seconds/shot. The standard deviation of shot length for the film as a whole is 2.66 seconds/shot, though the distribution is highly skewed and non-normal.) The 11.47 second shot that includes the two slaps in it is, out of over 5,800 shots in the film, the forty-fourth longest shot in the film, putting it in the top 0.76 per cent of shots. Many thanks to Ruhi Sah for annotating *Mankatha* for shot length.

41 Another reason Sakti Saravanan opted for a single-camera setup is that *Mankatha* was shot on film. When shooting on film, he noted, he always operates the camera himself, the reason being that with film you can't get an independent judgment on the frame except through the viewfinder. With digital cameras, by contrast, he said, you can judge the frame by the monitor output. The need to judge the image through the camera itself is compounded, of course, when one uses a handheld camera in a dynamic, free-flowing way, which Sakti Saravanan did with high frequency for *Mankatha* (as well as with Venkat Prabhu's earlier films *Chennai 600028* and *Saroja*). Having switched to using digital cameras, Sakti explained in 2016 that he had since given up actual camera operation, leaving it to his assistants. In addition, he said, he has become bored with handheld cameras. While in the past he and Venkat Prabhu were the only ones using handheld cameras with heavy frequency, now everyone is using them, he claimed.

42 Indeed, Venkat Prabhu directed the slap sequence rather than the "fight master" (stunt choreographer) Silva, precisely because it was not a "fight" at all but a (dramatic) "scene."

43 The planning of the slap sequence's shot selection was largely on the spot. This improvisational approach is common in the Tamil film industry, which places a premium on an openness to the particularity of the shooting event and its locations (Pandian 2011, 2015:111–12, 120; compare Ganti 2012:155–74, 225–32; Rossoukh and Caton 2021:21). This approach

doesn't mean that shoots are disorganized or not thought out, but rather that the filmmaking process is reflexively attuned to its inevitable contingencies. Given that this sequence had multiple takes (see the discussion in the main text below), however, we should take Sakti Saravanan's claim to complete extemporaneity as just that, a claim that entextualizes the image in a particular way: as a vérité "document" of his "touch."

44 Thanks to E. Summerson Carr for pointing out this dance-like quality to me. By "participatory" and "interactive," I am thinking of David MacDougall's discussion of the use of the camera in a way that "records its own interchanges with the subject" (2006:4) and thus can "become involved with his [here, Rouch's] subjects as he himself was involved – to see them through his experience as a participant as well as an observer" (251).

45 As Venkat Prabhu (2016) explained, if you took the scene in a "plain" way, with steady shots or tracking shots, then the tension of the scene has to be carried by the acting alone. If it was a steady shot, the scene would be "boring," Venkat Prabhu said. You should be watching it at "seat edge," he explained, which is why you need the handheld camera; with Sakti Saravanan wielding the handheld camera as a fourth performer/participant, the scene's tension increases. The result is what Pier Paolo Pasolini (1988) and Gilles Deleuze (1986[1983]:72–4, 1989[1985]:232) – following Vološinov (1986[1929]) and Bakhtin (1981) – called a "free indirect point-of-view shot," an image-text that is simultaneously an objective and subjective shot at once (see also Mitry 1997[1963]:215–16 on the "semisubjective" shot; see Browne 1999[1975]:156; Branigan 1984:122–38; Metz 2016[1991]:92–3, 130–2; and Schwartz 2005 for discussion). In such image-texts, we see the event from a third-person perspective, the indexical (spatial) "reference" of the image thus decentred from the subjectivity of the characters; yet, the shakes, movements in and outwards, and so on all affectively register the subjectivity of the characters precisely by iconically echoing indexical signs of their subjectivity. In the scene in question, for example, we find a parallelism between the emotional crescendos in Ajith's performance (his volume, speech quality, facial expressions) and the movement of the camera, which moves in as he explodes and moves out as he cools down, shifting slightly as he gestures, and the like. In effect, we see Ajith (in an objective mode of presentation) but see *as if* we are him, the camera's jittery motion capturing the emotional "chaos" and "rawness" (to paraphrase Sakti Saravanan) *from Vinayak's point of view*, blending an objective reporting style with the emotional centring (deictic origo) of first-person expression. The possibility not explored by Deleuze but that is looming in *Mankatha*'s slap sequence is how such complex "voicing" or "looking" structures are entextualized as enunciations whose performative entailments outstrip such analyses of subjectivity. As Schwartz (2005) notes, rather than turn towards

the social conditions of possibility (as Vološinov would have it) and empirical contexts of actuality of such tropes, Deleuze retreats back *into* the image and reads such tropes as expressions of the subjectivities of the auteur and his characters. It is precisely this ideology of authorship and diegesis that is articulated by Venkat Prabhu and Sakti Saravanan. Moreover, the image that this ideology entextualizes itself interpellates a particular kind of spectator-subject, a liberal subject who can construe the image *as* a *representation* as such, as an expression of a directorial author. Yet, as we will see, this image-act/text of the slaps harbours recognition of a radically different kind of image, production format, and image-act: namely, that of the fans who read such images as performative profanations of their *Thala*. This implies *another* set of voices and looks "in" this image not accounted for by this ideology. Such voices and looks cannot be excavated simply by a textual analysis or by attention to the intentions of the films' makers.

46 As Amanda Weidman suggested to me (personal communication, 2018), in Tamil cinema a slap always occurs at a moment when the moral compass of the diegesis gets reset across some hierarchical relation – for example, by age/generation or gender.

47 The "fight master" "Stunt" Silva (2016) noted that punching doesn't come naturally in real-life fights. Your first reaction when emotionally incensed will be to slap, he said, while punching is something that one mentally prepares for. A slap, thus, is more 'realistic' (*etārttam*) and emotionally powerful in this sequence, he explained.

48 While the first generation of mass heroes exclusively acted on celluloid film (for example, MGR, N.T. Rama Rao), the second and third generations (for example, Rajinikanth, Vijay, Ajith) have seen their image digitally captured and embellished in more and more profound ways. And while the mass hero's image is increasingly digitally mediated, as Rajan Kurai (2014) has argued, it still depends on the presumption of his physical body transduced through the indexicality of the image, be that through light on celluloid or digital sensor (Gunning 2008). This is why, Kurai argues, Rajinikanth's motion-capture animated film *Kochadaiiyaan* (2014, dir. Soundarya Rajinikanth Ashwin) failed among audiences: the actor's body was missing from the screen/theatre. The issue, this suggests, is less whether the image is analogue or digital (Prince 1996), manipulated or not, a physical trace or not, but rather how different images, in their aesthetic form and political pragmatics, figurate and are taken up as standing in contrastive ontological relations with others (presentist/representationalist, performative/constative, fantastical/realist, and so on). I thank a reviewer of an article draft of this chapter for prompting me to articulate this point.

49 As we watched the scene together in his home, Venkat Prabhu (2016) narrated, with some amusement and pride even, how when the scene was

shot Ajith's shirt got ripped from the action. When it was suggested that they stitch the shirt up, Venkat Prabhu insisted that they leave it as is ("Eh, why? It's natural man!"). As he explained, "they [other filmmakers, other heroes] won't let the hero have a kind of torn clothes … This is REAL torn. This is not um artificially made."

50 This contradiction of being asked to identify with a lesser character against the hero is interpreted in fan discourse both as a site of dissonance – resulting in the question of "Why is Vaibhav getting so much importance in this film?" (see note 36 in this chapter) – and as something to be relished (see note 37 in this chapter).

51 As Venkat Prabhu noted to me in 2016, this narrative centring of Vaibhav/Sumanth was an act of celebrity munificence, since Ajith, as an eminent hero-star, didn't have to concede any screen space to a junior actor like Vaibhav. See also note 57 in this chapter.

52 Indeed, the slap sequence boosted Vaibhav's career, as he told it (Vaibhav Reddy 2016), though he didn't expect this result at the time; in fact, quite the opposite. As he said to me, Ajith told him: "This slap is going to protect you [that is, your career] for five years." Vaibhav said that at the time he didn't know why Ajith told him that, but he was right. The scene got him attention from other filmmakers, which he might not have otherwise received, and thus, more film offers.

53 Although distancing himself from those who got mad at Vaibhav, when Anbu saw other fans' reaction in the theatre, it made him proud, he said, because he realized how much respect people have for Ajith, not just as an actor but as a human being. This "over emotional" reaction, as he put it, validated his own (rational, cool) appreciation for Ajith as a good person, and thus his own 'prestige' (*gettu*) as an Ajith fan – rather than disesteem – because it showed how Ajith was 'in everyone's hearts.'

54 With very few exceptions, since the late 1970s Tamil cinema doesn't use live sound (Nakassis and Weidman 2018). As a result, nearly all dialogues are dubbed. In this scene, Vaibhav and Ajith recorded their lines on separate occasions. When I asked Vaibhav if he had the same trepidation in scolding Ajith/Vinayak with curse words (which were eventually bleeped out), he said: "That was just dubbing, we can change anything. But *aṟaik-kiṟatu vantu* [when it comes to slapping] it's onscreen, no? People watch it." Notice, first, the different performative weight of sound versus visual imagery (and the seemingly more mediated quality of the former versus the putatively immediated quality of the latter); second, notice the importance of (for Vaibhav at least) the profilmic co-presence in the performance of the act, where the fact that Ajith wasn't co-present in the post-production act

of dubbing defuses Vaibhav from having "actually" scolded Ajith in the film; and third, note the lability of the aural profilmic versus the assumed unchangeability of the visual track.

55 Ajith's authority over but not responsibility for the image also explains the end credits out-take discussed at the outset of the chapter, which insists on Ajith's authority over the image so as to (ultimately unsuccessfully) dispel Vaibhav's responsibility for it (compare Dyer 1998[1979]:152–5). We similarly see this authority looming in the film's final image, reiterating that *Mankatha* was "A Film by Venkat Prabhu"; see note 29 in this chapter.

56 During the 2011 Sun TV special, Venkat Prabhu narrated a conversation between himself (VP) and Ajith (Aj):

Illa, nān Ajith sārukku aṅkēyē pēsinōm.	I spoke to Ajith sir right there (at the shooting spot).
Aṅkēyē vantu,	Right there, I said,
(VP:) *"Sir etō vantu etāvātu taḷḷi uṭuṟatā anta mātiri paṇṇikkalāmā? Aṭikkalāmā? Illa, fans-lām etāvatu piraccanai paṇṇuvāṅka?"*	(VP:) "Sir, can we have something like you getting pushed? Maybe getting hit? Will the fans make some problems?"
(Aj:) *"Illa ite* character-*ā pāru.* Character *nnā un poṇṭāṭṭi patti nān tappā pēsuṟēn. Atu vantu aṭikkalām. Tappē illai"*	(Aj:) "No, look [-HON.] at it as the character. For the character, I'm talking bad about your [-HON.] wife. For that (one) can hit. There isn't anything wrong in it."
appaṭi nnuṭṭu.	Like that, he said.

57 As Venkat Prabhu (VP) told me (CN) in 2016:

VP: Because it was just a PUsh (in the original scene). I didn't want him to slap slap [that is, really slap him]. It was like, <mouth click> he tries to first, he, he pulls him- he sl:::- slaps and-, he slaps and throws him off. And he just talks the dialogue. That was, that was the original (scene). And later what uh Ajith said is like "No, it's it's- let him hit me mo:re."

CN: Oh, so Ajith wanted it EVen //more?

VP: //Yeah, even more.

So the second slap which uh=

CN: =yeah yeah yeah //the second one//

VP: //that was // because Ajith told him to sl- hit him again.

Because he wanted to uh ELevate that, you know, the stardom of giving the liberty of another small actor to hit him.

58 See Kampa 2019 for a critical review of some such reportage.

59 Consider how Vaibhav (V) narrated to me in 2016 the way in which Ajith (Aj) pressured him (and Venkat Prabhu [VP]) to do the scene:

(Aj:) "*Itu pāru. Eh, eh-* Acting *vantuṭṭu, itu vantu oru* character. *Nān vantu anta Vinayakan, Vinayak* character. *Nī vantu anta Sumanth* character. *Un* wife-*e patti tappā pēsinā nī anta Vinayak aṭikkiṟe. Ajith-lām ille iṅkē. Vinayak aṭikkaṇum nī.* So you have to hit."	(Aj:) "Look [-HON.] here, Eh, eh- In acting, this is a character. I am Vinayakan, Vinayak character. You [-HON.] are the Sumanth character. If I talk bad about your wife, you're gonna hit Vinayak. There is no Ajith and all here. You have to hit Vinayak. So you have to hit."
appaṭi ṇṇāru. ((Nān)) vantu	He [+HON.] said like that. I was like,
(V:) "*Ille aṇṇā koñcam:: (1) vēṇā(m) ṇṇā, nā(n) paṇṇamāṭṭēn" appaṭi nnu.*	(V:) "No older brother, a little:: (1) I don't want to, older brother, I won't do it."
Oru two three times *sonnāru:*	About two or three times he said it:
(Aj:) "*Illelle paṇṇu. Appaṭi nnā* if you don't do it, you're not professional,"	(Aj:) "No no, do it. If you don't do it, you're not professional."
appaṭiṇṇāru.	He said like that.
(V:) "Let it be *aṇṇā* but *nān uṅkaḷe aṭikkiṟatu tappā irukkum. Vēṇām,"*	(V:) "Let it be older brother, but hitting you [+HON.] is wrong. I don't want to."
appaṭi nnuṭṭēn. (Venkat) Prabhu [VP] also got convinced and he said,	I said like that. (Venkat) Prabhu [VP] also got convinced and he said,
(VP:) "No no no. *Uṭṭu aṇṇā,* he'll just push you and *pōtum,"*	(VP:) "No no no. Let it be [-HON.], older brother. He'll just push you and that's enough."
appaṭi nnu. Atukku appuṟam he was like, you know,	He said like that. After that, he was like, you know,
(Aj:) "No no you you people are going to kill the scene. You have to do it. *Prabhu avan maṭṭum aṭikkale nnā nān uh* confirm(*(ṭṭā)*) *unnaiyum avaneyum reṇṭu pēr nān aṭippēn iṅkē. Nā(n)* uh- It's it's really very intense scene. *Itu nī vantu ennai avan aṭikkaṇum.* Whatever you've written has to be taken. *((Ille)) etāvatu* changes *iruntuccu nnā* I'm not going to keep quiet."	(Aj:) "No no no, you people are going to kill the scene. You have to do it. Prabhu, if he [-HON.] doesn't hit me, uh it's confirmed that I am going to beat up both you [-HON.] and him right here. I uh- It's really a very intense scene. You have to hit me. Whatever you've written has to be taken. If not, if there are any changes, I'm not going to keep quiet."

60 In contrast to Ajith, who was deep into his character Vinayak, the auratic presence and emanations of Ajith's star image was a blockage for Vaibhav to act in the fiction, even after he agreed to slap Ajith (Vaibhav Reddy 2016): the pressure of Ajith and Venkat Prabhu to get it done ('Do it fast! Do it fast!,' they yelled at him); knowing that he was holding up the shoot and making the other major star of the film, Arjun, wait on him; the idea that he had to hit one of his idols (who was threatening him with violence if he didn't do it!); the thought of fans chasing him down and attacking and scolding him if he did do it – all this made it difficult for Vaibhav to get into his character, he reported. Running through his mind, he said, was 'this is Ajith I'm hitting, this is Ajith I'm hitting …'

61 In the case of participation frameworks, such role fractions (or "footings") include (un)ratified addressee, audience, bystander, and the like. (Within the category of audience, we might partition, in the Tamil case, fan-stewards and heralds, non-addressed non-fan viewers, and so on.) As Judith Irvine (1996) has argued, such roles are essentially open-ended and in principle infinitely reticulatable. See Iyer 2020 and Weidman 2021 for discussion of some of the complex participation frameworks evinced in Indian cinemas.

62 Here, I find S.V. Srinivas's (2009) account of the mass film and its hero in Telugu cinema particularly provocative and brilliant. Srinivas suggests that the mass film positions/presupposes the spectator as a cinephilic subject for whom, and by whose will, the image appears. The author and animator of the image, ultimately, is the fan-spectator himself who is thereby immanently present *in* the film's form itself, indeed, as its enunciator (Metz 2016[1991]). This argument is useful and well-grounded in Srinivas's analysis, and complementary to my own. How might we think this argument with the materials presented in this chapter, where the actness of the image is animated not by but *for* the fan-spectator and which appears as a manifestation of a hero-star who transacts in a mode of alterity to the spectator (rather than as a manifestation of the fan's subjectivity projected onscreen)? It strikes me that we should consider the way in which the image is both an emanation of the (presentist, performative) hero-star and the (demanding, entitled) fan-spectator at one and the same time (each embedded in the other; Nakassis 2019), though sitting in a complex and unstable relation (Srinivas 2009:104).

63 A critical question is, What are such potentialities? Whatever they may be, such potentialities can only be known through their actualization in empirical events of usage and encounter (see discussion in the book's Introduction and Conclusions; in particular, see note 21 in the book's Conclusions). A second question is, What is *an* image (how is it bound

off from its surrounds) such there could be an ontology/being of *the* image (in general)? Here too, the reflexivity of ontologies, as claims on the being of images, is critical. Any ontology is a principle that (1) regiments processes of bounding off images from their contextual surround in particular events (an evenemential process of *entextualization*); and (2) imputes some set of properties and potentialities to such sign forms *as* images (whatever that might mean) in distinction from other similarly constituted ontic types (a process of *typification*). At the same time, every mode of being, as historical emergence, presupposes processes of entextualization and typification as its conditions of possibility. On this dialectical relation, see Silverstein and Urban 1996; Nakassis 2019; on consonant approaches in visual studies, see Mitchell 1986; Alloa 2011; Moxey 2011; Sonderegger 2011.

64 See Stam 1989 on an extension of Bakhtinian translinguistics into the study of cinema.

65 While, as I note in the main text, I am not interested to avow (or disagree with) Bazin's ethical position, important for me is that Bazin's normative approach to the question of being opens up for us a flexible space to productively think being in ways that outstrip Bazin's own account. This is in at least three ways. First, Bazin's ethical position on the world as ambiguous and contingent implies not an opening to *the* world (the reality from which images emanate) as if this world is already known as such – it is not, this non-determinateness being the basis of all ontological politics (see also Chapter 4). Rather, Bazin's ethical position provides an opening to other possible worlds, other possibilities that are otherwise foreclosed (including by Bazin's discussion); it also provides, as Bazin's characterization of Chaplin's realism indicates (see note 16 in this chapter), an openness to the multiple ways in which different flavours of "reality" are countenanced by the image beyond conventional (or enregistered) styles of representational realism. Second, this openness (as well as its medium non-specificity and its necessary metasemiotic, or ideological, framing) foregrounds, without quite answering, the critical empirical question of *how* and *for whom* presence is achieved; which is to say, the multiple routes to, and types of, filmic presence (Bazin's description being only one). In addition, it foregrounds the many different potential entailments to acts of presencing beyond Bazin's liberal hopes and worries. Finally, to speak of the ambiguity and alterity of the world is to recognize that any account of what an image is – especially a realist one – is a political act. Indeed, as noted, Bazin's ontology is both a claim on the nature of the world and the nature of cinematic representation, as well as a claim on what kind

of subject does/would/should construe and experience both (Rosen 2001). Yet if so, to repeat the argument, Bazin's account is only one such account among many. Note, then, how we are already dealing with the problematic of multiple ontologies, multiple claims on and for the image as they play out through multiple kinds of images and multiple enculturated subjectivities. How do we deal with these dialectically tangled multiplicities? And, to reframe Bazin's ethical position, how could we know and be open to them in their heterogeneity, ambiguity, and difference (especially when they counter our taken-for-granted assumptions for how things "are")? As noted above, I would argue that the only way to broach such questions is empirically and, further, through attention to the politics implied by them.

66 Similarly, consider Miriam Hansen's (1991:82–3) discussion of Frank Woods – or, in a different way, Rochona Majumdar's (2021:25–52) discussion of Marie Seton – as, not dissimilar to Bazin, a social agent in the ontological politics of realism (see also Dagrada 2014:35, as well as Metz's 1974[1971]:11 mention of the "theoretician"). Hansen's analysis powerfully shows how putative ontologies of the image and accounts of the medium per se (such as Bazin's and Metz's) are, in matter of fact, reanalyses of a historically particular textual form and industry metadiscourse that was waged by an emergent "classical" Hollywood in its attempts to gentrify and regiment an otherwise more ontologically open and unruly medium (see also Gunning 1991). Such accounts, thus, as I have been arguing, are an ontological politics.

Chapter 2. The Heroine's Stigma

1 While I don't develop it as an explicit theme in this chapter, the turn to the Goffmanian question of the production format and participation framework of filmic image-acts speaks to the concern in film theory (and beyond) to theorize how filmic representations have subjectivity effects (see also Casetti 1998[1986]:153n53, 154n59). As we see, the question of "the subject" has to be rethought in terms of the complex ways in which individuals may take "footings" (Goffman 1979) to swatches of cinematic semiosis, which are multiple, shifting, and perspectival, as well as being, at times, objects of political contestation. See note 64 in this chapter for more discussion.

2 On the repression of the dasi figure within 1930s and 1940s Tamil film narratives, see Sundar Kaali 2013. The stigma associated with women acting is not particular, of course, to Indian theatre or cinemas. As Christopher Wild (personal communication, 2015) noted to me at a

seminar presentation of an early draft of this chapter, some of the dynamics described in this chapter also characterize nineteenth-century German theatre (and later cinema), which endeavoured to make itself more respectable by instating a new kind of relationship between the viewer and the stage, separating them by creating a fourth wall that allowed the spectator to enter a representational space rather than a space of co-presence. This separation was prompted by worries about the inherent eroticism linked to co-presence with women who returned the gaze.

3 In mid-twentieth-century Tamil cinema, the vamp and the heroine existed as a division of sexual labour within a continuum of stigmatic performativity. In the 1990s, with the widespread advent of television and home-theatre technology, and their attendant effects on audience demographics and the political economy of film, this division collapsed and reappeared as the blurry distinction of heroine and item (often played by the same actresses, though not necessarily in the same film). (While the item number as a generic feature of Tamil cinema is typically dated to the 1980s and 1990s, see Eswaran Pillai 2015:111 on the term *item* as used to refer to a stand-alone dance number in the 1940s Tamil film industry.) This is not to say, however, that there is not still a sexual division of labour, on or off the screen, that marks the career trajectories and images of actresses. Indeed, the stigmatic performativity of the film image can be seen in the latent asymmetry that a heroine can dance item numbers, but someone who specializes in item numbers has difficultly inhabiting heroine roles. This asymmetry is also the case for former heroines, who may appear in item numbers as sites of *sight aṭikkiṟatu* (sexualized ogling) but not reappear in heroine roles as the site of *kanavu kanni pārvai* (a vision of a dream girl). See the main text below for more discussion.

4 Not all songs "interrupt" equally, of course. Background scores, as their name implies, displace almost nothing at all, interwoven as they are with the narrative. So-called montage sequences less so. The most intense breaks – often the bane or condescending delight of elite viewers – are the mass hero's "entry" and accompanying "introduction song" (Chapters 1, 3) and the "item number," two displacements that echo each other (compare Iyer 2020:42). These two intense moments, both scopically and erotically charged, both aesthetically marked off, both arresting and arrested (that is, narratively frozen), differ in many ways, of course. On this issue, see discussion in the main text below.

5 Scholars writing on the early history of American and European cinema (for example, Gunning 1986, 1991; Elsaesser 1990; Hansen 1991;

Gaudreault 2009[1999]) have worked against this ideological reduction of commercial cinema to narrative function by showing how the realist aesthetics, narrative-immersive forms of spectatorship, and associated modes of exhibition of classical Hollywood historically emerged as a political and economic intervention of the film industry. However, while scholars of early Euro-American cinema have posed narrative and attraction (and its associated binaries) as a historical development, or as a division of labour across genres (commercial versus avant-garde), my interest is to tease out representationality and performativity as co-constitutive, if ambivalently entangled semiotic potentialities underwriting film images more generally as they come to be reflexively construed (for example, by audiences, filmmakers) and entextualized, elaborated, institutionalized, managed, disavowed, and exploited. The question, then, is not just a comparative one but also a question of how to clarify the ways in which performativity and representationality come to be achieved, managed, dealt with, and used on and off the screen in and across images of various sorts. See discussion in Chapter 1.

6 Note how, while – as we see in this chapter – the principalship for the performativity of the item number often falls back to the female dancer, in moments when directors lament the pressures they feel to include item numbers in their films, they often deflect the responsibility for sequences to producers and male audiences, who they thereby figure as Goffmanian principals for the very existence of such sequences (see also Ganti 2012:87). I thank Amanda Weidman for pointing this out to me.

7 In this discourse, the degree to which the narrative reins in the non-diegetic illogic of such sequences is the measure of its director. Tejaswini Ganti tells us from her work in Hindi cinema: "The skill of a writer and/or director is demonstrated by how well the song situations are integrated into the screenplay. While there are plenty of examples of Hindi films where the songs seem either very loosely connected to the narrative or simply pop out of nowhere, such a lack of integration is considered 'sloppy,' 'lazy,' or simply 'bad filmmaking'" (Ganti 2004:80; also Ganti 2009:106; Gopalan 2002:127). The journalist Saibal Chatterjee (2003:16–17) writes:

> Songs serve a range of purposes in the narrative design of a Hindi film … When the mandatory song-and-dance sequences are utilized intelligently … they do manage to traverse time and space in a manner that only serves to enhance the dream quality that is so essential to the overall narrative format of a Hindi film. However, in less accomplished hands, they may, even when

> emotionally expressive, often be dragged down to the level of vulgarized portrayals of feelings and passions, especially sexual desire, which cannot be projected upfront owing to restrictions imposed by the censorship code and the pressures asserted by prudish middle-class mores.

As this quote shows, often the qualities of the song and dance may also be attributed to some external party – the government or public prudery – as if to exorcise responsibility for its unreason to some other less than rational principal (for example, the Censor Board; see also Ganti 2004:81; Mazzarella 2013).

8 This structure of ambivalence is often reproduced in accounts of item numbers written by scholars and film critics of Indian cinemas; in particular, in their stressing of the narrative function of such song-and-dance sequences: for example, to "express intense emotion" and "romance," to "evoke memories," "facilitate the passage of time," "represent fantasy," and the like (see, for example, Chatterjee 2003:16; Virdi 2003:146; Pinto 2006:85–118; Mazumdar 2007:89; Roy 2010:36). By assigning a function to such sequences, the coherence of film is retroactively reconstituted, the seeming challenge of the item to the narrative, its *public punctum* as William Mazzarella (2013:211), following Barthes (1981:27), might put it, kept in abeyance. Item songs do, of course, serve narratological functions. Further, pointing this fact out is important, so as to counter prejudicial discourse that would dismiss Indian cinemas out of hand because of the perceived illogic of item numbers. But if they serve such functions, it is, as noted in the main text, precisely as a dialogic response to a performativity and set of interests that sit uncomfortably with the representationality of narrative, diegesis, and their stewards (namely, directors; see note 7 in this chapter). If so, then the urge to reintegrate the item's interruption into the narrative and its diegetic rationality also perhaps reveals a problematic lacuna of the theory of Indian film itself (see Gopalan 2011:19; Kumar 2011; Iyer 2020:12, 29–31).

9 Indeed, there are many more elements of Tamil film that are often considered "illogical" vis-à-vis the narrative (for example, the separate "comedy track," action sequences, other songs, and so on), which do not irritate in the same way or to the same extent as the item number.

10 This imputation of titillation suffuses talk about Tamil film. One's alignment to film determines *where* one locates titillation. In that sense, this discourse is fractally recursive (Gal 2002) – that is, repeated across nested distinctions. Thus, for those most morally opposed to (commercial) cinema, it is cinema itself that titillates; for those who appreciate "good" cinema (for example, from the golden era of the past), contemporary youth cinema titillates; or within film texts, it is actresses (in commercial cinema) who

titillate; more specifically, vamps and items titillate; and most specifically, "vulgar"/"glamorous" lyrics/movements/shots enacted by particular item dancers in particular songs titillate.

11 On *darśan* and cinema, see note 28 in Chapter 1. On examples of the erotic tactility of vision in Western cinema, see Canby 1987; Narenmore 1988; Saner 2014.

12 In interrogating the image of female form as a problem of the text, Mulvey's (2009[1975]) classic essay does not attend to the complex extratextual labour that goes into maintaining the patriarchal regime of looking that she identifies and imputes to the apparatus and its texts. Here, my analysis is closer to Mulvey's (2009[1989]:215) later work on Clara Bow, which moves beyond the apparatus and film text to their social conditions of possibility.

13 Thanks to Daniel Morgan for drawing my attention to this reference in Gunning's article.

14 It is worth noting that at the time of my research, such a structure of looking and its textual manifestation in item numbers and the like were highly conventionalized, familiar, and routine. After some seventy-five years, sexually charged song-and-dance sequences, kissing scenes, and similarly normalized spectacles of femininity were not necessarily particularly transgressive. Their performative bite was more bark than bite or, to pun on the Tamil slang term for pornography, *bit*. This citational, and conventionalized, quality was evinced in the difference in spectator practices between, on the one hand, item numbers and romantic scenes and, on the other hand, pornography. Young men hooted and hollered at the screen when the hero and heroine embraced and (almost) kissed and when the item girl bared her body for the audience to see. They played up the stereotypes that respectable society has for debauched spectatorship. By contrast, they were *absolutely silent* while watching pornography as a group. The actually nude image was a true shock and attraction – and that, too, was one point of watching pornography, to engage in the shock of what one should or could never see in public. It is the liminal space that is of interest here, the way in which commercial cinema flirts with the transgressive, the way it cites and contains it, and the ways such sequences thereby do retain something of that bit(e), always threatening to push past their own conventional boundaries into a certain kind of transgressive excess.

15 Debates in feminist film scholarship in the 1970s and 1980s largely turned on the question of sexual difference and its relationship to the film image – as unrealistic depiction; as mode of patriarchal inscription, naturalization, and dissemination; or as site for patriarchy's ideological contradictions and potential feminist recuperation (see Doane et al. 1984; Mulvey 1989, 2015; Hollinger 2012:7–19 for discussion). Particularly contentious was

the question of the immanence of sexual difference to narrative cinema and its apparatus (such arguments largely being argued with or against psychoanalytic theories of subjectivity and their stipulation of a putatively active male gaze/subject versus a passive female image/object), and thus the question of what a non-patriarchal cinema might look like (Mulvey 2009[1975]; de Lauretis 1984). Importantly, such debates critically traversed the lines between film practice and criticism (Mulvey's work providing an exemplary instance), offering a clear example of the way in which we can productively see such theoretical debates as an ontological politics (for images), one that leaves its traces in images (that is, as a politics of images).

16 While this regime of visibility and its differential stakes for women crosscuts different modalities and media in South India – we find it at play on the street (Dickey 2013; Dean 2013), on stage (Weidman 2012), in theatre (Seizer 2005), on television (Nakassis 2015) – it is particularly intensified in cinema, the medium that since the 1930s has been understood as the primary site of modern mass publicity in South Asia and beyond (Hughes 1996; Mazzarella 2013; Prasad 2014), with all the attendant moral anxieties and desires entailed therein.

17 Actresses, in particular "glamorous" ones, must continually confront this conflation with anxious disavowals of any relationship between their onscreen and offscreen selves, disallowing the screen to contaminate them, detouring its semiotics away from their offscreen selves to the film image's narrative referent (Seizer 2005; Majumdar 2009; Ganti 2012:135–51; Pandian 2015:171, 176; see Pinto 2006:41 and Kasbekar 2001:300 on Helen; Farook 2012 on Bindu; Govindan and Dutta 2008:189 on Priyanka Chopra; Iyer 2020:112–20 on Azurie, 193 on Madhuri Dixit; compare Strassler 2020:133–66). See main text for discussion.

18 Consider a 2016 response by the heroine-star Nayanthara to the misogynistic statements of the director Suraj, who in an interview suggested that the function of actresses was to please low-class audiences by bearing their flesh. It is irrelevant whether or not the heroines are comfortable, he said, "because audiences pay money to see the heroines in such clothes." He is reported to have said, "with a smirk: 'Let heroines show their acting abilities in television serials. When it comes to commercial films, they are paid only to provide the required sizzle to the money paying audiences,'" a telling comparison as discussion in the main text below indicates. In response, Nayanthara is reported to have equally tellingly said: "Does he [Suraj] think that heroines are strippers who will come and shed their clothes just because they are paid money? Will he dare to speak such things about working women in his family? … At a time when [Hindi] films like *Pink* and *Dangal* speak about women empowerment and respect to women, in

which era does Suraj belong to? … And by making such comments that heroines take money to shed clothes, he is misleading the youngsters who will think this is what happens in cinema. I too have done my share of glamour in commercial films, not because my director wanted to please that particular 'low class' of audience but because it was my CHOICE. No one has the right to think that heroines can be taken for granted." It is important to note, as I discuss in the epilogue of this chapter, that it is precisely actresses like Nayanthara who in the last several years have taken charge in helming female-centred films that break with the sequestering and reduction of the heroine role to simply the actress's ogled body (see Moviebuzz 2016; on similar incidents, see Krishnan 2009:191–2).

Compare this exchange with statements about actresses by the so-called father of Indian cinema, Dada-Saheb Phalke (1870–1944); while over a hundred years old, they still have a current ring to them, even down to the kinship chronotope of reception he invokes (see discussion in main text below):

> It'd be better if female roles are enacted by women. This is the conclusion I have come to after spending 20 years in this (film) industry … God willing, if one day these prostitutes can be removed and replaced with women from good families, our studios will no longer be compared with whore houses and the prestige of the filmmakers and their teams will be salvaged … Then it will no longer be embarrassing to see films accompanied by one's mother, mother-in-law, daughter, or daughter-in-law. (quoted in Pande 2006:1649)

Similarly:

> Women from good Samskari families alone should act in films. Brothers, how would you feel if Sita and Draupadi were to be played by someone who is in the habit of using obscene gestures, making lewd eyes and has a half-revealed bosom and a wiggling behind? Would you not be enraged? … [S]tudios are not brothels … [W]ith their innate breeding and aura of a respectable marital status, women from good families (as actresses) will add a glow to the mythical days, my devis and to the atmosphere in and around our studios … Then no one shall feel bad watching our movies in the company of one's mother, mother-in-law, daughter-in-law, wife, or daughter. (quoted in Pande 2006:1649–50)

The problem of the stigma of the actress, and the felt need to be rid of it, has confronted the Indian film industries from their inception (Majumdar 2009; Mukherjee 2017:20–1, 110–19; Niazi 2019:345–7, 2021:52). See Pandian (1996:951) on the appeal by the Ceylonese Brahmin actress, Thavamani

Devi, in the 1930s that "women from respectable families should give up their reluctance and act in films" and the popular press's tellingly satiric rebuke (perhaps given her controversially glamorous onscreen image; see also Sabita Devi in Mukherjee 2017:119–22). See Nakassis 2015 on contemporary attempts to confront this stigma and reform the Tamil industry's lack of respectability; Ganti 2012:119–51 on questions of respectability in the Hindi cinema.

19 At play for those who hold this sexist stereotype that actresses are no more than "prostitutes" is an ideological loop that collapses being/appearing by blurring the presupposing and entailing relationship between the act of appearing onscreen and the actress's status as morally compromised (compare Žižek 1989:106–7). When I asked men I knew (including some working in the film industry) how they know that actresses are "prostitutes" (as they would put it), it wouldn't be uncommon for them to reply, as if it were self-evident, that actresses are prostitutes simply because they appear onscreen, for to appear onscreen as a heroine or an item is to have already performed a transgressive sexual act, one that itself presupposes another offscreen; or, to run the logic of this sociological realism in reverse, as a conservative friend put it (discussed in the main text below), what kind of 'family girl' would act?

20 Sangita Gopal (2011) dates the disappearance of the onscreen kiss to the 1930s and the shift to a reflexively Indian nationalist cinematic project and its bourgeois pedagogy.

21 See discussion in Dungan and Smik 2001 (53, 58, 66, 71, 100–1) for a series of remembrances of the American film director Ellis R. Dungan about on-set gender politics in the Tamil cinema of the 1930s and 1940s. Also see the short news clip, "Ellis Dungan Senior Report with Ken Kadar," posted on YouTube at https://www.youtube.com/watch?v=2pxFVdSnVHw, where Dungan recalls:

> See over there [Madras Presidency] the, the actors were not permitted to touch one another. And I introduced this (in the film *Ponmudi*), and I got panned by the local press, and the women, when they uh saw it in the, in the- this scene in the uh local film, film house they would always pull their sari <gestures pulling up the sari *paḷḷu* over the face> and turn their head around this (be) cause they didn't want to see that. That's something, it should go, happen behind closed doors, not on the screen.

22 Catharine MacKinnon's (1993) *Only Words* presents a distinct, if comparable, ethnometapragmatic logic of the performative image (in her case, the pornographic image). MacKinnon's reasoning about pornographic images as acts of sexual inequality similarly turns, on the one hand, on their seemingly rigid performativity (the effects they give rise to) and, on the other hand, their profilmic reality (an act of abuse had to have taken place before

the camera), echoing both Bazin's ontology of the photographic image and a familiar mass-society/media-effects narrative, as well as some of the ways of cultivating the image discussed in this chapter. While MacKinnon importantly argues that images act, it has – as her critics have pointed out – been at the cost of immediating the pornographic image as inherently performative. By doing so, this position obscures the complex historical, textual, and cultural mediation that is part and parcel of any performative act (Williams 1989). My suggestion here, then, is *not* that the image-act is inherently performative or that the problem of presence in Tamil cinema is pornographic, but to ask under what conditions it might come to be and for whom, with what political entailments and presuppositions, and with what frailties and vulnerabilities to being undone.

23 One veteran industry insider critical of this sexism suggested to me that this mode of vision isn't only for the screen and its viewers; it can also be an alibi for filmmakers themselves, who in the name of the film (and the "market") orchestrate their own profilmic scenes of *sight*ing the actress's body and, in certain cases he claimed, touching her (as when the director "has" to show the hero how to embrace her in a certain scene). Here, the actress's body is a pivot point around a set of entangled fraternal relays of vision and touch, each of which circulates through/in the name of the others: that of the hero, the director, the male spectator. Here, I'm less interested in the veracity of this insider's claim (though I don't doubt it either; see Pandian 2015:176) than in how it construes the image, not as representation but as a series of proxy looks and touches, on and off the screen, that inscribe themselves on the body of the actress and that construe appearance as itself an act with particular performative effect.

24 Consider, for example, the public outcries of obscenity against the 2007 film *New*, starring the actress Simran and directed, produced, and acted in by S.J. Surya; in particular, to its promotional photos that showed Simran and S.J. Surya kissing. In response, one media outlet reported, Simran denied that she had "actually" kissed the actor S.J. Surya. The kiss, it was declared, was simply computer graphics. Their lips never actually touched (see Behindwoods n.d.; also P.V. Satish Kumar 2005 for oblique references to censored elements of the film used in promotional materials, which included a still of S.J. Surya's head resting on Simran's breast). For his part, S.J. Suriya justified such "obscene" images and scenes by saying that the "storyline" demanded them (BBC News 2004). Similarly, consider the controversial "lip-lock" in Samantha's 2018 film *Rangasthalam*, in response to which she noted both that "it was not a true kiss" but a trick shot of a kiss on the cheek that was made to look like a kiss on the mouth and that, in any case, "the scene" needed it (*Gulte.com* 2018; see also Gopal 2011:160; Pandian 2016; Subhakeerthana 2018a). In such cases, the disavowal of the

actuality of the image's profilmic referent – and indeed, the attempt to shift the putative mode of being and type of indexical contact of the filmic image – points to a mode of spectatorship at play that construes such image-acts beyond questions of representation, that construes such images as performatively realistic forms of documentary evidence whose display makes them count as moral acts in the very fact/context of their display. See also note 17 in this chapter.

25 See Nakassis and Dean 2007 for a more detailed description of this scene and its dialogue.

26 The lighting contrast of dark to light parallels the asymmetric discursive control of the interaction (and events in the plot), with Anitha explaining to – indeed, illuminating – a confused, in-the-dark (!) Kathir, drawing him to the (well-lit) bed. This approach also parallels the way the film's director (Selvaraghavan 2005), critics, and viewers glossed the dynamics of the couple and the trajectory of the story (see Nakassis and Dean 2007).

27 In Figures 2.2 to 2.4, screen shots are roughly aligned with the lines adjacent to them. Notes about audience behaviour, in {curly brackets}, are from theatre shows that I attended in 2004 and 2005 in Madurai and Chennai, and from a film screening on a television for my male hostel mates in Madurai in 2008.

28 This partial integration was important for the director, Selvaraghavan (2005), and for the dance master, Kalyan Kumar (2011), as distinguishing their filmmaking practice from standard filmic fare; on this point, see discussion in main text above and note 7 in this chapter.

29 As the item number section proceeds, we see the pistol-brandishing gangster sitting in the audience; he is arguably, thus, a seeing subject of the item dancers within the nightclub (see Iyer 2020:66). While his look tightens the coherence with Anitha's dance for Kathir (and likens Kathir's look to the gangster's) and motivates some of the shots of the item dancers, most of the shots of the item dancers are unmotivated in terms of such a voyeuristic looking structure.

30 Compare how narrative and performativity interact here with fans' reactions to *Mankatha*'s (2011, dir. Venkat Prabhu) narrative justifying Vaibhav's slaps, as discussed in Chapter 1.

31 With this point in mind, we can see another reason why the post-Independence kiss, as discussed by Prasad (1998), has a different status than the cabaret song or item number: they have different production formats (Goffman 1974, 1979). The kiss arguably stands in a different relationship to the film text and its director than the item number. The kiss stands as *both* a transgressive profilmic/screened act *and* as a kind of "speech" act itself; which is to say, as an assertion by the film – and

thus, potentially, its director – of the acceptability of the expression of female desire and private conjugality. By contrast, the expiated item number doesn't stand in such a relation to the film text or to any authorial directing subject.

32 Here, we see another variant of the politics of the image discussed in the main text above, which locates the performativity of the image not only in the way it conflates actress and character but also in the way it figures narrative representations themselves as performative acts with certain "effects" on the audience (here, presumed-to-be impressionable youth). Often voiced through a developmentalist discourse of "social awareness" (and a nostalgia for a past where such awareness and social responsibility existed in the film industry), here the director as author is called on to *not* write stories that necessitate sexualized images, images that (re)present women in putatively degrading ways. Note, incidentally, the way in which the importance of the question of *who* it is that acts, that communicates, and that gives us the image stands in direct contrast to the view of Metz (2016[1991]:9) that cinema is "impersonal" and that the spectator is not concerned with what/who the enunciator (the image-maker) is, and instead simply "sees images" (compare Gunning 1991:23). See Chapter 4 for more discussion.

33 While I don't have positive evidence that Sonia Agrawal's ethnic identity mattered, one might conjecture that her non-Tamil identity as a North Indian Punjabi (see discussion in the second half of the chapter) might have also influenced Selvaraghavan being imputed as the principal of her character's actions. Thanks to Amanda Weidman for suggesting this point.

34 For example, see the film reviews at https://www.mouthshut.com/review/7/G-Rainbow-Colony-Movie-review-pqnnuuror.

35 Selvaraghavan (2005) put it in our interview:

> It's a flow. When you write a screenplay, you can't think about anything, you just have to go to the characters. So, you should put your characters in the particular situation and think about what they would do. Obviously, it is, will generally be ((???)). They will do this. So, it's not like you think "I want put this kind of scene"; then I can't write the rest of the screenplay and match the rest of scenes. I go from scene one. So, the scene you are saying [the lodge scene], it is almost the sixtieth scene or ((???)) scene. So, when it comes, you know the flow. It's going. So, parents won't have it, they ran away, so he just stayed with the girl alone in a hotel, then they talk about it, and then the fine moment she says, "So, let's have it."

Immediately after appealing, and ceding authorial agency, to the narrative and its "flow," Selvaraghavan commented:

> <getting louder:> I- I- I don't feel nothing wrong about it. There is not a rule in the whole world like only guys should have desires. Females have. They have, I mean, they have much strong(er) desires than the guys actually.

Or, as he put it earlier in the interview, defending himself against his critics:

> But still in South, it's typical even everybody starts scolding me, "What sort of female it is?" But still I want to resemble what females we have today. Today. Because Chennai or Tamil Nadu or even the whole of India has improved a lot. But still we have a huge gap between the people from that period and the people of the last ten years or last fifteen years. We have a huge gap. Those people want to put a mask and just pretend everything is fine. Our society is the most orthodox, every female is a very- I can't take that because we know what is happening out there. So, we- I don't want to just take a mask and put it on my face and act like I am just like a ((???)). We have. We have everything.

See Nakassis and Dean 2007 for more discussion.

36 See Chapters 1 and 4 on similar directorial deflections and deferrals.

37 Arguably, because the song sequence of "January Madham" in *7/G Rainbow Colony* juxtaposed and integrated/blended the diegetic chronotope and the chronotope of the item, its performative edge was more powerful than the standard-fare item number, which is generally detached completely from the film and its narrative. This amplification is because the song sequence in *7/G Rainbow Colony* poetically likens and thus forces the spectator to inhabit (that is, take a simultaneous footing to) both the space of narrative identification and the space of spectacle, of voyeurism and intimacy, exhibition and publicity; in doing so, the performative force of one is communicated to the other, and vice versa, the presence of the item prescencing the narrative, the realism and emotional impact of the narrative intensifying the item.

38 Of course, marriage is not always the cause of a heroine moving out of acting; in certain cases, it is the consequence of one's acting career as a popular heroine coming to an end (as with, for example, Latha, Suvalakshmi, and Rambha).

39 Through secondary print and online sources, I have surveyed 220 actresses, with a specific focus on heroines, who have acted in Tamil-language films from the late 1920s to the mid-2010s. (The total pool of actresses was 246. It included notable actresses from the Hindi industry who did not act in South Indian films and actresses who acted in Tamil-language films but about whom I could not find enough reliable information for useful comparison; this latter group included mainly actresses from the first decades of talkies.) The survey collected birth, wedding, and

divorce dates (if applicable); ethnolinguistic, religious, and caste background; the industries that the actress acted in and with which she was mainly associated; the kinds of roles she played; the years in which she was most active (in particular, as a heroine); as well as the trajectory of her career before, during, and after her marriage (as applicable). Biographical and historical information that was relevant but not part of these categories was also noted (for example, landmark films; heroes she was associated with; non-marital relationships; kinship relations). It is important to stress that these results are very much preliminary and tentative, and should be taken as a first step for more in-depth, systematic primary research. Key information was not always available, was sometimes unclear or ambiguous, or was inconsistent across sources. Further, the sample could be usefully enlarged and statistically treated in a rigorous way.

40 Some notable examples are, in the 1930s, T.P. Rajalakshmi; in the 1940s and 1950s, B.S. Saroja and P. Bhanumathi Ramakrishnan (though Bhanumathi did initially leave acting after her marriage, as her husband forbade her to act; Rāmaccantiran 2004:45); in the 1950s and 1960s, Savitiri (often paired in her Tamil films with her partner, Gemini Ganesan), Padmini (whose screen image became even more glamorous after her marriage), and Saroja Devi (who stopped acting with MGR not simply after he was shot by M.R. Radha but also after her marriage); in the 1970s, Lakshmi.

41 The issue here isn't that families (or women) no longer went to the cinema during this time, for they did. Rather, it is how shifting market and demographic dynamics involving the so-called family audience came to be construed by filmmakers, and how this mediated their textual and economic practices. While since the widespread advent of television, the "family" audience became, in fact, a smaller chunk of the theatre audience, just as important was the changing temporality of theatre attendance (Nakassis 2016a:221–3). With the spread of television and media (VHS) piracy in the 1980s and 1990s, satellite and cable television in the mid-to-late 1990s, digital piracy in the 2000s, and with the increase in numbers of films released in the 2000s, theatre runs significantly shortened. During the time of my research, films no longer serially circulated through so-called A, B, and C centres over the course of many months. Instead, they simultaneously released on a large number of screens over a relatively short time period. This timing made a film's opening critical to its success, for if a film didn't open strongly it would likely be quickly replaced. As producers noted, "family" audiences now wait for a week or two to see if a film is "good" (that is, popular, well-made, morally "decent"), leaving young men as the prime audience for a film's opening. This temporality, and how it registered as tiered target audiences within film texts, was critical to what emerged as an economics of the gaze and its politics, as discussed in the main text.

42 To this factor we can also add, as S.V. Srinivas (2016) has pointed out, the rise of the "blockbuster" in South Indian industries in the 1990s. As a response to this changing political economy, the appearance of the blockbuster indicates the increasing need for big-budget films to reach markets beyond specific regions (for example, Tamil Nadu, Andhra Pradesh, and the like) in order to justify their costs or to reach their target profits (symbolic or economic). Such films generally require mass heroes, and yet at the same time cannot only depend on them, insofar as hero-stars – unlike heroines, music directors, and villains – are tied to particular regions as (political) representatives of them (see Introduction and Chapter 1). On Srinivas's argument, then, the heroine becomes part of a spectacular assemblage that helps to compensate for the hero's immobility. And indeed, heroines' alterity (for example, coming from Bollywood, Kerala, Andhra Pradesh, or Europe) has long been part of their attraction. See discussion in the main text below.

43 In addition to the reorganization of the media landscape (discussed in note 41 in this chapter), we can mention a number of other factors. The mid- to late-1970s saw the rise of a new generation of young heroes (in particular, Kamal Haasan and Rajinikanth) and young heroines, both of whom were accepted by the audience with a readiness that, according to the late film historian and industry insider "Film News" Anandan (2008), was historically novel. This emergence of a new generation of actors and actresses was abetted by a significant increase in the number of films made (from 63 in 1977 to upwards of 100 to 130 per year in the 1980s), a change encouraged by MGR's departure from film; in addition to making space for other heroes in the industry, after taking office as chief minister of Tamil Nadu, MGR also provided the film industry with a number of concessions that helped bolster its growth.

44 In Tamil, the English borrowing "*loose*" (pronounced with an epenthetic *-u* at the end: /lus-ɯ/) refers to being crazy. The phrase *loosu poṇṇu* (crazy girl) denotes a ditzy heroine type that emerged in the 1990s who, as one commentary put it, "is very angelic and innocent, needs constant rescuing and cannot do the simplest things in life" (TNM Staff 2018b) and whose love for the hero, by being so overdetermined as a necessity of the narrative and yet so underdetermined in its narrative motivation, comes off as crazy. The film critic Baradwaj Rangan (2013) writes:

> The "loosu ponnu" trope became especially set when we began to get North Indian heroines who didn't speak a word of Tamil. They wouldn't move their lips according to the lines they were supposed to be speaking (and [had] to be filled in later by a dubbing artist). They'd end up gesticulating wildly to make a point. Their emotional reactions would be a bit "off." And all of this ended

up making them look like mad people ... i.e. women with a screw loose, i.e. "loosu ponnu."

This character type became the target of parody in the spoof *Thamizh Padam 2.0* (2018, dir. C.S. Amudhan), the sequel of the 2010 spoof film *Thamizh Padam* (2010, dir. C.S. Amudhan), discussed in Chapter 3.

45 Of course, the reasons for this post-marital division of acting and its historical emergence are complex and tangled, with a host of reasons not simply reducible to the historical semiotics of the screen and its changing economics. Jealous or status-conscious husbands, in-laws concerned about family reputation, or the increasing demands of post-marriage family life (for example, bearing and raising children, running a household) have all been cited over the decades by actresses and industry insiders as reasons for why actresses stop acting after marriage or shift to non-heroine roles ("Film News" Anandan 2008; Simran Bagga 2011; Shakeela 2013; Hooli 2015). And yet, as the example of Simran discussed in the main text below indicates, it is also more than these reasons.

46 Similarly, consider the case of Aruna Irani, the 1970s Hindi vamp-actress, whose career underwent a lull after people believed her to be married to the Hindi actor Mehmood (Joshi 2013). See Weidman 2016 on journalist parodies of such dynamics in the 1930s and 1940s; see also Dyer's (1998[1979]:98) discussion of Ingrid Bergman, whose career came to a standstill in the United States after she started making films with Rossellini and had his child out of wedlock.

47 The "aunty" figure is not stereotypically a *kanavu kanni* but instead a sexualized object of *sight aṭikkiṟatu*; moreover, actresses who act the "aunty" have not typically, as far as I know, acted as commercial heroines at the same time (for such a status already presupposes that the actress has moved out of, or is excluded from, heroine roles). A telling example is Ramya Krishnan who, while a heroine in 1990s commercial films, shifted to playing the protagonist in devotional films (whose primary target audience is women), character roles in commercial films, and then, most interestingly, the occasional item dancer (for example, in *Kaakha Kaakha* [2003, dir. Gautham Menon], *Kuthu* [2004, dir. A. Venkatesh], *Manmadhan* [2005, A.J. Murugan]). See note 70 in this chapter.

48 This avoidance of *sight*ing a married actress echoes Prasad's (1998) argument that a patriarchal compact mediates filmic representation: in Prasad's case, of the visible kiss; here, of *sight*ing another man's woman.

49 Consider the comments from the director Vasanth at a press meet for the reality television show *Tamil Pesum Kadhanayagi* (12 January 2013; see note 58 in this chapter). In describing his own responsibility for failing to cultivate and promote Tamil-speaking heroines, he referred to both Jyothika and Simran

(two non-Tamil heroines whom he introduced to the Tamil film industry) as today being daughters-in-law (*marumakaḷ*) to Tamil Nadu. When Vasanth made this comment, both actresses had since married and passed out of heroine roles, transformed from exterior objects of sexual desire to being semi-exterior affines to the larger Tamil community (and not, tellingly, consanguineal daughters, sisters, or mothers; compare Thomas 1989:24 on Nargis; also discussion in the book's Conclusion of Jayalalitha's post-filmic transformation into *Ammā*, 'Mother'). This affinal trope, of course, figurates the film industry and its publics as comprising consanguineally related men (Lakshmi 1990; Chinniah 2008:32–3).

50 In talking with friends and acquaintances in Chennai and Madurai, it was almost universally the case that the closer the act of *seeing* the actress came to home – that is, to kin relations – the more uncomfortable it got (see note 18 in this chapter), whether it be watching images *with* kin or watching images *of* kin. Here, we see another sociological aspect of this kinship chronotope: the participation framework implied in the act of seeing the image.

51 William Mazzarella (2009, 2013) has shown that it was precisely the complex of the foreign sexual that prompted increasing policing of the filmic image by the colonial state, a policing that, of course, already presupposes its awesome tendencies towards performative excess (see also Ramamurthy 2006:213–14).

52 Featuring transgressive modern characters – typists, telephone operators, and film actresses – such films focused on the spectacle and "implied nudity" (Majumdar 2009:101) of the (white) actress's body, featuring copious amounts of "indiscriminate" kissing and other transgressive bodily acts. As Priti Ramamurthy (2006) and Mrinal Pande (2006:1650) have argued, it was precisely their racial otherness that licensed such performative excesses and allowed such women to enter into the industry in the first place and grace the screen (see also Barnouw and Krishnaswamy 1980:169–72; Ganti 2012:124–30; Niazi 2019, 2021; Iyer 2020; in Tamil cinema in particular, see Baskaran 1996:8; Dungan and Smik 2001:72).

53 On the racial alterity of the vamp in Hindi cinema, see Rao 1989; Mazumdar 2007:86; Chowdhury 2010:66; Iyer 2020; in Tamil cinema, see Lakshmi 2008:18–19; Chinniah 2008. The "H-Bomb" Helen Richardson – and before her, Cuckoo Moray, who trained her – is often considered the paradigmatic vamp. Consider what Jerry Pinto (2006:10), a journalist and fan, writes: "We needed an Other around which to build fantasies and Helen was available, a white woman in a brown world, a woman who could produce sensuality out of golden cage flamingos, an excess of blue eyeshadow and oversized orange earrings" (see also Virdi 2003:168; Mishra 2020).

54 This association of film with hereditary performers was given as an explanation, for example, for the presence of Anglo women on the Indian screen in its early years. T. Rangachariar, the lawyer assigned by the British

colonial government to evaluate film censorship in 1928, noted on this subject: "The actresses are mainly recruited from the 'dancing girl' class. Indian women of the better class do not take up film-acting as a profession … Owing to the difficulty of obtaining suitable Indian actresses some Anglo-Indian girls have adopted the profession" (quoted in Ramamurthy 2006:215). See note 18 in this chapter.

55 Of course, the very notion of being ethnolinguistically Tamil should not be taken for granted as self-evident, given both the deep histories of multilingualism and mobility in South India and the relatively recent history of linguistically organized states (and film industries; see Introduction for more discussion), even if here I use this discursively constructed and historically emergent identity as a heuristic to track changing demographic patterns in their relationship to the ideological sense, within and outside the industry, that "Tamil" heroines are a minority in the Tamil film industry.

56 The early decades of talkies in South India – wherein the populist Dravidian articulations of ethnolinguistic identity and gender had yet to become hegemonic – featured a predominance of Brahmin producers (Hardgrave 1973:295), as well as, into the mid-century, many actresses from Brahmin backgrounds, whose increasing presence tracked with the marginalization of actresses from *devadāsī* backgrounds. Indeed, the former capitalized on their training in classicized forms of singing and dancing co-opted, and learned, from the latter (Weidman 2003; Soneji 2012; Krishnan 2019). By my tentative estimates, the absolute number of heroines from Brahmin communities has been relatively stable since the mid-century, though the relative percentages have declined as the number of heroines in the industry has risen.

The rise of the Dravidian movement also tracks alongside transformations in the *devadāsī* community itself in the first half of the twentieth century (as a result of the anti-*devadāsī* reform movements and legislation): on the one hand, the effacement and devaluing of the cinematic labour of actresses from the *devadāsī* community and, on the other hand, the increased importance of men from the community – who had taken on for themselves, or "birthed" (Soneji 2021), a novel community identity, using the non-Brahmin, upper-caste name *icai vēḷāḷar* (cultivators of music) – in both the political sphere (in particular, in the Dravidian movement) and in the cinema (Krishnan 2019:29, 162–3). The correlation between attempts to raise the respectability of the community by preventing its women from acting, the influx of men from the community into cinema *and* the Dravidian movement, and the decrease of Tamil(-speaking) actresses in the industry overall is worth noting.

57 In an industry that has long accepted actors and actresses (as well as technicians, directors, and producers) from elsewhere (Hughes 2011), the issue of linguistic (in)competence attracted some amount of attention from the film industry and its publics during my fieldwork, though this issue was

often conflated with questions of ethnolinguistic identity and anxieties about language loss (Nakassis 2015). Why actresses' speech competence becomes an issue in the post-liberalization period is a topic that requires more research, though my sense is that it is intimately linked to the decreasing half-life of actress's career spans, as well as to their marginalization from and sexualization in the narrative (as discussed in the main text above).

58 This dearth of Tamil(-speaking) heroine-actresses formed, for example, the conceit of a 2012 reality television contest, *Tamil Pesum Kadhanayagi*, to find its eponymous 'Tamil-speaking Heroine.' See Nakassis 2015 for discussion of the show.

59 In this context, consider how the veteran Tamil actress Vadivukkarasi framed her own career to me in 2011. She noted halfway through our conversation that she began her career doing "glamour" (sexy roles that involve exposing some amount of flesh). She was, as she pointedly emphasized, however, never a very good heroine. She was too embarrassed during romance scenes and would giggle while the camera was rolling, she said, adding that she was never a great dancer either. With time, she decided to move away from glamorous heroine roles. Most interesting for us, here, is how she framed this shift to a more respectable screen image as a move into the kin unit, not simply in terms of character types (sister, sister-in-law, mother roles) but also in terms of her relationship to the audience (as mediated by her screen appearance). As she put it, in Tamil: 'when people see me on the screen I should look like a homely woman (*vīṭṭu poṇṇā*), I should look like a woman whom they know. So if I'm their woman, would they like it if I'm acting in some kind of two piece (bikini) and all that?'

60 In discussing the 2008 realist film *Subramaniyapuram* (dir. Sasikumar; see Chapter 4), one hostel mate in Madurai even claimed that you could tell that the *actress* playing the female lead wasn't Tamil simply from how she smiled and looked at her love interest in the film: too widely, too directly, and not with enough embarrassment.

61 My point is not that this discourse is necessarily ethnolinguistically chauvinist or that the voices from which I elicited it are a homogeneous group. Indeed, actors like Sriman are not "Tamil" on hegemonic conceptions of ethnolinguistic Tamil identity. (Sriman is ethnolinguistically Telugu; see note 55 in this chapter.) The point, rather, is that the particularity of the Tamil cinema is figured in his and others' discourse by recourse to the absence of Tamil women onscreen as heroines, and that this absence carries with it valorized moral overtones linked to questions of "culture," kinship, respectability, and visibility.

62 By contrast, see Ramamurthy 1996; Majumdar 2009; Iyer 2020 on 1930s Indian film, where female stars *did* subordinate the narrative. Also see

the chapter's epilogue for discussion of the emergence of a crop of female-star–centred Tamil films in the 2010s.

63 The cases discussed in Chapters 1 and 2 also evince a parallel to what Luke Fleming (2011, 2014, 2018) theorizes as the "undecontextualizable," "rigid" performativity of tabooed acts. As Fleming points out, forms that become taboo – in his discussion, curse words, proper names of dead kin, gaze at or reference to particular affines or sacred objects – generate a seemingly intrinsic performative effect when enacted that cannot – unlike the explicit performativity discussed by Austin (1962) – be contained or defeased by reportively calibrated frames such as reported speech constructions (Nakassis 2013a) or reportively/nomically calibrated frames such as fictional narratives (Nakassis 2020). Even when so framed, the performative effect of such rigid performatives holds. Vaibhav's slaps of Ajith Kumar count as just such a profanation, indeed, a taboo-transgressing act of Ajith's sacral (nomically calibrated) personage. But if so, we might add, it is because the sacred, like the profane, has its own "rigid" performativity, one achieved not by avoidance but by insistent iteration (Butler 1993), in this case, of Ajith's presence across his film history (Nakassis 2016a:188–226). The seemingly inescapable performativity of the mass hero's "image trap" (Pandian 1992), thus, has its own kind of rigid performativity (for the social domain of his fans, at least), resistant to being decentred by a reportive/nomic calibration in the form of a narrative (denotational) text.

This is not to say that Ajith's image trap or a taboo form are unchangeable or ineluctable in their performative force, of course; heroes can lose their stardom just as taboo forms can be resignified and neutralized over historical time. The question is, At what temporal scale, through what kind of semiotic labour, and with what kinds of resistances? Rigidity, analytically, is gradient and is an achievement, even if, empirically and phenomenologically, it has a felt discreteness, ineluctability, and self-evidence.

The female cine-artists' act of appearance and acting in front of a camera and in a theatre (for that conservative social domain that would condemn her so, at least) similarly entails a kind of rigid performativity, indeed, is itself a form of taboo-breaking, a profanation of (nomically calibrated) axiological ideologies of gender and kinship. It is precisely such a deeply institutionalized performativity that regiments the entextualization of the heroine's and item's appearances onscreen, rupturing any reportively/nomically calibrated denotational entextualization of her qua fictional character as always still a reflexively calibrated act by the animating actress in the event of her appearance. This gaze, as we saw, extends beyond the narrative text, adhering to her as a form of negative value, carried in and by her marks of identity (name, face), threatening to interdiscursively follow her across her roles and beyond the theatre, a form of infamy (Munn 1986) that presents the exact inverse of the hero's auratic fame. Yet by comparison to the retrenched performativity of the mass hero – which has a rigidity only as the effect of a career of dozens and dozens of films, cultivated across them and beyond them through complex, continually repeated and ultimately tenuous, semiotic processes that would build up an image-text of auratic power (a star text) laminated onto a biographical person (the actor himself) – the performativity of the actress/item dancer's perforative act of appearance seems to hold automatically. Of course, such an effect is not automatic, or necessary, as I've argued in this chapter, but the effect of a whole "social apparatus" (Williams 1989) brought to bear as a virtual metapragmatics mediating various cinematic events. Where the hero and heroine differ is in such mediation, namely, where their performative potential is invested, where that potential's felicity conditions lie, how they are policed and cultivated (or challenged and changed), who are recruited to such sites of performativity, and with what effects and values.

A second dimension of comparison, as we've seen, centres on the relationship of narrative to performativity. Part of our point about the "build-up" of the mass hero's image is that the denotational text of the film works to amplify and make possible the performativity of his presence; indeed, what is enacted onscreen in the narrative (the hero's dominance, charisma, power, political sovereignty even, and so on) is an offscreen enactment of the personage of the star himself. Similarly, the naturalizing logic that would reason about narrative acts emplotted within a film – such as kissing, hugging, loving, and the like – *as* the basis for a stigma imputed to actresses is also not unresponsive to narrative framing, which may amplify such acts, though such acts often stand in tension with the main narrative movement of the films in which they occur. At the same time, as we saw, the narrative framing of the image-text can also work to defease or dampen filmic performativity, shifting it into an act of representation in a storied world. In Chapter 1, we saw how the filmmakers' framing of Ajith's image attempted to bracket it within a realist scene governed by the logic of its characters and story, marked by the filmmaker's "touch" rather than the hero's star image, knowing the whole while that the very possibility of such a framing turned on and presupposed that very star image and its performativity. In this chapter, we similarly see how narrative can envelop the actress with her character, defeasing the performativity of her appearance by subsuming it to an image-act that would redound not to the act-animating actress but to the story-authoring director. Yet, at one and the same time (and as we further see in Chapter 4), such reportive/nomic calibrations, such narrative frames, are themselves image-acts, entextualizable as acts of insult and profanation, be it as an attack on the mass hero's sacral image (to his fans, at least) *or* – in the case of Selvaraghavan's "pornographic" films (as denounced by his conservative critics, at least) – on the social itself.

What I would emphasize here is that these processes of entextualization are also political acts about what an image is or should be. These various acts of framing are an *ontological politics* of the image, one whose very terrain is waged across the possibilities and actualities of representationality and performativity, as the complex achievement of struggles over entextualization, over the alignments and disalignments of images, acts, and narratives as they play out on and off the screen (as I discuss more in the main text below). Such achievements do not only happen "on" the screen or "in" the film, for as I have argued, the process of entextualization traverses the screen, taking place on and off of it at once. Moreover, such effects/achievements of performativity or representationality are perspectival, situational, revisable, and open to contestation and internal heterogeneity. Independent of some ideology, some institutional frame, some textual aesthetics, some act of embodied uptake, an image-text is neither determinately performative nor representational. In other words, the performativity or representationality of the image is critically distributed across the image and its uptakes in a text-in-context that stretches beyond the localized, felt incident of its seeming "power" (Silverstein 1979; Agha 2007a). Images may come to be performative, but if so, it is because they are only the "leading incidents," as Austin (1962:8) put it, within larger meta-semiotic and institutional processes and structures – indeed, rituals – within which they come to be felt as the source of "power," "agency," and "force." See the book's Conclusions for more discussion.

64 At issue with such questions of performativity is how their perlocutionary fallout is distributed in particular ways; indeed, how it maps out and entails certain kinds of subjectivities in an array of positionalities and relationalities (Butler 1993; Kulick 2003). Implied in such relationalities are stipulations as to *what* the image in question is, in fact or by fiat; that is, the very question of the being of the image is itself a question of *how* different subjectivities are instated and related to each other *through* that very image-act/text. In short, performative or representational acts instate multiple subjectivities in the complex transactions in which they unfold: the authorizing subject of the hero-star, the principalship of Vaibhav (Chapter 1), the stigmatic subjectivity of the item, the fan subject, the disdainful elite liberal subject, and so on. Each of these subjectivities may be ambivalently and complexly articulated to each other vis-à-vis the biographical individuals who inhabit them at one and the same time: recall that Vaibhav himself was a fan-spectator, animator, and principal of the act; Ajith, a disdainful elite subject and hero-star, an authorizing agent and animator; and Anbu in Chapter 1, a disdainful liberal subject and a fan, and so on. This last point is particularly worth reiterating: *modes of being and footings*

are mutually constitutive; they presuppose and entail each other, and both are up for grabs in the unfolding pragmatics of events of entextualization. Footings in such cases, to reverse the formulation, *are* ontological politics, implicit and sometimes explicit claims on the nature of signs, and thus the first toe-hold, the foot in the door, as it were, to being.

65 In addition to acting, women also have sizeable representation in playback singing (Weidman 2021). We can similarly add stylists and marketing personnel as parts of the film industry where women are represented; both positions are relatively recent ones that displaced the male-dominated positions of the costumer and the public relations officer (PRO), respectively. Over the years there have also been some increases in female producers and directors, among other technicians (for example, editors), though they are far, far fewer than their male counterparts (see also Ganti 2012).

66 Here, de Lauretis (1984) is arguing with and against a psychoanalytic account of sexual difference that would oppose male and female as (unmarked) presence and (marked) lack (vis-à-vis the role of the phallus); by making the distinction of woman (ideal type) and women (historical subjects; fractally echoing the distinction of male spectator and female viewer), the *latter* of which are absented through the (re)presentation of the former, de Lauretis is changing the terms of the argument away from a rigid, essentialist, psychoanalytic account of sexual difference to a dialectical semiotic account of *how* historical subjects are swept up into processes that produce sexual difference, the question becoming how woman metapragmatically regiments the subject-formation of women *by* the absenting of the latter from cinema. See bell hooks's (1992) furthering of this critique, which points to the fractal replication of such dynamics within such abstracted categories of woman (in her case, by race; in the case discussed here, by caste and community); see also Stewart 2003.

67 In addition to other critiques, some commentators (Rao 2019) noted the especially problematic way in which *7/G Rainbow Colony* naturalizes male "stalking" (or eve-teasing) as an appropriate expression of romantic affection and thus promotes a form of misogynistic masculinity as a realistic depiction of female desire.

68 See, for example, Elena Dagrada's (2014:35–9) discussion of the concerted efforts by American film producers and film critics in the early part of the twentieth century to prohibit the look to the camera and the dialogic engagement of actors and spectators (see also Gunning 1991; Hansen 1991).

69 For coverage in the popular press of this "trend" of women-centred films, see *Moviecrow.com* 2018; Mridula 2018; Rajendran 2018c; Sreedhar Pillai 2018b. On scholarly discussions, see Kunapulli 2021:102–9; Zamboulingame 2021. Women-centred films, of course, are not new in

themselves (one thinks automatically of the films of K. Balachander in the 1970s and 1980s; Velayutham and Devadas 2021:5), even if films in the late 2010s have reversed a general trend (from the 1980s through the 1990s and 2000s) of minimizing (and sexualizing) the heroine. What is new, however, is (1) the number of such films and their success at the box office; (2) the way in which they ride on the star power of the heroine and not their male directors; and (3) the way in which they articulate a larger gender politics that is voiced *by* women, rather than always filtered through the figure of the male director (see, for example, the marketing posters for the 2018 film *Kaatrin Mozhi* [The Language of Air/Wind, dir. Radha Mohan], featuring ten commandments for female empowerment being held by a fiery Jyothika; see Subramanian 2018). A comparison of the 2008 film *Poo* (Flower, dir. Sasi) – a film centred on a female protagonist – is telling. As the director told me in an interview (Sasi 2009), the producer of the film felt that the film would fail without a known actor in a hero role, a request to which he had to submit (compare Ganti 2012:209–10). And while the film was critically acclaimed, it didn't do particularly well at the box office. One might argue that the film could have been viable with a bigger actress in the lead (rather than then-new-face Parvathy). But the point here is that the producer's sense at the time that the film needed a hero figure, rather than a bigger actress, contrasts with the new crop of films helmed by star actresses, which lack hero figure roles, as discussed in the main text.

70 Jyothika's *Kaatrin Mozhi* (2018, dir. Radha Mohan) can itself be read as an allegory about actresses, depicting and contesting the stigma and the conflicts created by a career in the industry. In the film, Jyothika's character has a particular line, "it's like being an actress," which she says to placate her conservative family – who would prevent her from fulfilling her desire to be a radio jockey – even if, in the instance, they reject her logic (precisely because of this connection, we might argue). As Jyothika has said, reflecting on her "second innings": "I'm not ready to stand near the hero and praise him anymore. I can't be like, 'thank you very much for giving me screen space, now let me praise you in five scenes.' I don't want to do that" (Rajendran 2018b). Similarly, consider the extended dialogue by Ramya Krishnan's character at the conclusion of *Super Deluxe* (2019, dir. Thiagarajan Kumararaja), where she explains and defends herself for acting in a pornographic film to her outraged, humiliated son. She says that she wanted to act in a blue film and in a goddess film (with a knowing wink to her intertexts; see note 47 in this chapter), and so she did. Neither role, she says, define her, nor is she ashamed of having acted in either. She did it by her own choice, knowingly, as she says in response to her son asking if she was forced to do it. Acting is a job like any other, she says, and why should actresses in blue films be made to feel shame when their viewers don't at all?

71 There is certainly an economic component to this shift – or at least a perception therein by producers – with the deepening of multiplex audiences and, as some have suggested, the rise in streaming platforms for films (Shiva Kumar 2019). While both these changes have been encouraging conditions (making such films appear more viable to producers), it shouldn't be inferred that it was economically impossible to have such films before such changes (as evidenced by heroine-centred films in the 1970s or the centrality of a female audience to commercial cinema before the 1990s); rather, the gender politics that have concerned this chapter are just as critical.

72 Of interest here is that Nayanthara's hit film, the thriller *Imaikkaa Nodigal* (Blinkless Seconds; 2018, dir. R. Ajay Gnanamuthu) was originally written for a male actor (reportedly, the Malayalam film star Mammootty; TNN 2018). Sreedhar Pillai (2018b) reports that the script was changed when the director decided to cast Nayanthara as the lead character. (See also Shekar and Thirumurthy 2018 on Trisha's 2018 film *Mohini*.) Similarly of interest is how Nayanthara's post-comeback films have garnered early morning first-day shows (Rao 2018), a practice typically reserved for hero-stars with large fan followings. And with a history of female stars like Khushboo becoming both the object of organized fan clubs and, later, politicians, one might reserve judgment on the cine-politics of the heroine. That said, what is lacking in both cases – for the moment at least – is the alignment of the denotational texts of the heroine's star-centred films with her offscreen political text.

73 Just as revealing as such counter-gestures, however, are their specific contours and the conservative responses to them. Nayanthara came back only when she became single again. Jyothika came back, still married, but in roles that were not focused on romantic love or sexual desire. And while the heroine Samantha insisted on acting across her marital status in heroine roles that still featured romance and sexuality, as a married woman she has received pointed criticism for doing romantic scenes that required kissing (Moviebuzz 2018; Subhakeerthana 2018a; Rajendran 2018b). Finally, Simran's comeback as a (second) heroine in *Petta* (2019, dir. Karthik Subbaraj) appears as a nostalgic gesture. *Petta* was itself touted as a throwback to a 1990s-style Rajinikanth film (but updated for today's generation) and as fulfilling a pairing – Simran with Rajini (and Trisha with Rajini in a flashback) – which had not happened in Simran's (or Trisha's) heyday.

Moreover, as Sreedhar Pillai (2018b) notes, the "market" and salaries of the top heroines remain much less than top heroes (for example, Nayanthara could, circa the late 2010s, reportedly command a salary of 4 to 5 crores for films she helmed, such films having budgets in the range of 10 to 15 crores and collecting around 15 to 20 crores; by comparison, the mass hero Vijay was reportedly paid 35 crores out of a 130 crore budget for the 2017 film *Mersal* [dir. Atlee], with the film reported to have collected 260 crores); rather, top heroine-stars compete with middle-level heroes.

74 Also worth noting is that in these new representational economies, as the centre of the onscreen and offscreen worlds of these films, a number of these heroine-stars (Samantha, Jyothika, Nayanthara – all non-native Tamil speakers) have begun to dub their own Tamil dialogues. While framed as an attempt to make the films more "natural" (Mridula 2018), it also indicates the anchoring in and possession of the film by the heroine-star. As has long been noted, hero-stars – with interesting, noteworthy exceptions (such as, for example, Mike Mohan or a young Ajith Kumar) – dub with their own voices (even if their Tamil is non-standard/non-fluent or their voices atypical) in order to "build up" their star image as a site of spectatorial identification and investment on and off the screen. With the success of films riding on such heroine-stars, it makes sense that they would invest the extra effort to do their own dubbing (often otherwise not expected of them) to align their image and voice, and thus to speak for themselves. As Amanda Weidman helpfully noted upon reading a draft of this book, the rise of female-centred films alongside (1) their heroine-stars dubbing for themselves and (2) a decrease in stand-alone songs animated by playback singers indexes the emergence of a new aural economy of gendered appearance and audition (see also Weidman 2021:196–202). An ontological politics of the image is not simply about the visual modality but also includes contestations and transformations in the aurality of cinema as well; indeed, as noted in the book's Introduction, images are not only visual but occur in and across any and every modality in which diagrammatic iconic aesthetic textuality is possible (Nakassis 2019).

Chapter 3. The Politics of Parody

1 At the time of my research, industry insiders explained this seeming paradox that Tamil cinema is all spoof with no spoofs by pointing to the self-seriousness of the industry or, alternatively, by suggesting that the film "spoof" is a foreign genre. (In a telling intergeneric comparison, during a conversation with me, one Tamil interlocutor from an elite Chennai college characterized *Thamizh Padam*, the spoof film discussed in this chapter, as "India's *Scary Movie*," a reference to the American franchise of spoof horror films.) Yet the industry has long made jokes at its own expense. Think, for example, of the comedian-actor Nagesh's memorable comedy track from C.V. Sridhar's classic 1964 romantic comedy *Kadhalikka Neeramillai* (No Time for Love), which turns on Nagesh's nascent film production: a parody of the film producer, Nagesh has everything lined up to make a film … except

a story. Or, consider a film like *Sivaji: The Boss* (2007, dir. Shankar), whose hero, the "Superstar" Rajinikanth, and comic sidekick, played by Vivek, are continually parodying Rajini's star image; the film is a smorgasbord of pastiche upon pastiche, parody upon self-parody. No exception to Tamil cinema, self-reflexive parody is and has long been its rule. But what is distinct about *Thamizh Padam* is that the whole of its textual body was a comedic cannibalization of the conventions and stereotypes, and specific texts, of Tamil cinema, rather than sequestering its parody to the narrative-external "comedy track" (Kunapulli 2021:113–14). Moreover, as we see below, *Thamizh Padam* refused to reinforce the "build-up" of the figure of the hero through its comedy; indeed, it launched a full-on attack on him.

In this attack, however, *Thamizh Padam* reflected wider post-millennial trends. Indeed, in addition to *Thamizh Padam*, 2010 saw the release of two other parodic films: Venkat Prabhu's *Goa* (which released on the same day as *Thamizh Padam* and whose first half was an extended parody of the 1980s nativity film) and Simbudevan's *Irumbukkottai Murattu Singam* (released 7 May 2010, a spoof of the Tamil Western genre from the 1970s). Further, a number of farcical, yet seemingly serious heroes emerged in the late 2000s: "Powerstar" Dr. S. Srinivasan, Sam Anderson (Soman 2012), and J.K. Ritesh. The self-anointed "Powerstar" went on to have a short-lived career as a comedian, (unintentionally, but then knowingly) parodying himself as a seriously delusional hero-star (which maybe he also was?). Giving us licence to parody Marx's adage that history repeats … first as spoof, then as farce, it was reported in the media that, in addition to personally producing his first film, *Lathika* (2011) and launching himself as a sui generis mass hero (financed presumably from his work as a medical doctor and pyramid schemer), he also paid viewers, or plied them with alcohol and biryani, to watch the film so as to run it, in one theatre at least, for 225 days (*IndiaGlitz* 2014). What is so strange about Dr. Srinivasan – besides his uncharismatic charisma, his absurd self-promotion (for example, his claims to being on par with industry stalwarts such as Rajinikanth), or the way in which he attracted ironic(?) "fans" (who seemed to love how bad he was at being a hero-star) – is the way in which, initially at least, he seemed not to understand that he was taken as a joke within the industry. (Revealingly, perhaps, his career ended with arrest for a number of scams that he was involved in; on his unlikely, yet perhaps predictable, career, see Kandavel 2013; Chitra B. 2015.) On a cinematic allegory of the self-serious actor who appears to all others as a self-parody (and thus is a parody of the industry itself), see Karthik Subbaraj's 2014 *Jigarthanda*, one of a number of "neo-noir" films that has followed in the wake of *Thamizh Padam* (see discussion in the main text below). Important precursors to the 2010 films noted above include Sakti Chidambaram's *Mahanadigan* (2004; and sequences from his

2005 *Englishkkaran*), the STAR Vijay TV spoof series *Lollu Sabha*, as well as Venkat Prabhu's 2007 *Chennai 600028* and 2008 *Saroja*. Dhananjayan (2011, 1:46–7) reports that *Naveen Vikramadityan* (1940, dir. K.S. Mani) was "the first full-length comedy spoof in Tamil cinema" (of a well-known folk story), followed by *Chandrahari* (1941, dir. K.S. Mani), a spoof of the story of *Harichandra*. Tamil cinema also has a long history of satire, for example, N.S. Krishnan's 1949 *Nalla Thambi* (dir. Krishnan–Panju) and Cho Ramasamy's 1971 *Muhammad bin Tughluq*.

2 Being a hit here means that *Thamizh Padam* turned a profit at the box office for its distributors (on producer's profits, see note 3 in this chapter), had a relatively long run in the theatres, and was popular with audiences. Its financial success, of course, was abetted by its lower budget (and expectations) in comparison to bigger-budget, hero-driven films.

3 Coming from an advertising background, *Thamizh Padam*'s director, C.S. Amudhan, framed himself as an outsider to the Tamil film world when he began writing the film. He put it to me this way in 2010:

> This was something that, you know, everybody who watches Tamil films thinks about these things, you know, what if the scene were like this? You know, this is what we tell our friends, this is what we, uh, when you're having a drink, this is what we do: how would it be if it were like this? So, I started writing, writing this more out of fun than anything else. And I absolutely had no intention of trying to find a backer for this to make (it) into a feature film … I had very low aspirations for it. I thought maybe it could go on television, or maybe be a DVD exclusive product.

He managed to hook up, however, with an acquaintance, S. Sashikanth, a Chennai architect with common clients as Amudhan's advertising company. Sashikanth had recently founded his own film production company, YNOT Studios (which Amudhan came to have a 25 per cent stake in, up until 2011). Sashikanth's aim for YNOT was to establish a film production house that created commercial content "alternative" to the standard fare of the industry. As Sashikanth told me in his Chennai home in 2011, part of his vision for YNOT Productions, even before he teamed up with Amudhan, included producing a spoof film. When Amudhan pitched him three concepts during a brainstorming session, one of which was a spoof, Sashikanth, as he told me, seized upon the idea of the spoof. From there, Amudhan narrated the film's "one-line" to Sashikanth's childhood friend Dayanidhi Alagiri, who had recently begun his own production company, Cloud 9 Movies. (Sashikanth [2011] told me that Red Giant Movies, the film production company of Dayanidhi Alagiri's cousin Udhayanidhi Stalin, was originally supposed to produce the film in conjunction with YNOT. However, since Udhayanidhi was busy with another project, he referred the project to his cousin's company, Cloud 9 Movies.) "Excited by it [the "big idea ... to do a spoof"]," as Amudhan (2010) put it, Cloud 9 bought the first copy rights of the film from YNOT, eventually going on to see the film to its theatrical release. *Thamizh Padam* was pre-sold to Cloud 9 for its actual cost to YNOT. Sashikanth (2011) reported to me that he sold it at cost because, as it was his first film, he was more concerned with producing sellable content, so as to presumably get his foot in the door of the industry and generate a name for his company as a bankable, reliable production house of alternative content. He narrated this to me in the context of criticizing the dominant mode of production of the industry, whereby windfall profits from huge hits are attempted to be made from hero-oriented films, rather than rationalizing the production process to create regular, if lower profit margins. See main text below for more discussion.

4 As K. Chandru (2010), one of the screenwriters of *Thamizh Padam* indicated to me, the film was written to have a narrative structure and plot just like any other (stereotypical) commercial Tamil film. With such a "one-line" set, Amudhan and his assistants then contemplated *which* particular film from the past had the "best," most "iconic" scene for every specific plot point ("line") of the story. If it is a confrontation with a villain, Chandru proffered, then the most "iconic scene" is from the Rajinikanth film *Baashaa* (1995, dir. Suresh Krissna); if it's the introductory scene of a heroine, then Radha Mohan's *Mozhi* (2007, starring Jyothika as the heroine); if it's a love scene, then Prabhu Deva's Bharatanatyam dance scene in *Kadhalan* (1994, dir. S. Shankar); and so on.

5 While film scholars who have focused on parody have noted that film parodies may take up any and every aspect of cinema, on or off the screen, in general this literature has focused on the film textuality of what such parodies spoof (see, for example, the May 1990 issue of *Quarterly Review of Film and Video*; see also Genette 1997[1982]). Here, my interest is not in how either the offscreen or the onscreen may be the target of parodic citation but rather in how the *entanglement between them* is.

6 Bakhtin's (1981, 1984[1963]) arguments, however, are not simply about genres or registers (or their historical unfolding, from parody to novelistic realism) but also, and more specifically, about how they combine multiple voices and genres within particular texts (that is, their voicing strategies); in the case of parody, the way in which its double voicing brings the object of its representation close to the reflexive voice of its enunciation, and thereby, to the readers themselves. This closeness, and the simultaneity of the present of enunciation with the object of enunciation (what is represented), Bakhtin suggests, is critical to a realist voicing structure and

chronotope, which polyphonically represents a heteroglossic world akin to, indeed that is, our own. And, of course, in the case of film studies, it has long been argued that narrative cinema is closer to the novel (and its realism) than other arts that would, on the surface, seem more closely allied to it (for example, theatre, photography). This proximity, we might suggest, has to do with the particular kind of realism at stake – voyeuristic, representationalist realism – and the capacity of narrative cinema to instate multiply embedded subjectivities and points of view (Browne 1999[1975]; Branigan 1984) – Bakhtinian voices, as it were – through its entextualizations. Here, however, my point is slightly different and simpler – namely, that the possibility of realism turns on a concept of what reality is and what an image is such that it could represent it; and both require a contrast between what is (1) typified as unreal and real, and (2) typified as an improper and a proper image. Parody is one way in which the denaturalization of one "regime of imageness" (Rancière 2007, 2009) and the naturalization of another (sometimes, the one that the parody putatively attempts to denaturalize!) may be attempted.

7 Fans' aggression towards the television station resulted in the station and show issuing an on-air apology letter to Vijay and his fans "for the anguish they caused through their controversial program," as well as a personal letter to the actor Vijay for the anger it caused for his "family, friends, relatives, and his thousands of fans" (see *Vijaynet* 2007). With this incident in mind, consider how Amudhan reported in an online interview (see BehindwoodsTV 2018) that he and his team were afraid of how the film would be received; but when Shiva, on a television special, received a phone call from Vijay joking with him about the film, then Amudhan knew that everything would be okay and that the industry would take the film well.

8 The 2019 film *Comali* (Clown, dir. Pradeep Ranganathan), to take another example, elicited calls for boycott from Rajinikanth fans for a scene in the film's trailer that poked fun at the Superstar's hesitations to enter electoral politics. In the trailer, we learn that the film's protagonist has just discovered, to his shock, that he has been in a coma for sixteen years. But upon seeing a clip on television of Rajinikanth's 2017 announcement that he will be forming a party (see the book's Conclusions), he protests that it must be 1996, a time when Rajinikanth was famously expected to enter electoral politics. Fans protested the joke, demanding its removal and an apology from the filmmakers. They succeeded in getting both; the scene was removed from the film, and the film's director and lead actor (Jayam Ravi) offered apologetic public remarks (see TNM Staff 2019; Sreedhar Pillai 2019a). Similarly consider a passage from Janaki Venkataraman (2004:45–7), writing about her time as a journalist:

> As for MGR, we never got to meet him, period. We wrote several stories criticizing his policies, and his leadership, but none of these got us into trouble. Then we published an innocuous piece on his personal habits, his sartorial preferences and his little vanities – and immediately attracted several threatening phone calls. Time and time again it was brought home to us that Madras VIPs could not bear to be laughed at. They didn't mind criticism as much. You could even get away with labelling someone a villain. But if you made fun of them – beware! … *Aside*'s film reviewers and, occasionally, book reviewers faced the same problem. The magazine's film reviews were always fun to read … but in the process of critiquing bad cinema (which was 90 per cent of the time), they also hurt egos.

9 Spurge milk is the emulsified sap from euphorbia plants. Here, the joke is that such a traditional, medicinal liquid (which is also poisonous and used in infanticide) would be packaged in a modern, aseptic packaging (typically reserved for expensive, branded comestibles like juice, milk, and so on).

10 The term *nativity* here refers to films that depict folk life in rural Tamil Nadu; regarding the particular genre of such films that emerged in the 1970s, the term also connotes the naturalism of their depictions. See Chapter 4 for more discussion.

11 A central element to *Thamizh Padam*'s comic parody is the actor Shiva's *offscreen* status as an up-and-coming comedic hero who had previously acted in Venkat Prabhu's non–hero-centred films, delivering all his lines with a smirking straight face that seems always on the edge of cracking up. As with the "Powerstar" (see note 1 in this chapter), the very idea of an unserious, relatively unstatusful actor taking on such a star image is laughable in the Tamil context (see Nakassis 2016a:196). As a critique of the onscreen/offscreen entanglement that *is* the mass-hero image, as I suggest in the main text below, *Thamizh Padam* of necessity partakes of precisely this sociological realism (as I put it in Chapters 1 and 2): the relevance of Shiva's offscreen status to the onscreen image is one example of this sociological (un)realism.

12 While *Thamizh Padam* parodizes it, whether or not the mass hero, his films, or his fans actually abide the idea that hero and star, character and actor are seamlessly collapsed into each other is another issue; arguably, *Thamizh Padam* reads the mass-hero figure more literally and seriously – that is, more univocally, more credulously – than his films or his fans; indeed, the former often reflect on and play with just this gap/slippage, and the latter are not the dupes that elitist discourse would characterize them as. Or, we might say, *Thamizh Padam* meta-parodically voices (what it takes to be) the credulous spectator's literalism. Or both.

13 Hence, for example, if Rajinikanth is the actor's name (the Goffmanian natural figure) and Baashaa, Billa, Padaiyappa, and so on are his characters' names (staged figures), it is the appellation "Superstar" (his star figure) that sutures actor and character, infusing each character with something of the others and conserving the iterated "build-up" of the actor-hero's "mass" so as to unleash his gravitational force elsewhere, on or off the screen (Nakassis 2016a:209). See note 31 in Chapter 1.

14 As Sudhish Kamath (2014), a journalist, parallel filmmaker, and film critic (and one of *Thamizh Padam*'s most vocal supporters), said to me (CN) in an interview:

> Well, it's a very rare thing for the film industry to not take itself seriously, you know? Because we're talking about an industry where everyone comes up with, you know, names for titles for themselves, like, it started with Rajinikanth ... And then slowly all these heroes started doing that, you know? They would just come up with their own thing that-, so that- at one point in time there was a "Top Star," a "Little Star"- no, "The Little Superstar," there was a "Universal Star," there was a "Supreme Star." There were all these different, you know, titles taken, so that finally there were not enough stars <CN laughs> uh <SK chuckles> that uh people could use. And it was sounding really ridiculous, you know, imagine "Little Superstar" and "Top Star" and stuff like that. And so, during- and- in fact, this is something that even *Thamizh Padam* makes fun of. So to actually make fun of the film industry, which doesn't laugh at itself, required quite a lot guts.

15 Both titles citationally invert the practice of using diminutivized sobriquets (for example, Little Superstar) for younger hero-stars, here using, for example, the augmentative *periya* (big, older) to modify *Taḷapati* (compare Vijay's title at the time, *Iḷaiya Taḷapati*, Young General), absurdly and thus humorously portraying Shiva as a bigger star than all other hero-stars (Rajinikanth, Kamal Haasan, Vijay, and so on). See note 11 in this chapter.

16 In this critique, perhaps we hear echoes of André Bazin's (2005[1958]) essay "The Evolution of the Language of Cinema" – wherein he critiques montage (in Soviet cinema and German expressionism) as destroying cinema's inherent ability to represent time in its substance, to embalm it in its reality – or even Mikhail Bakhtin's (1981) discussion of the parodic/realist chronopolitics of the novel vis-à-vis the "epic" chronotope.

17 Another parody later in the film – taken from *Annamalai* (1992, dir. Suresh Krissna) – features Shiva and his girlfriend's rich father, named Koodiswaran (Billionaire)! While waiting for his coffee, Koodiswaran tells Shiva that he will never marry his daughter to a poor guy like Shiva. In response, Shiva leaves the house to make his name and fame, becoming a

tycoon in a montage that features him working his way up from being a milkman to a magnate with IT parks, rail stations, beaches, airports, mortuaries(!), jails(!), and electricity boards named after him. We see scenes of him selling toys, then delivering newspapers, and finally constructing large engineering projects. He returns to his girlfriend's house before Koodiswaran's coffee has arrived, as his future father-in-law conspicuously notes, and wins his favour.

18 To use Metz's (1991[1971]:124–33) terms, here we have an intercalation of a conventional, perhaps clichéd "alternate (narrative) syntagma" with the satirization of the (unrealistic) ellipses that we often take for granted in an "ordinary sequence" involving a hero, to the point where the sequence begins to approach a "bracket syntagma."

19 This chronopolitics is not simply that mass-hero films have absurd representations of temporality. (As reflection reveals, most all narrative films do.) Rather, what *Thamizh Padam* takes issue with is the temporality of the onscreen/offscreen entanglement itself. This is the joke at play with Shiva's sidekick friends, played by Manobala, Vennira Adai Moorthy, and M.S. Bhaskaran, three veteran comedians in their sixties and seventies at the time. Dressed up as college students (Figure 3.8 – right), and with the same names as the teenage characters of S. Shankar's *Boys* (2003), these elderly comedians travesty the fact – as C.S. Amudhan (2010) noted regarding the comedian Vivek, who "must have grandchildren by now" – that whereas actors age (in the chronotope of biological time), they keep playing the same young characters in films. In a similar joke, Shiva asks his adopted grandmother about his parents. When he asks if they are still alive, she – who has not aged since his birth – says: 'If I'm still alive, won't they be too?' To which Shiva responds: 'Okay grandma, but how is it that after all these years you're exactly the same [that is, haven't aged]?' (*Atu sari pāṭṭi, ittanai varuṣaṅka nī ippaṭi ippaṭiyē irukke?*). She says: 'You can be forty and still go to college (in the movies), so why shouldn't I be that way [that is, unaged]?' (*Āmām nāppatu vayasu college-kku pōkalām, nān appaṭi irukkakkūṭātu?*). Here, we might read the parodied figure as the actor Murali, who long acted as a college hero after his success in his 1991 film *Idhayam* (dir. Kathir). Thanks to Perundevi Srinivasan for suggesting this last point to me.

20 *Thamizh Padam* also offers a number of parodic figurations of credulous spectators; see, for example, Figures 3.2 and 3.3 for images of text-internal spectators adulating and gazing at (images of) Shiva, offering up figures for the film's viewer to disalign with. It is relative, of course, to this credulous subject that the critically aware subject – the drunk fan – most forcefully asserts the excess of the mass hero, for *even the mass hero's fans* can't seem to stand his over-the-top antics.

21 Given the caste-linked stereotypes of image uptake that *Thamizh Padam* was parodying and the class location of the filmmakers, we might ask about the role of caste in this politics of the spoof. While there is a certain logic that would lead us from class to caste, distinguishing the stereotyped quality of this logic from its reality is complex. My research data didn't warrant any particular conclusion on this issue. On its textual surface, *Thamizh Padam* has no overt caste politics of its own, nor did caste appear as an issue in either media reportage about the film, in my conversations with viewers, or (expectedly) in its makers' talk about the film. In a context, however, where screen image and caste are deeply imbricated (Damodaran and Gorringe 2017), we might see such an omission as itself articulating a particular (non)politics of the image, in particular, given that the "golden era" of "nativity films" that Amudhan praises in the main text below was precisely a period where an explicitness about valorizing particular dominant castes was enregistered as "realism" (see Chapter 4). We might point out how the film's sequel, *Thamizh Padam 2.0* (2018, dir. C.S. Amudhan), however, opens with a parody of a filmic depiction of a caste riot, reflecting Tamil cinema's increased, explicit focus on caste violence as such (see the book's Conclusions) and thus, by comparison, the first *Thamizh Padam*'s lack of attention to questions of caste.

22 The issue, of course, is not just performativity or presence as such but the enregisterment of certain kinds of performative image-acts and certain kinds of presencing for certain kinds of spectator-subjects as problematically illiberal. See Chapters 1 and 4 for discussion.

23 For the director, C.S. Amudhan, the temporality of this narrative was less a linear history than an interrupted one, with the mass hero as an interloper into the proper domain of cinema: the story (on which, see more below in the main text). When prompted by me with a quote from producer Dayanidhi Alagiri that "the Tamil film industry needed a film like this [*Thamizh Padam*], and it needed it right now," Amudhan (2010) responded by saying:

> I think it has always needed it. I think it's needed it for the past thirty years. Because see, the hero thing has not always been there. This mega-hero has not always been here. It came along with MGR [M.G. Ramachandran]. Until then the story was like it should be, the narrative was the main party of the story, and then there was a guy who played the lead. But this whole thing about films being centred around a hero is a relatively new thing.

24 Or, we might say, while the film did not offer a realist image of the non-cinematic world, it did presume to offer a reflective image of the mass

hero's (self)regard, a realist image of Narcissus's (subjective regard for his) mirror reflection.

25 A key figure anticipating such films is the director Venkat Prabhu, whose popular films have wed a deep (if playful) investment in the Tamil film canon with a cosmopolitan orientation to (realist) Hollywood cinema and tongue-in-cheek hero parody. See Chapter 1.

26 Such neonativity films of the early 2000s – what Lalitha Gopalan (2008) has dubbed "cruel cinema" and K. Hariharan "the new Madurai genre" (K. Hariharan 2011, cited in Leonard 2015:156) and "the cinema of disgust" (K. Hariharan 2013) – are marked by their gritty realism, male violence, and distrust of Dravidian(ist) politics, as well as by a particular cohort of directors (for example, Balu Mahendra's former assistant directors, Vetrimaaran and Bala, as well as Bala's former assistant directors, Ameer and Sasikumar; Eswaran Pillai 2015:272–88). Becoming a recognizable "formula" by the late 2000s (see Chapter 4), it is with respect to such increasingly stereotyped films that the new crop of absurdist, hyper-reflexive "neo-noir" films have to be situated, both in continuity and difference. While Amudhan (2014), for example, found path-breaking neonativity films like *Paruthiveeran* (2007, dir. Ameer) and *Subramaniya-puram* (2008, dir. Sasikumar) "brilliant," he went on to say: "It's spawned this genre altogether now which is getting really irritating ... This is the problem we have with Tamil cinema, they won't leave well enough alone. When you've done something you have to move on. But they won't."

27 As Amudhan (2014) noted to me, despite their parody, many of the scenes of *Thamizh Padam* turn on an intimate knowledge and care ("loving detail-ing," as he put it) that only a cinephile of Tamil cinema could have.

28 Both Venkat Prabhu (2010) and C.S. Amudhan (2010) noted to me that, while comedy and shock were central to their cinematic style, both in-tended to make more "serious" films in the future (at the time of the interview with Venkat Prabhu, he was referring to *Mankatha*, discussed in Chapter 1), films that their previous comedic films would, they hoped, open the space for. As Amudhan (2014) noted, *Thamizh Padam* "was an idea ... whose time had come ... a long time ago and had never been done." Regarding his then-to-be second film, Amudhan (2010) noted that "the second movie around ... is when I would try and do what I always thought how filmmaking should be and the kind of thing that needs to be done ... That [*Thamizh Padam*] was not about me making a film. It was me giving structure to an idea. Hereafter is when I would try to make movies the way I want to make them." The way Amudhan (2010, 2014) charac-terized this second film, entitled *Rendavathu Padam* (Second Film), abided precisely with the "neo-noir" aesthetic that followed in *Thamizh Padam*'s wake (see Kailasam 2017). While *Rendavathu Padam* was completed by our

2014 interview, as of the time of writing it has yet to be released due to financial reasons. In the interim, Amudhan teamed up again with Sashikanth and Shiva to make a sequel to *Thamizh Padam* (*Thamizh Padam 2.0* [2018]), which went on to be a success like the first film.

29 Thanks to Amanda Weidman for impressing upon me the importance of this point. See also Kunapulli 2021:138.

30 While the film's 2018 sequel, *Thamizh Padam 2.0*, attempted to correct for this issue, and was hailed as speaking "the truth about female characters in Kollywood" (Rajendran 2018a) – in particular, by parodying the so-called *loosu poṇṇu* (see note 44 in Chapter 2) – it was also noted that the film's parody of the "item number" (as narratively illogical) simply reproduced its structure of looking and gender stereotypes without any real critique of them. Indeed, its parody of the item number was simply … *an item number*: autonomous from the narrative, non-diegetic, and sexualized and objectifying of women. While this reproduction points to the difficulty of bracketing and citing the rigid performativity of "*sight*," as discussed in Chapter 2, it also indicates that *Thamizh Padam 2.0* overlooked the fact that the transgressiveness and regressive gender politics of the item number is not about narrative coherence but about the performativity of presence and "titillation." An item number featuring the less-than-lean hero, Shiva, *as* (a representation of) an item, for example, would have been a fabulous burlesque of the item number.

31 This faux rivalry between C.S. Amudhan and Venkat Prabhu continued with the publicity of *Thamizh Padam 2.0* (2018), which spoofed the posters of Venkat Prabhu's then-in-production film, *Maanaadu* (2021), in which Simbu – who the reader will recall was a brutal target of *Thamizh Padam*'s satire – was cast.

32 Venkat Prabhu is seen within and outside the industry as an easygoing filmmaker who doesn't have any "ego," on or off the set, and whose "team" of directors and technicians is run in a relatively egalitarian manner, in contrast to the stereotyped hierarchy of the industry. One (parodic) sign of this relaxed culture is how Venkat Prabhu and his team continually use the word *sār* (sir) with each other on and off the screen, parodying the norm of *sār* usage among industry insiders as a symmetrical address term of respect.

33 I would underline how this prank puts into joke form an otherwise serious critique of the organization of the industry. Amudhan's original "critique" of Venkat Prabhu on NDTV's *Hands Up*, which kicked off the prank, was that "just because Prabhu is from an industry family doesn't mean that he owns the industry." More than just a lampoon of the sensitive offscreen egos of its principle players, part of the prank was the assertion that such egos organized the political economy of the industry itself. Indeed, note how Amudhan's original print advertisement figured the difference

between him and Venkat Prabhu as between a director "on a holiday" and a director on a "working day" (Figure 3.8), that is, between those who have to work their way up and struggle, and those who are simply handed things because they, and their family members, are big names in the industry. (Venkat Prabhu's father is the director and music director, Gangai Amaran; one of his paternal uncles, the legendary musical director, Ilayaraja; two cousins, Yuvan Shankar Raja and Karthik Raja, music directors; another, Vasuki Bhaskar, a stylist; and his brother, Premji Amaren, a notable comedian.) The prank seemed to say that cinema is just for fun, don't take it seriously, *precisely because* those who take it seriously have organized the industry in a way that turns on the reverence of authority and hierarchy (that is, to them), and this is not a good thing – and don't you see, even those who seem not to, even they still do take themselves too seriously.

34 I would stress that this argument is not a personalist critique of the individuals involved but about structural dynamics – in particular, of masculine privilege and feminine absencing – that are reproduced in the texts and events discussed.

35 Casual drinking, for example, is taboo for proper middle-class femininity (though norms in elite, cosmopolitan circles are laxer). Jocular ribbing between men and women risks being interpreted as (unwanted, sexualized) familiarity or as threats to the male "egos" involved, and thus as indicating the "arrogance" of the women involved. Similarly, public irreverence and too-quick indignance are also likely interpreted as arrogance and improper comportment for women. The point isn't that women can't or don't engage in any of these practices, but that, again, the stakes are higher and interpretations tend to be more negative for women than men.

36 For example, the films *Rasigan* (1994), *Deva* (1995), *Vishnu* (1995), *Maanbumigu Maanavan* (1996), and *Once More* (1997) – all directed by Vijay's father, the director and producer S.A. Chandrasekhar – are so referenced.

37 Though, we may also argue that this first image-text figurates the film qua enunciator in a (personalized) fan-relation to the hero-star, telling us of the prowess of the star, who not only can act but can sing as well! See Nakassis 2019 on the notion of film as an image-act of praise of the hero-star. On this analysis, the second image-text parodies this form of fan-enunciation.

38 In another example from the second half of *Thamizh Padam*, Shiva alights upon how to find his parents: ask the railway master. Shiva then calls for a "cut" to the railway station (where they will be going in the diegetic world). At that point, we hear the director's voice from behind the camera, saying in Tamil: 'We're the ones who take care of editing, you pay attention to your own work!' Shiva apologizes, and we again hear the voice of the director muttering to himself: 'He doesn't even know how to act but he is now trying to direct too!' In both examples, note that what is at issue, and is thus

parodied, is the inability of the film to be impersonally enunciated/entextualized qua *histoire* (symbolically abstracted, nomically calibrated denotational text authored by the filmmakers) because of the personalized enunciation/entextualization of the film qua *discours* ("deictically" anchored, reflexively calibrated interactional text ordered/authorized by the hero).

39 Consider C.S. Amudhan's (2014) comment on the relationship of the hero to the story, using the example of Rajinikanth:

> Rajini's style started as something being unique. Now it's a caricature. Now it's become very-, now he's become only the style. He used to be about performance and then style was cherry on the cake. Now there's only the cherry, there's no cake. So, you need to have (a) good story ... you still need, the basics of filmmaking need to be there. It needs to be good- (there has to be a) basically good screen play.

40 In 2014, C.S. Amudhan noted:

> We're not seriously trying to revolutionize or anything like that. We're just guys having fun ... But what it [*Thamizh Padam*] ultimately does is that it also shows them [mass heroes] in a certain light in which they are not comfortable being seen in, which is like, big spoof time. You know, they are, they've always (been) accustomed to being put on a pedestal. And this kind of approach irks them, and it questions their very-, because that's that's how movies get made, you know, they have this formula of how to make movies. You know, you have a bankable star. And then, you have a story which has a love portion and a glamour portion. It's a formula, right? So if you question that formula and the audiences start to think about this then they would not know how to function, because then the formula doesn't apply. And they would really not know how to function. I'm talking about heroes, producers, directors who work like that. I have nothing against them. I enjoy uh watching those kinds of movies too sometimes. But, the kind- the spoof genre does actually threaten them.

At the same time, Amudhan was sanguine as the extent of this threat. In 2014, he said:

> I don't think that *Thamizh Padam* changed anything <chuckles>. I mean, let's be realistic, we're talking about a hundred years of cinema. I don't think it changed anything, but I think it would have woken up certain stakeholders in the industry like assistant directors, for example, into- okay, this stuff is actually ridiculous and has been done so many times. So, in movie discussions I think this will feature to some extent. But we'll need dozens of *Thamizh Padam*s <chuckles> before we can actually make a dent in the mainstream thinking.

The journalist Sudhish Kamath (2014), however, was more optimistic, noting that the mainstream has shifted since/because of films like *Thamizh Padam*. As evidence, he observed that after such films, Venkat Prabhu began making films with big heroes such as Surya, Ajith, and Karthi. See also Kailasam 2017.

41 See Kamath 2012: "As a producer, Sashikanth has never ever sat through a narration. 'It has to be in a written form. Unless it's on paper, I don't even want to know about it.'" Also part of Sashikanth's lament was that there was no clear notion of an efficient, rational division of modular labour in the film industry. In particular, he noted that it is often assumed in the Tamil film industry that the director has to also be the scriptwriter, screenplay writer, author of the story, and so on. Instead, he said, direction and scriptwriting are different tasks and different roles in the production process, and should be filled by different individuals. For discussion of similar critiques of the production format of filmmaking in Indian film industries, see Prasad 1998; Vasudevan 2010; on the concept of modularity in film production, see Rossoukh and Caton 2021.

42 Sashikanth (2011) here voices a longer-standing discourse about the need to corporatize the Tamil film industry, to render it transparent and rationalized (see also Ganti 2012:176–9; S.V. Srinivas 2016). One can also hear his experience as a corporate architect bleed into his speech here – initially using "build" to refer to the "product," then repairing with the more film-appropriate verb "make."

43 C.S. Amudhan (2010, 2014) and Sashikanth (2011) framed finding such a producer to be, if lucky (both noted that most film producers wouldn't touch such a project with a ten-foot pole), a relatively straightforward process with few hiccups. The hero-actor, Shiva (2014), however, humorously narrated to me a different story. He spoke of a failed narration with a producer who didn't understand the spoof concept:

Ēnnā niṟaiya pēru ottukka māṭṭāṅka. Producer *ottukka māṭṭāru.* In fact, *Amudhan avaṅkakiṭṭayellām pōyiṭṭu katai sollum pōtu oru* producer full-*ā uṭkārntu tūṅkiṭṭāru. Atukku appuṟam eḻuntu "Enna sār paṭam eppaṭi irukkum" nnu kēṭṭā "Ennappā ellā* scenes-*um* already *vantiruccu. Itu eppaṭi namma paṭamā paṇṟatu" appaṭi nnu anuppiccu viṭṭuṭṭāru.* As a spoof *appaṭiṇā ennannē teriyale!* <laughing> So *atanālē*

Because a lot of people didn't/won't accept it [*Thamizh Padam*]. Producers didn't/won't accept it. In fact, Amudhan went to all of them, and when he narrated the story, one producer even slept through the whole thing. Afterwards, he got up, and when Amudhan asked: "How is the film, sir?" he said: "What is this, son? All these scenes have already been done (in other films)? How could we make this into a film?," and sent him off.

romba varuttamā iruntatu. But *namma ennannā yārum*- we want to break something, *putusā etāvatu paṇṇaṇumē nṟa oru* interest *tān*.

He had no idea what a spoof was! <laughing> So it was really discouraging. But what our-, anyone- we want to break something, we want to do something new. That's what our interest is.

44 Indeed, with the exception of Shiva, none of the actors were told that the film was a spoof during its production. Simply telling them it was a "funny film," Amudhan only told the actors what they needed to know scene by scene, often to their confusion when they were asked to do silly things or speak absurd lines. As Amudhan (2014) said, "we didn't tell them what they're doing. They wouldn't appear on set if I told them." For those actors who were in many scenes (such as Manobala, M.S. Bhaskar, Vennira Adai Moorthy), at first it didn't occur to them that this project was a full-on spoof film. Amudhan (2014) noted:

> [Those kinds of comedy scene are] not that remarkable because spoof scenes are there in literally every movie, I mean. So the fact that we're doing an entire movie which is spoof based was the surprise. So on day one, on day two, on day three, on day four you wouldn't realize this. But then as you keep shooting and everything, these guys are doing *only* this stuff. They're not doing anything else. Then it's, then they start coming to me and asking me: "So, so what's actually happening here?" <chuckles; breaths in> Uh, eh-uh "See it's mostly funny, so it's spoof based, and especially your portions are fully funny, maybe there are other serious <starts laughing> portions in there." <claps> Just told them that. But they go- by the end of the, I think the second schedule they were on to it.

See note 45 in this chapter for more discussion.

45 While *Thamizh Padam* was written to be irreverent to the industry, this effort did *not*, its makers claimed, aim to "hurt" anyone, that is, was not directed at specific *persons*. (That no one was hurt personally was also one of Shiva's conditions on doing the film, as he told me in 2014.) Drawing the line, and cutting the knot, between the personage and the image, then, required a fine balance that, again, turned on and ended at the personal name. As Amudhan (2014) noted, rather than calling out someone by name (for example, like Simbu in the panchayat scene), he might simply be referred to obliquely (for example, as 'that little brother' who does that thing with his hands; see Figure 3.1). Similarly, the dance master, Kalyan Kumar (2011), noted to me that in choreographing the opening song, he

felt Amudhan had gone a little too far in certain respects, individuating *persons* rather than stereotypes. He said:

> When I was doing that, *inta* [that] song, that opening song of Shiva dancing, his cut-outs and everything. Actually, they- a lot of Ajith's- this thing, Vijay's cut-out and everything and they had put *Thala illai, talavali* [Not the Head but a headache]. I said: "Avoid certain things. You can't go overboard." I said: "Don't go overboard, like insulting a person personally, maybe a character he has done." <mouth click> You know, you can *kalācc*-ify [make fun of] the character, not the PERSON. And (so) I had to cut a little bit here and there, and I said, then it is okay.

Similarly, when he choreographed the opening song, Kalyan Kumar said he didn't take specific steps identifiable with a particular person, but just did things that typically happen in opening songs. Yet, as he also said: "I only did one thing where finally this guy comes and dances (with the hero), this choreographer [a reference to a particular dance master], I would have done also that … <laughing> That I did." As this discussion suggests, despite any stated intention not to hurt anyone personally, in parodying an image that is inherently about how the image is caught up with the person, we can see how the inevitable (and even intended) effect of *Thamizh Padam* was precisely to do just this, for to disaggregate the ego of the artist from the performative pragmatics of the image *is* to attack their cinematically extended person(age). (Hence the whole discourse about the industry being unable to "take a joke," discussed in the main text above.) After the comedians Manobala, M.S. Bhaskar, and Vennira Adai Moorthy, for example, figured out that the *whole* film was a spoof (see note 44 in this chapter), they came to Amudhan:

> They(('d say)) "Please-" They woul- if they, if I gave them a controversial dialogue they would come up to me and say: "Do you really want me to say this? Can I maybe say this? It might offend them [the targets of the parody] directly. Those- it's like underlining *the name* so can we not do that?" … In some places I put my foot down and said: "No please, you have to say this." And in certain places I said: "Okay, it doesn't make much of a difference, so-." (Amudhan 2014; my italics)

Here, the issue was that the person they were making fun of would get mad *at the actor* for saying the lines. When I queried Amudhan (2014) on this logic – for wasn't Amudhan the one responsible for the film and its dialogues? – he responded by saying:

> I'm on the same side as you, because (as an actor) I would think it's "I had nothing to do with that, I was just mouthing the lines." But they [the targets of the parody] would think: "You could have said no! When it's so insulting to me you could have just said no. I know you so well, you're my friend, you could have said no." They would think that.

See Chapters 1, 2, and 4 for discussions of this logic of principalship.

46 One example of someone who suffered from being satirized, perhaps, is the particular dance master who is parodied in Shiva's introduction song (see note 45 in this chapter). It was suggested to me that, because of *Thamizh Padam*, his popularity waned. While I have not been able to confirm any such effect, my own avid filmgoing friends noted to me that, indeed, since *Thamizh Padam*, the dance master dancing with the hero – now defamiliarized as absurd – has lessened (see Genette's epigraph in this chapter).

47 As noted in the main text, we might point to the success of a new wave of realist and experimental, small-budget films since the early 2000s (see Chapter 4), along with a slew of new directors, producers, and technicians. We may also point to changes within mass-hero films themselves in the twenty-first century (Kurai 2012; Nakassis 2016a:221–3; Kailasam 2021; Kunapulli 2021:82–3) – for example, as discussed in Chapter 1 and the book's Conclusions, hero-stars like Ajith and Rajinikanth in the 2010s began attempts to break with (or at least loosen the grip of) their "image traps" (Pandian 1992) by playing characters with muted heroism in relatively realist narratives (for example, Rajini's 2016 film *Kabali*) or by playing negative roles (for example, Ajith's 2011 *Mankatha*) in films directed by filmmakers known for their non–hero-based films (Pa. Ranjith and Venkat Prabhu, respectively). Similarly, we can point to the highly self-reflexive irony of the mass hero's image in films like *Sivaji* (2007, dir. Shankar; see note 1 in this chapter).

48 When *Thamizh Padam 2.0* was released in 2018, some Twitter users raised the question of whether the film was soft on the DMK because C.S. Amudhan's father-in-law is a senior cadre of the party. The director denied on Twitter being soft on anyone, including the DMK (see Dhiwaharan 2018). When the first *Thamizh Padam* was released in 2010, while Sashikanth's DMK affiliation was mentioned in the press, the political connections of Amudhan did not come up in my discussions or in press coverage of the film. On kinship relations mediating the cinematic mode of production of the Hindi film industry, see Ganti 2012:195–202.

49 While my fieldwork didn't indicate whether this fact had a chilling effect on protests of the film by fans or their lampooned heroes (many of whom have personal connections to the DMK), given industry reaction it is not unreasonable to assume it did.

50 Rancière's (2007, 2009) concern is to shift our image of politics, away from the questions of cause and effect (how does this representation cause this effect in audiences, how can such a cause–effect relation be unmasked and undone?) and towards the question of how what is experienceable and intelligible is redistributed, that is, how new "regimes of imageness" are opened up and transformed in non-deterministic ways. *Thamizh Padam*'s politics engages both such images of politics: it attempts to unmask one regime of imageness (and in service of a particular kind of representationalism) but with the hope of opening up a different topography of the possible. Rancière is useful for his productively broad conception of the political. But while Rancière would have us (normatively) choose one (image of) politics or the other, here my interest is empirical and alive to the diversities of such regimes: What does image politics look like in different times and places? How are we to site it and theorize it?

51 These are not the only such politics for the image involved, of course. We might also add, for example, the ethnolinguistic politics of belonging; a comparison of the reception of *Thamizh Padam* with Shah Rukh Khan's Bollywood spoof of Tamil cinema (and faux homage of Rajinikanth) in *Chennai Express* (2013, dir. Rohit Shetty) in the song sequence "Lungi Dance" – which was widely criticized in Tamil Nadu – reveals the politics of cultural intimacy (Herzfeld 1997) at play here. By contrast, the possibility of *Thamizh Padam* was it being made in the Tamil film industry by Tamil filmmakers. I thank Amanda Weidman for raising this comparison.

52 In addition to the way in which *Thamizh Padam*'s lampooning of the mass hero's performative image entails its own forms of performative screen-crossing, we can also note the heavy reliance on forms of direct "deictic" address in the film (Casetti 1998[1986]; Dagrada 2014), though not of the presenced hero-star to his fans but of the director to the aware audience. Think, for example, of the numerous instances in the film where we can hear Amudhan's voice seeming to collude with the film's spectator to decry the hero-star as "Too much!" and so on (for example, the drunk fan, the young Shiva's disbelief, the scolding director, song lyrics during the bullet-shot sequence).

Chapter 4. The Politics of the Real

1 Unless otherwise modified, as discussed in note 35 of Chapter 1, I use the term *realism* to denote some variety of *representational realism*, following its usage among film theorists, Tamil film directors, producers, actors, critics, and viewers. This contrasts with what I have called in previous chapters *sociological realism*. As the reader will recall from Chapter 1, *sociological realism* is not an ethnographic term but an analytic coined precisely to

destabilize and open up the term *realism* and point up its representationalist ideological basis.

2 For Bakhtin (1981, 1984[1963]), the realist novel through its dialogism opens a space for the recognition of the unfinalizability of man, in particular, by rendering the hero character himself unfinalizable and autonomous vis-à-vis the author's voice. Realism, thus, is staged vis-à-vis the polyphony of discourse and self-consciousness, both because, for Bakhtin, man and his world are themselves shot through and constituted by this discursive heteroglossia and polyphony, and because discourse is the very medium of literature. For Bazin, as discussed in Chapter 1, realism in the cinema registers and (re)presents the unfinalizability of the world as autonomous, ambiguous, and contingent vis-à-vis any particular consciousness. In doing so, realism gives over the process of meaning-making and experience to the spectator, with whom it can enter into a dialogue of sorts; and this, we might add, because – for Bazin at least – the medium and object of cinema is reality itself. And just as for Bakhtin the character comes into a (seeming) existence that is independent of the novel (he has a life and personality of his own), for Bazin the uniqueness of the cinema is the way in which its world exists beyond the frame. Both accounts are existentialist, humanist ideologies of realism (such ideologies are also immanent in many kinds of realist texts) and, further, an ontological politics. Regarding the unfinalizability of the world and image, and their dialectical (or dialogic) relation, we might consider (with a different sense), Dostoevsky's statement, as cited by Bakhtin (1984[1963]:90): "Reality in its entirety is not to be exhausted by what is immediately at hand, for an overwhelming part of this reality is contained in the form of a still *latent, unuttered future Word*" (italics in Bakhtin).

3 The importance of realism to film studies stretches beyond Bazin's writings (see Chapter 1), of course, including so-called Screen theory's characterization of realism as ideologically naturalizing Enlightenment epistemologies (Baudry 1986[1970], 1986[1975]; Comolli 1986[1971]; Metz 1986[1975]; see also Snyder 1980), as well as cognitivist accounts of realism (Carroll 1996:78–93, 224–52; Currie 1996; Prince 1996) and the resurgent interest in Bazin (Margulies 2003; Morgan 2006; Andrew 2011; Schoonover 2012; Hassan 2017) in light of the challenges of the digital.

4 Interestingly, when I spoke with the director of *Kaadhal*, Balaji Sakthivel, in October 2018, he characterized his way of filmmaking as a "realistic approach," one among many approaches to filmmaking. To make this point, he began to animate different speech registers of Tamil: at first, he spoke with the voice and register of the town crier – affective, exaggerated, even theatrical – and then with an intimate, colloquial, understated voice. He then said: "*Itu vantu* [this (realism) too is] a kind of speech," a "realistic

approach" in contrast to a "make-believe approach." The latter, he then animated through exaggerated oratorical speech evocative of the films of Sivaji Ganesan and M.G. Ramachandran of the previous generation.

5 This referential relation may take many forms – stipulated as an ontological identity (Bazin 2005[1945]), a mimetic illusion (Baudry 1986[1970], 1986[1975]; Metz 1991[1971]), an isomorphism to "natural" (Prince 1996; compare Bazin 2005[1951]b; Mitry 1997[1963]:29–33; Branigan 1984:198–208, 2006:77–80) or habitual (Goodman 1976) perception (compare Mitchell 1986:72), or as narrative believability and plausibility (Perkins 1980[1972]; Aumont et al. 1992[1983]:114–17). In each case, at stake for discourses of realism, including those of the directors and viewers I discuss in this chapter, is some claim to the truth-functional correspondence between sign and object to some spectatorial subject.

6 Just as realisms are part of contrast sets (whose cultural phenomenology and academic theorization often turn on an ideological erasure of this fact), so too are the realities they represent and presence (and similarly ideologically reduce as well, we might add). See discussion in the main text below. While this claim might be (wrongly) taken to suggest an extreme relativism, perhaps even nominalism, I do not see it as in tension with the semiotic realism advocated in this book, for my point isn't that there is not a(n ultimate) "reality," or that such a reality is only relative to some form of (cultural, historical, ideological, that is, semiotic) mediation. The point, rather, is that whatever we experience and understand to be reality is already apprehended semiotically (indeed, it is, in large swathes, itself semiotic insofar as it is so mediated) and thus in principle multiple (and no less real for it), both epistemologically (open to doubt and error – and thus improvable – and perspectival) and ontically (open to chance, self-difference, change). See also note 5 in the book's Introduction.

7 Moreover, such contrast sets are fractal in nature (Gal and Irvine 2019); see, for example, Mitchell's (1994:324) discussion of realism versus illusionism, in addition to naturalism, to say nothing of the various flavours of fantasy (see also Jakobson 1971[1921]).

8 As Bakhtin (1981) argued in the context of literature and the novel, realism is inherently intergeneric and intertextual (see also Bauman and Briggs 1990; Briggs and Bauman 1992). The same principle is at play in cinematic realisms, having to do both with the multiplicity of subjectivities and perspectives in which cinema traffics (Branigan 1984) *and*, more importantly, the way in which realisms always ground themselves through *contrast* with what they thereby typify as non-realist, a differentiation that, as we will see, appears *within* realist texts.

9 In the Tamil cinema, for example, the auteur-director C.V. Sridhar (1933–2008) was an innovator whose dialogues were considered realistic and

natural – in contrast to the high, efflorescent oratorical styles of the (DMK) cinema of the time (Pandian 1996:952–3; Gangai Amaran 2008) – just as were his use of makeup-less actors and camera-driven storytelling (C.V. Rajendran 2009), despite his contrived plot structures sourced from urban middle-class plays (Chitralaya Gopu 2009). Similarly, while Bharathiraja's "nativity" films of the 1970s and 1980s are replete with (non-realist) symbolist imagery, high melodrama, and genred depictions of village life and its places (Srinivas and Sundar Kaali 1998:208; Kurai 2012:44; see also Sundar Kaali 2000:176; Pandian 2008:132; Chakravarthy 2018:17–31), his move to outdoor sets in rural areas (and thus away from the studios and urban middle-classes of Sridhar's films), use of local non-standard colloquial dialects and other (caste) emblems of "authenticity," casting of "new face" actors (as was also the practice of Sridhar), among other stylistic innovations, all led to films of his such as *Pathinaaru Vayathileyee* (1976) to be typified among reviewers of the time as realistic (Eswaran Pillai 2012:84).

10 It is not only realism as register that presupposes and entails an ontological politics. Note how the ideological constitution of speech registers as "different ways of saying the same thing" already makes an ontological claim as to the nature of language (it is a denotational system for referring), even as it splits itself by also, secondarily, making a claim that language is an indexical system of signalling social difference. The point here isn't that language is one or the other, but that the very notion of register, and thus the processes of enregisterment through which this ambivalence unfolds, belies an ontological politics of language, one that, not unrelatedly to realism, is based in a referentialist ideology. (This point perhaps bears out the history of register as an analytic, insofar as the focus on registers emerges out of a concern to characterize sociolinguistic variation in language communities dominated by a culture of standard.)

11 Theatre was itself already divided at the end of the nineteenth century in Tamil Nadu into mass-oriented "company dramas" that staged mythological plays in Tamil and elite, amateur theatre that staged Indian and European content (for example, Shakespeare; Baskaran 1996:75–6; Hughes 1996:33–4, 2018; Ebeling 2019). The former were often characterized (from an elite perspective) as unrealistic and the latter as more realistic, anticipating (indeed, later being taken up as) the ideological cleavage within cinema between (the possibility of) a fully modern realist cinema and (the actuality of) popular "escapist" cinema.

12 A fuller account of the enregisterment of realism in Tamil cinema would certainly have to take into account (1) its dialogic engagement with (a) commercial and experimental European and American filmic traditions (see note 23 in the Introduction) via the post-war dissemination of Italian neorealist aesthetics (which influenced figures as diverse as C.N.

Annadurai and Satyajit Ray; Krishnan 2009:295; Majumdar 2011; Majumdar 2016) and, later, (b) Iranian, Korean, and Brazilian "global" or "world" cinema (with vectors of influence also going from India outwards); (2) ongoing contact with other regional commercial and art realisms (for example, Bengali cinema, "parallel" or "new" [Hindi] cinema, Malayali cinema, and so on); and (3) institutions such as film festivals, film societies, film schools, as well as the financial support of the government (Prasad 1998; Majumdar 2021).

13 As Swarnavel Eswaran Pillai (2012) has argued, while the studios finally collapsed in the 1970s with the fading of Sivaji and the disappearance of MGR into politics, their atrophy was itself driven by the rise and dominance of these stars and the studios' increasing dependence on them. See the Introduction for more discussion.

14 This shift to shooting outside with newer, lighter cameras also precipitated the shift to non-sync sound and the use of dubbing (as it also did with Italian neorealism), an aural mode of production that arguably – at least to some today (Ganti 2012:227, 229) – is less realistic than sync-sound. As this judgment indicates, realisms are internally structured in complex ways (here, for example, revealing a hierarchy of senses, with a privilege for the visual over the aural) and often feature forms of ideological erasure (Gal and Irvine 2019) and historical/technological contingency that reveal their mediatedness and conventionality. In my experience, few mention the shift to dubbing in the context of nativity films as making such films less realistic, but instead focus on the change in visual aesthetics as a shift to a more realistic filmmaking.

15 Regarding the link of "nativity" and realism in the 1970s, the urban, middle-class films of K. Balachander (1930–2014) provide an important exception. Balachander pioneered the director as auteur in this period, as well as broke from existing formulas with his selective use of realist stylistic elements. Here, upper-caste background and a relationship to urban, middle-class theatre are relevant to Balachander's differences from other directors of this moment (also in this regard, consider C.V. Sridhar).

16 Note, of course, how the notion of an "image trap" (Pandian 1992) is voiced from a subject position that normatively assumes a representationalist ontology and ontological politics (precisely the one critically described by Pandian 1996), since such a trap binds the actor and prevents him from doing other types of films (such freedom being assumed to be a good thing), in particular, "serious" "class" cinema. The inability of character actors to inhabit the figure of the mass hero, by contrast, is typically not described in my experience as a "trap," even if many up-and-coming actors desire to become mass heroes.

17 In *Baba*'s climax, Rajini's character, Baba, turns back to "the people" (after deciding to renounce material life for a life of spirituality) when the evil villain, and ex-chief minister, assassinates the honest man whom Baba installed (with one of his seven wishes) as the chief minister of the state. As Baba turns back, a song sings, among other things, that while Baba/Rajini doesn't desire political positions or parties, he cannot turn away from the Tamil soil. The final frame freezes on Rajini, with 'to be continued' (*toṭarum*) inscribed on the image as the end credits begin to roll.

18 Karthick Ram Manoharan (n.d.) suggests, however, that Murugan's Dalit identity is open to interpretation, as we might also read Murugan as Vanniyar. Nevertheless, most commentators and viewers took the story up as one narrating Thevar–Dalit conflicts.

19 In the films *7/G Rainbow Colony* (2004, dir. Selvaraghavan) and *Subramaniyapuram* (2008, dir. Sasikumar), the low-class and illiberal rowdy nature of the protagonists is shown to the audience in scenes of boisterous fan activity in the movie theatre; in *7/G Rainbow Colony*, it is Rajinikanth's 2002 *Baba* that sends the protagonist and his friends into apoplectic fits (in the Telugu version, it is Palwan Kalyan's remake of the A.M. Ratnam–produced, Vijay-starring Tamil film *Kushi* [2001, dir. S.J. Surya]; thanks to S.V. Srinivas to clarifying this for me); in *Subramaniyapuram*, it is Rajini's 1980 smash hit *Murattu Kaalai* (dir. S.P. Muthuraman). In both cases, the scenes end in fist fights, tellingly in *7/G Rainbow Colony* with theatre-goers who complained about the illiberal mode of spectatorship of the protagonist and his friends.

20 In addition to this visual frame, the flickering bands created by filming a video and the attenuated bass frequencies and lo-fi sound of the embedded film (from the small television speaker) place the mass hero within the profilmic and diegetic space of *Kaadhal*, bracketing Rajini's image and decentring its otherwise reflexively calibrated image. Of course, as one friend in Madurai opined, in regards to the film *Subramaniyapuram* (2008), directors put such scenes *for* Rajinikanth fans, since seeing his image (even embedded within another image) gives them pleasure and increases the enjoyment of the embedding film (see also Pandian 2014:ix). As this friend's statement suggests, decentring the image of the mass hero is an accomplishment that presumes upon, but can never guarantee, the uptake of its viewers as such (see also Chapter 1 for discussion).

21 Earlier, the scene introduced Rajini's *Baashaa* in a non-subjective shot (that is, not from anyone's point of view in particular), intercut with shots of the bus and its interior. Here, the shot of Murugan reframes the deictic, interpellative look of Rajini in the previous shot as the object of Murugan and the bridegroom's gaze (thereby constituting it as a kind of "discovered" point-of-view shot; Branigan 1984:111). Interestingly, however, while

we are seeing what they see (the television image of the filmic image), the angle and distance of the "discovered" shot is *not* from their point of view in space, since the image is relatively straight-on (it is at a slight low angle) rather than shot from below. This angle replicates (or figurates), I would argue, the fan-spectator's experience of directly seeing the star looking at him from within a theatrical screening of such a film (that is, it is a renvoi to an experience of having already seen *Baashaa* or a film like it in the theatre), *even as*, as we noted, the editing and profilmic content (as a recording of the television) motivates the image as a point-of-view shot of the characters in the bus (in the diegesis of *Kaadhal*). The result of the superposition of these two reflexive sketches of looking is a kind of double-voiced discourse (see note 45 in Chapter 1), a shot simultaneously entextualizing two distinct points of view: namely, we see *as* those in the bus (Murugan, the bridegroom, and others) *and* from a vantage that recalls a timespace outside of the bus and the film itself, that is, *as* a fan-spectator of a Rajini film in a theatre. The result is multiple: on the one hand, it imputes to the characters a *way* of looking at the image (that is, they are looking *as* fans whose looks interdiscursively harken back to seeing Rajini films in the theatre on other occasions); on the other hand, it appeals to our own experiences of seeing such films as fan-spectators in the theatre. Murugan's subsequent turn to the right, to looking at the bridegroom looking at Rajini, shifts the site of subjectivity and narration to Murugan's point of view, suggesting that this earlier shot is not really Murugan's, but rather that of the bridegroom. In that way, it also invites us to alienate ourselves from looking *as* fan-spectators, even as (or rather, because) it makes us see *as* them. As the object of a sequence of point-of-view shots, then, Rajini's own look, and its engagement with the bridegroom (qua Rajini fan-spectator), anchors Murugan's own gaze as the metapragmatic frame for the sequence as a whole – as a judgment on cinematic (fan-)spectatorship itself. Arguably, this look, or voice, is not just Murugan's but also the director's and, so the text invites through a complex kind of interpellation, ours as well.

22 In this shot, the bridegroom offers his bride some of the snacks he is eating, interpreting her desire for amorous interaction as a mundane request for some food. In the next shot of them, the bride lightly slaps her forehead in a metapragmatic evaluation of her groom's unbelievable behaviour that echoes Murugan's own evaluation; she then gives up on him and turns away.

23 From here, Murugan's gaze falls onto a photograph of Aiswarya's family as she is crying; seeing her cry, he turns to her (echoing, in difference, the bridegroom's failure to turn to his wife and the wife's turn away from her husband). With this, the scene shifts gears into a conversation about her difficulties in leaving her family but her commitment to being with him.

24 We might say more: *Kaadhal*'s persistent use of film to frame its realist world is – as the director indicated to me (Balaji Sakthivel 2018b) – an attempt to "travel" in the "mind" of the "masses" who watch commercial cinema (*inta* movie *pākkuṟavaṅka* – mass *irukkāṅka, illaiyā?* – *anta* mind-*leyē tān nān* travel *ākuṟēn*) while, at the same time, opening up a critical space of difference from that very "mind." The film, thus, suggests – as I discuss more in the main text below – that people in Tamil Nadu think about life *as* cinema while at the same time refusing to act in everyday life as they do in cinema (for example, regarding women's sexuality or caste), this contradiction being the tension and hypocrisy the film hopes to point out to its audiences. This space of difference and critical awareness is linked, most clearly, to Murugan's character, the primary site of intended identification at this point in the film. Murugan's character, thus, offers a site of interpellative identification that is also the very voicing of the film's ontological politics of realism, in this case, the director's own voice – hence, Murugan's judging gaze at his fellow bus-traveller but also, as Balaji Sakthivel noted, his relationship to Aiswarya. Aiswarya believes, we learn in a later scene – following the cinematic logics of films like *Kaadhalukku Mariyadai* (as shown in an earlier scene; see the main text for discussion) – that if they get married then no one can split them apart; yet Murugan is more doubtful and less credulous of commercial cinema's relationship with the real. "He's raising questions," Balaji Sakthivel put it to me, precisely what he hoped the film would do among audiences. Here, too, Murugan sees things as they (presumably) are, unlike the cinema-blinded bridegroom or the naïve Aiswarya.

25 Interestingly, the Telugu version of *Kaadhal* (dubbed as *Premisthe*) opens with a preamble from the famous commercial director S. Shankar, who produced the film. The preamble begins with a smiling still of Shankar giving, in Telugu, his 'greetings to my dear Telugu audience' and recognizing that his previous films 'were enjoyed and made successful by you!' He goes on to say that 'it's long been my desire to make realist (*yadarthamaina*, translated by the subtitles on the print as 'logical'), quality, and different kinds of movies.' As he says these words, we see posters of *The Bicycle Thief* (1948, dir. de Sica), *Children of Heaven* (1997, dir. Majidi), *The Gold Rush* (1925, dir. Chaplin), *Life is Beautiful* (1997, dir. Benigni), and *Love Story* (1970, dir. Hiller). 'The result of that desire,' he goes on to say, 'is *Kaadhal*.' We then see stills from the film (including a 100-day poster that says, in Tamil, 'A world cinema film in Tamil'); then we see a picture of Shankar and Balaji Sakthivel sitting on the floor talking while Shankar says: 'My friend Balaji Sakthivel has directed this film.' As we see images of Madurai's canonical places and its everyday spaces, Shankar says: 'Taking a real incident in the Madurai district of Tamil Nadu, he has directed

this film greatly.' We again see Shankar, who says: 'For three days I was unable to forget/overcome the feeling I experienced while watching it.' He goes on to explain that in order to maintain the 'naturalness' of the film and the 'life' and space it depicted, he decided *not* to remake it but to dub it, leaving in all of the Tamil boards and locations. He concludes by saying: 'This film may not have the scale (*bharitanam*) or fantasy of my earlier films, but my conviction is that the film will move you much more than those.' The image returns to the first smiling still of his face and he says: 'I remain yours forever.' His signature, hand-written in Telugu, along with the phrase 'always yours,' appears below his face. (Thanks to S.V. Srinivas for translation clarifications. Srinivas indicates that such prologues are not typical for dubbed films into Telugu.) See note 51 in this chapter.

26 As two recognizable chronotopes of the everyday experience of narration, the bus and the railway function to further authenticate the filmic realism of *Kaadhal*. (On cinema and the railway as linked media in India and elsewhere, see Chakravarthy 1993:83; Schivelbusch 2014[1977]:42; Larkin 2008:75.) Interestingly, note how the railway chronotope of face-to-face narration – where a "real" story is told by a "real" person – is situated outside of the film proper and yet is anchored by (that is, comes from) a character(-person) within the filmic narrative, while the bus chronotope of cinematic narration – within which an un-real story is enacted by the fantastical hero – is situated within the film narrative proper, such that the putative historical reality of the film (the railway chronotope) frames and envelops the mass hero and his own narrative text (the bus chronotope) within itself. Thanks to Jürgen Spitzmüller for pushing me to articulate these contrasting chronotopes, and to Martin Lefebvre and Daniel Morgan for pointing out the "found manuscript" or "message in a bottle" quality of this frame and its "reality effect."

27 We may argue the more general point that realist metapragmatic function always goes hand in hand with realist metapragmatic discourse (the distinction is from Silverstein 1993), be it through the metadiscourse of the film itself, processes of being socialized to the discourse of realism (see note 14 in Chapter 1), or marketing materials and other press materials that discuss the making of some film or other.

28 Recall from Chapter 1, for example, how the director Venkat Prabhu, in discussing the slap sequence of his 2011 film *Mankatha*, noted that if Vaibhav had punched rather than slapped Ajith the scene would become fake (*poyyā iruntirukkum*) and turn into "cinema"; here falsity and "cinema" are equated with each other in opposition to how such a fight would be 'in reality' (*nijamā irukkum*). Similarly consider, in this context, Bazin's comment on *The Bicycle Thief* (1948, dir. de Sica): "No more actors, no more story, no more sets … no more cinema" (Bazin 2005[1949]:60). As Aumont et al.

(1992[1983]:114) note, this formulation pits "no more cinema" (or "pure cinema," as Bazin also puts it elsewhere) against "the pejorative sense of 'it is cinema,'" that is, against cinema itself (see also Wollen 1969:87, 89).

29 *Dicent* and *dicisign* are Charles Sanders Peirce's (1931–35:2:§251, 309–22) terms for a sign construed by its interpretant as a sign of existence, or Secondness, that is, as an index. *Dicentization*, on Ball's (2014) coinage, is the process through which a sign – which may, from some other perspective, not be so construed – is construed as an index. When putative symbols are dicentized, for example, we speak of naturalization; ritual performativity, similarly, turns on construing iconic representations as efficacious in entailing states of existence in the events of their happening. Compare *dicentization* with Susan Gal's and Judith Irvine's notion of *rhematization* (Gal 2018; Gal and Irvine 2019), from Peirce's (1931–35:2:§250) *rheme* – the construal of an (indexical) sign as an icon, for example, as the essence or quality shared with the thing it indexes (what Parmentier 1994:18 calls "downshifting"). We might similarly construe *argumentization* (from the third term of Peirce's 1931–35:2:§250–3 rheme-dicent-argument trichotomy) – or perhaps less awkwardly if more ambiguously, *conventionalization* – as the (re)construal (and entailing) of an icon or index as a symbol (Parmentier 1994:19), a process common in academic critique.

30 As discussed in the 2014 documentary *The Invisible Other: Caste in Tamil Cinema* (dir. Suresh-ET; https://www.youtube.com/watch?v=GOoI4zNEOmI), the Censor Board's policy has been to censor any explicit, definite representations of particular castes that are denigrating, though representations that valorize particular castes (without denigrating other castes) are allowed. "Dalit," one former regional board director avers in the documentary, is an intrinsically denigrating term (because Dalits are denigrated), and hence explicit representations of Dalits qua Dalits are not allowed. Here, note how a casteist, anti-Dalit politics, by framing a term of uplift and political mobilization against casteist domination by dominant upper castes *as* a taboo term, figures it as having a performative power that allows for state intervention of censorship. (Also note how it conflates the oppressed status of the referent of the term for the pragmatics of the term itself.) The activist, Dalit director Pa. Ranjith has also spoken about the difficulties he faced from producers who worried that depicting Dalit heroes and symbols would result in the economic failure of his films due to non-Dalit audiences rejecting such images (see Pa. Ranjith 2018b; Damodaran and Gorringe 2021:32; see also discussion by directors Thangabachan and S.P. Jananathan in *The Invisible Other*, as well as by Chakravarthy 2018).

This avoidance was apparent in my empirical materials as well. In our interviews, for example, Balaji Sakthivel studiously avoided ever uttering the word "Dalit," even when I had introduced the term in our discussion.

Similarly, in discussing *7/G Rainbow Colony* with a group of my Madurai hostel mates after a screening of the film in the hostel in 2008, the discussion of realism turned to *Kaadhal*. After noting that the film depicts the love story as it would have proceeded in real life (that is, with violence and tragedy), one of the students (who was not Dalit), after a pregnant three second pause in an otherwise lively conversation, switched into English to say: "That story is based on caste." He later reiterated, in full Tamil, that "*jāti*" (caste) is the basis of the story. When another student disagreed, saying that you can't say that it's about caste per se, he interrupted in Tamil: 'It is only about caste! You can't tell from seeing it? Just that. Caste. BC [Backwards Caste] and:: (2) you can tell what's the caste, can you not tell?' (*Jāti tān! Atule pāttā teriyaleyā? Atān.* Caste. BC *vantu*:: (2) *atē teriyutu enna* caste *teriyāmalā irukkutu*). Note the euphemist codeswitch to the English word "caste" and later the avoidance of saying either the words Dalit or SC (that is, scheduled caste). In its place appear the filler word *vantu::* with an elongated epenthetic vowel and a long two second pause, and then an appeal to the obviousness of Murugan's caste identity.

Naming and depicting the Brahmin has a long and continuous history in Tamil cinema, one linked post-1940s to the place of the Brahmin as the constitutive internal other of the Dravidian movement (Ramaswamy 1997; Pandian 2007). Similarly, certain dominant castes in 1970s "nativity" films have a history of being so named and depicted – see the main text and note 35 in this chapter for discussion.

31 Note how the "on record" indexicality of the kiss as relayed by film – that is, the presumption that if we see it onscreen it happened offscreen – is assimilated to the rigid designation of the proper caste name; it is the secured interdiscursive chain from profilmic/baptismal origin to theatre that renders both image-acts "explicit" and thus performatively potent. See discussion in Chapter 2.

32 The distinction of reproducing reality versus representing society is taken from K. Hariharan (2008); see also Mitry 1997[1963]:15.

33 In this 2008 interview, Balaji Sakthivel did not ask me to put his admission off the record, as directors often did when making sensitive admissions or criticisms. Nevertheless, in our 2018 interviews, I explicitly told him I would not write about his "script," offering to efface it in my own "script," since it was his right to disclose it. In response, he said that it was fine for me to write about it, that he had made his own peace with it. Initially, while he knew the audience would believe his "script," he did not think it would take on the proportions it did. He was scared for a long time, he said, because people kept asking him where Murugan was, what hospital he was staying in, so that they could help him, send him money, and so on (for example, at the London Film Festival, where *Kaadhal* was screened

in 2005). He began to develop a "guilty conscience" about it, though it's been long enough, he said, that the truth could come out. It's important, he said, for the audience to trust a filmmaker, to believe they aren't trying to cheat them. Now that he has made two further films, *Kalloori* (2007) and *Vazhakku Enn 18/9* (2012), which are known to be fictionalizations of actual incidents, the audience, he said, trusts him and the 'purity' of his politics. He can now say, he said, that 'this was a technique, don't think it was to cheat you, this happens,' because he's continuously made films that aren't "make believe." 'I can say it now,' he said, 'but if I had said it then people might have thought, "we were so engaged by the film and then at the end he cheated us."'

34 Balaji Sakthivel put it this way in September 2018:

Atāvatu, this is not my own story. This is his story. I have cooked this story as a screenplay, as *Kaadhal*, and I have given to you. *Appaṭi nnu atu pōṭṭa pōtu tān, itu varai pārttuṭṭu iruntatu paṭam kiṭaiyātu*, this is a real story, *avarṭṭa yārō sollirukkāru.*

That is to say, this is not my own story. This is his story. I have cooked this story as a screenplay, as *Kaadhal*, and I have given to you. When it's said like that, (they'll think) what's seen up until now is not a film, this is a real story, someone told it to him.

Note the voicing shifts here, where Balaji Sakthivel (BS) moves from his own disclaiming – "this is not my$_{BS}$ story" – to figurating its uptake by a viewer – "this is a real story, someone told it to him$_{BS}$."

35 This risk of interpellation also explains why, despite being replete with realist depictions of caste (in particular, of Thevar identity; Murugan's Dalit identity is only indirectly indicated; Rajangam 2016; see note 18 in this chapter), *Kaadhal* completely avoided uttering the name of any particular caste. This avoidance contrasts with films from the late 1970s to 1990s (where dominant-caste names were used in the names of the films and their characters) but not with an earlier generation of films, which, as Prasad (1998) points out, studiously avoided any mention of caste. To utter the name of the caste in a film would risk its representations being taken up as accusation and insult.

Similarly, consider how the director Sasikumar answered a question I asked in a 2008 interview about how he chose to depict caste relations in his film *Subramaniyapuram* (2008) – in particular, about his placement of a picture of a Pillaimar nationalist leader, V.O. Chidambaram Pillai, in the house of the politicians who cheat the lower-caste protagonists. Sasikumar responded with a burst of laughter, a break in his otherwise low-pitched, monotone voice, followed by a statement of surprise: 'You really watched the film closely' (*Bayaṅkaramā* watch *paṇṇirukkīṅka*). When I followed up, asking why he brought that particular picture into the film, he (SK) responded by saying to me (CN):

> SK: (1.5) *Hmm(h)* (2) *Atu:::*↓ (.5) *he he* <laughing voice:> *atu* art director *vacciṭṭāru=(h)ava(h)ḷō t(h)ān*. (3) [That::: the art director put that. That's all.]
> CN: *Sari* [Okay].

Here, Sasikumar's otherwise brisk speech came to a standstill, with a 1.5 second pause before he begins his turn. He elongates the end of "*Atu*" (the distal neuter deictic 'that'), the 2 second gap before he finishes the sentence filled by 0.5 seconds of silence and two bursts of laughter (*he he*). It was as if he was searching for what he should say, whether he should say anything at all. He follows with an explanation: 'That was the art director, that's all,' an utterance threaded by bursts of uncomfortable laughter and followed by a long 3 second silence. After I say, 'Okay,' closing his turn (he didn't self-select to take the next turn at talk), his speech returned to its normal pitch and cadence, giving a politic explanation that the film is not about caste: 'If I said that this guy is that caste and that guy that caste, then the film would've become a caste film [*jāti paṭam*], about how this caste does this like this, this caste are good guys, this caste-' <he cuts off, presumably to say 'bad guys'>. '(But) I didn't say anything that like that. The groups of the film are the uneducated youth and the politicians. This is a film for everyone and not for a particular caste; that is why I didn't identify any caste in any detail' (*Atanāle tān nān jātiyai romba* detail-*ā kāmikkale, inta jāti anta jāti nnu sollale*). 'It is a film about four friends,' he continued, 'and could be about any caste; that if you do this, this would happen to you (independent of your caste), no matter what their caste they [politicians] will cheat you; so because I wanted to say this I didn't "concentrate" on caste.' Here, caste is denied precisely at the moment of its enunciation. Also note how sensitive, and avoidant, Sasikumar is to the performativity of audience uptakes of depictions of caste.

36 Balaji Sakthivel put it this way to me (CN) in September 2018:

Avan emote *āki kaṭaisiyile "itu uṇmaiyileyē naṭantuccu" appaṭiṅkum pōtu* they feel more than *itu, uh, atāvatu uh innum ((romba)) vantu avaṅkaḷukku valikkum*, (CN: hmm) *ēnnā itu oru mukkiyamāna* matter, *oru jātiye pārkka kūṭātu appaṭiṅkuṟatu mukkiyamāna* matter.	He's [the viewer] become emotional, at the end when he hears/thinks, "this really happened," they'll feel more than this, uh, that is, uh, it'll hurt even more to them, (CN: hmm) because this is a really important matter, it's a really important matter that you shouldn't observe caste.

Note here the shift in perspective from the spectator's (reportively calibrated) perspective to a general moral frame (that is nomically calibrated).

37 The necessity of Balaji Sakthivel's "disclaimer" reveals the extent to which Benveniste's (1971:206–15) notion of *histoire* as a discourse that effaces its own marks of enunciation such that the story "seems to tell itself" (Aumont et al. 1992[1983]:96) cannot be assumed in this context, or in general (which is to say, the story never tells itself; Gunning 1991:21–2; Metz 2016[1991]:143–5). This is because *histoire* is not a function of effacing reflexively calibrated deixis per se but is the *outcome* of a process of entextualization (whereby deictics of various kinds are nomically calibrated). In the case of *Kaadhal*, in order for the story to be told at all requires an explicit intervention by the director's enunciated "I" into the film text, an intervention that, retroactively, allows the story to seem to have "told itself."

38 Here, notice the contrast between Murugan as a subject who can *see* – as discussed in the main text above – with Murugan after he has gone crazy. The trauma of his being separated from Aiswarya and her ripping off her thali has made him unable to recognize her, the break of their conjugal love and his capacity for vision going hand in hand. I thank Christopher Ball for highlighting this contrast to me.

39 To allow Murugan and Aiswarya to have sex would also potentially trigger a rejection of the heroine's character ('How could she have sex with one man and then go and marry another?' Balaji Sakthivel rhetorically voiced the spectator inside himself) and thus the film itself. He said:

Anta poṇṇa vantu keṭuttu, itā ākiṟuccu nnu vaccukkōṅka, ellāmē muṭiñciruccu nnu vaccukkōṅka, automatic-*ā "Evvaḷavu (timiru) … ippaṭi vantu innoruttanōṭa pōy* sex *ellām vaccukkiṭṭu oru kalyāṇam paṇratuṅkṟate" vantu* mind *vantu* viewers-*ōṭa* mind *ēttukkavē ēttukkātu.*

Suppose that this happened, that the girl is spoiled, that everything was finished, then automatically, "How (arrogant) she is to go and have sex with one man, to do everything, then to go and get married (to someone else)," the mind, the viewer's mind would never accept that.

40 In *7/G Rainbow Colony*, though, we can note that the lovers' sexual encounter takes place not in Chennai (the space of kinship and sexual policing in the film) but in the "hill station" of Ooty, a place that is both tucked away in the wild forest and evocative of colonial British pasts and contemporary Indian vacations, fractally replicating the Madurai and Chennai distinction as a distinction of Chennai and Ooty.

41 Balaji Sakthivel's comparison of himself to Selvaraghavan is telling, given that my interviews with youth viewers of both films in 2004–05

and 2007–09 revealed that while both films were cited as showing the contemporary realities of love and sexuality in Tamil Nadu, the reality of *7/G Rainbow Colony*'s depiction of the sex act (indeed, the whole climax sequence) was much more contested as to its believability (see Nakassis and Dean 2007). By contrast, *Kaadhal* was much more likely to be cited as realistically depicting the impossibility of (inter-caste) premarital love and the sorrowful affects therein, indicating the fraught intersection of realism and the moral imaginaries of caste and female sexuality.

42 Here, we might observe that in contrast to the performative force of *7/G Rainbow Colony*, the representation in *Kaadhal* was more explosive, because castes are organized into political groups – and, in some cases, willing to engage in forms of violence – in ways that Indian feminisms, to my knowledge, have not. Indeed, the liberal discourse on female sexuality has to separate sexuality out from caste – to make it liberal, conjugal, urban, cosmopolitan. Female sexuality, thus, becomes a source of violent controversy most often when it comes to be taken as the emblem of larger corporate, masculinist groups (castes, ethnolinguistic groups, religious groups, the nation) rather than as a problem on its own terms (that is, on the terms of liberal individualism). I thank Amanda Weidman for pushing me to make this point.

43 In *Bharathi Kannamma*, while the protagonist only unites with the heroine on her funeral pyre (she has committed suicide because of her inability to marry him), her father, the headman of the village, realizes his error and marries his relative's (Thevar) son to the dead hero's (Dalit) sister, as well as falls at the feet of the village's Dalits in atonement.

44 When I asked Balaji Sakthivel in 2018 if he feared reprisals from Thevar groups if he had been more "bold" in his depiction (that is, not avoided having Aiswarya and Murugan have sex), he brushed it off; yet in 2008, he seemed less confident, indicating that if he had shown the couple having had sex that 'they' (what I understood him to mean, protesting Thevars) would not let the film release.

45 As Stalin Rajangam (2016) argues, *Kaadhal*, like a number of other realist films of this type, essentializes a set of indexical (enregistered) signs of dominant-caste identity, in particular Thevar identity (as violent, dominant, honourable), and by implication Dalit identity (as meek, victimized, subservient; see also Leonard 2015). As he also points out, violence in *Kaadhal* is reserved only for the dominant caste, while in reality Dalits respond to Thevar aggression by defending themselves; further, the film resolves itself by figuring the second husband, a Thevar, as a martyr of sorts, effacing any critical Dalit voice in the film. See discussion in the main text.

46 Of course, this is not to say that all viewers necessarily felt this way, or even felt one way or the other. For example, when I chatted with a group

of Tamil MA students at a Madurai college in March 2008, they said that *Kaadhal* was a "super" film. And while it was so true (*uṇmai*), especially its conclusion, they couldn't accept it (*ēttukkamuṭiyale*; that is, they couldn't deal with how tragic it was). They would rather have had a happy ending, like in *Kaadhalukku Mariyadai*, they said, a film that has a "super" ending.

47 Damodaran and Gorringe (2017) report numerous other such instances of the uptake of caste-based films (be they critical of caste domination or not), indicating their socially regular nature; they cite examples such as the use of songs from films like the 1992 Thevar-valourizing, yet also critical *Thevar Magan* (Son of Thevar, dir. Bharathan) during the yearly public (and often violent) birthday celebrations of the caste-hero/leader Muthuramalinga Thevar; cases of Thevars singing the songs on school or college campuses when encountering Dalit classmates; as well as the screening of the film to mobilize caste violence against Dalits in preparation for organized attacks (something of a macabre pep rally; see also Srinivas and Sundar Kaali 1998:224–5n17; for more recent examples, see the 2014 documentary *The Invisible Other: Caste in Tamil Cinema*, 0:22:50).

48 Notice in the English translation the work of the deictics – "this," "our" (likely, the addressee-excluding *eṅka*), and "you," as well as the vocative address term "Fuckers" (co-referential with "you") and the second-person imperative – to anchor the denotational and image text of the screen onto the interactional text of the screening such that Dalit viewers are likened to Murugan's character and Thevar viewers to Aiswarya's family. (To whatever extent the translation is pragmatically accurate, some such deictic anchoring was in effect in the reported Tamil original.) This lamination of a nomically calibrated denotational text, framed by a reportively calibrated realist style, onto a reflexively calibrated set of deictics renders the film-scene itself a performative image-act of threat, whose perlocutionary uptake is characterized in Anand's quotation as "intimidation." See Chapters 1 and 2 on the semiotics of performativity.

49 See Metz's (2016[1991]:46–51) interesting survey of such enunciatory uses of titles in Euro-American cinema.

50 This communicative exchange of moves provides a counter-argument to Metz's (2016[1991]) narrow view of film as "non-deictic," "monodirectional," and "unresponsive" to empirical uptake (compare Stam 1989; Dagrada 2014:34–9).

51 As discused in note 25 in this chapter, the Telugu version of *Kaadhal* begins with the director and producer S. Shankar's face, voice, name, and signature, grounding the film in this citational chain of auteur-director authority. This preamble anticipates Balaji Sakthivel's own epistle and signature at the end of the film, suturing him into a lineage featuring Shankar and Bharathiraja, as well as the auteurs called out in Shankar's preamble. That the film is brought

to us by Shankar is also inscribed in the Tamil version, both by his production banner at the beginning of the film and by the marketing materials (film posters, press commentary), which tell us that it is produced by him.

While I do not pursue it explicitly in this book (though see the main text for various exemplifications), the discussion of enregisterment and realism in this chapter suggests not only a more general account of film style but also how to think semiotically about auteurism (Sarris 2007[1962]; Wollen 1969:74–115) and film stardom (Dyer 1998[1979]; Barry 1985). All three are species of enregisterment. The latter two involve cinematic repertoires of signs whose indexicality have a unique value and functionality: they rigidly index a particular agent, the auteur-director or the star-actor (compare the notion of rigid designation; Kripke 1980). (This focus on the enregisterment of rigidly indexing semiotic repertoires suggests a more general approach to questions of identity and fame/celebrity; on the former, see Wortham 2006; on the latter, see Munn 1986; Nakassis 2012.) Of course, it is not only directors and stars who can be so enregistered/indexed; in principle, anyone who may be recruited to a footing in the production format of a film can be so enregistered. Film form may come to rigidly index a film editor, a cinematographer (Sakti Saravanan's "touch" in Chapter 1), a production house, a dialogue writer, a dubbing artist, a dance or fight choreographer, and so on and so forth.

52 It is important to note, as mentioned in Chapter 3, that the distinct roles of dialogue writer, screenplay writer, and director are often collapsed in contemporary Tamil cinema, especially in realist, auteur films, where the "director" officially fills all of these roles at once, a pattern that dates to at least K. Balachander (whom many credit with beginning such a trend). I say officially, since all directors in the Tamil industry work with a number of assistant and associate directors who participate in the scripting and dialogue writing of the film. The monopolization of (credit for) these distinct roles is itself, of course, part of the politics of production format.

53 While this claim – that it is the director, and not the hero, who is the rightful mediator of the real and the audience via his "story" – manifests in *Kaadhal* as the director's signature, it also appears as a more general fashion of speaking in the industry and among audiences. Consider the often-uttered phrase "the story is the hero" or "content is the hero" (see Majumdar 2021:73), which appeared in both my conversations with directors and audiences to describe films like *Kaadhal*, *7/G Rainbow Colony*, and *Subramaniyapuram*, films that either lack a hero figure or negate his heroism. Such a phrase is a trope of (de)personification, taking the predicate "is the hero" and putting a subject that is not and cannot be construed as a "hero" on the term's default semantics and prototypy (that is, a human who is an actor; for example, "Bharat is the hero of the film"), as if to

replace the hero by the story and thus, ultimately, by the director and his privileged relationship to the story. Here, as we have seen throughout the book, "the story" articulates a particular ontological politics of the image and its production format (and thus political economy). This ontological politics is not dissimilar from Miriam Hansen's (1991) discussion of the institutionalization of classical cinema and its spectator – the very basis for much of what constitutes the object of film theory – out of the more open and unruly tendencies of early cinema, wherein "the story" and its coherent narrative became the central vehicle to discipline the viewer (qua spectator), the exhibition space, and the industry itself (see also Gunning 1991; Hughes 1996 on early cinema in South India; Ganti 2012:276 on 1990s Hindi cinema).

In my interviews with directors (like Selvaraghavan 2005; Balaji Sakthivel 2008, 2018a, 2018b; Sasikumar 2008; Mysskin 2008; Balu Mahendra 2008; and others) – as we have had occasion to see in Chapters 1 and 2 – questions about why some or another important if contentious element was in or absent from a film (Why does the heroine die at the end? Why did you show the sex scene in this way? How did you handle caste in the film? and so on) would often be answered by deferring responsibility and agency onto the script, the story, and the world it represents. In this discourse, script, story, and world make their own demands and require the entextualization and emplotment of the film just as it is. Yet ultimately, the appeal to the script, story, or world was an appeal to the subjectivity of the director.

Consider *7/G Rainbow Colony* in this regard. When Selvaraghavan (2005) reported to me that people in the theatre yelled and scolded *him*, the director, when the heroine died ('Why did you kill her?!' he reported them yelling), he simply said to me: "It was a real story. I have to present it the way I saw it." Recall as well that, like *Kaadhal*, *7/G Rainbow Colony* begins its first frame with its own disclaimer: "Based on a True Story" (see Figure 4.7). At the same time, all the metadiscourse about the film (press coverage, film reviews, interviews with its actors, producer, and director) emphasized that it was not just *a* true story; it was *Selvaraghavan*'s true story: he too had loved and lost a Punjabi girl when he was studying; he too was a wastrel loser; he too – like his films' predominantly male audience – felt the uplift and loss of love. Here, the disavowal of the responsibility to show (I had to show it like this because that is how it is/was, because that is the "flow" of the script, or the psychology of its characters) comes along with the director's privileged relationship to all of the above ("This is my experience, my story"; "It happened to me, I saw it"; or in *Kaadhal*, "He told it to me").

This privileged relationship was reflected in the discourse of the film's sixtieth-day celebrations that I attended on 12 December 2004 at the Devi

Kalaivani Theatre in the south Madurai neighbourhood of Tirunagar. The theatre was bristling with excitement (something like a first-day film show; see Chapter 1 for description), the almost exclusively male audience yelling and whistling at the appearance and mention of the film's actors and its director. Indeed, the intensity and duration of such extended bouts of whistling and screaming singled out, in particular, two persons: (1) Selvaraghavan ('the respectable, modern director who has the pulse of the youth,' as the emcee for the event called him in Tamil; in the English-language press, Baradwaj Rangan [2004] has referred to him as the "poet laureate" for the "slackers and losers of Tamil Nadu") as the audience's site of praise and identification; and (2) the 'dream girl' Sonia Agrawal (as the emcee put it in Tamil), the film's heroine, as the object of their desire. In a speech praising the film, the All-India Radio director and Tamil scholar Ilasai Sundaram praised the director for putting his 'stamp' (*muttirai*) on every department of the film, tellingly saying in Tamil that 'while in those days a film was referred to as an MGR film, a Sivaji film, a Rajini film, or a Kamal film,' 'this film can only be called a Selvaraghavan film.' For his part, Selvaraghavan's own speech turned precisely on identifying himself with (1) the male audience (for example, by talking about how he too is from Madurai, he too struggles with English [see Nakassis 2016a:89–155], he too has loved and lost like they have) and (2) his films' protagonists. Indeed, as he said in his speech, 'you all always call out for the *characters* of my films (Kathir and Anitha) and not the actors (Ravikrishnan and Sonia Agrawal), which tells us that the artists are not what is important.' He went on say, to riotous applause and yelling from the audience, that his protagonists in *Kaadhal Kondein* and *7/G* are 'no one else but the one who is standing before you.'

There is much to say about this event, but my point here is that the event figurates, and is taken up by the other speakers at the event and the audience, as a claim on the story and world of *7/G* as being, in the first instance, the director's and, as a function of that, the audience's as well. Further, not only is it his film, he is its hero and the lover of the heroine (indeed, he married the actress Sonia Agrawal in 2006 after working with her on three films). "He's me, and nobody else," Selvaraghavan (2004a) said when asked in an interview on whom he based the protagonist of *7/G*, earlier described in the interview as an average, "normal guy," "50 or 60" of whom you might bump into if "you walk for a mile in Chennai": insecure, vulnerable, imperfect, and yet still worthy to be the hero of a film (Susan 2016). In this world, the actor is incidental and the hero secondary. For it is a director's world, and – in this case – the story and its characters are him and his alone; see note 57 in this chapter, as well as discussion in Chapter 1 and the book's Conclusions.

54 While casting hero-stars affords bigger budgets (and director salaries), and thus more scope for grander sets, more effects, better technicians, and so on, for most of the directors with whom I spoke (the exception being those who exclusively thought of themselves as "commercial" directors; for example, K.S. Ravikumar 2018), the hero-star was also framed as a burden and a blockage (Srinivas 2009; Ganti 2012:211–13). All of my discussions with such directors featured stories of (1) humiliating rejection by producers for lack of named heroes or hero-roles; or (2) compromises that had to be made to producers by introducing hero-type roles or casting established actors. Needless to say, directors often had little good to say about producers, painting them as crass, uneducated philistines (a discourse that could be elicited among certain producers themselves; see Chapter 3). (For their part, producers complained about directors' pretentiousness, their indifference to the financial struggles of producers and ignorance of the financial necessities to make films, their taking advantage of producers by living on their dime, and so on.)

For those interested to pursue "experimental," realist subjects, casting a hero-star wasn't possible anyway. Most established heroes would refuse to act in a film like *Kaadhal* or *7/G Rainbow Colony* – films that not only lack much "heroism" or "build-up" but whose male protagonists are mediocre, meek losers – just as most producers would hesitate to produce such films. In a context where films are pre-sold to distributors, where theatre dates are reserved for screening, and where financiers invest based on whether or not a particular hero is on board, a film without a hero is a risk. It is not without reason, then, that *Kaadhal* was produced by another director, S. Shankar (with the desire to bring "world cinema" to the Tamil industry), that *7/G Rainbow Colony* was produced by the lead actor's father (who was using the film to introduce his son into the industry), or that *Subramaniyapuram* was self-produced by the director and his kin (and with no expectations of turning a profit; Sasikumar 2008). Casting the kin of financiers or producers is a strategy that Balaji Sakthivel repeatedly exploited to get financing for his films, describing his films to me as "grade schools" for new actors, a place where producers drop off their kids (Balaji Sakthivel 2018b). He teaches them how to act, he said, and then passes them off to higher grades (that is, bigger-budget productions).

Regarding *Kaadhal*, Balaji Sakthivel noted that the film is less about characters than about a situation, starting with focus on one character (Murugan) but ending with another (Aiswarya's Thevar husband); there is no stable space, he explained, for a hero character as the basis of the film or as the site for audience identification, which is to say, for the *actor* to be "in" the film; hence, he said in October 2018, "no star will come forward to work with my movie, it's obvious, because my story will twist and turn, not because of the character (but) because of the story." Interestingly, the context of this statement was Balaji Sakthivel distinguishing himself from Bala, another auteur-director, whose films, he said, are character driven (see Eswaran 2021:166). Such films can accommodate heroes – and indeed, Bala has (re)launched a number of hero-stars such as Vikram, Suriya, Vishal, Arya – because his films focus on a particular character that the film structures an identification with, opening up a space in the film for the actor. In such a film, with such a hero, you will be focused on watching the character (and thus the hero-star): who he is, what he does, what task he has ahead of him. "When he cries you cry, when he laughs you laugh, when he reacts you react," Balaji Sakthivel put it. "These are the things a hero wants (from his films)." Note, here, the fractal recursion of the distinctions of presencing/representation and hero/story, with the distinction drawn here by types of directors, narratives, and the identifications they afford.

55 Balaji Sakthivel (2018b), for example, made this point by likening professional and non-professional actors to plastic and real fruits, saying:

Plastic *paḻam, pakkattule vantu* natural *paḻam reṇṭumē vaccōm nnu vaccukkōṅka,* juxtaposed *vaccukōṅka. Uṅkaḷukku* easy-*ā teriñcu pōyiṭum. Itu* plastic *nnu ēnnā* plastic *vantu more* colourful-*ā irukkum.* Natural *tān* color *kammiyā irukkum* … Like that, new face *pakkattule inta mātiri āḷuṅka irukkum pōtu romba* organic-*ā irukkum.*	Suppose you take a plastic and a natural fruit and juxtapose them. You can easily tell the difference. This is plastic because it's more colourful. The natural fruit will be less colourful … Like that, when a new face is close, when a guy like this is close, it'll be very organic.

Elsewhere in the same interview, Balaji Sakthivel made the same comparison, but with flowers, saying that the plastic flower will be more colourful but only the real flower will smell. It is this "freshness," he said, that he is after with "new faces" (compare Jakobson 1971[1921]:26).

56 The director Mysskin (2008) said to me:

> So see, that's [casting heroes/new faces] a big problem here. See, if I have to go with any big people [that is, actors], then I have to have the same set of principles that they have, actually. First, ((???)) they get introduced, they should have a dance, they should be having a fight. And they should be having a very sexy heroine. With all these things, I don't want to do deal with any big heroes. Because I believe- I am very happy to work with amateurs because I get (a) very spontaneous thing.

57 Many have noticed, for example, how Selvaraghavan's early protagonists act with the same mannerisms (see note 53 in this chapter). Neither Selvaraghavan nor Balaji Sakthivel, for example (the former saying so in public interviews [Selvaraghavan 2004b:34–5], the latter in our own discussions), profess a need for actors who have training since, they say, they know how each of the actors' actions, expressions, emotions should be executed. As Selvaraghavan has said, his actors don't need to know how to act as "in my mind I have acted each scene of my film, even as I script," allowing him to show his actors how to perform the scene "by acting it [the scene] out (for them) 15 to 20 times" before a take (Selvaraghavan 2004b:35).

58 Directors like K. Balachander, Selvaraghavan, and Balaji Sakthivel all emphasized that once they made a few successful films, they could sell their films on *their* names. Similarly, Chitralaya Gopu (2009) and C.V. Rajendran (2009), in speaking to me about the director C.V. Sridhar, with whom they worked, emphasized the "value" of Sridhar's name, worth as much as MGR or Sivaji, they said (with some hyperbole), to produce a film and draw a crowd. As the director K. Balachander put it to me in an interview in 2005, he "entered filmdom when the old films were only hero oriented" and where the female characters – indeed, all the characters – only existed to "glorify his character" as "props." Hence, he explained, he wanted to break with that norm and make films with strong female characters at their core. He went on to say: "Probably I made a mark, I made a distinction … because I made a mark of this kind I was noticeable, I was noticed, and I became a director of my own fame, my own making … I have not worked as (someone) subservient to the hero. I have been keeping my identity intact and making all the other characters intact." Notice here how the diegetic "characters" and the director's identity are "kept intact" against the threat of subservience to the hero, a conflation of production format and image ontology that goes to the point of this chapter. Elsewhere in the interview, he also said: "So I wanted to portray that way because I wanted to make my presence felt in filmmaking, in filmmaking. And I think I succeeded to a very great extent and all."

59 As one of my Madurai hostel mates put it in a group discussion of *7/G Rainbow Colony* after a screening in the hostel in February 2008: 'The film became realistic because they put in a new hero in the film' (*Putu hero pōṭṭatāle tān paṭam etārttamā pōccu*). If a big hero-star like Vijay, Ajith, or Rajini had acted in it, it would not have been. Agreeing with him, another hostel mate said: 'They'll watch for their image, if it's a big actor, they'll watch for his image' (Image *pāppāṅka, periya naṭikan nnā* image *pāppāṅkka*). If Rajini had acted in *7/G Rainbow Colony*, he said, the film would have been a huge "flop."

60 Balaji Sakthivel's narration of this alternate version is all the more interesting given the resonance with the 2019 film *Asuran*, directed by

Vetrimaaran and starring Dhanush as a violence-averse Dalit who eventually, after repeated atrocities and provocations by the local dominant castes, rises in just such a (star-building) manner in a sand-pluming fight to massacre all the bad, dominant-caste guys (see also Mari Selvaraj's 2021 film *Karnan*, also with Dhanush). (*Asuran*, incidentally, stars Balaji Sakthivel as a dominant-caste police officer.) In this post–*Kabali* and *Kaala* moment (see the book's Conclusions), however, the hero is not revealed to be a Thevar (as in Balaji Sakthivel's narration) but rises up *as* a Dalit.

61 See Lalitha Gopalan's (2021:214–26) detailed and insightful reading of *Subramaniyapuram* in the context of what she calls "the cinema of cruelty" and the "Tamil new wave"; see also Leonard 2021:37.

62 As Karthikeyan Damodaran (personal communication, 2018) pointed out to me, one might see the backstory of *Subramaniyapuram* narrating the rise of Thevars by politically displacing other upper-caste non-Brahmins in Madurai (in particular, Pillaimars), depicting the very historical conditions of possibility for the rise of the film's genre and aesthetic style – a casted realism – in an intensely, meticulous realist style, which it participates in and naturalizes.

63 For a critical reading of the role of gender and masculine supremacy in *Subramaniyapuram*, see Divya 2021.

64 Sasikumar (2008) said in our interview: "But I kept that length (of the Steadicam shot) because I want to show the emotion of that Kasi" (see also Sasikumar 2014:252–3). Consider how Sasikumar voiced the audience:

"Kāsi enna ṭā īppaṭiyellām itu paṇṇinān?" "Iṅka ennennā" Kāsiyum yōsicciṭṭu varṟān. Aṅkēyum oru kolai naṭantirukku. Audience point of (view)- audience *yōsikka ārambikkiṟān, "Enna ṭā ivanai ippaṭi paṇṇiṭṭān," avan yōsikkiṟān anta* time. *"Enna ṭā ippaṭi paṇṇiṭṭān, ivanā ippaṭi paṇṟān?" Atanāle tān tiṭṭuṟāṅka. Tiṭṭuṟatukku "ṭēy vā!" tiṭṭuvāṅka. Tiṭṭuṟatellām anta* emotion *tān. "Ippaṭiyellām kūṭa iruntiya ṭā, ippaṭi paṇṇiṭṭiya ṭā,"* emotion *āki sila pēru tiṭṭuṟāṅka, sila pēru yōsiccu irukkāṅka.* Audience-*um yōsikkiṟāṅka,* character-*um avaṅkaḷōṭa* emotion-*ai ((kāmikka vaikkiṟāṅka/ kāmiccatu)).*

"Why the hell did Kasi do all that?" "What's going on here," Kasi is also coming, thinking. A murder has happened over there (on the riverbed). Audience point of (view)- the audience will start to think: "Why the hell did he do this to him?" he's thinking at that time. "Why the hell did he do this? Is it him who did that?" That's why they curse him. "Come here, man!" they'll scold. All that scolding is (from) that emotion only. "You did all that, man, you did that man," some people will get emotional and scold him, some people will be thinking. The audience will also be thinking, the character will make them show their emotions.

65 This discourse of realism and the credulous, overly affective spectator recalls, of course, precisely the class politics that M.S.S. Pandian (1996) and Stephen Hughes (1996) date to the advent of cinema in South India. But it is more. It is symptomatic of the ambivalent structure of realism as an aesthetic style that affirms and negates itself at once, as committed to an ontological politics of the image that always admits those counterforces that it must and yet always fails to completely master.

66 I thank Amanda Weidman for suggesting this point and its phrasing.

67 Compare Sasha Newell's (2012:21–2) quoting of Harry West's anecdote about an anti-witchcraft theatre troupe in Mozambique, that acting out sorcery entailed the belief among audiences that, given their accuracy, the actors must have been sorcerers themselves:

> "You see the way they eat human flesh?!" He asked me, genuinely scandalized.
>
> "But surely they are just acting out what they imagine sorcerers do?" I responded.
>
> "Exactly … Who can imagine such a thing without doing it!?" he asked me, clinching his case. (West 2008:54)

68 This logic is a variant of the sociological realism of the image discussed in Chapters 1 and 2, a spectatorial engagement with the image that asks who must one be to animate an image. It is a realism where not only does the image emanate from the sociological reality of the actor (Chapter 1) but also returns in reverse, where the image radiates and refracts back as an indexical sign of the actor as a moral subject (Chapter 2). It is not uncommon to hear from MGR fans (or Ajith, Vijay, Vijayakanth, Rajinikanth fans), for example, that he was/is a good man, a strong man, a moral man, and that his films provide evidence for this very fact (Pandian 1992:121; Dickey 1993a; Rogers 2009:83). This conflation of onscreen and offscreen image might be written off as an effect of MGR's propagandistic films on impressionable, uneducated, and immature audiences. Yet, as I was told by those partial to him, those presumed dupes, MGR was known to be a good man, not because the onscreen representation of MGR reflected who he was or what he did in some sort of direct way but because MGR *chose* to portray good, moral, just characters (just as Vaibhav "chose" to slap Ajith, the item dancer "chose" to get in front of the camera, the comedian "chose" to utter the insulting lines, or the villain "chose" to enact evil, as discussed in the chapters across the book). Note how far we are from confusion of the real and reel, for such a spectatorial logic is based precisely on a clear distinction between the two, one taken as the sign of the other (Srinivas 2009:238–9)! Based on a

set of assumptions about how MGR picked his films, here such fans deduce reality from image. Hence, as they explained, MGR made sure his characters didn't smoke, drink, cheat women, and the like, because he didn't do, or condone, such things. And knowing the power of cinema to potentially affect the (credulous) audience, he took social responsibility for his "mass" appeal. Here, through an ironic reversal, it is precisely by inhabiting a (liberal) media ideology of "effects" that would frame the fan-spectator as a credulous dupe (but projected on others, as always) that such putative dupes come to know the moral character of the actor from the role he chooses to essay on the screen, precisely the conclusion from the elite point of view that qualifies them as those very impressionable subjects, yet for all the wrong reasons.

69 From this theoretical point follows a methodological point: namely, that realism isn't an answer to a question that can be answered on its own terms from some single point of view. It is an empirical question about what counts as realism for/across some heterogeneous social domain of persons. Of course, as noted at the outset of this chapter, this relativist point isn't news to visual studies, cinema and media studies, or media anthropology (see, for example, Goodman 1976; Carroll 1988; Kulick and Willson 1994; Staiger 1992; Mitchell 1994). And yet – and here we detect that we are in the presence of ideology (Snyder 1980; Žižek 1989) – despite the recognition of the import of this point, much of the scholarly discourse on realism proceeds as if the point hadn't been made. While many would agree that realisms are relative, anyone who actually pursues this question quickly discovers that not only does what "realism" entails shift across historical period, medium, culture, social class, and so on, but that within any such culture, period, and so on, within even any single viewer's "reception" of a film, there is internal contestation about what realism is or should or could be, indeed, what an image is or should or could be. This is because what counts as reality, and what counts as the most realistic way of representing it, are deeply political questions, as argued in Chapter 1. That the empirical obviousness of all this for any who has cared to look hasn't stopped critics and theorists from offering accounts of what realism "is" is itself empirical evidence of precisely this point: realism is a site of political struggle and contestation as much as it is a *medium* of political struggle and contestation.

This relativity does not commit us, however, to an unproductive relativism. For having surveilled the complexity of what realisms might involve – in different times, places, political positions, media, and so on; as a contested field that folds heterogeneity within itself – we can ask: are there comparative grounds and contours across *different* realisms *from which* one might posit some more general account? I think so, and my comments in this chapter, and the book more generally, should be taken in this light. But to see this point requires taking the methodological point as a first principle for our theoretical propositions. See the book's Conclusions for more discussion.

Conclusions: Ends and Openings

1 According to Swarnavel Eswaran (personal communication, 2020), Jayalalitha's affectionate, diminutive nickname from her mother was *Ammu*, which was taken up by MGR and Sivaji Ganesan to address/refer to her, even in published interviews (see also Ramki 2008). As Swarnavel put it, "from the innocent, joy-free, child-woman Ammu, she later became the *Amma* of the AIADMK and Tamil Nadu." Following discussion in Chapter 2, this transition was an effacement of her cinematic past, enacted through, among other things, her sartorial style – a dark green, monochrome sari/cape that wrapped around and covered every part of her body – and public demeanour as a matronly and strong, steely female politician, both of which de-eroticized her (Prasad 2014:186–92; Venkatachalapathy 2018:78). Such an effacement was all the more necessary due to the DMK's attempts to undermine her through demeaning, misogynistic attacks on her status as a former actress.

2 After foregoing the 2019 Indian general elections and delaying formally constituting the party, Rajinikanth finally announced his intention to form his party and run candidates in the 2021 Tamil Nadu Legislative Assembly elections in December 2020. Citing ongoing health concerns under conditions of the global COVID-19 pandemic and following a hospitalization, on 29 December 2020, almost three years to the day of his original declaration, Rajinikanth announced via Twitter that he would not, ultimately, be forming a party or entering electoral politics.

3 Of course, Dravidianism in Tamil Nadu has long focused on a linguistic politics of Tamil purism and chauvinism. Here, however, Seeman has "grafted" (Gal 2018) a Dravidianist linguistic politics of identity onto an *ethnic* identity politics while, at the time, cynically critiquing Dravidianism as a ruse for non-Tamil South Indians to rule over Tamils.

4 With his 2017 film *Mersal* (dir. Atlee), Vijay dropped the adjective *Iḷaiya* (Young) from his epithet, perhaps making a claim to his maturation into the next phase of his stardom, arguably ascending to the level of the pre-eminent mass hero, Rajinikanth. It is reported that Vijay was given the epithet *Iḷaiya Taḷapati* in 1994 with the film *Rasigan* (dir. S.A. Chandrasekhar) because he was a huge fan of Rajinikanth, whose film *Thalapathi* (1991, dir. Mani Ratnam) had come out when Vijay entered the industry (Aiyappan 2018).

5 See Ranjith's comments in a 2018 interview on Radio City India (Pa. Ranjith 2018a).

6 Ranjith, as well as one of his associate directors on the film, indicated to me in 2018 that they didn't know when making *Kaala* that Rajinikanth had any definite plans on entering politics, saying that he only informed them in the final stage of the film's production.
7 This politics for the image extends to Pa. Ranjith's efforts at promoting Dalit filmmakers and films about Dalit lives (as with Mari Selvaraj's 2018 *Pariyerum Perumal*, which Ranjith produced), his construction of a public library of books on cinema and politics for aspiring and assistant directors, his support for anti-caste popular musical groups (such as the Casteless Collective; Diwakar 2022), creation of a publishing house and cultural centre, as well as his general participation in public debates and protests about questions of representation, film, and social inequality.
8 On how Ranjith's *Kaala* "breaks gender moulds in Tamil cinema," see Rajendran 2018d; Shinde 2018; see Rangan 2014 on the "misogyny in Rajinikanth's cinema" from the 1980s and 1990s.
9 Following its release, many articles came out on the internet "decoding" the anti-caste politics of *Kaala*; see, for example, Mejel 2018; Samos 2018; Shinde 2018; Surendhar 2018.
10 M.S.S. Pandian (1992:46) writes of the flopping of the 1962 MGR film *Paasam* due to the hero's death, an outcome MGR predicted but the director, T.R. Ramanna, ignored. And knowing that MGR's 1975 film *Pallandu Vazhga* (dir. K. Shankar) – a remake of the Hindi film *Do Aankhen Barah Haath* (1957, dir. V. Shantaram) – would involve the hero's death, MGR's fans "became restive and the director of the film had to change the end to present an invincible and deathless MGR" (Pandian 1992:46; compare Srinivas 2009:38).
11 The usage of the *Ramayana* in *Kaala* has deep cultural significance, not simply as a Hindu story that demonizes the Dravidian but also as a reference to Periyar's own subversive exegesis of this Hindu story as Aryanist, anti-Dravidian ideology that misrepresents Ravana; it also invokes the Dravidian writer Pulavar Kuzhanthai's retelling of the *Ramayana* with Ravana as the hero in his 1946 *Raavana Kaviyam* (a copy of which we see on Kaala's table in the film). Here, Ranjith reaches out to a Periyarite, Dravidianist, and an Ambedkarite politics while offering a critique of a Hindutva and North Indian politics of caste exclusion and discrimination against South India. As Stalin Rajangam (2018) argues, *Kaala* differs from the Dravidianist retellings, however, by allowing Ravana to be revived as the people themselves; rather than killed off, Ravaana lives on. On the relation of Ranjith's politics to Dravidianism, see Ram Manoharan 2021.
12 Compare this dialogue to his pre-climactic dialogue in the 1999 super-hit *Padaiyappa* (dir. K.S. Ravikumar), which features the line 'Take a look at all these people willing to die for this single man' (see Nakassis 2017, 2019).

13 There is much debate on the internet whether Kaala really dies in the film, revealing a deep anxiety over the possibility of the mass hero's death. It is interesting, if not unexpected, that there would be such a wide variety of interpretations, particularly since the film text leaves this question open. Part of this speculation was because – as an assistant director on the film told me in 2018 – the producer of the film, the actor and son-in-law of Rajinikanth, Dhanush (and thus presumably Rajinikanth himself), asked that a shot that disambiguated the question (in favour of clarifying his death) be removed.

14 We can also consider the director S. Shankar's two science fiction films with Rajinikanth, *Enthiran* (Robot, 2010) and *2.0* (2018), which similarly assault the body of the star. In both films, the star is split into two characters: a meek, human scientist and a super-powerful robot (here, diegetizing the power of the hero-star by "explaining" it through the character's status as a robot), the latter of whom is destroyed. In *Enthiran*, the Rajini-robot is dismantled at the end of the film. In *2.0*, the Rajini-robot is dismembered and decapitated by the villain in a grotesque scene, even as, in the climax, he is resurrected as a miniature of himself, literally diminished by the narrative. I thank S.V. Srinivas for a stimulating email exchange on these films. I thank Meghanne Barker for bringing the Eisenstein reference in the main text to my attention.

15 Ranjith's films also represent a shift in political economy; as Venkatesh Chakravarthy (2018) points out, Ranjith's films aren't the first to put the Superstar into a directorially helmed realist frame (consider, for example, Mani Ratnam's 1991 *Thalapathi*), though they are the first to produce and market such a film *as* a successful blockbuster (see also Prasad 2020). This success became possible because of what we might call the "Kollywoodization" (compare Rajadhyaksha 2003, 2009) of Tamil cinema, that is, the expansion of Tamil film markets beyond single-screen Tamil Nadu (S.V. Srinivas 2016). This expansion should also be considered against what Amrutha Kunapulli (2021) has referred to as the "worlding" of post-millennial Tamil cinema, that is, its (re)imagination as simultaneously an indigenous regional cinema (as *Tamil* cinema) and part of, and in conversation with, a global, world cinema (versus within the nation-state frame of "Indian cinema"), with structures of addressivity to both a Tamil and a non-Tamil, non-Indian audience.

16 Others speculated that it was Ranjith who was using Rajini to unite the Dalit vote, but presumably not to vote for Rajini.

17 I read this disalignment as also indicating the complex politics between directors and stars. Ranjith, and also S. Shankar (who made Rajini's *Enthiran* and *2.0*), have made director-authored films, not star-authored films like Rajini's mass films from the 1990s (and here we might add K.S.

Ravikumar's 2014 *Lingaa*). In such cases, what is critical is the stance of the director to the star. My sense is that neither Ranjith nor Shankar, unlike a director like K.S. Ravikumar in the 1990s (see Nakassis 2019), have a deep stake in Rajini coming to politics. And without that pull from the filmmaker (as advocate for the hero-star's fans and as fan himself), Rajini's films have no clear relationship to his offscreen political activity, revealing something of the complexity and variability in the production format of Rajinikanth's mass films of this period (compare MGR, who had a much tighter control over his films' production).

18 Here, we are reminded of Peirce's comments in a different context: "We naturally make all our distinctions too absolute. We are accustomed to speak of an external universe and an inner world of thought. But they are merely vicinities, with no real boundary between them" (Peirce 1958:7:§438).

19 This point bears on a number of Metz's (2016[1986], 2016[1991]) arguments about filmic enunciation (see also Browne 1999[1975]; Branigan 1984:66; Aumont et al. 1992[1983]:86). Of course, Metz is right to suggest that processes of enunciation/entextualization and the text so-enunciated/entextualized stand independently of any *particular* empirical person (author, viewer), and thus texts can circulate far beyond their contexts of enunciation/entextualization. But while such processes and their products are independent of any particular person, they are not independent of *semiotic agents* in general, that is, they cannot exist without being taken up in some context or other by some semiotic agent or other (see also de Lauretis 1984:44; Gledhill 1999[1988]:169). A text exceeds any particular person (and hence is "impersonal"), but it does not exceed communication in general.

Aspects of this theoretical point have been made by a number of film scholars. For example, Casetti points to the importance of the empirical "inhabiting" of the virtual roles inscribed by enunciation; Browne (1999[1975]) complicates the "position" of the spectator (as not simply implied by the position of the camera, the spatial relations in a scene, and so on) by reference to the "experience" of a spectator beyond the text; and similarly, Edward Branigan (1984) indicates the centrality of psychological inferences of the spectator. Ultimately, however, this theoretical point is toothless without being cashed out methodologically. What is required of us, thus, is to follow out how our theoretical discourse demands a particular mode of inquiry and vice versa. Indeed, the authors cited above do not seriously follow the methodological implications of this theoretical point; that is, none make such inhabiting, experience, or psychological inference their object of empirical investigation or analysis. Rather, each remains content with the internal/external shoring up of the film text (Stam 1989; Jost 1995; Srinivas

2009:5). Metz (2016[1991]:17–18, 23, 163, 167) himself points this out, arguing in effect that textual analysis is, and should remain, a methodologically individualist endeavour of entextualization, simply relying on the film's texture and the analyst's own empirical reception of it. If you want to know about a viewer, he notes, you have to go and talk to them! Yet, he implies, this has nothing to do with film analysis. But in actually doing such analysis, Metz recurrently relies on what actual viewers likely (and actually) think when seeing a film, implicitly making *empirical* claims about reception to argue for what he otherwise frames as a non-empirical elucidation of the autonomous structure of cinema's impersonal enunciation (for example, Metz 2016[1991]:9, 17; though see also 137, 167; compare Branigan 1984:207; Gunning 1991:23; Nakassis 2009).

20 Consider, for example, Dudley Andrew's (1998) praise of Francesco Casetti's (1998[1986]) brilliant book *Inside the Gaze*. Andrew (1998:xviii) notes that Casetti's focus on the text-internality of spectatorship (while still attentive to "socio-cultural realities that activate a text in any given viewing of it") can help protect film scholarship from "entering the waters patrolled by sociology, or of just floundering in the vast sea of the anecdotal, the tendentious, and the merely 'interesting.'" Casetti's theorization is needed, according to Andrew (1998:xvii), "to anchor reception studies, to keep it from floating free of the flimsy breakwater that cinema studies keeps constructing so as to harbour its work" (similarly, see Metz 2016[1986]:§86; compare Gledhill 1999[1988]:172, 174; Stewart 2003). Note, here, the presupposition of the sui generis text, which gets "activated in any given viewing of it," as well as the nautical chronotope of the choppy open seas of empirical reality and the perilously floating ship of reception, dogged dangers harboured and kept at bay by the discipline and its textual analysis. Revealed with some clarity is that such investments in the text are as much about, and perhaps always about, disciplinary politics and, in particular, the need to carve out an object of analysis with its own proper ontology and methodology, distinct from neighbouring disciplines (here, sociology, cultural studies, mass communications, anthropology, but also, we might add, as is so apparent in the early writings of Metz and others, linguistics and literary studies).

21 There are no "internal" positions of spectatorship that can be intuited independently of events of "external" viewers engaging a text, in construing and "reading" it *as* a text, that is, *entextualizing* it. This is because text-internal "positions" are projections out of text-external *events*, a reversal of the assumption in some film theory that methodologically (if not theoretically) assumes a sui generis, bound text that can then be "read" in an act that disavows the empirical situatedness of the act of reading *as itself an act of entextualization* (see note 19 in this chapter).

My argument, however, is not the theoretical claim that there is no text independent of "reception" or that texts don't have their own rhetorics, strategies, and even autonomy in any particular event of their engagement. They do. Rather, mine is an epistemological and methodological – and thus ultimately theoretical – claim that *what* a text *is* – and thus what its possible "internal" spectatorship positions are – cannot be determined independently of investigating *events* of viewership, even ones that *imagine* possible viewers as simply "in" the text; it is the claim that one cannot study a text without studying its "context" (to put it too crudely; Nakassis 2020), which is to say, without studying those events of *entextualization* that would constitute a text *as such*: as both context dependent and independent, as engaging us even as, in that moment, it is constituted in part by, and in part independently of, us.

I see this position as a realization of the implications of Casetti's (1998[1986]) argument with Metz (2016[1991]), even if such implications are not themselves fully followed through by Casetti. Yet despite any differences from Metz and Casetti, I believe that both authors' interests in enunciation intersect with linguistic anthropology's explorations of the process of entextualization. As Metz put it in a 1990 interview (Blüher and Tröhler 2018:465; see also Metz 2016[1991]:163): "Enunciation refers to the activity, the abstract [though ultimately thoroughly concrete, we would add] process, that creates the perceivable text." But where Metz's theorization of enunciation falls short for us is (1) it too quickly reduces *linguistic* enunciation to deixis, and deixis to personal pronouns (even as he, in other moments, critiques this reduction in the study of cinema; Metz 2016[1991]:171), and thus to the issue of exchangeability; based on that reduction, it creates a too-strong distinction of linguistic and cinematic enunciation (namely, that the latter turns on reflexivity and metadiscourse, and the former on deixis), failing to see that each (metadiscourse and deixis) implies the other as a species of indexicality (though, see Metz 2016[1991]:172); and (2) it wrongly cordons off enunciation as a purely text-internal phenomenon (Boillat 2018), which is to say, it narrowly constrains the borders of film textuality to what appears on the screen (see also Metz 2016[1986]:§70–1) rather than including semiotic processes that happen on set, in post-production, in the theatre, and beyond (see, for example, Metz's similarly narrow reduction of "semiology" to the "internal structure of the film" [Blüher and Tröhler 2018:462]; compare Metz 2016[1991]:156, where he tellingly, and to my mind damningly, writes [my emphasis]: "In every discursive system the subject and the object are absent, and they reappear *only if the social context of the system is taken into account*," only to then reiterate the necessity of differentiating enunciation from communication and thus, in effect, allowing the analyst to *not* take social context into account). All this is wrong, it seems to me, because (1) there *is* exchange and communication through cinema, though it doesn't happen with the same temporality, scale, or through the same media as face-to-face conversation (compare Mitry 1997[1963]:14; see Nakassis 2016a:219); and (2) because so-called face-to-face conversation is not as simple as Metz seems to assume (indeed, when it comes to discourse, Metz ascribes to an implicit metaphysics of presence), as shown by (a) Goffman's (1974, 1979) deconstructions of the speaker and hearer in interactional ritual (which Casetti, from his citations to Goffman – all in endnotes [Casetti 1998[1986]:153n53, 154n59] – appreciates, even if he doesn't fully work them through his analysis) and (b) the explorations of reflexivity and metapragmatics in real-time discourse by linguistic anthropologists (compare Metz 2016[1991]:172–3). (Recall that Benveniste's comments on enunciation are derived, in part, in dedication to Jakobson's work on shifters; but Jakobson's own turn to shifters and deixis was, in part, inspired from his reading of Peirce on indexicality. The import, then, of deixis has to lie in the larger category of indexicality, which accounts of cinematic enunciation fail to fully engage. Similarly, recall that the focus on reflexivity in deixis, face-to-face interaction, and entextualization – that is, metapragmatics – in linguistic anthropology similarly derives from Jakobson's [1987(1935), 1960(1958)] writings on the aesthetic/poetic function, the latter of which is not explicitly taken up in cinematic enunciation theory as such, even if it appears in other aspects of Metz's work [for example, Metz 1974(1971):166, 177].)

To truly realize investigations into enunciation, then, requires us to break down the distinctions of inside/outside the text and to radically rethink, thus, the notions of text, communication, and semiosis (which is the very import, in my opinion, of Jakobson's and Benveniste's turn to deixis as a deconstruction of post-Enlightenment semiotic ideologies of word/world, of which inside/outside of the text is a variant). And this rethinking, in turn, requires us to bring an empirical, ethnographic account of indexicality and metapragmatics *into* the theory of film and cinema. This theoretical reorientation, thus, implies/requires a methodological shift. And it is on this point in particular that my discussion diverges from Metz's position, as noted above and as is apparent from Metz's (2016[1986]; Buckland and Fairfax 2017:200–1) critiques of the notion of pragmatics and communication in the work on film in the 1970s and 1980s (a critique I don't completely disagree with) and the possibilities of an empiricist, Peircean film semiotics (a semiotic approach that I do completely agree with). I thank Martin Lefebvre for bringing Metz 2016[1986] to my attention.

22 A further reason that I insist on the phrase *linguistic anthropology of cinema* is that it forces linguistic anthropology to interrogate the ways in which, despite its (aspirationally) pan-semiotic horizons, its productively deconstructive engagements with "language," while opening up a space to think semiosis beyond the linguistic, have also – through that very critique – blinkered and thus limited the field by implicitly yoking it to "language" as its (non)object of analysis (on this point, see also Hull 2012). Linguistic anthropology's in-principle openness to an account of images coupled with its (to date) in-practice lack of any systematic account of images is, I would contend, one indication of such a limit (Barker and Nakassis 2020).

References

Interviews

Balaji Sakthivel (director). 2008. Interview with the author, 10 December 2008, Chennai, India.

– 2018a. Interview with the author (by phone), 30 September 2018, India.

– 2018b. Interview with the author, 16 October 2018, Chennai, India.

Balu Mahendra (director, cinematographer). 2008. Interview with the author, 15 September 2008, Chennai, India.

Chitralaya Gopu (dialogue writer, director). 2009. Interview with the author, 30 January 2009, Chennai, India.

C.S. Amudhan (director). 2010. Interview with the author, 30 June 2010, Chennai, India.

– 2014. Interview with the author, 3 July 2014, Chennai, India.

C.V. Rajendran (director). 2009. Interview with the author, 17 January 2009, Chennai, India.

"Film News" Anandan (film historian, public relations officer). 2008. Interview with the author, 3 November 2008, Chennai, India.

Gangai Amaran (director). 2008. Interview with the author, 25 October 2008, Chennai, India.

Kalyan Kumar (dance choreographer). 2011. Interview with the author, 22 August 2011, Chennai, India.

Kamath, Sudhish (journalist, television host, filmmaker). 2014. Interview with the author (by phone), 27 July 2014, India.

K. Balachander (director, producer). 2005. Interview with the author, 28 June 2005, Chennai, India.

K. Chandru (screenwriter, assistant director). 2010. Interview with the author, 13 July 2010, Chennai, India.

K.S. Ravikumar (director). 2018. Interview with the author, 15 October 2018, Chennai, India.

Manobala (director, producer, actor). 2010. Interview with the author, 16 July 2010, Chennai, India.
Mysskin (director). 2008. Interview with the author, 24 November 2008, Chennai, India.
Pa. Ranjith (director, producer). 2018a. Kaala Movie Review with Kaala Team – Pa Ranjith | Santhosh Narayanan | Easwari Rao … Interview on *Radio City India* (YouTube channel), 11 June 2018. https://www.youtube.com/watch?v=RMQrsqCElUY.
– 2018b. Pa Ranjith Exclusive on Casteism, Dalits, Cinema and Politics & #MeToo Movement | #ConclaveSouth18. Interview at *India Today Conclave* (YouTube channel), 22 December 2018. https://www.youtube.com/watch?v=qcqMw5IlPG4.
Rajiv Menon (cinematographer, director). 2009. Interview with the author, 10 March 2009, Chennai, India.
Rambala (comedy writer). 2011a. Interview with Pagal Kanavu blog, 8 February 2011. http://englishtamil.blogspot.com/2011/02/day-dream-making-mockery-with-lollu.html.
– 2011b. Interview with the author, 7 September 2011, Chennai, India.
S.A. Chandrasekhar (director, producer). 2010. Interview with the author, 14 July 2010, Chennai, India.
Sakti Saravanan (cinematographer). 2016. Interview with the author, 1 September 2016, Chennai, India.
Sasi (director). 2009. Interview with the author, 6 January 2009, Chennai, India.
Sasikumar (director, producer, actor). 2008. Interview with the author, 25 September 2008, Chennai, India.
– 2014. "The Locality Is the Real Hero": An Interview with S. Sasikumar. Interview by Rajan Kurai Krishnan. In *Subramaniyapuram: The Tamil Film in English Translation*. Ed. A. Pandian. Chennai: Blaft Publications, pp. 243–54.
Selvaraghavan (director). 2004a. "7-G Rainbow Colony is My Story." Interview by Shoba Warrier. *Rediff.com*, 15 October 2004. https://www.rediff.com/movies/report/selv/20041015.htm.
– 2004b. Young Love. Interview by Vasanthi Sankaranarayanan. *Cinema in India*, April–June 2004, pp. 35–6.
– 2005. Interview with the author, 1 February 2005, Chennai, India.
Shakeela (actress). 2013. *Ṣakīlā Akkā Cinimā Turaiyin Cērntatu Eppaṭi?* (How Did Shakeela Sister Enter the Cinema Field?) Shakeela – A Brief Biography. Interview with Dalit Camera, 15 November 2013. https://www.youtube.com/watch?v=DAtoUT6Ij-A.
Shiva (actor). 2014. Interview with the author, 7 July 2014, Chennai, India.
Simran Bagga (actress). 2011. Interview with the author, 13 September 2011, Chennai, India.

Sriman Reddy (actor). 2008. Interview with the author, 24 September 2008, Chennai, India.
S. Sashikanth (producer). 2011. Interview with the author, 24 August 2011, Chennai, India.
"Stunt" Silva (stunt choreographer). 2016. Interview with the author, 28 July 2016, Chennai, India.
Vaibhav Reddy (actor). 2016. Interview with the author, 30 July 2016, Chennai, India.
Venkat Prabhu (director). 2010. Interview with the author, 13 July 2010, Chennai, India.
– 2016. Interview with the author, 1 August 2016, Chennai, India.

References

Agha, Asif. 2005. Introduction: Semiosis across Encounters. *Journal of Linguistic Anthropology* 15(1):1–5. https://doi.org/10.1525/jlin.2005.15.1.1.
– 2007a. *Language and Social Relations*. Cambridge: Cambridge University Press.
– 2007b. The Object Called "Language" and the Subject of Linguistics. *Journal of English Linguistics* 35(3):217–35. https://doi.org/10.1177/0075424207304240.
– 2011. Commodity Registers. *Journal of Linguistic Anthropology* 21(1):22–53. https://doi.org/10.1111/j.1548-1395.2011.01081.x.
– 2017. Money Talk and Conduct from Cowries to Bitcoin. *Signs and Society* 5(2):293–355. https://doi.org/10.1086/693775.
Aiyappan, Ashameera. 2018. Happy Birthday Vijay: From Ilayathalapathy Vijay to Thalapathy Joseph Vijay. *The Indian Express*, 22 June 2018. https://indianexpress.com/article/entertainment/tamil/happy-birthday-vijay-from-ilayathalapathy-vijay-to-thalapathy-joseph-vijay-5228095/.
Alloa, Emmanuel. 2011. Intensive, Not Extensive. In J. Elkins and Maja Naef, eds., *What Is an Image?* University Park: Pennsylvania State University Press, pp. 148–51.
Anand, S. 2005. Politics, Tamil Cinema Eshtyle. *Outlook*, 30 May 2005. https://web.archive.org/web/20101123153129/http://www.outlookindia.com/article.aspx?227523.
Ananda Vikadan. 2005a. Kātal: *Cinimā Vimarcanam* [*Kaadhal*: Film Review]. *Ananda Vikadan*, 27 February 2005, pp. 92–5.
– 2005b. Kātal … *Kalaṅkaṭitta Rayil Rāttiri* [*Kaadhal* … The Night on the Train That Disturbed Me]. *Ananda Vikadan*, 9 January 2005, pp. 34–40.
Andrew, Dudley. 1998. Preface to the English Edition. In Francesco Casetti, *Inside the Gaze: The Fiction Film and Its Spectator*. Trans. N. Andrew with C. O'Brien. Bloomington: Indiana University Press, pp. vii–x.

–, ed. 2011. *Opening Bazin: Postwar Film Theory and Its Afterlife*. New York: Oxford University Press.
Annamalai, E. 2011. *Social Dimensions of Modern Tamil*. Chennai: Cre-A.
Armstrong, Robert Plant. 1971. *The Affecting Presence: An Essay in Humanistic Anthropology*. Urbana: University of Illinois Press.
– 1981. *The Powers of Presence: Consciousness, Myth, and Affecting Presence*. Philadelphia: University of Pennsylvania Press.
Aumont, Jacques, Alain Bergala, Michel Marie, and Marc Vernet. 1992[1983]. *Aesthetics of Film*. Trans. and revised by R. Neupert. Austin: University of Texas Press.
Austin, J.L. 1962. *How to Do Things with Words*. Oxford: Clarendon.
Babb, Lawrence. 1981. Glancing: Visual Interaction in Hinduism. *Journal of Anthropological Research* 37(4):387–401. https://doi.org/10.1086/jar.37.4.3629835.
Bakewell, Liza. 1998. Image Acts. *American Anthropologist* 100(1):22–32. https://doi.org/10.1525/aa.1998.100.1.22.
Bakhtin, Mikhail. 1981. *The Dialogic Imagination: Four Essays*. Ed. M. Holquist. Trans. C. Emmerson and M. Holquist. Austin: University of Texas Press.
– 1984[1963]. *Problems of Dostoevsky's Poetics*. Ed. and Trans. C. Emmerson. Minneapolis: University of Minnesota Press.
– 1984[1965]. *Rabelais and His World*. Trans. H. Iswolsky. Bloomington: Indiana University Press.
Ball, Christopher. 2014. On Dicentization. *Journal of Linguistic Anthropology* 24(2):151–73. https://doi.org/10.1111/jola.12046.
– 2017. Realisms and Indexicalities of Photographic Propositions. *Signs and Society* 5(S1):S154–77. https://doi.org/10.1086/690032.
Ball, Christopher, Meghanne Barker, Elizabeth Edwards, Tomáš Kolich, W.J.T. Mitchell, Daniel Morgan, and Constantine V. Nakassis. 2020. Opening Up the Indexicality of the Image, Again: A Virtual Roundtable. In M. Barker and C.V. Nakassis, eds. *Images* (Special Issue). *Semiotic Review* 9. https://www.semioticreview.com/ojs/index.php/sr/article/view/62.
Ball, Christopher, and Nicholas Harkness, eds. 2015. *Kinship Chronotopes* (Special Collection). *Anthropological Quarterly* 88(2). https://aq.gwu.edu/aq-spring-2015-toc.html.
Barker, Meghanne, and Constantine V. Nakassis, eds. 2020. *Images* (Special Issue). *Semiotic Review* 9. https://www.semioticreview.com/ojs/index.php/sr/issue/view/9.
Barnouw, Erik, and S. Krishnaswamy. 1980. *Indian Film*. 2nd ed. New York: Oxford University Press.
Barthes, Roland. 1981. *Camera Lucida*. New York: Hill and Wang.
– 1986[1968]. The Reality Effect. In *The Rustle of Language*. Trans. R. Howard. New York: Farrar, Straus, Giroux, pp. 141–8.

– 1986[1975]. Leaving the Movie Theater. In *The Rustle of Language*. Trans. R. Howard. New York: Farrar, Straus, Giroux, pp. 345–9.

Baskaran, S. Theodore. 1996. *Eye of the Serpent: An Introduction to Tamil Cinema*. Madras: EastWest Books.

Bate, Bernard. 2009. *Tamil Oratory and the Dravidian Aesthetic*. New York: Columbia University Press.

Bateman, John, and Karl-Heinreich Schmidt. 2012. *Multimodal Film Analysis: How Films Mean*. New York: Routledge.

Baudry, Jean-Louis. 1986[1970]. Ideological Effects of the Basic Cinematographic Apparatus. In P. Rosen, ed., *Narrative, Apparatus, Ideology: A Film Theory Reader*. New York: Columbia University Press, pp. 281–98.

– 1986[1975]. The Apparatus: Metapsychological Approaches to the Impression of Reality in Cinema. In P. Rosen, ed., *Narrative, Apparatus, Ideology: A Film Theory Reader*. New York: Columbia University Press, pp. 299–318.

Baumach, Nico. 2019. *Cinema/Politics/Philosophy*. New York: Columbia University Press.

Bauman, Richard, and Charles Briggs. 1990. Poetics and Performance as Critical Perspectives on Language and Social Life. *Annual Review of Anthropology* 19:59–88. https://doi.org/10.1146/annurev.an.19.100190.000423.

Bazin, André. 1985[1950]. The Stalin Myth in Soviet Cinema. In B. Nichols, ed., *Movies and Methods: An Anthology*. Vol. 2. Berkeley: University of California Press, pp. 29–40.

– 2005[1945]. The Ontology of the Photographic Image. In H. Gray, ed., *What Is Cinema?* Vol. 1. Berkeley: University of California Press, pp. 9–16.

– 2005[1946]. The Myth of Total Cinema. In H. Gray, ed., *What Is Cinema?* Vol. 1. Berkeley: University of California Press, pp. 17–22.

– 2005[1948]. An Aesthetic of Reality: Cinematic Realism and the Italian School of the Liberation. In H. Gray, ed., *What Is Cinema?* Vol. 2. Berkeley: University of California Press, pp. 16–40.

– 2005[1949]. *Bicycle Thief*. In H. Gray, ed., *What Is Cinema?* Vol. 2. Berkeley: University of California Press, pp. 47–60.

– 2005[1951]a. De Sica: Metteur en Scène. In H. Gray, ed., *What Is Cinema?* Vol. 2. Berkeley: University of California Press, pp. 61–78.

– 2005[1951]b. Theater and Cinema – Part Two. In H. Gray, ed., *What Is Cinema?* Vol. 1. Berkeley: University of California Press, pp. 95–124.

– 2005[1952]. In Defense of Mixed Cinema. In H. Gray, ed., *What Is Cinema?* Vol. 1. Berkeley: University of California Press, pp. 53–75.

– 2005[1955]. In Defense of Rossellini. In H. Gray, ed., *What Is Cinema?* Vol. 2. Berkeley: University of California Press, pp. 93–101.

– 2005[1957]. Marginal Notes on *Eroticism in the Cinema*. In H. Gray, ed., *What Is Cinema?* Vol. 2. Berkeley: University of California Press, pp. 169–75.
– 2005[1958]. The Evolution of the Language of Cinema. In H. Gray, ed., *What Is Cinema?* Vol. 1. Berkeley: University of California Press, pp. 23–40.
BBC News. 2004. "Obscene" Tamil Film Angers Women. *BBC News*, 29 July 2004. http://news.bbc.co.uk/2/hi/south_asia/3935795.stm.
Behindwoods. n.d. Ten Smooches of Tamil Cinema. *Behindwoods.com* (website). http://www.behindwoods.com/tamil-movies-slide-shows/movie-1/tamil-cinema-kiss/tamil-movie-kiss-new.html.
– 2008. Lollu Sabha Is Threatened. *Behindwoods.com* (website), 11 July 2008. http://www.behindwoods.com/tamil-movie-news-1/july-08-02/lollu-sabha-11-07-08.html.
BehindwoodsTV. 2018. Thalapathy Vijay's Phone Call after Tamil Padam | C S Amudhan Reveals! | Tamizh Padam 2. *BehindwoodsTV* (YouTube channel), 21 April 2018. https://www.youtube.com/watch?v=8gcwYpwb8QA.
Bellour, Raymond. 2000[1979]. *Analysis of Film*. Ed. C. Penley. Bloomington: Indiana University Press.
Belting, Hans. 1994[1990]. *Likeness and Presence: A History of the Image before the Era of Art*. Trans. E. Jephcott. Chicago: University of Chicago Press.
Benjamin, Walter. 1968[1935]. The Work of Art in the Age of Mechanical Reproduction. In H. Arendt, ed., *Illuminations: Essays and Reflections*. Trans. H. Zohn. New York: Schocken Books, pp. 217–51.
Benveniste, Émile. 1971. *Problems in General Linguistics*. Coral Gables, FL: University of Miami Press.
Bhrugubanda, Uma Maheswari. 2018. *Deities and Devotees: Cinema, Religion, and Politics in South India*. New Delhi: Oxford University Press.
Blüher, Dominique, and Margit Tröhler. 2018. "I Never Expected Semiology to Thrill the Masses" (Interview with Christian Metz). In M. Tröhler and G. Kirsten, eds., *Christian Metz and the Codes of Cinema*. Amsterdam: University of Amsterdam Press, pp. 459–72.
Boillat, Alain. 2018. "'Theorize,' He Says …" Christian Metz and the Question of Enunciation: A Theory in (Speech) Acts. In M. Tröhler and G. Kirsten, eds., *Christian Metz and the Codes of Cinema*. Amsterdam: University of Amsterdam Press, pp. 369–90.
Bordwell, David. 1985. *Narration in the Fiction Film*. New York: Routledge.
– 2009[1979]. The Art Cinema as a Mode of Film Practice. In L. Braudy and M. Cohen, eds., *Film Theory and Criticism*. 7th ed. New York: Oxford University Press, pp. 649–57.
Boyer, Dominic, and Alexei Yurchak. 2010. American Stiob: Or, What Late-Socialist Aesthetics of Parody Reveal about Contemporary Political Culture in the West. *Cultural Anthropology* 25(2):179–221. https://doi.org/10.1111/j.1548-1360.2010.01056.x.

Branigan, Edward. 1984. *Point of View in the Cinema: A Theory of Narration and Subjectivity in Classical Film*. Berlin: Mouton Publishers.

– 2006. *Projecting a Camera: Language-Games in Film Theory*. New York: Routledge.

Bredekamp, Horst. 2018[2010]. *Image Acts: A Systematic Approach to Visual Agency*. Ed. and Trans. E. Clegg. Berlin: De Gruyter.

Briggs, Charles, and Richard Bauman. 1992. Genre, Intertextuality, and Social Power. *Journal of Linguistic Anthropology* 2(2):131–72. https://doi.org/10.1093/OBO/9780199766567-0171.

– 2003. *Voices of Modernity: Language Ideologies and the Politics of Inequality*. Cambridge: Cambridge University Press.

Browne, Nick. 1999[1975]. The Spectator-in-the-Text: The Rhetoric of *Stagecoach*. In L. Braudy and M. Cohen, eds., *Film Theory and Criticism*. 5th ed. New York: Oxford University Press, pp. 148–64.

Bucholtz, Mary. 2011. Race and the Re-embodied Voice in Hollywood Film. *Language & Communication* 31:255–65. https://doi.org/10.1016/j.langcom.2011.02.004.

Bucholtz, Mary, and Kira Hall. 2005. Identity and Interaction: A Sociocultural Linguistic Approach. *Discourse Studies* 7(4–5):585–614. https://doi.org/10.1177/1461445605054407.

Buckland, Warren, and Daniel Fairfax, eds. 2017. *Conversations with Christian Metz*. Amsterdam: Amsterdam University Press.

Burket, Walter. 1985. *Greek Religion*. Malden, MA: Blackwell Publishing.

Butler, Judith. 1993. *Bodies that Matter: On the Discursive Limits of "Sex."* New York: Routledge.

Cadena, Marisol de la. 2010. Indigenous Cosmopolitics in the Andes: Conceptual Reflections beyond "Politics." *Cultural Anthropology* 25(2): 334–70. https://doi.org/10.1111/j.1548-1360.2010.01061.x.

Canby, Vincent. 1987. Sex Can Spoil the Scene. *New York Times*, 27 June 1987, Section 2, p. 17.

Carroll, Noël. 1988. *Philosophical Problems of Classical Film Theory*. Princeton, NJ: Princeton University Press.

– 1996. *Theorizing the Moving Image*. Cambridge: Cambridge University Press.

Casetti, Francesco. 1998[1986]. *Inside the Gaze: The Fiction Film and Its Spectator*. Trans. N. Andrew with C. O'Brien. Bloomington: Indiana University Press.

– 2009. Filmic Experience, Part 2. *Screen* 50(1):56–66. https://doi.org/10.1093/screen/hjn075.

Caton, Steven. 2021. "The Most Reluctant of Romantic Cities": Dis-location Film Shooting in the Old City of Sana'a. In R. Rossoukh and S. Caton, eds., *Anthropology, Film Industries, Modularity*. Durham, NC: Duke University Press, pp. 129–61.

Cavell, Stanley. 1979. *The World Viewed: Reflections on the Ontology of Film*. Cambridge, MA: Harvard University Press.

Chakrabarty, Dipesh. 2001. Clothing the Political Man: A Reading of the Use of Khadi/White in Indian Public Life. *Postcolonial Studies* 4(1):27–38. https://doi.org/10.1080/13688790120046852.

Chakravarthy, Sumitha. 1993. *National Identity in Indian Popular Cinema, 1947–1987*. Austin: University of Texas Press.

Chakravarthy, Venkatesh. 2002. Locating the Star as Sinthome – Rajnikant – A Case Study. In U. Khattab and F. Ibrahim, eds., *Communication and Media Studies in ASEAN*. Bangi, Malaysia: School of Media and Communication Studies, pp. 223–41.

– 2018. *Cuvaṭukaḷ* [*Traces*]. Chennai: Pragnai.

Chatterjee, Partha. 1993. *The Nation and Its Fragments: Colonial and Postcolonial Histories*. Princeton, NJ: Princeton University Press.

Chatterjee, Saibal. 2003. Overview: Hindi Cinema through the Decades. In *Encyclopaedia of Hindi Cinema*. New Delhi: Encyclopedia Brittanica (India), pp. 3–23.

Chinniah, Sathiavathi. 2008. The Tamil Film Heroine: From a Passive Subject to a Pleasurable Object. In S. Velayutham, ed., *Tamil Cinema: The Cultural Politics of India's Other Film Industry*. New York: Routledge, pp. 29–43.

Chitra B. 2015. Rise & Fall of Powerstar. *Deccan Herald*, 15 September 2013. https://www.deccanherald.com/content/357075/rise-fall-powerstar.html.

Chowdhury, Purna. 2010. Bollywood Babes: Body and Female Desire in the Bombay Films since the Nineties and *Darr*, *Mohra*, and *Aitraaz*: A Tropic Discourse. In R.B. Mehta and R.V. Pandharipande, eds., *Bollywood and Globalization: Indian Popular Cinema, Nation, and Diaspora*. London: Anthem Press, pp. 51–73.

Chumley, Lily. 2017. Qualia and Ontology: Language, Semiotics, and Materiality; an Introduction. *Signs and Society* 5(S1):S1–20. https://doi.org/10.1086/690190.

Cody, Francis. 2015. Print Capitalism and Crowd Violence beyond Liberal Frameworks. *Comparative Studies of South Asia, Africa, and the Middle East* 35(1):50–65. https://doi.org/10.1215/1089201X-2876092.

– 2018. Media Involution. Paper presented at the Chicago Tamil Forum – Mass Publicity and Mediation in Tamilagam (24–26 May 2018), University of Chicago.

– 2019. Millennial Turbulence: The Networking of Tamil Media Politics. *Television and New Media Studies* 21(4):392–406. https://doi.org/10.1177/1527476419869128.

Coleridge, Samuel Taylor. 1817. *Biographia Literaria*. Vols. 1–2. London: Rest Fenner.

Colin, Michel. 1995. Film Semiology as Cognitive Science. In W. Buckland, ed., *The Film Spectator: From Sign to Mind*. Amsterdam: Amsterdam University Press, pp. 87–112.

Comolli, Jean-Louis. 1986[1971]. Technique and Ideology: Camera, Perspective, Depth of Field (Parts 3 and 4). In P. Rosen, ed., *Narrative, Apparatus, Ideology: A Film Theory Reader*. New York: Columbia University Press, pp. 421–43.

Cooper, Timothy. 2018. Cinema *Itself*: Cinephobia, Filmic Anxieties, and Ontologies of the Moving Image in Pakistan. *Visual Anthropology* 31(3): 253–67. https://doi.org/10.1080/08949468.2018.1445394.

Currie, Gregory. 1996. Film, Reality, and Illusion. In D. Bordwell and N. Carroll, eds., *Post-Theory: Reconstructing Film Studies*. Madison: University of Wisconsin Press, pp. 325–46.

Dagrada, Elena. 2014. *Between the Eye and the World: The Emergence of the Point-of-View Shot*. Bruxelles: P.I.E. Peter Lang.

Damodaran, Karthikeyan, and Hugo Gorringe. 2017. Madurai Formula Films: Caste Pride and Politics in Tamil Cinema. *South Asia Multidisciplinary Academic Journal* (online: free standing article). https://doi.org/10.4000/samaj.4359.

– 2021. Contested Narratives: Filmic Representations of North Chennai in Contemporary Tamil Cinema. In S. Velayutham and V. Devadas, eds., *Tamil Cinema in the Twenty-First Century: Caste, Gender, and Technology*. London: Routledge, pp. 19–35.

Davis, Richard. 1999. *Lives of Indian Images*. Princeton, NJ: Princeton University Press.

Dean, Melanie. 2013. From "Evil Eye" Anxiety to the Desirability of Envy: Status, Consumption and the Politics of Visibility in Urban South India. *Contributions to Indian Sociology* 47(2):185–216. https://doi.org/10.1177/0069966713482999.

de Lauretis, Teresa. 1984. *Alice Doesn't: Feminism, Semiotics, Cinema*. Bloomington: Indiana University Press.

Deleuze, Gilles. 1986[1983]. *Cinema 1: The Movement-Image*. Trans. H. Tomlinson and B. Habberjam. Minneapolis: University of Minnesota Press.

– 1989[1985]. *Cinema 2: The Time-Image*. Trans. H. Tomlinson and R. Galeta. Minneapolis: University of Minnesota Press.

Dent, Alexander. 2009. *River of Tears: Country Music, Memory, and Modernity in Brazil*. Durham, NC: Duke University Press.

Derrida, Jacques. 1988. *Limited Inc*. Ed. G. Graff. Trans. J. Mehlman and S. Weber. Evanston, IL: Northwestern University Press.

Devadas, Vijay, and Selvaraj Velayutham. 2021. Tamil Platform Cinema. In S. Velayutham and V. Devadas, eds., *Tamil Cinema in the Twenty-First Century: Caste, Gender, and Technology*. London: Routledge, pp. 194–208.

Dhananjayan, G. 2011. *The Best of Tamil Cinema: 1931 to 2010*. Vols. 1–2. Chennai: Galatta Media.

Dhiwaharan. 2018. C.S. Amudhan Bashes People Who Accused That He Is Belong To DMK!! Says Had A Scene That Trolled "SEYAL"!! *Chennai Memes* (website), 16 July 2018. http://www.chennaimemes.in/c-s-amudhan-bashes-people-who-accused-that-he-is-belong-to-dmk-says-had-a-scene-that-trolled-seyal/.

Dickey, Sara. 1993a. *Cinema and the Urban Poor in South India*. New York: Cambridge University Press.

– 1993b. The Politics of Adulation: Cinema and the Production of Politicians in South India. *The Journal of Asian Studies* 52(2):340–72. https://doi.org/10.2307/2059651.

– 2001. Opposing Faces: Film Star Fan Clubs and the Construction of Class Identities in South India. In R. Dwyer and C. Pinney, eds., *Pleasure and the Nation: The History, Politics and Consumption of Popular Culture in India*. New Delhi: Oxford University Press, pp. 212–46.

– 2009. Fantasy, Realism, and Other Mixed Delights: What Have Film Analysts Seen in Popular Indian Cinema? *Projections* 13(2):1–19. https://doi.org/10.3167/proj.2009.030202.

– 2013. Apprehensions: On Gaining Recognition as Middle Class in Madurai. *Contributions to Indian Sociology* 47(2):217–43. https://doi.org/10.1177/0069966713482963.

Dinamalar. 2018. *Ēmāntatu Rajiniyā, Rañcittā?* Kālā: *Ōr Alacal* [Who Was Disappointed/Cheated, Rajini or Ranjith? *Kala*: An Analysis]. *Dinamalar* (YouTube channel), 9 June 2018. https://www.youtube.com/watch?v=f8JIzJx4bIk.

Dinathanti. 2010. *Alṭimēṭ Sṭār Paṭṭattai Ini Payanpaṭutta Māṭṭēn – Naṭikar Ajīt Kumār Pēṭṭi* [I Won't Use "Ultimate Star" Title in My Films Hereafter – Actor Ajith Kumar Interview]. *Dinathanti*, 9 January 2010. http://www.ajithfans.com/media/media-news/2010/01/09/i-wont-use-ultimate-star-title-in-my-films-here-after-ajithkumar/.

Divya, A. 2021. "He Made Me Fall at the Feet of a Woman": Masculine Anxieties and Dysfunctional Romance in Tamil Cult Film *Subramaniyapuram* (2008). *Rupkatha Journal on Interdisciplinary Studies in Humanities* 13(2):1–11. https://doi.org/10.21659/rupkatha.v13n2.38.

Diwakar, Pranathi. 2022. *Resounding Caste: Practices of Distinction, Urban Segregation, and Musical Politics in Chennai, India*. PhD dissertation, University of Chicago.

Doane, Mary Ann. 1988. Woman's Stake: Filming the Female Body. In C. Penley, ed., *Feminism and Film Theory*. New York: Routledge, pp. 216–28.

– 2002. *The Emergence of Cinematic Time: Modernity, Contingency, the Archive*. Cambridge, MA: Harvard University Press.

Doane, Mary Ann, Patricia Mellencamp, and Linda Williams. 1984. Feminist Film Criticism: An Introduction. In M. Doane, P. Mellencamp, and L. Williams, eds., *Re-Vision: Essays in Feminist Film Criticism*. Los Angeles, CA: American Film Institute, pp. 1–15.

Dungan, Ellis, with Barbara Smik. 2001. *A Guide to Adventure: An Autobiography*. Pittsburgh, PA: Dorrance Publishing Company.

Dyer, Richard. 1998[1979]. *Stars*. London: BFI Publications.

Ebeling, Sascha. 2019. The Many Shakespeares of Rao Bahadur Pammal Campanta Mutaliyar (1873–1964): Shakespeare in Colonial South India and the History of Modern Tamil Drama. Paper presented at the Chicago Tamil Forum – Never Alone: Linguistic Ecologies of Tamil (23–25 May 2019), University of Chicago.

Eck, Diana. 1997. *Darśan: Seeing the Divine Image in India*. New York: Columbia University Press.

Eisenstein, Sergei. 1943. *The Film Sense*. Trans. J. Leyda. London: Faber and Faber.

– 1977[1949]. *Film Form: Essays in Film Theory*. Trans. J. Leyda. New York: Harcourt Brace Jovanovich.

Elkins, James, and Maja Naef, eds. 2011. *What Is an Image?* University Park: Pennsylvania State University Press.

Elsaesser, Thomas, ed. 1990. *Early Cinema: Space. Frame, Narrative*. London: BFI Publications.

Eswaran, Swarnavel. 2021. Post-Millennial Tamil Cinema: Transitional Generation and the Traces of Continuity. In S. Velayutham and V. Devadas, eds., *Tamil Cinema in the Twenty-First Century: Caste, Gender, and Technology*. London: Routledge, pp. 161–78.

Eswaran Pillai, Swarnavel. 2012. 1970s Tamil Cinema and the Post-Classical Turn. *South Asian Popular Culture* 10(1):77–89. https://doi.org/10.1080/14746689.2012.655109.

– 2015. *Madras Studios: Narrative, Genre, and Ideology in Tamil Cinema*. London: Sage Publications.

Evreinov, Nicolas. 1927. *The Theater in Life*. Trans. A. Nazaroff. New York: Brentano.

Evreinov, Nikolai. 1973. *Life as Theater: Five Modern Plays*. Trans. C. Collins. Ann Arbor, MI: Ardis.

Farook, Farhana. 2012. "The Gaalis Were My Awards" – Bindu. *Filmfare.com* (website), 9 November 2012. http://www.filmfare.com/interviews/the-gaalis-were-my-awards=bindu-1645.html.

Feld, Steven, Meghanne Barker, and Constantine V. Nakassis. 2020. Spectral Signage: A Conversation with Steven Feld. In M. Barker and C.V. Nakassis, eds. *Images* (Special Issue). *Semiotic Review* 9. https://www.semioticreview.com/ojs/index.php/sr/article/view/63.

Feld, Steven, and Carol Williams. 1975. Toward a Researchable Film Language. *Studies in Visual Communication* 2(1):25–32. https://repository.upenn.edu/svc/vol2/iss1/3/.

Fleming, Luke. 2011. Name Taboos and Rigid Performativity. *Anthropological Quarterly* 84(1):141–64. https://doi.org/10.1353/anq.2011.0010.

– 2014. Whorfian Pragmatics Revisited: Language Anti-structures and Performativist Ideologies of Language. SALSA (Symposium about Language and Society – Austin) XXII Proceedings (11–12 April 2014). *Texas Linguistics Forum* 57:55–66. http://salsa.ling.utexas.edu/proceedings/2014/index.html.

– 2018. Undecontextualizable: Performativity and the Conditions of Possibility of Linguistic Symbolism. *Signs and Society* 6(3):558–606. https://doi.org/10.1086/699599.

– 2020. The Elementary Structures of Kinship Interaction: Corporeal Communication in Joking-avoidance Relationships. SALSA XXVII Proceedings. *Texas Linguistics Forum* (forthcoming). http://salsa.ling.utexas.edu/proceedings/.

Fleming, Luke, and Michael Lempert. 2014. Poetics and Performativity. In N.J. Enfield, P. Kockelman, and J. Sidnell, eds., *The Cambridge Handbook of Linguistic Anthropology*. Cambridge: Cambridge University Press, pp. 469–95.

Freedberg, David. 1989. *The Power of Images: Studies in the History and Theory of Response*. Chicago: University of Chicago Press.

Gal, Susan. 2002. A Semiotics of the Public/Private Distinction. *differences* 13(1):77–95. https://doi.org/10.1215/10407391-13-1-77.

– 2005. Language Ideologies Compared: Metaphors of Public/Private. *Journal of Linguistic Anthropology* 15(1):23–37. https://doi.org/10.1525/jlin.2005.15.1.23.

– 2018. Registers in Circulation: The Social Organization of Interdiscursivity. *Signs and Society* 6(1):1–24. https://doi.org/10.1086/694551.

Gal, Susan, and Judith Irvine. 2019. *Signs of Difference: Language and Ideology in Social Life*. Cambridge: Cambridge University Press.

Ganti, Tejaswini. 2004. *Bollywood: A Guidebook to Popular Hindi Cinema*. New York: Routledge.

– 2009. The Limits of Decency and the Decency of Limits: Censorship and the Bombay Film Industry. In R. Kaur and W. Mazzarella, eds., *Censorship in South Asia: Cultural Regulation from Sedition to Seduction*. Bloomington: Indiana University Press, pp. 87–122.

– 2012. *Producing Bollywood: Inside the Contemporary Hindi Film Industry*. Durham, NC: Duke University Press.

Garoo, Rohit. 2016. Prabhu Deva Marriage: The Affair That Ended It All. *The Bridal Box* (website), 1 August 2016. https://www.thebridalbox.com/articles/prabhu-deva-marriage_0051458/.

Gaudreault, André. 2009[1999]. *From Plato to Lumière: Narration and Monstration in Literature and Cinema*. Toronto: University of Toronto Press.

Gell, Alfred. 1998. *Art and Agency: An Anthropological Theory*. Oxford: Oxford University Press.

Genette, Gerard. 1997[1982]. *Palimpsests: Literature in the Second Degree*. Trans. C. Newmand and C. Dubinsky. Lincoln: University of Nebraska Press.

Gerritsen, Roos. 2012. *Fandom on Display: Intimate Visualities and the Politics of Spectacle*. PhD dissertation, Leiden University.

– 2019. *Intimate Visualities and the Politics of Fandom in India*. Amsterdam: Amsterdam University Press.

– 2021. Will the Real Kollywood Fan Please Stand Up? Tamil Film Fandom in the New Millennium. In S. Velayutham and V. Devadas, eds., *Tamil Cinema in the Twenty-First Century: Caste, Gender, and Technology*. London: Routledge, pp. 147–60.

Gershon, Ilana. 2010. Media Ideologies: An Introduction. *Journal of Linguistic Anthropology* 20(2):283–93. https://doi.org/10.1111/j.1548-1395.2010.01070.x.

Gershon, Ilana, and Joshua Malitsky. 2011. Documentary Studies and Linguistic Anthropology. *Culture, Theory and Critique* 52(1):45–63. https://doi.org/10.1080/14735784.2011.621667.

Gledhill, Christine. 1999[1988]. Pleasurable Negotiations. In S. Thornham, ed., *Feminist Film Theory: A Reader*. Edinburgh: Edinburgh University Press, pp. 166–79.

Goffman, Erving. 1974. *Frame Analysis: An Essay on the Organization of Experience*. Cambridge, MA: Harvard University Press.

– 1979. Footing. *Semiotica* 25(1–2):1–30. https://doi.org/10.1515/semi.1979.25.1-2.1.

Goodman, Nelson. 1976. *Languages of Art*. Indianapolis, IN: Hackett Publishing Company.

Gopal, Sangita. 2011. Sealed with a Kiss: Conjugality and Hindi Film Form. *Feminist Studies* 37(1):154–80. https://doi.org/10.1353/fem.2011.0021.

Gopalan, Lalitha. 2002. *Cinema of Interruptions: Action Genres in Contemporary Indian Cinema*. London: BFI Publishing.

– 2008. Film Culture in Chennai. *Film Quarterly* 62(1):40–5. https://doi.org/10.1525/fq.2008.62.1.40.

– 2021. *Cinemas Dark and Slow in Digital India*. Cham, Switzerland: Palgrave MacMillan.

Gopalan, Ravindran. 2011. Singing Bodies and "Movement" Images in a 1937 Tamil Film: A Deleuzian Perspective. *Journal of Creative Communications* 6(1–2):15–33. https://doi.org/10.1177/0973258613499107.

Gopinath, Arun. n.d.-a. "Formulaic Realism" – The New Tamil Cinema. *Behindwoods.com* (website). http://www.behindwoods.com/features/column/index-43.html.

– n.d.-b. Thamizh Padam's Only Cliché! *Behindwoods.com* (website). http://www.behindwoods.com/features/column/index-27.html.

Govindan, Padma, and Bisakha Dutta. 2008. "From Villain to Traditional Housewife!" The Politics of Globalization and Women's Sexuality in the

"New" Indian Media. In A. P. Kavoori and A. Punathambekar, eds., *Global Bollywood*. New York: NYU Press, pp. 180–202.

Gross, Larry. 1981. Introduction: Sol Worth and the Study of Visual Communication. In Sol Worth, *Studying Visual Communication*. Ed. L. Gross. Philadelphia: University of Pennsylvania Press, pp. 1–35.

Gulte.com. 2018. Rangasthalam Lip Lock: It's Not True a Kiss. *Gulte.com* (website), 10 April 2018. https://archive.gulte.com/movienews/65747/Rangasthalam-Lip-Lock-Its-Not-True-A-Kiss.

Gunning, Tom. 1986. The Cinema of Attractions: Early Cinema, Its Spectator and the Avant-Garde. *Wide Angle* 8(3–4):63–70.

– 1989. An Aesthetic of Astonishment: Early Film and the (In)credulous Spectator. *Art and Text* 34(1):31–45.

– 1991. *D.W. Griffith and the Origin of American Narrative Film*. Urbana: University of Illinois Press.

– 2008. What's the Point of an Index? Or Faking Photographs. In K. Beckman and J. Ma, eds., *Still/Moving: Between Cinema and Photography*. Durham, NC: Duke University Press, pp. 23–40.

Hansen, Miriam. 1991. *Babel and Babylon: Spectatorship in American Silent Film*. Cambridge, MA: Harvard University Press.

Hardgrave, Jr., Robert. 1973. Politics and the Film in Tamilnadu: The Stars and the DMK. *Asian Survey* 13(3):288–305. https://doi.org/10.2307/2643038.

– 1993[1975]. When Stars Displace the Gods: The Folk Culture of Cinema in Tamil Nadu. In *Essays in the Political Sociology of South India*. New Delhi: Usha, pp. 92–114.

Hardy, Kathryn. 2014. *Becoming Bhojpuri: Producing Cinema and Producing Language in Post-liberalization India*. PhD dissertation, University of Pennsylvania.

Harikrishnan, Charmy. 2018. Can Tamils Reconcile Rajini's Politics with His Art? *The Economic Times*, 10 June 2018. https://economictimes.indiatimes.com/news/politics-and-nation/rajinikanth-vs-kaala-how-do-tamils-reconcile-rajnis-art-with-his-politics/articleshow/64523721.cms.

Harkness, Nicholas. 2021. *Glossolalia and the Problem of Language*. Chicago: University of Chicago Press.

Harries, Dan. 2000. *Film Parody*. London: BFI Publications.

Hassan, Feroz. 2017. Total War, Total History, Total Cinema: André Bazin on the Political Perils of Cinematic Realism. *Screen* 58(1):38–58. https://doi.org/10.1093/screen/hjx013.

Hastings, Adi, and Paul Manning. 2004. Introduction: Acts of Alterity. *Language & Communication* 24(4):291–311. https://doi.org/10.1016/j.langcom.2004.07.001.

Henderson, Brian. 1972. The Structure of Bazin's Thought. *Film Quarterly* 25(4):18–27. https://doi.org/10.2307/1211273.

Herzfeld, Michael. 1997. *Cultural Intimacy: Social Poetics in the Nation-State.* New York: Routledge.

Hoek, Lotte. 2013. *Cut-Pieces: Celluloid Obscenity and Popular Cinema in Bangladesh.* New York: Columbia University Press.

Hollinger, Karen. 2012. *Feminist Film Studies.* London: Routledge.

hooks, bell. 1992. The Oppositional Gaze: Black Female Spectators. In *Black Looks: Race and Representation.* Boston: South End Press, pp. 115–31.

Hooli, Shekhar H. 2015. 3 Reasons Why We Think Trisha and Varun May Have Broken Up. *International Business Times,* 6 May 2015. https://www.ibtimes.co.in/3-reasons-why-we-think-trisha-varun-may-have-broken-631487.

Hughes, Stephen. 1996. *Is There Anyone Out There? Exhibition and the Formation of Silent Film Audiences in South India.* PhD dissertation, University of Chicago.

– 2007. Music in the Age of Mechanical Reproduction: Drama, Gramophone, and the Beginnings of Tamil Cinema. *The Journal of Asian Studies* 66(1):3–34. https://doi.org/10.1017/S0021911807000034.

– 2011. What Is Tamil about Tamil Cinema? In S. Dickey and R. Dudrah, eds., *South Asian Cinemas: Widening the Lens.* London: Routledge, pp. 8–24.

– 2018. Social Sense and Embodied Sensibility: Towards a Historical Phenomenology of Film Going. Paper presented at the Chicago Tamil Forum – Mass Publicity and Mediation in Tamilagam (24–26 May 2018), University of Chicago.

Hull, Matthew. 2012. *Government of Paper: The Materiality of Bureaucracy in Urban Pakistan.* Berkeley: University of California Press.

Hutcheon, Linda. 2000[1985]. *A Theory of Parody: The Teachings of Twentieth-Century Art Forms.* Urbana: University of Illinois Press.

Hymes, Dell. 1964a. General Introduction. In D. Hymes, ed., *Language in Culture and Society: A Reader in Linguistics and Anthropology.* New York: Harper & Row, pp. xxi–xxxii.

– 1964b. Introduction: Towards Ethnographies of Communication. *American Anthropologist* 66(6), part 2:1–34. https://doi.org/10.1525/aa.1964.66.suppl_3.02a00010.

– 1973. Speech and Language: On the Origins and Foundations of Inequality among Speakers. *Daedalus* 102(3):59–85. https://www.jstor.org/stable/20024146.

IndiaGlitz. 2007. Tamil *Kireedam* Changes Climax. *IndiaGlitz* (website), 3 August 2007. https://www.indiaglitz.com/tamil-kireedam-changes-climax-malayalam-news-32775.html.

– 2011. Ajith Dismantles His Fan Clubs! *IndiaGlitz* (website), 29 April 2011. https://www.indiaglitz.com/ajith-dismantles-his-fan-clubs--tamil-news-66256.html.

– 2014. Power Star Srinivasan Distributed Quarter and Biriyani to Run His Film Lathika for 225 days | Comedy. *IndiaGlitz* (YouTube channel), 24 November 2014. https://www.youtube.com/watch?v=jmtSQVcKry4.

IndiaToday.in. 2018. Pa Ranjith on Directing Rajinikanth in Kaala and Kabali. *IndiaToday.in* (website), 21 December 2018. https://www.indiatoday.in/movies/regional-cinema/story/pa-ranjith-on-directing-rajinikanth-in-kaala-and-kabali-1414834-2018-12-21.

Irvine, Judith. 1996. Shadow Conversations: The Indeterminacy of Participant Roles. In M. Silverstein and G. Urban, eds., *Natural Histories of Discourse*. Chicago: University of Chicago Press, pp. 131–59.

Iyer, Usha. 2020. *Dancing Women: Choreographing Corporeal Histories of Hindi Cinema*. New York: Oxford University Press.

Jacob, Preminda. 2009. *Celluloid Deities: The Visual Culture of Cinema and Politics in South India*. Lanham, MD: Lexington Books.

Jain, Kajri. 2007. *Gods in the Bazaar: The Economies of Indian Calendar Art*. Durham, NC: Duke University Press.

Jakobson, Roman. 1960[1958]. Closing Statement: Linguistic and Poetics. In T. Sebeok, ed., *Style in Language*. Cambridge, MA: MIT Press, pp. 350–77.

– 1971[1921]. On Realism in Art. In L. Matejka and K. Pomorska, eds., *Readings in Russian Poetics: Formalist and Structuralist Views*. Cambridge, MA: MIT Press, pp. 38–46.

– 1981. Poetry of Grammar and Grammar of Poetry. In S. Rudy, ed., *Selected Writings of Roman Jakobson*. Vol. 3. The Hague: Mouton, pp. 87–97.

– 1987[1935]. The Dominant. In *Language in Literature*. Ed. K. Pomorska and S. Ruby. Cambridge, MA: Harvard University Press, pp. 41–9.

– 1990[1957]. Shifters and Verbal Categories. In *On Language*. Ed. L. Waugh and M. Monville-Burston. Cambridge, MA: Harvard University Press, pp. 386–92.

Jespersen, Otto. 1922. *Language: Its Nature, Development and Origin*. New York: Henry Holt.

Joshi, Meera. 2013. Aruna Irani: Mehmood & I Never Got Married. *IDIVA* (website), 13 October 2013. https://www.idiva.com/entertainment/celebrity-news/mehmood-and-i-never-got-married-aroona-irani/24865.

Jost, Francois. 1995. The Polyphonic Film and the Spectator. In W. Buckland. ed., *The Film Spectator: From Sign to Mind*. Amsterdam: University of Amsterdam Press, pp. 181–91.

Kailasam, Vasugi. 2017. Framing the Neo-Noir in Contemporary Tamil Cinema: Masculinity and Modernity in Tamil Nadu. *South Asian Popular Culture* 15(1):1–17. https://doi.org/10.1080/14746689.2017.1351788.

– 2021. Redefining the Mass Hero: The Rise of the Engineer as "Hero" in Contemporary Tamil Cinema. In S. Velayutham and V. Devadas, eds., *Tamil Cinema in the Twenty-First Century: Caste, Gender, and Technology*. London: Routledge, pp. 84–98.

Kamath, Sudhish. 2010. Double Blast of Irreverence. *The Hindu*, 6 February 2010. https://www.thehindu.com/features/cinema/Double-blast-of-irreverence/article11628376.ece.

– 2012. Why Not? *The Hindu*, 1 March 2012. https://www.thehindu.com/features/cinema/why-not/article2949904.ece.

Kampa, Samuel. 2019. Is Acting Hazardous? On the Risks of Immersing Oneself in a Role. *Aeon*, 18 April 2019. https://aeon.co/ideas/is-acting-hazardous-on-the-risks-of-immersing-oneself-in-a-role.

Kanchibhotia, Srinivas. n.d. Some Ramblings on *Kaadhal. Idlebrain.com* (website), http://www.idlebrain.com/research/ramblings/ramblings-kaadhal.html.

Kandavel, Sangeetha, and Jarshad NK. 2013. Mind It: Rajinikanth Gets a Rival in Unlikely Hero "Power Star" S Srinivasan. *The Economic Times*, 26 January 2013. https://economictimes.indiatimes.com/industry/media/entertainment/mind-it-rajinikanth-gets-a-rival-in-unlikely-hero-power-star-s-srinivasan/articleshow/18189722.cms.

Kapur, Geeta. 1987. Mythic Material in Indian Cinema. *Journal of Arts and Ideas* 14–15:79–108.

Karr, Jean-Baptiste Alphonse. 1862[1848]. *Les Guèpes*. Nouvelle édition. Paris: Michel Lévy Frères.

Karupiah, Premalatha. 2017. Voiceless Heroines: Use of Dubbed Voices in Tamil Movies. *Asian Women* 33(1):73–98. http://e-asianwomen.org/xml/10075/10075.pdf

Kasbekar, Asha. 2001. Hidden Pleasures: Negotiating the Myth of the Female Ideal in Popular Hindi Cinema. In R. Dwyer and C. Pinney, eds., *Pleasure and the Nation: The History, Politics and Consumption of Popular Culture in India*. Oxford: Oxford University Press, pp. 286–308.

Keane, Webb. 2003. Semiotics and the Social Analysis of Material Things. *Language & Communication* 23(3–4):409–25. https://doi.org/10.1016/S0271-5309(03)00010-7.

– 2009. Freedom and Blasphemy: On Indonesian Press Bans and Danish Cartoons. *Public Culture* 21(1):47–76. https://doi.org/10.1215/08992363-2008-021.

K. Hariharan. 2008. On Gender Violence and Cinema. Paper presented at the L.V. Prasad Film Academy (2 December 2008), Chennai, India.

– 2011. Getting on the Virtual Bridge. *The Hindu* (*Sunday Magazine*), 1 January 2011, https://www.thehindu.com/features/magazine/Getting-on-the-virtual-bridge/article15502170.ece.

– 2013. After the Cinema of Disgust: A Close Reading of the Renegade New Wave of Tamil Cinema. *Open Magazine*, 10 August 2013. https://openthemagazine.com/art-culture/after-the-cinema-of-disgust/.

King, Barry. 1985. Articulating Stardom. *Screen* 26(5):27–51. https://doi.org/10.1093/screen/26.5.27.

Kirk, Gwendolyn. 2016. *Uncivilized Language and Aesthetic Exclusion: Language, Power, and Film Production in Pakistan*. PhD dissertation, University of Texas – Austin.

Kracauer, Siegfried. 1960. *Theory of Film: The Redemption of Physical Reality*. New York: Oxford University Press.

Kripke, Saul. 1980. *Naming and Necessity*. Cambridge, MA: Harvard University Press.

Krishnan, Hari. 2019. *Celluloid Classicism: Early Tamil Cinema and the Making of Modern Bharatanatyam*. Middletown, CT: Wesleyan University Press.

Krishnan, Rajan (Kurai). 2008. Imaginary Geographies: The Makings of "South" in Contemporary Tamil Cinema. In. S. Velayutham, ed., *Tamil Cinema: The Cultural Politics of India's Other Film Industry*. London: Routledge, pp. 139–53.

– 2009. *Cultures of Indices*. PhD dissertation, Columbia University.

Kuhn, Annette. 1984. Women's Genres: Melodrama, Soap Opera and Theory. *Screen* 25(1):18–28. https://doi.org/10.1093/screen/25.1.18.

Kuleshov, Lev. 1974[1929]. Art of the Cinema. In R. Levaco, ed., *Kuleshov on Film: Writings of Lev Kuleshov*. Berkeley: University of California Press, pp. 41–123.

Kulick, Don. 2003. No. *Language & Communication* 23(2):139–51. https://doi.org/10.1016/S0271-5309(02)00043-5.

Kulick, Don, and Margaret Willson. 1994. Rambo's Wife Saves the Day: Subjugating the Gaze and Subverting the Narrative in a Papua New Guinean Swamp. *Visual Anthropology Review* 10(2):1–13. https://doi.org/10.1525/var.1994.10.2.1.

Kumar, Hemanth. 2018. Kaala Marks Advent of Rajinikanth 2.0 – Pa Ranjith's Vulnerable Protagonist Is Not a Man of the Masses. *First Post* (website), 8 June 2018. https://www.firstpost.com/entertainment/kaala-marks-advent-of-rajinikanth-2-0-pa-ranjiths-vulnerable-protagonist-is-not-a-man-of-the-masses-4502155.html.

Kumar, Ranjith. 2011. The Theory of Pleasure-Pauses: Making Sense of "Interruptions" in the Indian Film Narrative. *Journal of Creative Communications* 6(1–2):35–48. https://doi.org/10.1177/0973258613499106.

Kunapulli, Amruta. 2021. *Situating Tamil Cinema*. PhD dissertation, Michigan State University.

Kurai (Krishnan), Rajan. 2012. *Katānāyakanin Maraṇam* [*Death of the Hero*]. Chennai: Kayal Kavin.

– 2014. Naṭikan, Uṭal, Asaivu: *Kōccaṭaiyān* Putir Vilakkum Marmaṅkaḷ [Actor, Body, Movement: The Mysteries that Explain the Enigma of *Kochadaiiyaan*]. *Kāṭcippiḻai* 2(6).

Lakshmi, C.S. 1990. Mother, Mother-community and Mother-politics in Tamil Nadu. *Economic and Political Weekly* 25(42–43):WS72–83. https://www.jstor.org/stable/4396895.

– 2008. A Good Woman, A Very Good Woman: Tamil Cinema's Women. In S. Velayutham, ed., *Tamil Cinema: The Cultural Politics of India's Other Cinema*. New York: Routledge, pp. 16–28.

Larkin, Brian. 2008. *Signal and Noise: Media, Infrastruction, and Urban Culture in Nigeria*. Durham, NC: Duke University Press.

Latour, Bruno. 2005. *Reassembling the Social: An Introduction to Actor-Network-Theory*. Oxford: Oxford University Press.

Lee, Benjamin. 1997. *Talking Heads: Language, Metalanguage, and the Semiotics of Subjectivity*. Durham, NC: Duke University Press.

Lefebvre, Martin. 2021. A Peircean Lens on Cinematic Special Effects. In M. Barker and C.V. Nakassis, eds., *Images* (Special Issue). *Semiotic Review* 9. https://semioticreview.com/ojs/index.php/sr/article/view/71.

Lefkowitz, Daniel. 2005. On the Relation between Sound and Meaning in Hicks' *Snow Falling on Cedars*. *Semiotica* 2005(155):15–50. https://doi.org/10.1515/semi.2005.2005.155.1-4.15.

– 2019. A Discourse-Centered Approach to Sound and Meaning in Spike Lee's *Chi-Raq*. *Journal of Linguistic Anthropology* 29(2):231–8. https://doi.org/10.1111/jola.12246.

Leonard, Dickens. 2015. Spectacle Spaces: Production of Caste in Recent Tamil Films. *South Asian Popular Culture* 13(2):155–73. https://doi.org/10.1080/14746689.2015.1088499.

– 2021. Conscripts of Cinema: The Dangerous and Deviant Third Wave. In S. Velayutham and V. Devadas, eds., *Tamil Cinema in the Twenty-First Century: Caste, Gender, and Technology*. London: Routledge, pp. 36–51.

Levaco, Ronald. 1974. Introduction. In R. Levaco, ed., *Kuleshov on Film: Writings of Lev Kuleshov*. Berkeley: University of California Press, pp. 1–37.

López, Ana. 1990. Parody, Underdevelopment, and the New Latin American Cinema. *Quarterly Review of Film and Video* 12(1–2):63–71. https://doi.org/10.1080/10509209009361340.

Lotman, Jurij. 1976. *Semiotics of Cinema*. Trans. M. Suino. Ann Arbor: University of Michigan Press.

MacDougall, David. 2006. *The Corporeal Image: Film, Ethnography, and the Senses*. Princeton, NJ: Princeton University Press.

MacKinnon, Catharine. 1993. *Only Words*. Cambridge, MA: Harvard University Press.

Majumdar, Neepa. 2009. *Wanted Cultured Ladies Only: Female Stardom and Cinema in India, 1930s–1950s*. Urbana: University of Illinois Press.

– 2011. Importing Neorealism, Exporting Cinema: Indian Cinema and Film Festivals in the 1950s. In S. Giovacchini and R. Sklar, eds., *Global Neorealism: The Transnational History of a Film Style*. Jackson: University Press of Mississippi, pp. 178–93.

Majumdar, Rochona. 2016. Art Cinema: The Indian Career of a Global Category. *Critical Inquiry* 42(3):580–610. https://doi.org/10.1086/685605.

– 2021. *Art Cinema and India's Forgotten Future*. New York: Columbia University Press.

Malitsky, Joshua. 2010. Ideologies in Fact: Still and Moving-Image Documentary in the Soviet Union, 1927–1932. *Journal of Linguistic Anthropology* 20(2):352–71. https://doi.org/10.1111/j.1548-1395.2010.01074.x.

Manghani, Sunil, Arthur Piper, and Jon Simons. 2006. General Introduction. In S. Manghani, A. Piper, and J. Simons, eds., *Images: A Reader*. London: Sage, pp. 1–18.

Margulies, Ivone, ed. 2003. *Rites of Realism: Essays on Corporeal Cinema*. Durham, NC: Duke University Press.

Mazumdar, Ranjani. 2007. *Bombay Cinema: An Archive of the City*. Minneapolis: University of Minnesota Press.

Mazzarella, William. 2009. Making Sense of Cinema in Late Colonial India. In R. Kaur and W. Mazzarella, eds., *Censorship in South Asia: Cultural Regulation from Sedition to Seduction*. Bloomington: Indiana University Press, pp. 63–86.

– 2013. *Censorium: Cinema and the Open Edge of Mass Publicity*. Durham, NC: Duke University Press.

Meek, Barbra. 2006. And the Injun Goes "How!": Representations of American Indian English in White Public Space. *Language in Society* 35(1):93–128. https://doi.org/10.1017/S0047404506060040.

Mejel, Prince. 2018. Politics that Kaala Speaks – A Detailed Analysis. *Currently Globally* (website), 7 June 2018. https://web.archive.org/web/20180610114836/http://www.currentlyglobally.com/2018/06/politics-that-kaala-speaks-detailed-analysis.html.

Mertz, Elizabeth. 2007. Semiotic Anthropology. *Annual Review of Anthropology* 36:337–53. https://doi.org/10.1146/annurev.anthro.36.081406.094417.

Metz, Christian. 1974[1971]. *Language and Cinema*. Trans. D. Umiker-Sebeok. The Hague: Mouton.

– 1980. The Perceived and the Named. Trans. S. Feld and S. Robertson. *Studies in Visual Communication* 6(3):56–68. https://repository.upenn.edu/svc/vol6/iss3/4/.

– 1982[1975]. Story/Discourse (A Note on Two Kinds of Voyeurism). In *The Imaginary Signifier: Psychoanalysis and the Cinema*. Trans. C. Britton. Bloomington: Indiana University Press, pp. 91–8.

– 1986[1975]. The Imaginary Signifier (Excerpts). In P. Rosen, ed., *Narrative, Apparatus, Ideology: A Film Theory Reader*. New York: Columbia University Press, pp. 244–80.

– 1991[1971]. *Film Language: A Semiotics of the Cinema*. Trans. M. Taylor. Chicago: University of Chicago Press.

– 2016[1986]. Théorie de la Communication *versus* Structuralisme: Sur la Notion de Communication. *Mise au Point* (online) 8. https://doi.org/10.4000/map.2121.

– 2016[1991]. *Impersonal Enunciation, Or the Place of Film*. New York: Columbia University Press.

Mines, Diane. 2005. *Fierce Gods: Inequalities, Ritual, and the Politics of Dignity in a South Indian Village*. Bloomington: Indiana University Press.

Mines, Mattison. 1994. *Public Faces, Private Voices: Community and Individuality in South India*. Berkeley: University of California Press.

Mishra, Sudesh. 2020. Helen: The Chin Chin Chu Girl. In M. Lawrence, ed., *Indian Film Stars: New Critical Perspectives*. London: BFI Publications, pp. 151–62.

Mitchell, Lisa. 2009. *Language, Emotion, and Politics in South India*. Bloomington: Indiana University Press.

Mitchell, W.J.T. 1986. *Iconology: Image, Text, Ideology*. Chicago: University of Chicago Press.

– 1994. *Picture Theory: Essays on Verbal and Visual Representation*. Chicago: University of Chicago Press.

– 2004. *What Do Pictures Want? The Lives and Loves of Images*. Chicago: University of Chicago Press.

– 2015. *Image Science: Iconology, Visual Culture, and Media Aesthetics*. Chicago: University of Chicago Press.

Mitry, Jean. 1997[1963]. *The Aesthetics and Psychology of the Cinema*. Bloomington: Indiana University Press.

Mol, Annemarie. 1999. Ontological Politics: A Word and Some Questions. *Sociological Review* 47(S1):74–89. https://doi.org/10.1111/j.1467-954X.1999.tb03483.x.

Mondzain, Marie-José. 2005. *Image, Icon, Economy: The Byzantine Origins of the Contemporary Imaginary*. Trans. R. Franses. Stanford, CA: Stanford University Press.

Morgan, Daniel. 2006. Rethinking Bazin: Ontology and Realist Aesthetics. *Critical Inquiry* 32(3):443–81. https://doi.org/10.1086/505375.

– 2013. Bazin's Modernism. *Paragraph* 36(1):10–30. https://doi.org/10.3366/para.2013.0075.

– 2018. Bazin and His Legacies. In M. Temple and M. Witt, eds., *The French Cinema Book*. 2nd ed. London: British Film Institute, pp. 234–40.

Moviebuzz. 2016. We Are Not Strippers Mr Suraj: Nayanthara Lashes Out! *Sify.com* (website), 16 December 2016. https://www.sify.com/movies/we-are-not-strippers-mr-suraj-nayanthara-lashes-out-news-tamil-qm0oSIeggfdjd.html.

– 2018. Samantha: I Always Wanted a Family, Be a Good Mother and Wife. *Sify.com* (website), 8 May 2018. https://www.sify.com/movies/samantha

-i-always-wanted-a-family-be-a-good-mother-and-wife-news-tamil-sfioMfbcggdgh.html.

Moviecrow.com. 2018. Women Power Soaring in Kollywood: Ten Upcoming Films Bear Testimony to This Fact. *Moviecrow.com* (website), 11 September 2018. https://www.moviecrow.com/News/21327/women-power-soaring-in-kollywood-ten-upcoming-films-bear-testimony-to-this-fact.

Moxey, Keith. 2011. Lost in Translation. In J. Elkins and Maja Naef, eds., *What Is an Image?* University Park: Pennsylvania State University Press, pp. 122–5.

Mridula, R. 2018. Like Nayanthara and Anushka, Samantha Proves She's Ready to Lead Films with "U Turn." *The News Minute* (website), 18 September 2018. https://www.thenewsminute.com/article/nayanthara-and-anushka-samantha-proves-shes-ready-lead-films-u-turn-88533.

Mukherjee, Madhuja, ed. 2017. *Voices of the Talking Stars: Women of Indian Cinema and Beyond*. Los Angeles, CA: Sage.

Mukherjee, Madhuja, and Monika Mehta. 2021. Introduction: Detouring Networks. In M. Mehta and M. Mukherjee, eds., *Industrial Networks and Cinemas of India: Shooting Stars, Shifting Geographies and Multiplying Media*. London: Routledge, pp. 1–17.

Mulvey, Laura. 1989. British Feminist Film Theory's Female Spectators: Presence and Absence. *Camera Obscura* 7(2–3 [20–21]):68–81. https://doi.org/10.1215/02705346-7-2-3_20-21-68.

– 2002. Afterword. In R. Tapper, ed., *The New Iranian Cinema: Politics, Representation, and Identity*. London: I.B. Tauris, pp. 254–61.

– 2009[1975]. Visual Pleasure and Narrative Cinema. In *Visual and Other Pleasures*. 2nd ed. London: Palgrave Macmillan, pp. 14–27.

– 2009[1989]. Thoughts on the Young Modern Woman of the 1920s and Feminist Film Theory. In *Visual and Other Pleasures*. 2nd ed. London: Palgrave Macmillan, pp. 213–32.

– 2015. Introduction: 1970s Feminist Film Theory and the Obsolescent Object. In L. Mulvey and A. Backman Rogers, eds., *Feminisms: Diversity, Difference and Multiplicity in Contemporary Film Culture*. Amsterdam: Amsterdam University Press, pp. 17–26.

Munn, Nancy, 1986. *Fame of Gawa: A Symbolic Study of Value Transformation in a Massim (Papua New Guinea) Society*. Cambridge: Cambridge University Press.

Naficy, Hamid. 1994. Veiled Visions/Powerful Presences: Women in Postrevolutionary Iranian Cinema. In M. Afkhami and E. Friedl, eds., *In the Eye of the Storm: Women in Postrevolutionary Iran*. Syracuse, NY: Syracuse University Press, pp. 131–50.

Nakassis, Constantine V. 2009. Theorizing Realism Empirically. *New Cinemas* 7(3):211–35. https://doi.org/10.1386/ncin.7.3.211/1.

– 2010. *Youth and Status in Tamil Nadu*. PhD dissertation, University of Pennsylvania.
– 2012. Brand, Citationality, Performativity. *American Anthropologist* 114(4):624–38. https://doi.org/10.1111/j.1548-1433.2012.01511.x.
– 2013a. Citation and Citationality. *Signs and Society* 1(1):51–78. https://doi.org/10.1086/670165.
– 2013b. Youth Masculinity, "Style," and the Peer Group in Tamil Nadu, India. *Contributions to Indian Sociology* 47(2):245–69. https://doi.org/10.1177/0069966713482982.
– 2015. A Tamil-speaking Heroine. *Bioscope* 6(2):165–86. http://doi.org/10.1177/0974927615600625.
– 2016a. *Doing* Style: *Youth and Mass Mediation in South India*. Chicago: University of Chicago Press.
– 2016b. Linguistic Anthropology in 2015: Not the Study of Language. *American Anthropologist* 118(2):330–45. https://doi.org/10.1111/aman.12528.
– 2017. Rajini's Finger, Indexicality, and the Metapragmatics of Presence. *Signs and Society* 5(2):201–42. https://doi.org/10.1086/692128.
– 2018. Indexicality's Ambivalent Ground. *Signs and Society* 6(1):281–304. https://doi.org/10.1086/694753.
– 2019. Poetics of Praise and Image-Texts of Cinematic Encompassment. *Journal of Linguistic Anthropology* 29(1):69–94. https://doi.org/10.1111/jola.12217.
– 2020. Deixis and the Linguistic Anthropology of Cinema. In M. Barker and C.V. Nakassis, eds., *Images* (Special Issue). *Semiotic Review* 9. https://www.semioticreview.com/ojs/index.php/sr/article/view/65.
Nakassis, Constantine V., and E. Annamalai. 2020. Linguistic Diversity in South Asia, Reconsidered. In J. Stanlaw, ed., *The International Encyclopedia of Linguistic Anthropology*. Wiley Blackwell. https://doi.org/10.1002/9781118786093.iela0237.
Nakassis, Constantine V., and Melanie Dean. 2007. Youth, Desire, and Realism in Tamil Cinema. *Journal of Linguistic Anthropology* 17(1):77–104. https://doi.org/10.1525/jlin.2007.17.1.77.
Nakassis, Constantine V., and Amanda Weidman. 2018. Vision, Voice, and Cinematic Presence. *differences* 29(3):107–36. https://doi.org/10.1215/10407391-7266494.
Nambath, Suresh. 2003. The Politics of Art. *The Hindu*, 28 December 2003. https://web.archive.org/web/20200706090435/https://www.thehindu.com/todays-paper/tp-national/tp-tamilnadu/the-politics-of-art/article27818048.ece.
Narenmore, James. 1988. *Acting in the Cinema*. Berkeley: University of California Press.
Nathan, Archana. 2018. Do Sun Music's Anchors Deserve the Hate for Taking Potshots at Actor Suriya's Height? *Scroll.in* (website), 20 June 2018.

https://scroll.in/reel/865495/do-sun-musics-anchors-deserve-the-hate-for-taking-potshots-at-actor-suriyas-height.

Neale, Stephen. 2000[1983]. Masculinity as Spectacle: Reflections on Men and Mainstream Cinema. In E. Ann Kaplan, ed., *Feminism and Film*. Oxford: Oxford University Press, pp. 253–64.

Newell, Sasha. 2012. *Modernity Bluff: Crime, Consumption, and Citizenship in Côte d'Ivoire*. Chicago: University of Chicago.

Niazi, Sarah Rahman. 2019. White Skin/Brown Masks: The Case of "White" Actresses from Silent to Early Sound Period in Bombay. *Culture Unbound* 10(3):332–52. https://doi.org/10.3384/cu.2000.1525.2018103332.

– 2021. Sabita's Journey from Calcutta to Bombay: Gender and Modernity in the Circuits of Cinema in India. In M. Mehta and M. Mukherjee, eds., *Industrial Networks and Cinemas of India: Shooting Stars, Shifting Geographies and Multiplying Media*. London: Routledge, pp. 48–60.

Odin, Roger. 1995. For a Semio-Pragmatics of Film. In W. Buckland. ed., *The Film Spectator: From Sign to Mind*. Amsterdam: University of Amsterdam Press, pp. 213–26.

– 2018. Christian Metz for Today. In M. Tröhler and G. Kirsten, eds., *Christian Metz and the Codes of Cinema*. Amsterdam: University of Amsterdam Press, pp. 91–114.

Pande, Mrinal. 2006. "Moving beyond Themselves": Women in Hindustani Parsi Theatre and Early Hindi Films. *Economic and Political Weekly* 41(17):1646–53. https://www.jstor.org/stable/4418142.

Pandian, Anand. 2008. Cinema in the Countryside: Popular Tamil Film and the Remaking of Rural Life. In S. Velayutham, ed., *Tamil Cinema: The Cultural Politics of India's Other Film Industry*. New York: Routledge, pp. 124–38.

– 2011. Reel Time: Ethnography and the Historical Ontology of the Cinematic Image. *Screen* 52(2):193–214. https://doi.org/10.1093/screen/hjr003.

– 2014. Introduction. In A. Pandian, ed., *Subramaniyapuram: The Tamil Film in English Translation*. Chennai: Blaft, pp. vii–x.

– 2015. *Reel World: An Anthropology of Creation*. Durham, NC: Duke University Press.

Pandian, Avinash. 2016. Randeep Clarifies on Kajal Aggarwal Lip Lock Controversy! *Behindwoods.com* (website), 17 May 2016. https://www.behindwoods.com/tamil-movies-cinema-news-16/randeep-hooda-clarifies-on-kajal-aggarwal-lip-lock-controversy.html.

Pandian, M.S.S. 1991. *Parasakthi*: Life and Times of a DMK Film. *Economic and Political Weekly* 26(11–12):759–70. https://www.jstor.org/stable/4397433.

– 1992. *The Image Trap*. New Delhi: Sage Publications.

– 1996. Tamil Cultural Elites and Cinema: Outline of an Argument. *Economic and Political Weekly* 31(15):950–55. https://www.jstor.org/stable/4404028.

– 2005. Picture Lives. In D. Blamey and R. de Souza, eds., *Living Pictures: Perspectives on the Film Poster in India*. London: Open Editions, pp. 55–62.

– 2007. *Brahmin and Non-Brahmin: Genealogies of the Tamil Political Present.* Ranikhet: Permanent Black.

Panofsky, Erwin. 1959[1936]. Style and Medium in the Motion Pictures. In D. Talbot, ed., *Film: An Anthology*. Berkeley: University of California Press, pp. 15–32.

– 1991[1927]. *Perspective as Symbolic Form*. New York: Zone Books.

Parmentier, Richard. 1994. *Signs in Society: Studies in Semiotic Anthropology.* Bloomington: Indiana University Press.

Pasolini, Pier Paolo. 1988. *Heretical Empiricism*. Ed. L. Barnett. Trans. B. Lawton and L. Barnett. Washington, DC: New Academia Publishing.

Peirce, Charles Sanders. 1931–35. *Collected Papers of Charles Sanders Peirce*. Vols. 1–6. Eds. C. Hartshorne and P. Weiss. Cambridge, MA: Harvard University Press.

– 1958. *Collected Papers of Charles Sanders Peirce*. Vols. 7–8. Ed. A. Burks. Cambridge, MA: Harvard University Press.

Perkins, V.F. 1980[1972]. Understanding and Judging Movies. In C. Williams, ed., *Realism and the Cinema: A Reader*. London: Routledge and Kegal Paul, pp. 69–79.

Peterson, Leighton. 2014. Made Impossible by "Viewers Like You": The Politics and Poetics of Native American Voices in US Public Television. In D. Macey, K. Ryan, and N. Springer, eds. *How Television Shapes Our Worldview: Media Representations of Social Trends and Change*. Lanham, MD: Lexington Books, pp. 247–65.

Pinney, Christopher. 1997. *Camera Indica: The Social Life of Indian Photographs*. Chicago: University of Chicago Press.

– 2002. The Indian Work of Art in the Age of Mechanical Reproduction; Or, What Happens When Peasants "Get Hold" of Images. In F. Ginsburg, L. Abu-Lughod, and B. Larkin, eds., *Media Worlds: Anthropology in New Terrain*. Berkeley: University of California Press, pp. 355–69.

– 2004. *Photos of the Gods: The Printed Image and Political Struggle in India*. London: Reaktion Books.

Pinto, Jerry. 2006. *Helen: The Life and Times of a Bollywood H-Bomb*. New Delhi: Penguin Books.

Pongiyannan, Dhamu. 2015. *Film and Politics in India: Cinematic Charisma as a Gateway to Political Power*. Bern, Switzerland: Peter Lang.

Power, Cormac. 2006. *Presence in Play: A Critique of Theories of Presence in the Theatre*. PhD dissertation, University of Glasgow.

Prasad, M. Madhava. 1998. *Ideology of the Hindi Film: A Historical Construction*. Delhi: Oxford University Press.

– 2014. *Cine-Politics: Film Stars and Political Existence in South India*. Hyderabad: Orient Blackswan.

– 2020. Political Surplus in Retrospect: On the Decline of Cinematic Sovereignties. In S. Anandi, K. Ram Manoharan, M. Vijayabaskar, and A. Kalaiyarasan, eds., *Rethinking Social Justice*. Hyderabad: Orient Blackswan, pp. 319–32.

Prince, Stephen. 1996. True Lies: Perceptual Realism, Digital Images, and Film Theory. *Film Quarterly* 49(3):27–37. https://doi.org/10.2307/1213468.

P.V. Satish Kumar. 2005. High Court Revokes Censor Certificate for S.J. Surya's "New." *Now Running* (website), 6 August 2005. https://www.nowrunning.com/news/tamil/high-court-bans-s-j-suryas-new/3908/story.htm.

Rajadhyaksha, Ashish. 2003. The "Bollywoodization" of the Indian Cinema: Cultural Nationalism in a Global Arena. *Inter Asia Cultural Studies* 4(1):25–39. https://doi.org/10.1080/1464937032000060195.

– 2009. *Indian Cinema in the Time of Celluloid: From Bollywood to the Emergency*. Bloomington: Indiana University Press.

Rajagopal, Arvind. 2001. *Politics after Television: Hindu Nationalism and the Reshaping of the Public in India*. Cambridge: Cambridge University Press.

Rajanayagam, S. 2015. *Popular Cinema and Politics in South India: The Films of MGR and Rajinikanth*. New Delhi: Routledge.

Rajangam, Stalin. 2016. *Tamil Cinimā* [*Tamil Cinema*]. Chennai: Pirakñai.

– 2018. Pa Ranjith's "Kaala" Turns the Ramayana on Its Head – By Making Raavana the Hero. *Scroll.in* (website), 14 June 2018. https://scroll.in/reel/882609/pa-ranjiths-kaala-turns-the-ramayana-on-its-head-by-making-raavana-the-hero.

Rajendran, Sowmya. 2018a. CS Amudhan's "Tamizh Padam 2" Speaks the Truth about Female Characters in Kollywood. *The News Minute* (website), 13 July 2018. https://www.thenewsminute.com/article/cs-amudhans-tamizh-padam-2-speaks-truth-about-female-characters-kollywood-84716.

– 2018b. Don't Want to Do Films Where I Stand Near the Hero and Praise Him: Jyothika to TNM. *The News Minute* (website), 14 November 2018. https://www.thenewsminute.com/article/don-t-want-do-films-where-i-stand-near-hero-and-praise-him-jyothika-tnm-91526.

– 2018c. "Me Too": How Women in South Cinema Are Considered Commodities on Screen and Off It. *The News Minute* (website), 9 November 2018. https://www.thenewsminute.com/article/me-too-how-women-south-cinema-are-considered-commodities-screen-and-it-91258.

– 2018d. The Women of "Kaala": How Pa Ranjith's Film Breaks Gender Moulds in Tamil Cinema. *The News Minute* (website), 8 June 2018. https://www.thenewsminute.com/article/women-kaala-how-pa-ranjiths-film-breaks-gender-moulds-tamil-cinema-82706.

– 2019. The "Item" Song in Tamil Cinema: Who Started It and Is It on Its Way Out? *The News Minute* (website), 18 January 2019. https://www.thenewsminute.com/article/item-song-tamil-cinema-who-started-it-and-it-its-way-out-95228.

Ram, Kalpana. 2008. Bringing the Amman into Presence in Tamil Cinema: Cinema Spectatorship as Sensuous Apprehension. In S. Velayutham, ed., *Tamil Cinema: The Cultural Politics of India's Other Film Industry*. London: Routledge, pp. 44–58.

Rāmaccantiran, Varicai Ki. 2004. *Sṭārs* [*Stars*]. Chennai: Sarupriya Publications.

Ramamurthy, Priti. 2006. The Modern Girl in India in the Interwar Years: Interracial Intimacies, International Competition, and Historical Eclipsing. *Women's Studies Quarterly* 34(1–2):197–226. https://www.jstor.org/stable/40004749.

Ramaswamy, Sumathi. 1997. *Passions of the Tongue: Language Devotion in Tamil India, 1891–1970*. Berkeley: University of California Press.

Ramki, J. 2008. *Jeyalalitā – Ammu Mutal Ammāvarai* [*Jayalalitha: From Ammu to Amma*]. Chennai: Kizhakku Pathippagam.

Ram Manoharan, Karthick. n.d. Love, Caste, and Ideology: Notes from a Tamil Film. Unpublished Manuscript.

– 2021. Being Dalit, Being Tamil. In S. Velayutham and V. Devadas, eds., *Tamil Cinema in the Twenty-First Century: Caste, Gender, and Technology*. London: Routledge, pp. 52–65.

Rancière, Jacques. 2007. *The Future of the Image*. Trans. G. Elliott. London: Verso.

– 2009. *The Emancipated Spectator*. Trans. G. Elliott. London: Verso.

Rangan, Baradwaj. 2004. Review of *7/G Rainbow Colony*. *The Economic Times, Madras Plus*, 21 October 2004. https://groups.google.com/forum/#!topic/rec.arts.movies.local.indian/cLqM67NVeOU.

– 2013. Comment, 7 November 2013, on "Arrambam" … Mission to "Mass." *Baradwaj Rangan Blog*, 4 November 2013. https://baradwajrangan.wordpress.com/2013/11/04/arrambam-mission-to-mass/.

– 2014. Readers Write In #2: The Misogyny in Rajinikanth's Cinema. *Baradwaj Rangan Blog*, 19 December 2014. https://baradwajrangan.wordpress.com/2014/12/19/the-misogyny-in-rajinikanths-cinema/.

– 2016. Kabali: An Unsatisfying Clash between the Impulses of Star and Director. *The Hindu*, 22 July 2016. https://www.thehindu.com/features/cinema/cinema-reviews/Kabali-An-unsatisfying-clash-between-the-impulses-of-star-and-director/article14515117.ece.

Ranganathan, Maya. 2021. A Rumble in the Movie Halls: Cinema in the "Orphaned" State. In S. Velayutham and V. Devadas, eds., *Tamil Cinema in the Twenty-First Century: Caste, Gender, and Technology*. London: Routledge, pp. 179–93.

Rao, Leela. 1989. Woman in Indian Films – A Paradigm of Continuity and Change. *Media, Culture & Society* 11(4):443–58. https://doi.org/10.1177/016344389011004007.

Rao, Subha J. 2018. Nayanthara: The Story of How an Actress Became a Star. *Silverscreen India* (website), 17 August 2018. https://silverscreenindia.com/movies/features/the-growth-of-nayanthara-into-a-superstar/.

– 2019. Selvaraghavan's Films Through the Eyes of a Woman. *Filmcompanion.in* (website), 17 June 2019. https://www.filmcompanion.in/selvaraghavans-films-through-the-eyes-of-a-woman-subha/.

Rodowick, D.N. 1994[1988]. *The Crisis of Political Modernism: Criticism and Ideology in Contemporary Film Criticism*. 2nd ed. Berkeley: University of California Press.

Rogers, Martyn. 2009. Between Fantasy and "Reality": Tamil Film Star Fan Club Networks and the Political Economy of Film Fandom. *South Asia: Journal of South Asian Studies* 32(1):63–85. https://doi.org/10.1080/00856400802709284.

– 2011. From the Sacred to the Performative: Tamil Film Star Fan Clubs, Religious Devotion and the Material Culture of Film Star Portraits. *Journal of Religion and Popular Culture* 23(1):40–52. https://doi.org/10.3138/jrpc.23.1.40.

Romig, Rollo. 2015. What Happens When a State Is Run by Movie Stars? The Frenzied Fanatical Politics of Tamil Nadu. *New York Times*, 1 July 2015. http://www.nytimes.com/2015/07/05/magazine/what-happens-when-a-state-is-run-by-movie-stars.html.

Rosen, Philip. 2001. *Change Mummified: Cinema, Historicity, Theory*. Minneapolis: University of Minnesota Press.

Rossoukh, Ramyar, and Steven Caton. 2021. Introduction. In R. Rossoukh and S. Caton, eds., *Anthropology, Film Industries, Modularity*. Durham, NC: Duke University Press, pp. 1–39.

Roth, Christopher. 2008. *Becoming Tsimshian: The Social Life of Names*. Seattle: University of Washington Press.

Roy, Anjali Gera. 2010. Is Everybody Saying "Shava Shava" to Bollywood Bhangra? In R.B. Mehta and R.V. Pandharipande, eds., *Bollywood and Globalization: Indian Popular Cinema, Nation, and Diaspora*. London: Anthem Press, pp. 35–50.

Russell, Kamala. 2020. Facing Another: The Attenuation of Contact as Space in Dhofar, Oman. *Signs and Society* 8(2):290–318. https://doi.org/10.1086/708145.

Sahlins, Marshall. 1981. *Historical Metaphors and Mythical Realities: Structure in the Early History of the Sandwich Islands Kingdom*. Ann Arbor: University of Michigan Press.

Samos, Sumeet. 2018. Kaala Is Not a "Rajinikanth Movie": A Dalit-Bahujan Reading of the Anti-Caste Politics in Pa Ranjith's Film. *First Post* (website), 11 June 2018. https://www.firstpost.com/entertainment/kaala-is-not-a-rajinikanth-movie-a-dalit-bahujan-reading-of-the-anti-caste-politics-in-pa-ranjiths-film-4505063.html.

Saner, Emine. 2014. From Nymphomaniac to Stranger by the Lake, Is Sex in Cinema Getting Too Real? *The Guardian*, 21 February 2014. https://www.theguardian.com/film/2014/feb/21/nymphomaniac-stranger-by-the-lake-sex-cinema.

Sarris, Andrew. 2007[1962]. Notes on the Auteur Theory in 1962. In L. Braudy and M. Cohen, ed., *Film Theory and Criticism: Introductory Readings*. 7th ed. New York: Oxford University Press, pp. 451–4.

Saussure, Ferdinand de. 1986[1916]. *Course in General Linguistics*. Trans. R. Harris. Peru, IL: Open Court.

Schechner, Richard. 1988. *Performance Theory*. New York: Routledge.

Schiffman, Harold. 1998. Standardization or Restandardization: The Case for "Standard" Spoken Tamil. *Language in Society* 27(3):359–85. https://doi.org/10.1017/S0047404500020017.

– 1999. *A Reference Grammar of Spoken Tamil*. Cambridge: Cambridge University Press.

Schivelbusch, Wolfgang. 2014[1977]. *The Railway Journey: The Industrialization of Time and Space in the Nineteenth Century*. Oakland: University of California Press.

Schoonover, Karl. 2012. *Brutal Vision: The Neorealist Body in Postwar Italian Cinema*. Minneapolis: University of Minnesota Press.

Schwartz, Louis-Georges. 2005. Typewriter: Free Indirect Discourse in Deleuze's *Cinema*. *SubStance* 34(3):107–35. https://www.jstor.org/stable/3685735.

Searle, Llerena Guiu. 2016. *Landscapes of Accumulation: Real Estate and the Neoliberal Imagination in Contemporary India*. Chicago: University of Chicago Press.

Seizer, Susan. 2005. *Stigmas of the Tamil Stage: An Ethnography of Special Drama Artists in South India*. Durham, NC: Duke University Press.

Shekar, Anjana, and Priyanka Thirumurthy. 2018. Trisha Starrer "Mohini" Will Redefine "Mass" Movies, Promises Director. *The News Minute*, 19 January 2018. https://www.thenewsminute.com/article/trisha-starrer-mohini-will-redefine-mass-movies-promises-director-74992.

Shinde, Ravikiran. 2018. How Kaala Upended the Caste and Colour Paradigm. *Newslaundry* (website), 11 June 2018. http://www.newslaundry.com/2018/06/11/kaala-caste-colour-paradigm-indian-films#disgus_thread.

Shiva Kumar, S. 2019. Now, Women Take Centrestage in South Indian Films. *The Hindu*, 12 July 2019. https://www.thehindu.com/entertainment/movies/now-women-take-centrestage-in-south-indian-films/article28402037.ece.

Shklovsky, Viktor. 1965[1917]. Art as Technique. In L. Lemon and M. Reiss, eds., *Russian Formalist Criticism*. Lincoln: University of Nebraska Press, pp. 3–24.

Shulman, David. 2012. *More than Real: A History of the Imagination in South India*. Cambridge, MA: Harvard University Press.
– 2016. *Tamil: A Biography*. Cambridge, MA: Harvard University Press.
Silverman, Kaja. 1988. *The Acoustic Mirror: The Female Voice in Psychoanalysis and Cinema*. Bloomington: Indiana University Press.
Silverstein, Michael. 1976. Shifters, Linguistic Categories, and Cultural Description. In K. Basso and H. Selby, eds., *Meaning in Anthropology*. Albuquerque: University of New Mexico Press, pp. 11–55.
– 1979. Language Structure and Linguistic Ideology. In R. Cline, W. Hanks, and C. Hofbauer, eds., *The Elements: A Parasession on Linguistic Units and Levels*. Chicago: Chicago Linguistic Society, pp. 193–247.
– 1992. The Indeterminacy of Contextualization: When Is Enough Enough? In P. Auer and A. Di Luzio, eds., *The Contextualization of Language*. Amsterdam: John Benjamins, pp. 55–76.
– 1993. Metapragmatic Discourse and Metapragmatic Function. In J. Lucy, ed., *Reflexive Language: Reported Speech and Metapragmatics*. Cambridge: Cambridge University Press, pp. 33–57.
– 1996. The Secret Life of Texts. In M. Silverstein and G. Urban, eds., *Natural Histories of Discourse*. Chicago: University of Chicago Press, pp. 81–105.
– 1998. Contemporary Transformations of Local Linguistic Communities. *Annual Review of Anthropology* 27:401–26. https://doi.org/10.1146/annurev.anthro.27.1.401.
– 2000. Whorfianism and the Linguistic Imagination of Nationality. In P. Kroskrity, ed., *Regimes of Language: Ideologies, Polities, and Identities*. Santa Fe, NM: School for Advanced Research Press, pp. 85–138.
– 2003a. Indexical Order and the Dialectics of Sociolinguistic Life. *Language & Communication* 23(3–4):193–229. https://doi.org/10.1016/S0271-5309(03)00013-2.
– 2003b. Translation, Transduction, Transformation: Skating Glossando on Thin Semiotic Ice. In P. Rubel and A. Rosman, eds., *Translating Cultures: Perspectives on Translation and Anthropology*. Oxford: Berg, pp. 75–105.
– 2004. "Cultural" Concepts and the Language-Culture Nexus. *Current Anthropology* 45(5):621–52. https://doi.org/10.1086/423971.
– 2005a. Axes of -Evals: Token versus Type Interdiscursivity. *Journal of Linguistic Anthropology* 15(1):6–22. https://doi.org/10.1525/jlin.2005.15.1.6.
– 2005b. Languages/Cultures are Dead! Long Live the Linguistic-Cultural! In D. Segal and S. Yanagisako, eds., *Unwrapping the Sacred Bundle: Reflections on the Disciplining of Anthropology*. Durham, NC: Duke University Press, pp. 99–125.
– 2013. Discourse and the No-thing-ness of Culture. *Signs and Society* 1(2):327–66. https://doi.org/10.1086/673252.

– 2021. The Dialectics of Indexical Semiosis: Scaling Up and Out from the "Actual" to the "Virtual." *International Journal of the Sociology of Language* 2021(272):13–45. https://doi.org/10.1515/ijsl-2021-2124.

Silverstein, Michael, and Greg Urban. 1996. The Natural History of Discourse. In M. Silverstein and G. Urban, eds., *Natural Histories of Discourse*. Chicago: University of Chicago Press, pp. 1–18.

Sivathamby, Karthigesu. 1981. *The Tamil Film as a Medium of Political Communication*. Madras: New Century Book House.

Snyder, Joel. 1980. Picturing Vision. *Critical Inquiry* 6(3):499–526. https://doi.org/10.1086/448062.

Soman, Sandhya. 2012. Sam Anderson from Erode Goes Viral. *Times of India*, 4 November 2012. https://timesofindia.indiatimes.com/city/chennai/sam-anderson-from-erode-goes-viral/articleshow/17083300.cms.

Sonderegger, Ruth. 2011. Private, Social, or Political? In J. Elkins and Maja Naef, eds., *What Is an Image?* University Park: Pennsylvania State University Press, pp. 173–5.

Soneji, Davesh. 2012. *Unfinished Gestures: Devadāsīs, Memory, and Modernity in South India*. Chicago: University of Chicago Press.

– 2021. Birthing a Caste: The Gendered Political Origins of the *Icai Vēḷāḷar* in Modern Tamil Nadu. Paper presented at the Chicago Tamil Forum – Caste and Community in Modern Tamilagam (13–15 May 2021), University of Chicago.

Sreedhar Pillai. 2018a. Kolamaavu Kokila Movie Review: Nayanthara Is Riveting as a Drug Peddler in a Film Laced with Dark Humour. *First Post* (website), 17 August 2018. https://www.firstpost.com/entertainment/kolamaavu-kokila-movie-review-nayanthara-is-riveting-as-a-drug-peddler-in-a-film-laced-with-dark-humour-4984691.html.

– 2018b. These Women Mean Business. *The Hindu*, 5 September 2018. https://www.thehindu.com/entertainment/movies/kollywood-these-women-mean-business/article24869809.ece.

– 2019a. Comali: Buzz around Jayam Ravi Film Rises, Particularly Due to the Now-Deleted Rajinikanth Reference in Trailer. *First Post* (website), 19 August 2019. https://www.firstpost.com/entertainment/comali-buzz-around-jayam-ravi-film-rises-particularly-due-to-the-now-deleted-rajinikanth-reference-in-trailer-7162591.html.

– 2019b. "Jackpot" to "Kolaiyuthir Kaalam": How Actresses are Questioning Status Quo in Tamil Cinema. *The Hindu*, 31 July 2019. https://www.thehindu.com/entertainment/movies/why-should-guys-have-all-the-fun/article28773058.ece.

Srinivas, K. Ravi, and Sundar Kaali. 1998. On Castes and Comedians: The Language of Power in Recent Tamil Cinema. In A. Nandy, ed., *The Secret Politics of Our Desires: Innocence, Culpability and Indian Popular Cinema*. New Delhi: Oxford University Press, pp. 208–27.

Srinivas, Lakshmi. 2016. *House Full: Indian Cinema and the Active Audience*. Chicago: University of Chicago Press.

Srinivas, S.V. 2009. *Megastar: Chiranjeevi and Telugu Cinema after N.T. Rama Rao*. Delhi: University of Oxford Press.

– 2016. Rajinikanth and the "Regional Blockbuster." *Working Papers of the Chicago Tamil Forum – Politics of Media, Media of Politics* (19 May 2016). Version 12.15.2016. http://chicagotamilforum.uchicago.edu/working-papers/.

Srinivasan, Perundevi. 2016. Love Meets Death: "Honour," Caste, and the Female Subject. Paper presented at the Chicago Tamil Forum – Politics of Media, Media of Politics (19–21 May 2016), University of Chicago.

SS Music Blog. 2013. Hansika Finally Answers Marriage Reports with STR. *SS Music Blog* (website), 18 July 2013. http://ssmusictheblog.blogspot.com/2013/07/hansika-finally-answers-marriage.html.

Stacey, Jackie. 1999[1991]. Feminine Fascinations: Forms of Identification in Star-Audience Relations. In S. Thornham, ed., *Feminist Film Theory: A Reader*. Edinburgh: Edinburgh University Press, pp. 196–209.

Staiger, Janet. 1984. Theorist, Yes, but What of? Bazin and History. *Iris* 2(2):99–109.

– 1985. The Hollywood Mode of Production: Conditions of Existence. In D. Bordwell, J. Staiger, and K. Thompson, *The Classical Hollywood Cinema: Film Style and Mode of Production to 1960*. New York: Columbia University Press, pp. 87–95.

– 1992. Securing the Fictional Narrative as a Tale of the Historically Real: *The Return of Martin Guerre*. In J. Gaines, ed., *Classical Hollywood Narrative: The Paradigm Wars*. Durham, NC: Duke University Press, pp. 107–28.

Stam, Robert. 1989. *Subversive Pleasures: Bakhtin, Cultural Criticism, and Film*. Baltimore, MD: Johns Hopkins University Press.

Stasch, Rupert. 2011. Ritual and Oratory Revisited: The Semiotics of Effective Action. *Annual Review of Anthropology* 40:159–74. https://doi.org/10.1146/annurev-anthro-081309-145623.

– 2014. Linguistic Anthropology and Sociocultural Anthropology. In N. Enfield, P. Kockelman, and J. Sidnell, eds., *The Cambridge Handbook of Linguistic Anthropology*. Cambridge: Cambridge University Press, pp. 604–21.

Stewart, Jacqueline. 2003. Negroes Laughing at Themselves? Black Spectatorship and the Performance of Urban Modernity. *Critical Inquiry* 29(4):650–77. https://doi.org/10.1086/377724.

Stoppard, Tom. 1967. *Rosencrantz and Guildenstern Are Dead*. London: Faber and Faber.

Strassler, Karen. 2020. *Demanding Images: Democracy, Mediation, and the Image-Event in Indonesia*. Durham, NC: Duke University Press.

Subhakeerthana, S. 2018a. "It's High Time We Had a Movement Like the WCC Here": In Conversation with Samantha Akkineni. *Silverscreen India* (website), 5 September 2018. https://silverscreen.in/features/interviews/samantha-interview-u-turn/.

– 2018b. You Won't See Nayanthara in My Film: "Kolamaavu Kokila" Director Nelson Dilipkumar. *The New Indian Express*, 16 March 2018. https://www.newindianexpress.com/entertainment/tamil/2018/mar/16/you-wont-see-nayanthara-in-my-film-kolamaavu-kokila-director-nelson-dilipkumar-1788280.html.

Subramanian, Anupama. 2018. On I-day, Jyothika Reveals "Ten Commandments" for Women. *Deccan Chronicle*, 15 August 2018. https://www.deccanchronicle.com/entertainment/kollywood/150818/on-i-day-jyothika-reveals-ten-commandments-for-women.html.

Sudhir, T.S. 2018. Sorry Rajinikanth – Protests Make India a Vibrant Democracy, Not a Graveyard. *The News Minute* (website), 31 May 2018. https://www.thenewsminute.com/article/sorry-rajinikanth-protests-make-india-vibrant-democracy-not-graveyard-82229.

Sundar Kaali. 2000. Narrating Seduction: Vicissitudes of the Sexed Subject in Tamil Nativity Film. In R. Vasudevan, ed., *Making Meaning in Indian Cinema*. New Delhi: Oxford University Press, pp. 168–90.

– 2013. Disciplining the *Dasi*: *Cintamani* and the Politics of a New Sexual Economy. *BioScope* 4(1):51–69. https://doi.org/10.1177/097492761200483062.

Surendhar, M.K. 2018. Rajinikanth's Kaala, Pa Ranjith Busts Clichés Regarding Dalit Representation in Mainstream Tamil Cinema. *First Post* (website), 10 June 2018. https://www.firstpost.com/entertainment/with-rajinikanths-kaala-director-pa-ranjith-busts-cliches-regarding-dalits-in-mainstream-tamil-cinema-4504135.html.

Susan, Nisha. 2016. Spitting on Heroes: The Curious Case of Dhanush and Selvaraghavan. *Papercuts Magazine* 16 (Summer). http://desiwriterslounge.net/articles/papercuts-selva/.

Taussig, Michael. 1993. *Mimesis and Alterity: A Particular History of the Senses*. New York: Routledge.

Taylor, Woodman. 2003. Penetrating Gazes: The Poetics of Sight and Visual Display in Popular Indian Cinema. In S. Ramaswamy, ed., *Beyond Appearances? Visual Practices and Ideologies in Modern India*. New Delhi: Sage Publications, pp. 297–322.

Thomas, Rosie. 1989. Sanctity and Scandal: The Mythologization of Mother India. *Quarterly Review of Film and Video* 11(3):11–30. https://doi.org/10.1080/10509208909361312.

Thompson, Kristin. 1988. *Breaking the Glass Armor: Neoformalist Film Analysis*. Princeton, NJ: Princeton University Press.

TNM Staff. 2018a. How Rajinikanth's Politics Is Playing Out at Cinema Halls amidst Kaala. *The News Minute* (website), 8 June 2018. https://www.thenewsminute.com/article/how-rajinikanth-s-politics-playing-out-cinema-halls-amidst-kaala-82679.

– 2018b. The "Loosu Ponnu" in Tamil Cinema and Why She Should Retire. *The News Minute* (website), 30 September 2018. https://www.thenewsminute.com/article/loosu-ponnu-tamil-cinema-and-why-she-should-retire-89332.

– 2019. #BoycottComali Trends as Trailer of Jayam Ravi Film Mocks Rajini's Political Entry. *The News Minute* (website), 4 August 2019. https://www.thenewsminute.com/article/boycottcomali-trends-trailer-jayam-ravi-film-mocks-rajinis-political-entry-106640.

– 2021. Ajith Asks Fans, Media Not to Call Him "Thala." *The News Minute* (website), 1 December 2021. https://www.thenewsminute.com/article/ajith-asks-fans-media-not-call-him-thala-158252.

TNN. 2017. Hansika-Simbu Marriage on Hold. *Times of India*, 15 January 2017. http://timesofindia.indiatimes.com/entertainment/tamil/movies/news/Hansika-Simbu-marriage-on-hold/articleshow/22761251.cms.

– 2018. Did You Know Mammootty Was Approached for "Imaikkaa Nodigal"? *Times of India*, 7 September 2018. https://timesofindia.indiatimes.com/entertainment/tamil/movies/news/did-you-know-mammootty-was-approached-for-imaikkaa-nodigal/articleshow/65718348.cms.

Trautmann, Thomas. 2006. *Languages and Nations: The Dravidian Proof in Colonial Madras*. Berkeley: University of California Press.

Tröhler, Margit. 2018. Christian Metz and Film Sociology. In M. Tröhler and G. Kirsten, eds., *Christian Metz and the Codes of Cinema*. Amsterdam: University of Amsterdam Press, pp. 15–66.

Tweedie, Jeff. 2018. The Genius of the System, or, André Bazin's Design Thinking. Paper presented at Bazin@100 (12 October 2018), University of Chicago.

Urban, Greg. 1989. The "I" of Discourse. In B. Lee and G. Urban, eds., *Semiotics, Self, and Society*. Berlin: Mouton de Gruyter, pp. 27–51.

Vasudevan, Ravi. 1995. Addressing the Spectator of a "Third World" Cinema: The Bombay "Social" Film of the 1940s and 1950s. *Screen* 36(4):305–24. https://doi.org/10.1093/screen/36.4.305.

– 2010. *The Melodramatic Public: Film Form and Spectatorship in Indian Cinema*. Ranikhet, India: Permanent Black.

Vega, Lope de. 1986[1607–08]. *Acting Is Believing*. Trans. M. McGaha. San Antonio, TX: Trinity University Press.

Velayutham, Selvaraj, and Vijay Devadas. 2021. Introduction: Tamil Cinema in the Twenty-First Century: Continuities and Changes. In S. Velayutham and V. Devadas, eds., *Tamil Cinema in the Twenty-First Century: Caste, Gender, and Technology*. London: Routledge, pp. 1–16.

Venkatachalapathy, A.R. 2018. *Tamil Characters: Personalities, Politics, Culture*. London: Pan Macmillan.

Venkataraman, Janaki. 2004. A Voice from *Aside*. In C.S. Lakshmi, ed., *The Unhurried City: Writings on Chennai*. New Delhi: Penguin, pp. 37–49.

Vijaynet. 2007. Apology from "Lollu Sabha" and Vijay TV. *Vijaynet* (website), 7 April 2007. https://vijaynet.wordpress.com/2007/04/08/apology-from-lollu-sabha-and-vijay-tv/.

Virdi, Jyotika. 2003. *The Cinematic ImagiNation: Indian Popular Films as Social History*. New Brunswick, NJ: Rutgers University Press.

Vološinov, Valentin. 1986[1929]. *Marxism and the Philosophy of Language*. Trans. L. Matejka. Cambridge, MA: Harvard University Press.

Waugh, Patricia. 1984. *Metafiction: The Theory and Practice of Self-Conscious Fiction*. London: Routledge.

Weidman, Amanda. 2003. Gender and the Politics of Voice: Colonial Modernity and Classical Music in South India. *Cultural Anthropology* 18(2):194–232. https://doi.org/10.1525/can.2003.18.2.194.

– 2012. Voices of Meenakumari: Sound, Meaning, and Self-Fashioning in Performances of an Item Number. *Journal of South Asian Popular Culture* 10(3):307–18. https://doi.org/10.1080/14746689.2012.706027.

– 2015. The Voice of Dravidianism? The Star Power of T.M. Sounderajan. Paper presented at the Chicago Tamil Forum – Margins of Dravidianism (21–23 May 2015), University of Chicago.

– 2016. Circulating Voices: The Gendered Beginnings of Playback. *Working Papers of the Chicago Tamil Forum – Politics of Media, Media of Politics* (19–21 May 2016). Version: 12.15.2016. http://chicagotamilforum.uchicago.edu/working-papers/.

– 2021. *Brought to Life by the Voice: Playback Singing and Cultural Politics in South India*. Oakland: University of California Press.

West, Harry. 2008. *Ethnographic Sorcery*. Chicago: University of Chicago Press.

Whorf, Benjamin. 1956[1939]. The Relation of Habitual Thought and Behavior to Language. In J. Carroll, ed., *Language, Thought, and Reality: Selected Writings of Benjamin Lee Whorf*. Cambridge, MA: MIT Press, pp. 134–59.

Willemen, Paul. 1994. The Fourth Look. In *Looks and Frictions: Essays in Cultural Studies and Film Theory*. Bloomington: Indiana University Press, pp. 99–104.

Williams, Linda. 1984. When the Woman Looks. In M. Doane, P. Mellencamp, and L. Williams, eds., *Re-Vision: Essays in Feminist Film Criticism*. Los Angeles, CA: American Film Institute, pp. 83–99.

– 1989. *Hard Core: Power, Pleasure, and the "Frenzy of the Visible."* Berkeley: University of California Press.

Wollen, Peter. 1969. *Signs and Meaning in the Cinema*. London: British Film Institute.

Woolard, Kathryn. 1998. Introduction: Language Ideology as a Field of Inquiry. In B. Schieffelin, K. Woolard, and P. Kroskrity, eds., *Language Ideologies: Practice and Theory*. New York: Oxford University Press, pp. 3–50.

Worth, Sol. 1969. The Development of a Semiotic of Film. *Semiotica* 1(3): 282–321. https://doi.org/10.1515/semi.1969.1.3.282.

– 1974. Toward an Anthropological Politics of Symbolic Forms. In D. Hymes, ed., *Reinventing Anthropology*. New York: Vintage Books, pp. 335–64.

– 1981. *Studying Visual Communication*. Ed. L. Gross. Philadelphia: University of Pennsylvania Press.

Worth, Sol, and John Adair. 1972. *Through Navajo Eyes: An Exploration in Film Communication and Anthropology*. Bloomington: Indiana University Press.

Wortham, Stanton. 2006. *Learning Identity: The Joint Emergence of Social Identification and Academic Learning*. Cambridge: Cambridge University Press.

Yamunan, Sruthisagar. 2017. The Daily Fix: As Fans Hound Woman Journalist, Actor Vijay's Statement Is Too Late and Too Weak. *Scroll.in* (website), 10 August 2017. https://scroll.in/article/846719/the-daily-fix-as-fans-hound-woman-journalist-actor-vijays-statement-is-too-late-and-too-weak.

Zamboulingame, Shakila. 2021. When Madhi Dances Like Dhanush: Gender Representation in *Irudhi Suttru*. In S. Velayutham and V. Devadas, eds., *Tamil Cinema in the Twenty-First Century: Caste, Gender, and Technology*. London: Routledge, pp. 69–83.

Žižek, Slavoj. 1989. *The Sublime Object of Ideology*. New York: Verso.

Index

Page numbers in italics represent figures or tables.